Blackstone's Guide to the

HOUSING ACT 1988

Stuart Bridge MA, Barrister

Lecturer in Law, University of Leeds

First published in Great Britain 1989 by Blackstone Press Limited,
9-15 Aldine Street, London W12 8AW. Telephone 01-740 1173

© Stuart Bridge, 1989

ISBN: 1 85431 045 3

British Library Cataloguing in Publication Data
A CIP catalogue record for this book is available from the British Library.

Typeset by Style Photosetting Ltd, Mayfield
Printed by Livesey Ltd, Shrewsbury

Contents

Preface

The Housing Act 1988 received royal assent on 15 November 1988, at the very end of the fourth longest Parliamentary session this century. Although the services of the guillotine were required to curtail final discussion of the 270 Lords amendments, the Bill could not complain of a lack of close attention to its details, as it kept Parliament occupied for a grand total of over 250 hours. To put it mildly, the Act does not represent a consensus of opinion on housing policy, and was fiercely and at times bitterly contested by the opposition parties in the course of its passage. Rarely do political controversy and practical impact combine in such equal measure as in the Housing Act 1988, such that every practitioner with a clientele on either side of the housing market-place will need to become acquainted with the effect of its provisions — and sooner rather than later.

As a statute, the Housing Act 1988 does not have a single identifiable theme, although the modern Conservative's implicit, some might say blind, faith in market forces is its largest motivating factor. There is hardly an area of residential housing law left untouched. Part I is the most important for the housing (or general) practitioner, phasing out rent controls and introducing a new form of tenure in the assured tenancy (chapters 1 to 7), but the rest of the statute must not be neglected. Part IV is the most controversial, enabling council tenants to opt out of local authority control and encouraging certain private sector landlords to take up the challenge of buying up the freeholds of such tenants (chapter 10). It may well be the source of as much litigation as discontent. Part III (chapter 9) provides for the establishment of housing action trusts (HATs) charged with the duty of revitalising designated run-down inner city estates, and Part II (chapter 8) effects major changes to the housing association movement. The housing associations are identified as central to government housing policy, benevolent landlords which will let to the underprivileged at relatively low rents and which will relieve councils (and therefore the ratepayer) of at least some of the burden of owning and managing a substantial housing stock. Finally, but significantly, Part V (chapter 11) enacts sundry disparate provisions on matters as diverse as the tenant's right to buy, rent officers, covenants to repair and improvement grants.

Faced with a measure of 141 sections and 18 schedules, totalling nearly 200 pages in all, a statute which does nothing to simplify an already complex area of the law, a book of this size can only do so much. It seeks to explain the structure of the Parts of the Act, and concentrate on the conceptual difficulties which will face practitioners in their early dealings with it. It cannot hope, and does not aim, to answer every possible ambiguity which is likely to arise. It is particularly important that reference is made to the statutory regulations and circulars which will begin to emanate from the Department of the Environment, the Housing Corporation and Housing for Wales in due course, for they will put the meat on the bones of the somewhat skeletal Parts II, III, and IV. So too with case law, of which it is anticipated the Act will spawn a not inconsiderable amount.

The writing of this book would have been impossible without the support of my family and friends, who have tolerated my 'voluntary' absenteeism even more than usual. Without prejudice to the generality of the foregoing, as they say, I must single out the patience of my students and colleagues at the Leeds Law Faculty throughout a busy autumn term, and the assistance and encouragement at home of Jane and David.

Stuart Bridge
Skelton, Yorkshire

January 1989

Table of Statutes

Table of Statutory Instruments

Table of Cases

Chapter One
Rented Accommodation: A General Introduction

Part I of the Housing Act 1988 introduces arguably the most radical attempt to regenerate the private rented housing market, not only of the present government, but of any Parliament this century. It appears at a time when that sector is unquestionably in decline. In a nation which once had the majority of its population occupying homes with a private landlord, the proportion is now of the order of 8%. The years of decline, commencing shortly before the First World War, have coincided with years in which protective legislation, the Rent Acts, has been in force, and the Housing Act targets that legislation as being the primary cause for the current malaise. There are other reasons for the loss of faith in the private sector, and the expansion of council ownership of homes following the great post-war building programmes is one of them. Public ownership, whether it be of national utilities, or of homes, is not a major theme at the heart of central policy-making in the 1980s, and the revitalisation of the private housing sector is no doubt seen by some as a means by which political power can be transferred from the local authorities. This wish for a transfer of power is seen more clearly in Parts III and IV of the Housing Act, but it underlies much of the thinking behind Part I as well.

The Conservative government has made earlier attempts to increase the housing available in the private sector by improving the incentives to let property. This has seen a gradual erosion of the effect of the Rent Acts, but nothing approximating to the significance of this latest measure. The Housing Act of 1980, at the same time as conferring the celebrated 'right to buy' on tenants in the public sector, gave landlords wishing to let on a short-term basis a right to repossess their properties at the termination of the agreement. Together with this so-called 'protected shorthold tenancy' was introduced a tenure known as 'assured tenancy' whereby landlords intending to build new homes were invited to put them on to the rental market free from the obligations, imposed by the Rent Acts, of charging a 'fair', below-market rent. These two tenures required the landlord to 'contract in' (he would need to observe very carefully prescribed conditions for their effective creation, the penalty for non-compliance being full Rent Act protection for the tenant) and their popularity, particularly the protected shorthold, has not been great.

Part I of the Housing Act 1988 sees a change of tack. It perceives the need, as before, to increase the incentives for private landlords to put their property on the market, but, unlike the earlier measures, considers that the only effective way to do so is to free the market altogether from Rent Act control. What is required is to allow homes to become an investment once more, with an acceptable level of capital return. The Rent Acts, with their insistence on a 'fair rent' being paid, and the possibility of registration of that rent binding the landlord in the case of future lettings, inhibit the process, and so they must go. In their place, the Housing Act 1988 allows the landlord to charge a market rent for lettings entered into after the Act commences, the Rent Act 1977 remaining in full force as far as existing tenancies are concerned.

It is an inevitable, indeed an intended, consequence, of the coming into force of Part I of the Housing Act 1988 that rents will rise. The government has acknowledged that this may cause hardship to individual tenants, but such genuine hardship will be offset by an increase in housing benefit payable to those people. The opposition doubts that sufficient money will be injected into the housing benefit scheme to make this undertaking crystallise, and sees this Part of the Act as driving another wedge between the property-owning privileged and the property-seeking underprivileged. As the effect of the Act begins to be felt among those looking for property to rent, the pressure will mount on the Treasury to release adequate funds to meet the needs which will arise, and only then will the extent of the financial commitment required to deal with its consequences be apparent.

The Housing Act 1988 does not directly attack the view, implicit in the Rent Acts since 1915 and necessary to make a system of rent control work effectively, that a tenant of a private landlord should be given a considerable degree of security in his home. The agreement under which he rents the house or flat will allow him to stay for as long: Parliament should add some statutory protection to that, entitling the landlord to repossess only where he satisfies the court that he has a need to do so, a need encapsulated in one or other of the so-called statutory grounds for possession. This extra-contractual 'security of tenure' is an important constituent of Rent Act protection (it has a public sector counterpart in the 'secure tenancy'), and security of tenure will continue to be a right of tenants of private sector landlords in most cases. The Housing Act 1988 replaces Rent Act tenancies as the major tenure for privately owned residential property by assured tenancies, confusingly given the same name (but having a quite different role) as the tenure created by the Housing Act 1980. The new assured tenancy will accord similar security of tenure on its holders as was conferred on Rent Act protected and statutory tenants. The potentially huge inroad into the principle of security of tenure for residential properties made by Part I of the Housing Act 1988 is not made by the assured tenancy, but by its brother the assured shorthold.

Landlords have since 1980 been able to 'contract out' of Rent Act security of tenure by granting protected shorthold tenancies to their tenants, but these tenures have been unpopular, probably owing to the formal complexity of the statutory provisions as much as to the fact that the tenant was entitled to the benefit of a 'fair rent'. The place of the protected shorthold is now taken by the (somewhat inaccurately named) 'assured shorthold tenancy', a tenure which, the government hopes, with some justification, will be considerably more popular than its predecessor among would-be private landlords. A landlord can now let property for as short a term as six months, and be free to recover possession at any time thereafter on giving two months' notice. He may charge a market rent with impunity. The tenure remains one which the landlord must contract into, and therefore he must act with care or on advice at the outset, but its potential for the investor who wishes a reasonable, low-risk return on his capital is considerable. For the tenant, the assured shorthold has few attractions: as we shall see, he has a right to apply to have the rent reduced, but the disparity of his bargaining position relative to that of his landlord is such that the right will often be merely notional.

The potential investor in the housing market should be aware of tax incentives which have been newly created. The 1988 Budget extended the Business Expansion Scheme (which offers income tax relief to individuals investing in new businesses) to investment in companies which specialise in letting residential property on assured (but not assured shorthold) tenancy. The provisions are complex and there are several important exclusions (see Income and Corporation Taxes Act 1988, Part VIII, Chapter III and Finance Act 1988, s. 50 and schedule 4).

The government recognises that Part I of the Housing Act 1988 may be seen as something of a charter for the less desirable subspecies of private landlord identified in the past with Mr Rachman. There will certainly be a strong incentive to landlords whose houses are let on Rent Act tenancies at the commencement of the Act to move those tenants on and thereby 'deregulate' their properties. The Housing Act 1988 responds by enabling civil courts to make substantial awards of damages in certain cases of unlawful eviction, and by making amendments to the Protection from Eviction Act 1977, which facilitate convictions for the criminal offences of unlawful eviction and unlawful harassment. However, other amendments to that Act are less liberal, and will enable landlords who let on certain kinds of tenancy and licence to recover possession where the tenancy or licence has come to an end without the need for a possession order.

Part I of the Housing Act 1988 also effects major changes to the regime under which agricultural workers presently hold their 'tied cottages', the Rent (Agriculture) Act 1976 now being replaced as far as new agreements are concerned by a new tenure, a form of assured tenancy known as the assured agricultural occupancy. Under the statutory scheme, landlords of these occupiers will also be free to obtain a market rent.

A wider policy evident elsewhere in the Act (see Part II) is the removal of governmental 'restraints' from housing associations, which are now being pushed firmly into the private sector arena. As part of this policy, housing associations are to be put on an equal footing with other private landlords, and they too will now be able, at least in theory, to charge their tenants a commercial rent, unhampered by the restrictions of the Rent Act 1977 (in the case of housing associations, Part VI of that Act).

Chapters 2 to 7 which follow outline these highly significant reforms to private sector housing law. The assured tenancy, as the tenure which is central to the regime of deregulation and which in the event of a landlord failing to 'contract out' will be applicable, is first considered: how the statute defines assured tenancy, the terms of such tenancies, recovery of possession and the rent provisions. The assured shorthold, which could well prove to be as popular with landlords as it will be despised by tenants, follows, and then the assured agricultural occupancy. Significant amendments are made to the law of statutory succession as it affects existing Rent Act protected and statutory tenants: this is the subject of chapter 6. The effect of Part I of the Housing Act on such Rent Act tenancies, and existing tenancies and licences subject to other statutory regimes is then considered. Chapter 7 is concerned with the reforms of the anti-eviction laws.

For a guide to a new statute, this book incorporates what might appear to be an excessive amount of case law, much of it decided under provisions of the Rent Acts. No apologies are made for this as there is no doubt of the relevance of this law. A passing glance at Part I of the Housing Act 1988, in particular Schedules 1 and 2, by one who is acquainted with the Rent Act 1977, will confirm that much of the terminology is virtually identical with that of the older statute. In construing the newly enacted sections and schedules, the first principle of statutory interpretation must be the ascertainment of the intention of Parliament by analysis of the words Parliament has used. Where words and expressions in the Housing Act 1988 have been plainly taken from a similar context in the Rent Act, in which context they have received a certain judicial interpretation, it may be assumed that Parliament was aware of that interpretation, and (in the absence of anything in the 1988 Act indicating a contrary intention) intended it to be followed (see further, on construing the statutes affecting private sector residential tenants Megarry, *The Rent Acts,* 11th ed, p. 12 et seq).

Chapter Two
Assured Tenancies: Definition and Terms

2.1 Introduction

The major new form of tenancy introduced by the Housing Act 1988 is the assured tenancy, which bears little similarity to the tenancy of the same name which was introduced in the Housing Act 1980 as an attempt to encourage the erection of new houses for private sector lettings. The 'new' assured tenancy will confer a security of tenure, modelled in some respects on the Rent Acts, although with some significant differences, and will allow landlords to charge their tenants a market rent. It will take the place of the protected tenancy as the major private sector form of letting. Save in certain exceptional circumstances, a tenancy cannot be assured if it was entered into before 15 January 1989.

2.2 Definition of assured tenancy (section 1)

2.2.1 'Tenancy'
An assured tenancy must be a tenancy (or 'lease'). Section 45 gives a partial definition of 'tenancy': it includes a subtenancy and an agreement for a tenancy or subtenancy. However, to establish the full meaning of tenancy, it will be necessary to look to the existing case law. The classic definition of tenancy is to be found in *Street* v *Mountford* [1985] AC 809: there must be a grant of exclusive possession for a term at a rent. If these three factors are present, there will be a tenancy whether or not that was the legal result intended by the parties unless there is some special circumstance indicating that something short of a tenancy, that is, a licence, has in fact been created.

Such special circumstances are:

(a) the intention of the parties not to enter a legally enforceable relationship of any kind (see, for example, *Marcroft Wagons Ltd* v *Smith* [1951] 2 KB 496);

(b) the intention of the parties to enter into a legal relationship distinct from a tenancy (for example, a contract of sale: *Isaac* v *Hotel de Paris Ltd* [1960] 1 WLR 239);

(c) a service occupancy, under which an employee occupies a property pursuant to his contract of employment for the better performance of the duties of that employment: *Smith* v *Seghill Overseers* (1875) LR 10 QB 422.

A major practical problem is working out exactly what the 'landlord' and 'tenant' did decide. The 'tenant' may have gone into occupation having been told by word of mouth what rent he must pay, when he must pay it, and nothing else: there may be no written agreement at all. On the other hand, there may be a lengthy document which purports to inform the occupier in detail what his rights (if any) are, and what his (somewhat more extensive) obligations are. Or the situation may be one where some of the terms of the agreement are oral, and some are in writing. Ultimately, the question is the same: does the agreement as a whole grant exclusive possession of the premises to the occupier, that exclusive possession being for a term at a rent? If the answer to this question is yes, and there are no other 'special circumstances', the occupier will be a tenant. If the answer is no, the occupier will be at best a licensee.

It was almost expected of landlords who operated under the shadow of the Rent Acts to attempt to obviate their effect. The conferment on the occupier, to use a neutral term, of a licence or some interest falling short of a tenancy was a common tactic of written agreements. There may not be the same incentive to defeat the statute under the new regime, but landlords who do not wish to confer a security of tenure, and have not yet come to grips with assured shortholds (see chapter 4), may wish to ply their old trade. It is likely that the courts will show them even less sympathy than did Lord Templeman in *Street* v *Mountford:*

> Although the Rent Acts must not be allowed to alter or influence the construction of an agreement, the court should, in my opinion, be astute to detect and frustrate sham devices and artificial transactions whose only object is to disguise the grant of a tenancy and to evade the Rent Acts.

A 'sham' in its strictest sense connotes 'acts done or documents executed by the parties to the "sham" which are intended by them to give to third parties or to the court the appearance of creating between the parties legal rights and obligations different from the actual legal rights and obligations (if any) which the parties intend to create' (per Diplock LJ in *Snook* v *London and West Riding Investments Ltd* [1967] 2 QB 786, 802). As the parties to a purported licence will have a common intention to create a licence rather than a tenancy, this test will rarely be satisfied. It does not follow that if a court finds that a written agreement is not a sham it must go on to apply the terms of the agreement as committed to writing. The court must apply the same rules of construction as it would apply to any other legal document, bearing in mind that the situation may be as envisaged by Mustill LJ in *Hadjiloucas* v *Crean* [1987] 3 All ER 1008, 1019, that is:

> . . . one in which the document does precisely reflect the true agreement between the parties, but where the language of the document (and in particular its title or description) superficially indicates that it falls into one legal category whereas when properly analysed in the light of the surrounding circumstances it can be seen to fall into another.

In *AG Securities* v *Vaughan* [1988] 3 WLR 1205, Lord Templeman adopted a rather less legalistic approach to sham agreements than was the case in *Street* v *Mountford,* being of the view that fewer misunderstandings would have been caused if he had used the word 'pretence' to describe a written agreement or clause which was intended to act as a smokescreen obscuring the parties' real intentions. It is now clear that, in determining whether an agreement or clause is a 'pretence', the court may look at the conduct of the parties subsequent to the agreement in question as evidence of whether they genuinely intended to act upon it (*AG Securities* v *Vaughan,* per Lord Oliver of Aylmerton at 203). Practitioners should note that a further important case on sham agreements in the field of agricultural holdings (but with wider implications) is at the time of writing on appeal to the House of Lords: see *Gisborne* v *Burton* [1988] 3 WLR 921.

2.2.1.1 Multiple occupiers

A landlord may allow more than one person into occupation of the same dwelling-house. The Housing Act 1988 makes express provision for joint tenants but reference must be made to case law to determine whether an agreement or agreements conferring rights of occupation over the one property to two or more persons creates a tenancy or a licence. The term 'non-exclusive occupation agreement' defined the relatively common practice whereby a landlord would issue joint occupiers with standard form licence agreements under which each occupier agreed that he or she would share the dwelling-house with the other, or, in some cases, with whomsoever the landord might nominate. The landlord would argue that such occupiers could not be tenants as their agreements did not grant them exclusive possession of the dwelling-house, and therefore fell outside the Rent Act regime.

Support was given to the proponents of such documents by the Court of Appeal decision in *Somma* v *Hazelhurst* [1978] 1 WLR 1014, which denied the status of tenant to an unmarried couple who had signed two such agreements even though the accommodation consisted of a bed-sitting room and the thought of the landlord unilaterally introducing a third party of his choice to share the occupiers' love-nest was somewhat far-fetched. *Somma* v *Hazelhurst* was overruled in *Street* v *Mountford* on the basis that the Court of Appeal had failed to address itself to the sham nature of the documents signed by the occupiers, who were on a true construction joint tenants of the dwelling-house.

The leading authority on non-exclusive occupation agreements is now the decision of the House of Lords in *Antoniades* v *Villiers* [1988] 3 WLR 1205, where the agreements which fell to be construed were very similar to those in *Somma* v *Hazelhurst.* This time the accommodation consisted of a flat with a bedroom (containing a double bed), a bed-sitting room, a kitchen and a bathroom. The occupiers, a young man and his girlfriend, signed agreements each of which stipulated that 'the licensor' was entitled at any time to use the rooms together with the licensee and to permit other persons to use all of the rooms together with the licensee. The House of Lords held that this clause was a sham (or, per Lord Templeman, a 'pretence') as the landlord did not genuinely intend it to be a true statement of the nature of the possession to be enjoyed by the occupiers. Evidence of its sham nature was provided by the physical arrangement of the premises (unsuited for the sharing the agreements contemplated), the lack of any discussion between the parties as to how the clause might operate and the fact that the landlord never made any attempt to obtain increased income from the flat by introducing further occupiers as by the agreement he was allegedly entitled to do. The true effect of the agreement between the parties was to confer on the licensees a joint right to exclusive possession of the flat, and they were accordingly joint tenants.

Not all written agreements to share property are sham, however. In *AG Securities* v *Vaughan,* consolidated with *Antoniades* v *Villiers* for the purposes of the House of Lords hearing, the agreements were held to confer separate licences on the occupiers rather than a joint tenancy. The facts were completely different from those in *Antoniades* v *Villiers.* A company entered into four separate agreements with four separate persons between 1982 and 1985 for the occupation of a large flat which consisted of four bedrooms, a sitting-room, a lounge, a kitchen and a bathroom. The agreements were independent, and each occupier had come individually to the flat. Each agreement was in the same form but the rent payable by each occupier was different, as they had arrived at the flat at different times. When one occupier left the flat, the three remaining would decide whether they wished to change their bedrooms, and the replacement occupier would be offered the room the others did not want.

The House of Lords held that the occupiers were not joint tenants of the flat. The agreements were not pretences, but accurately reflected the flexible relationship between the landord company and the occupiers. Construing the written agreements, their lordships held that there was no grant of exclusive possession to the occupiers jointly as, in the event of one of the occupiers leaving, the three remaining could not exclude a fourth person nominated by the company. It was not contended that each occupier had a tenancy of his own bedroom, as there was no grant of an identifiable part of the flat to any one individual. If each occupier had a tenancy of his bedroom and the Housing Act were applicable (i.e., the tenancy was entered into on or after 15 January 1989), the tenants would probably fall within s. 3 of the Housing Act 1988 (see 2.2.3).

2.2.2 'Dwelling-house'

By s. 45, a dwelling-house may be a house or part of a house, and clearly flats fall within this provision. Little is likely to turn on whether a particular house is a *dwelling*, that is, a house which is capable of being inhabited, as the tenant will only be assured where he occupies the house as his only or principal home, and if he does so occupy it, it is surely inevitable that it is a dwelling so called. The proper interpretation of 'house' may be more problematical. In *R* v *Nottingham Rent Officer, ex parte Allen* (1985) 17 HLR 481, the Divisional Court held that a caravan was capable of being a dwelling-house, the question being essentially one of fact and degree. The dominant factor was the extent to which the caravan could be moved: if, as was not the position in *ex parte Allen,* the caravan was completely immobile, it was the more likely to come within the term 'dwelling-house'.

2.2.3 'Let as a separate dwelling'

'Let' does not, by itself, add anything to the requirement that there must be a tenancy. The dwelling-house must be let as a dwelling, not, by inference, as a shop or an office. Schedule I, Part I, excludes from assured tenancy status four types of what might be generically termed 'non-residential' tenancy, namely, business tenancies, public-house tenancies, tenancies of agricultural land, and tenancies of agricultural holdings: see further 2.3.4, 2.3.5, 2.3.6 and 2.3.7.

The dwelling-house must be let as a separate dwelling: it must be possible for the 'ordinary activities of existence' to go on in the property let. The question is ultimately one of degree, but the cases under the Rent Acts provide some guidance. For example, it is not enough if the only activity which can be carried on in the demised property is sleeping (*Curl* v *Angelo* [1948] 2 All ER 189): nor will it suffice if the tenant does not sleep there at all (*Wimbush* v *Cibulia* [1949] 2 KB 564).

In *Kavanagh* v *Lyroudias* [1985] 1 All ER 560, the tenant was granted at different times tenancies of adjoining houses. The house of which possession was sought was used by the tenant for sleeping in, and occasionally doing work which he brought home from his place of business. The house had no hot water, and the tenant never cooked or ate there; he would do those things in the adjoining house. The house was not let as a separate dwelling, clearly evidenced by the fact that the tenant did not occupy it as a complete home.

It is occasionally the case that the landlord will let two physically separate properties to the tenant, the intention being that the tenant will occupy them as a single dwelling. Despite the reference in s. 1 to '*a* dwelling-house', it is likely that the courts would follow the lead of the case law on the identical expression in s. 1 of the Rent Act 1977 and hold that a dwelling-house need not be in one location only (*Langford Property Co. Ltd* v *Goldrich* [1949] 1 KB 511).

2.2.3.1 Tenants who share accommodation Consideration has already been given to the possibility that an occupier who shares his accommodation with others may not be a tenant at all as he has not been granted exclusive possession. In most cases the occupier will be able to show that he is a tenant. However, the tenant (of perhaps one room) who is unable to show that he is a joint tenant of the whole dwelling unit with the others might, without more, have difficulty in proving that the part of which he has exclusive possession is a separate dwelling.

A frequent sharing arrangement is one where the individual tenants are given possession of a bedroom but share the kitchen, living-room, bathroom and so forth as common facilities available for the use of all the tenants in the house. The individual occupier will be tenant of his own room, which would qualify as part of a house under s. 45. The room could not, however, be said to be let as a separate dwelling, because the tenant will not cook, eat or wash there: in other words the ordinary activities of daily existence will be carried on in the house as a whole rather than in the room.

What would be a relatively easy avoidance of assured tenancy status is denied to the landlord by ss. 3 and 10. Section 3 creates an exception to s. 1 by deeming certain units which would not otherwise fall within the definition of a dwelling-house let as a separate dwelling to be let on assured tenancies. The tenancy of the separate accommodation (the bedroom in the above example) will be deemed to be an assured tenancy if the following conditions are satisfied:

(a) the tenant must have exclusive occcupation of the bedroom;

(b)   the terms on which he holds that room must include the use of the other accommodation (the kitchen, living-room and bathroom) in common with others, not the landlord;

(c)   the letting of the bedroom must not be excluded from assured tenancy status by any provision other than s. 1, for example, the exclusions listed in sch. 1, Part I.

The landlord would, in the absence of express statutory provision to the contrary, be able to make the tenant's position in his separate accommodation somewhat precarious, not to say uncomfortable, by invoking a term of the tenancy that he could stop him using certain parts, or indeed the entirety, of the shared accommodation. However, ss. 10(2) and 3(3) seek to prevent such abuse.

By s. 10(2), the court is prohibited from making an order for possession of the shared accommodation while the tenant remains in possession of his separate accommodation. Only when the court makes, or has made, a possession order relating to the accommodation held separately by the tenant will it gain the necessary jurisdiction to order that possession of the shared accomodation be given up. The court will only be able to make a possession order relating to premises held under an assured tenancy (such as the separate accommodation) on certain tightly prescribed statutory grounds: see chapter 3.

By s. 3(3), any term of the tenancy terminating or modifying the tenant's right to use the shared accommodation, or allowing the landlord so to terminate or modify is of no effect whilst the tenant remains in possession of his separate accommodation. The landlord who seeks to prevent the tenant from using common rooms without authority in the tenancy agreement would be acting in breach of contract, and a tenant in such a situation would be well advised to apply for an injunction against him. Section 3(3) will frustrate the landlord who has inserted a contractual term permitting him to stop the tenant from using common rooms. The landlord who seeks to use such a contractual term to the same effect could be similarly enjoined, as the term is of no effect.

However, there are exceptions to the above:

(a)   The landlord is able to invoke a term in the lease allowing him to terminate or modify the tenant's right to use shared accommodation insofar as that accommodation is not 'living accommodation', as defined in s. 3(5).

(b)   If, under the lease, the landlord is entitled to increase the number of persons with whom the tenant has to share, he will be free to invoke such a term, despite the fact that by increasing the number of sharers the landlord will be to some extent modifying the use of the shared accommodation by the existing tenants.

The landlord is entitled to apply to the court to enforce the above contractual rights, and on such application the court may make such order as it thinks just (s. 10(3)).

Where a sharer of the dwelling-house is a subtenant to whom has been let part of the dwelling-house, he will not be excluded from being an assured tenant by reason only that he has the contractual right to use some shared accommodation (s. 4(1)). None of the above provisions applies where the tenant is sharing accommodation with his landlord, or with his landlord and other persons (s. 3(1)(a)). In such a case, the tenancy may not be assured at all, being excluded from protection by sch. 1, para. 10, on which see 2.3.10.

2.2.4 Tenant must be an 'individual'

A tenancy is only assured if and so long as the tenant, or in the case of joint tenancy, each of the joint tenants, is an individual. This provision is intended to prevent companies or other institutions from claiming the benefits of the new legislation. It is probably unnecessary as the next requirement, that the tenant occupies the dwelling-house as his home, would seem to be appropriate only to individuals (see *Hiller* v *United Dairies (London) Ltd* [1934] 1 KB 57). Whether landlords will seek to use the so-called 'company let' to prevent the application of Part I of the Housing Act 1988 is a moot point: one would have thought that the assured shorthold tenancy gave to the landlord all the practical advantages which a licence falling outside the Act altogether would give. However, the company let has a certain following amongst landlords, and they may remain loyal to it. Nothing in Part I of the 1988 Act appears to affect the workings of this device, and the express requirement that the tenant be an individual encourages it.

In its simplest form, the company let involves the landlord letting the property to a limited company (which undertakes to pay the rent and comply with the covenants) and the company then allows a person into occupation as licensee. The company cannot be an assured tenant, as it is not an individual, and the occupier is not an assured tenant either: he may not be a tenant at all, or he may be paying no rent. Similar schemes have succeeded in avoiding Rent Act protection, although a pre-existing connection between the limited company and the individual has generally been present: see, for example, *Firstcross Ltd* v *East West (Export/Import) Ltd* (1981) 41 P & CR 145; *Estavest Investments Ltd* v *Commercial Express Travel Ltd* (1988) 44 EG 73. However, the most recent authority upheld a company let where the occupier had been required by the landlord to purchase an 'off the shelf' company with the sole motive of Rent Act avoidance: *Hilton* v *Plustitle Ltd* [1988] 3 All ER 1051. Whether company let schemes prosper in the future will depend on the enthusiasm with which the courts analyse agreements which are created with the avoidance of statutory control as their primary object: see, for example, *Gisborne* v *Burton* [1988] 3 WLR 921 (itself considered in *Hilton* v *Plustitle Ltd.*)

2.2.5 Tenant must 'occupy'

The above conditions having been satisfied, a tenancy will only be assured if and so long as the tenant occupies the dwelling-house as his only or principal home. This marks a change of terminology from the Rent Acts, under which a tenant whose contractual tenancy had terminated remained a statutory tenant if and so long as he occupied the dwelling-house *as his residence* (Rent Act 1977, s. 2(1)(a)). It is derived from the condition which a public sector tenant must satisfy to qualify as a secure tenant (Housing Act 1985, s. 81). The Rent Act case law must be applied with some caution, but the distinction between the terminology may be of little import in practical application.

To occupy a dwelling-house, it is quite clearly unnecessary to remain inside it

24 hours a day, 365 days a year (*Brown* v *Brash* [1948] 2 KB 247, 254). A tenant will be away, sometimes overnight, sometimes for weeks on end, on business, on holiday and so forth, and absences of this kind will not bring the status of the assured tenancy into question. However, where the absence is so prolonged or uninterrupted as to compel the prima facie inference of a cesser of occupation (this being a question of fact and degree), the tenant will, if possession is sought of the premises, have the burden of proving that he had not in fact ceased to occupy. How will he do this? He must show an intention to return to the premises after his absence, coupled with some physical manifestation of that intention on the premises: elements which are referred to as '*animus possidendi*' and '*corpus possessionis*' respectively (*Brown* v *Brash*).

The intention to return need not be immediate, and it may be conditional. In *Gofor Investments Ltd* v *Roberts* (1975) 29 P & CR 366, the tenant went away, intending to return in eight to ten years' time: the Court of Appeal held that the judge was entitled to find a sufficient *animus possidendi*. In *Tickner* v *Hearn* [1960] 1 WLR 1406, despite emphasising the need for there to be 'a real hope [of return to the dwelling-house] coupled with the practical possibility of its fulfilment within a reasonable time', it was held that a patient in a mental home, who had been absent owing to her illness for over six years, and would be very unlikely to leave hospital, had nevertheless established an intention to return such that she preserved her statutory tenancy.

The physical manifestation of the intention to return was referred to in *Brown* v *Brash* as 'some visible state of affairs in which the *animus possidendi* finds expression'. The Court of Appeal in that case considered that the most obvious 'symbol of continued occupation' would be a 'caretaker' (using the word in its widest sense) or other representative, charged with the function of preserving the premises for the tenant's ultimate homecoming. Later cases (*Gofor Investments Ltd* v *Roberts*; *Hoggett* v *Hoggett* (1980) 39 P & CR 121) have decided that leaving furniture on the premises may be a sufficient *corpus possessionis*. The importance of the absent tenant leaving some indication of his intention to return is exemplified by *Brown* v *Brash* itself. The tenant was sentenced to two years' imprisonment for stealing tea. He intended at all times to return to the premises on his being free to do so. For six months after his incarceration, the property was inhabited by his common law wife and two children. When they left the premises, the tenant thereupon ceased in law to occupy, and his statutory tenancy terminated, despite the fact that he still had an intention to return.

2.2.5.1 '*Only or principal home*' Not only must the tenant occupy the dwelling-house, he must occupy it as his only or principal home. The absent tenant may lose his assured tenancy, not because he has ceased to occupy the premises in law, but because he is living somewhere else during that time of absence, and that somewhere else is found to be his principal home. A possible approach to this provision is as follows:

(a)   Is the tenant, despite being 'absent', nevertheless occupying the dwelling-house as his home (see above)?

If the answer to (a) is no then the tenant is not assured.

If the answer to (a) is yes then ask:
(b)   Is the tenant occupying anywhere else as his home?

If the answer to (b) is no then the tenant satisfies the occupation requirement and (all other things being equal) will be an assured tenant.
If the answer to (b) is yes then ask:

(c)   Of the two homes which the tenant occupies, is this dwelling-house the principal one?

It was the intention of this provision to eradicate the anomaly whereby persons with two (or more) homes could claim the protection of social legislation which was not aimed at benefiting those with ample resources. In fact, under the old law, the courts were reluctant to hold that a person was occupying two homes at once (see, for example, *Hampstead Way Investments Ltd* v *Lewis-Weare* [1985] 1 WLR 164). It is anticipated that deciding which of two homes is the principal one will not be an exercise which will be frequently conducted as, in almost all cases, the court will be able to hold that X, who is occupying Y house as his home, is not also occupying Z house as his home (*Richards* v *Green* (1983) 11 HLR 1).

Where there is a genuine case of a tenant occupying two homes, it will be a question of fact to determine which of the two is the principal, and the issue will almost certainly be seen as one for the judge in the county court rather than the Court of Appeal (cf. *Hampstead Way Investments Ltd* v *Lewis-Weare*).

2.2.5.2 Husband and wife Where the tenanted property is occupied by husband and wife, only one of whom is tenant, different considerations apply. The tenant who goes away for a time leaving his spouse in occupation (to keep the exposition simple it will be assumed that the tenant is the husband) will, as long as he intends to return to the house, remain an assured tenant (*Brown* v *Brash* [1948] 2 KB 247). The tenant who leaves the house with no intention to return (in other words abandoning his wife) will nevertheless remain an assured tenant. The Matrimonial Homes Act 1983, s. 1(6) as amended by the Housing Act 1988, sch. 17, para. 33, provides that the occupation of the wife would in these circumstances be treated as the occupation of the husband. Accordingly, as long as the wife continues to occupy the dwelling-house (and as long as she continues to be the wife of the tenant), the assured tenancy will persist. She will be entitled to make rent and rate payments herself (Matrimonial Homes Act 1983, s. 1(5)) and would be advised to do so, if necessary and practicable, as otherwise the landlord may have grounds for seeking possession (see Housing Act 1988, sch. 2, Grounds 8, 10 and 11, and chapter 3).

The deserted wife is therefore given some degree of protection. However, the operation of the Matrimonial Homes Act 1983 depends on her being the spouse of the tenant. If the parties have been divorced, the Act no longer applies, and the wife may be left without remedy (see *Metropolitan Properties Ltd* v *Cronan* (1982) 44 P & CR 1). Where divorce is to occur, the proper course for the wife residing in the former matrimonial home which is let to the husband under an assured tenancy is to apply in the ancillary relief proceedings for the tenancy to be transferred to her: see 2.4.3.2).

If the wife is provided with a house by her husband, of which house the husband is tenant, she will not be able to invoke the 1983 Act unless the house has been at some time their matrimonial home (Matrimonial Homes Act 1983, s. 1(10)). In such a situation the husband would never become an assured tenant, as he would not himself be occupying the house as his home, and his wife's (or ex-wife's) occupation would not suffice (see *Hall* v *King* [1988] 1 FLR 376).

2.2.6   Extent of the property subject to assured tenancy
The physical structure of the house or flat is not the only property leased by the landlord which will be subject to the assured tenancy. If, under the terms of the lease, the dwelling-house is let together with other land (for example, a garden, outhouses or even a small paddock) that other land will also be let on assured tenancy, if and so long as the main purpose of the letting is the provision of a home for the tenant (or one of joint tenants) (s. 2(1)(a)). The question of 'main purpose' will involve balancing the various purposes of the letting concerned. Where a camp site was let to the tenant, together with a bungalow for his personal occupation, it was held that the main purpose of the letting was the use of the site for the tenant's business of camp-site proprietor (*Feyereisel* v *Turnidge* [1952] 2 QB 29). If it is held that the main purpose of a letting of a dwelling-house and land is not the provision of a home for the tenant, then not only the land but also the dwelling-house will be excluded from assured tenancy status (s. 2(1)(b)).

However, where the other land consists of agricultural land (as defined in the General Rate Act 1967, s. 26(3)(a)) exceeding two acres, the tenancy cannot be an assured tenancy (sch. 1, para. 6). Note also in this context the exclusion from Housing Act protection of tenancies of agricultural holdings by sch. 1, para. 7.

2.2.7   Accommodation for homeless persons
Where accommodation is provided in pursuance of the statutory duties to house the homeless, the landlord will usually be the local housing authority itself, and express provision has been made in sch. 1 to the Housing Act 1985 that the applicant for housing will not become a secure tenant of the accommodation concerned until the expiry of one year from the date he receives his notification of the local housing authority's decision on the question whether he is homeless or threatened with homelessness, or of the name of the authority which has the duty to house him (Housing Act 1985, sch. 1, para. 4). It may be, however, that the authority does not house him but seeks accommodation for him. In particular, housing associations registered with the Housing Corporation are under a duty to cooperate with local housing authorities in the discharge of their homelessness functions (Housing Act 1985, s. 72). In such cases, where the tenancy is not with a landlord which satisfies 'the landlord condition' within the Housing Act 1985, s. 80, the tenancy could be an assured tenancy within Part I of the Housing Act 1988. However, s. 1(6) makes similar provision for the letting by the landlord who is assisting the local authority as is provided for the authority itself. Where the tenancy is granted in pursuance of arrangements between the authority and some other person to provide accommodation for the homeless, there will be a one-year period during which the tenancy cannot be assured. The period does not run from the date the tenancy is entered into, but from the date the tenant receives notification under Part III of the 1985 Act. If the one-year period expires

before the landlord terminates the tenancy, the tenancy may of course become assured, and the landlord is unlikely to succeed in arguing that, the accommodation being of an essentially temporary nature, the occupier is a licensee rather than a tenant (*Eastleigh Borough Council* v *Walsh* [1985] 1 WLR 525, HL). As long as the agreement granted exclusive possession of the dwelling-house for a term at a rent, then by an application of the ordinary principles of construction, the occupier will have a tenancy (*Street* v *Mountford* [1985] AC 809). If the tenant is notified by the landlord in the one-year period that the tenancy is to be regarded as an assured tenancy, then it will no longer be excluded from assured status by s. 1(6): not quite the same thing as becoming an assured tenancy.

2.2.8 Joint tenants

The Rent Act 1977 made no specific provision for joint tenants, or for that matter joint landlords, and occasioned a considerable amount of litigation as a result (see, e.g., *Lloyd* v *Sadler* [1978] QB 774; *Tilling* v *Whiteman* [1980] AC 1). The Housing Act 1988 does at least learn from this mistake, and throughout makes express provision to cater for joint tenants. Where only one of two or more joint tenants occupies the dwelling-house as his only or principal home, the tenancy will nevertheless be assured (s. 1(1)(b)). The provisions concerning joint tenants will not be discussed in this book in relation to each aspect of Part I: the Act itself is quite explicit. However, it should be noted that in those rare cases where the Act is silent, it must be implied that a reference to 'the tenant' (or 'the landlord') is a reference to both or all joint tenants (or joint landlords) (s. 45(3)).

2.3   Tenancies which cannot be assured tenancies (schedule 1)

Assuming that a tenancy has satisfied the conditions of s. 1 which have been discussed above, it may nevertheless be excluded from assured tenancy status as falling within one of the categories listed in sch. 1, succinctly titled 'Tenancies which cannot be assured tenancies'. A tenancy cannot be an assured tenancy 'if and so long as' it falls within one of the paragraphs of sch. 1, thus giving rise to the possibility that a tenancy may change its status during the course of its existence. For example, a tenancy which satisfies all the other statutory requirements may be excluded from being an assured tenancy because the rent payable is less than two thirds of the rateable value of the dwelling-house (sch. 1, para. 3). If the rent under the tenancy is then increased, so that it exceeds two thirds of the rateable value, the tenancy, being no longer excluded by para. 3, will become an assured tenancy.

The sch. 1 exclusions bear a close resemblance to those of ss. 4 to 16 of the Rent Act 1977, but they are not identical. In particular, a letting which includes payments in respect of board or attendance, exempt from protected status under the Rent Act 1977 (s. 7), is not prevented from being an assured tenancy on that ground. Lettings by housing associations, largely excluded from Rent Act security of tenure (Rent Act 1977, s. 15), will not be prohibited from being assured tenancies, save for tenancies entered into by the so-called 'fully mutual' associations. It should also be noted that with the repeal of the restricted contract provisions, there will be no residual 'diluted' security of tenure for tenancies which are excluded from assured status by sch. 1.

2.3.1   Pre-commencement tenancies

Tenancies entered into before 15 January 1989, the day Part I of the Housing Act 1988 came into force, or pursuant to a contract made before that date, cannot be assured tenancies (sch. 1, para. 1). It is the policy of the legislation to continue to subject such tenancies to their old regime. However, there are exceptions to this general rule. For instance, assured tenancies subject to the provisions of the Housing Act 1980, ss. 56 to 58 ('1980 Act assured tenancies'), will be converted into 1988 Act assured tenancies although they will by definition have been entered into before the commencement of the 1988 Act: see 6.3. More important is the exception contained in s. 38, which will now be considered.

In the months and years which follow the coming into force of the Housing Act 1988 many tenants will see the identity of their landlords change. The controversial Part IV grants to approved persons (so-called 'social landlords') the right to acquire houses presently occupied by public sector tenants, and these tenants will consequently be transferred from the public to the private sector. The less contentious Part III will see a similar, more gradual exodus, as housing action trusts, having revitalised inner city estates in accordance with their duties, sell off the one-time council properties in their improved state. In each of these situations, the purchaser of the reversion must be in the 'social landlord' category, the Housing Corporation being responsible for policing the approval system. In many cases, the purchaser will be a housing association (treated now as being a private sector landlord). The policy of the legislation is that tenants who move from the public to the private sector, whether in one of these ways or by a voluntary disposal of the reversion by their one-time landlord, will become assured tenants on transfer irrespective of the dates their tenancies were entered into, and this policy is put into effect by s. 38.

Example 2.1   In January 1986, district council L lets a house on secure tenancy to T. L sells the house to P, a private sector purchaser (which is not a housing association) in March 1989. On the date the sale is completed, T will cease to be a secure tenant, as the Housing Act 1985, s. 80 ('the landlord condition') , is no longer satisfied. The tenancy will become assured (as long as it is not otherwise excluded from assured status) although it was entered into prior to the commencement of the 1988 Act (s. 38(3)). If the purchaser was a housing association, the same principles would apply, save that the tenancy could not become assured if the new landlord was a fully mutual housing association (sch. 1, para. 12(1)(h), and see definition in Part I of the Housing Associations Act 1985). Although many housing associations are within the Housing Act 1985, s. 80, with respect to tenancies entered into before 15 January 1989, in this situation the tenancy would lose its secure status because the housing association is not within the definition of 'public body' contained in s. 38(5) and so, on the district council selling the property, the interest of the landlord ceases to be held by a public body (s. 38(1)(b)).

Example 2.2   Housing association H lets a house to T in June 1987. The tenancy is secure, and it is a 'housing association tenancy' within Part VI of the Rent Act 1977, entitling the tenant to the benefit of the fair rent provisions. In March 1989, H sells the house to Q, a private sector landlord. The tenancy will thereupon cease to be secure, and it will also cease to be a housing association tenancy (ss. 38(1)(b) and 38(2)(b)). The tenancy will become assured (as long as it is not otherwise excluded from assured tenancy status) although entered into prior to the commencement of the 1988 Act (s. 38(3)).

Note that if s. 38 did not intervene in these circumstances, the likelihood is that the tenant would hold from the new private sector landlord as a protected tenant under the Rent Act 1977. If the purchaser was a housing association, the tenancy would not be likely to be protected (see Rent Act 1977, ss. 15 and 16) but it would probably be a 'housing association tenancy' within Part VI of the Rent Act. Section 38(3)(a) ensures that this will not be the case.

Slightly different rules apply where the landlord disposing of its interest is a new town corporation (i.e., the Commission for the New Towns or a development corporation established by an order made, or having effect as if made, under the New Towns Act 1981: see Housing Act 1985, s. 4). Section 38 will only operate to 'convert' a tenancy to assured status in the way outlined above where the landlord disposes of its interest after 15 November 1990 (or such other date as the Secretary of State may specify by order (s. 38(4)). If, prior to that date, a new town corporation were to sell housing subject to tenancy to a private sector landlord, the likelihood is that the tenant would become protected under the Rent Act.

2.3.2 Tenancies with high rateable values

Few dwelling-houses will be excluded from assured tenancy protection by para. 2, the rateable value ceiling being high: over £1,500 in Greater London, over £750 elsewhere. Where the dwelling-house forms part only of a hereditament, its rateable value should be ascertained by apportioning the rateable value for the hereditament among its constituent parts. In the event of a failure to agree a proper apportionment, the county court is to decide (sch. 1, para. 14). The rateable value is generally to be ascertained from the valuation list, and alterations to that value are to be taken account of (sch. 1, para. 15). In assessing rateable value, account must be taken of any land which is let with the dwelling-house (s. 2(1)(a) and sch. 1, para. 16).

2.3.3 Tenancies at a low rent

Despite the enumeration of the necessary elements for a tenancy in the leading authority of *Street* v *Mountford* [1985] AC 809 as the grant of exclusive possession for a term *at a rent,* the Court of Appeal has since denied that the reservation of a rent is essential for the creation of a tenancy (see *Ashburn Anstalt* v *W. J. Arnold & Co.* [1988] 2 WLR 706). However, just as a tenancy under which no rent was reserved could not be protected under the Rent Acts, so too it cannot be an assured tenancy (sch. 1, para. 3).

Following the formula used in relation to the Rent Acts, a tenancy at a low rent cannot be an assured tenancy (sch. 1, para. 3). A low rent is one which is less than two thirds of the rateable value of the dwelling-house for the time being, the rateable value being ascertained by reference to the principles outlined in 2.3.2. Schedule 1, para. 3(2) gives guidance on sums which must be disregarded in determining the amount of rent payable.

'Rent', for the purposes of the analogous s. 5 of the Rent Act 1977, did not include the value of services rendered by the tenant for the benefit of the landlord (*Barnes* v *Barratt* [1970] 2 QB 657). However, where the tenant was employed by his landlord, occupying rent-free accommodation provided by his employer, and received a smaller wage as a result, it was proper to quantify the rent by reference to the reduction in wages (*Montagu* v *Browning* [1954] 1 WLR 1039). It is likely that similar principles will be used when the courts apply para. 3.

In considering whether a tenancy falls within para. 3, the court must beware of the danger of sham agreements. In *Samrose Properties Ltd* v *Gibbard* [1958] 1 WLR 235, the tenant paid a large premium for the grant of a fixed term of one year's duration, and then a weekly rent which was in itself less than two thirds of the rateable value of the dwelling-house. The written agreement was headed by a recital that the landlord was not desirous of granting a lease such that the Rent Acts would apply to it. The Court of Appeal held that the agreement was a sham, and that the true level of the rent should be calculated by adding the premium to the annual total of the weekly rent. Note that there are no provisions in the Housing Act 1988 outlawing the demand of a premium prior to entry into an assured tenancy. The government is content for the free market to dictate whether premiums can be charged as part of the consideration for the tenancy being granted.

2.3.4   Business tenancies

Schedule 1, para. 4, states that a tenancy to which Part II of the Landlord and Tenant Act 1954 applies cannot be an assured tenancy. Part II of the 1954 Act applies:

> to any tenancy where the property comprised in the tenancy is or includes premises which are occupied by the tenant and are so occupied for the purposes of a business carried on by him or for those and other purposes (Landlord and Tenant Act 1954, s. 23(1)).

'Business' is widely defined, including a trade, profession or employment, and it 'includes any activity carried on by a body of persons, whether corporate or unincorporate' (Landlord and Tenant Act 1954, s. 23(2)). Premises are only occupied by the tenant for the purposes of a business where business user forms a significant purpose of the occupation and is not merely incidental to residential occupation. In *Royal Life Saving Society* v *Page* [1978] 1 WLR 1329, a doctor rented a maisonette as his home. With the consent of the landlords, he saw the occasional patient at his home in an emergency and he used the telephone in the flat for the purposes of his profession. He was held to be a protected tenant of the maisonette and, were the Housing Act 1988 jurisdiction applicable, he would be an assured tenant (cf. *Cheryl Investments Ltd* v *Saldanha* (1978] 1 WLR 1329).

Although the definition of assured tenancy in s. 1 of the Housing Act 1988 requires the court to look at the use of the property contemplated at the time of the letting, the definition of business tenancy requires the court to look at the use in fact made of the property while the tenant is in occupation. This distinction has an important effect when it comes to ascertaining whether a given tenancy is an assured tenancy or a business tenancy.

If a property is initially let as a dwelling but the tenant occupies it for the purposes of his business, then the tenancy will cease to be assured and will become subject to the provisions of the 1954 Act (see *Cheryl Investments Ltd* v *Saldanha*). If, however, a property is initially let for the purposes of the tenant's business but then the tenant's business user ceases, it will not 'automatically' become an assured tenancy (*Wolfe* v *Hogan* [1949] 2 KB 194). In such a situation, the tenancy will become assured only if landlord and tenant have, since the initial letting, entered into a new contract providing for residential user *or* the tenant's change of user from business to residence has been acknowledged by the landlord so that a subsequent contract to let as a dwelling-house can be inferred: see per Slade LJ in *Russell* v *Booker* (1982) 263 EG 513.

There is a slight difference in wording between the Rent Act 1977 and the Housing Act 1988 (and the cases listed above are Rent Act authorities) but not, it is thought, a significant one. By s. 1(2) of the 1988 Act, a tenancy cannot be assured '*if and so long as*' it falls within para. 4. The italicised words do not appear in the 1977 Act, and it could be argued that once business occupation ceases, and para. 4 no longer applies, the tenancy will become an assured tenancy 'automatically'. However, such an argument would give insufficient weight to s. 1(1) of the 1988 Act which requires the dwelling-house to be 'let as a . . . dwelling'. This expression relates to the contract of letting between the parties, and if the contract was initially for the occupation of business premises the letting will remain for that purpose, and will not be a letting as a dwelling, unless and until there is a variation of the initial contract giving rise to the inference that the parties are now holding on a new contract altogether.

With the coming into force of the Housing Act 1988, it may not always be in the tenant's interest to argue that he is an assured tenant rather than a business tenant. Under both regimes, the landlord is able on termination of the contract to charge a market rent, and the assured tenant will not have the advantage of the protected tenant who could claim a 'fair' (that is, below market) rent. The procedure for obtaining possession of premises let on a business tenancy is highly technical and fraught with pitfalls: it may be that a tenant may on advice see himself in a stronger bargaining position as a business tenant than as an assured tenant. The old assumption that the tenant is better off claiming statutory rights as a residential tenant rather than trusting his chances with the 1954 Act may be undermined somewhat should such tenants first consider what benefits the new assured tenancy confers.

2.3.5   Licensed premises

'On-licences' cannot be assured tenancies (sch. 1, para. 5). Although public houses are clearly occupied for the purposes of a business, theirs are not tenancies to which Part II of the Landlord and Tenant Act 1954 applies: s. 43(1)(d) of that Act excludes them from business tenancy status. Schedule 1, para. 4, of the 1988 Act does not therefore effectively prevent them from being assured, and express exclusion is required. Off-licences cannot be let on assured tenancies either: they are within Part II of the Landlord and Tenant Act 1954, and so para. 4 excludes them from being assured tenancies.

2.3.6   Tenancies of agricultural land

Where agricultural land exceeding two acres, as defined in the General Rate Act 1967, s. 26(3)(a), is let together with the dwelling-house the tenancy cannot be an assured tenancy (sch. 1, para. 6). The tenant will not be able to argue that the dwelling-house alone has assured status: the statute clearly infers that one cannot arbitrarily divide up the property let. The tenancy as a whole must stand or fall within the definition.

2.3.7   Tenancies of agricultural holdings

'Agricultural holding' is defined in the Agricultural Holdings Act 1986, s. 1. Where the dwelling-house is comprised in an agricultural holding and is occupied by the person responsible for the control of the farming of the holding, any tenancy under which that dwelling-house is held cannot be assured (sch. 1, para. 7). Such tenancies will come within the protective umbrella of the Agricultural Holdings Act instead.

A property which is initially let as a dwelling-house, with no, or purely subsidiary, use as agricultural land, may be converted from being an assured tenancy to a tenancy within the Agricultural Holdings Act 1986 by a change of user. A dwelling-house which is initially let as part of an agricultural holding will, on a cesser of agricultural use, no longer be within the Agricultural Holdings Act 1986, but it does not follow that it will thereupon convert into an assured tenancy as a matter of course. To qualify as an assured tenancy, the dwelling-house must be let as a dwelling, and the tenant would need to prove that a new contract had come into being, either on the parties' express agreement or by inference from the landlord's tacit acceptance of the position (*Russell* v *Booker* (1982) 263 EG 513, and see 2.3.4).

2.3.8   Lettings to students

The heading to sch. 1, para. 8, is misleading. Two elements must be satisfied before assured tenancy status will be denied, and the fact that the tenant is a student is but one. The exclusion is of tenancies granted to students by 'specified educational institutions', and thus the private landlord whose eyes might light up on seeing para. 8 will be disappointed. The 'student' need not be full-time: he must merely be pursuing, or intending to pursue, a course of study provided by a 'specified educational institution'. It is not necessary that the educational institution of which he is a student is the same institution which is his landlord under the tenancy. Educational institutions are specified by the Secretary of State for the Environment, by statutory instrument. He may specify a class of institutions, and he has now used this power to specify (as under the Rent Act 1977, s. 8) universities, university colleges, most further educational establishments, sundry satellite bodies and certain named housing associations: see SI 1988 No. 2236.

Note that provision is made for mandatory recovery of possession of accommodation generally covered by para. 8 which is let on a short fixed term, perhaps during the vacations: see Ground 4 of sch. 2, dealt with in 3.2.4.

2.3.9   Holiday lettings

A tenancy cannot be an assured tenancy if its purpose is to confer on the tenant the right to occupy the dwelling-house for the purposes of a holiday (sch. 1, para. 9). 'Holiday' is not defined in the statute. It has been said, in the context of the Rent Act 1977 (s. 9 of which is practically identical to para. 9), that 'holiday' implied 'a period of cessation of work or a period of recreation' (*Buchmann* v *May* [1978] 2 All ER 993).

In *Buchmann* v *May*, a dancer from New Zealand had occupied the dwelling-house in question for two years when she signed a new agreement which stated 'that the letting hereby made is solely for the purposes of the tenant's holiday'. The Court of Appeal held that the onus was upon the tenant to displace the prima facie evidence of the parties' true purpose which the written agreement provided. This she had failed to do and so the tenancy was unprotected. However, the courts must now be astute to detect shams and artificial devices whose only object is to avoid the application of protective statutes such as the Housing Act 1988 (*Street* v *Mountford* [1985] AC 809, 825). In the light of this, one should be careful of placing too much weight on the authority of *Buchmann* v *May*.

In *R* v *Camden Rent Officer, ex parte Plant* (1980) 257 EG 713, the landlord let to four student nurses, the written agreement stating that the letting was for the purposes of a holiday. In view of clear evidence that the landlord knew that the tenants were nurses, Glidewell J held that the tenancy was protected.

2.3.10 Resident landlords

The resident landlord exception, never the most coherent or straightforward provision in the Rent Act 1977, applies to assured tenancies too. Whereas tenants of resident landlords enjoyed restricted contract status under the Rent Acts, under the Housing Act 1988 they will have no such residual protection. It will first be necessary to establish which code is to be applied. The date of the tenancy is crucial. If the tenancy was entered into before 15 January 1989 (or pursuant to a contract made before that date), the Rent Act 1977 will be applicable, and the provisions of s. 12 and sch. 2 thereof must be consulted. If the tenancy is denied protection by virtue only of the Rent Act 1977, it will be a restricted contract (Rent Act 1977, s. 20).

Once satisfied that the tenancy is prima facie assured, sch. 1, para. 10, and possibly paras 17 to 22, must be carefully considered. Three conditions must be fulfilled before the resident landlord exception will be established. The conditions to be fulfilled depend on whether the dwelling-house let to the tenant forms part of a building which is a purpose-built block of flats. 'Purpose-built block of flats' is defined in sch. 1, para. 22. It must *as constructed* contain two or more flats. The date of construction is the relevant time to consider, and a distinction is drawn between conversions of existing buildings (which can only in the most exceptional circumstances constitute 'purpose-built blocks of flats') and constructions of new buildings (which if they consist of two or more flats will be within the definition) (see *Bardrick* v *Haycock* (1976) 31 P & CR 420; *Barnes* v *Gorsuch* (1981) 43 P & CR 294).

If the building is not a purpose-built block of flats:
   (a)   The dwelling-house let to the tenant must form part only of the building.
   (b)   The person who granted the tenancy (the first landlord) must have been

an individual (i.e., not a company or institution) and he must have occupied another dwelling-house in the same building as his only or principal home.

(c) At all times, each of the persons who had the landlord's interest (the later landlords) must have been an individual and he must have occupied another dwelling-house in the same building as his only or principal home.

If the building is a purpose-built block of flats:

(a) The dwelling-house let to the tenant must form part of one of the flats.

(b) The first landlord must have been an individual, and he must have occupied another dwelling-house *in the same flat* as his only or principal home.

(c) At all times, each of the later landlords must have been an individual and must have occupied another dwelling-house in the flat as his only or principal home.

Whether the dwelling-house let to the tenant forms part of the same building (or flat) as the dwelling-house occupied by the landlord is a question of fact and degree. In *Bardrick* v *Haycock* (1976) 31 P & CR 420, a substantial house was converted into six flats, occupied by tenants. The landlord lived in a two-storey extension which, although physically attached to the house, did not have any internal means of communication to it. It was held on the facts that the landlord did not occupy a dwelling-house forming part of the same building as that of which the tenants' dwelling-houses formed part.

2.3.10.1 Joint landlords The Rent Acts were silent on whether the occupation of one of a number of joint landlords would suffice for the purposes of the resident landlord exception, and the matter had to be resolved judicially, in favour of the landlord (see *Cooper* v *Tait* (1984) 15 HLR 98). Part I of the Housing Act does not leave the matter to the courts: the occupation of one 'joint landlord' will do (para. 10(2)).

2.3.10.2 Regrants The landlord is prevented from sidestepping the sometimes heavy burden of satisfying para. 10 by the simple ruse of granting the tenant a new tenancy of the same flat (or by the rather more subtle one of rearranging his tenants within the building and granting each of them new tenancies). If he grants a new tenancy to a person who, immediately before it was granted, was a tenant under an assured tenancy of the same dwelling-house or another dwelling-house in the same building, then the resident landlord exception will not apply to the new tenancy (para. 10(3)). This provision may not be watertight. If there is a hiatus between the termination of the former tenancy and the grant of the new one, the landlord may be able to argue that the tenant was not an assured tenant 'immediately before' the new tenancy was granted. Less easy to engineer is to grant the assured tenant a tenancy in a different building altogether, the difficulty being to ensure that there is a resident landlord in that building at the relevant times. The difficulty would be soluble where the landlord's interest was held jointly: one of the joint landlords could go to the new building.

What if the landlord seeks to grant to a *protected* tenant (whose tenancy commenced before 15 January 1989) a new tenancy so as to fuel the resident landlord exception? Although para. 10(3) is silent, the tenant would be able to rely on s. 34(1)(b). If the landlord grants a tenancy to a person who, immediately before the tenancy was granted, was a protected or statutory tenant, and the landlord is the landlord (or one of joint landlords) under the protected or statutory tenancy, then the new tenancy will also be protected even though it is entered into after 15 January 1989. The landlord would have the same argument as above in the event of a hiatus, but offering the tenant different accommodation, even in a different building, would probably be of no avail as s. 34(1)(b) does not require the new tenancy to be of the old dwelling-house.

2.3.10.3 Occupation by the landlord Part III of sch. 1 must be examined with care. Paragraphs 17 to 20 add a gloss to the condition in para. 10(1)(c) ('condition (c)') that there should be continuous occupation of a part of the building (or flat) by the prevailing landlord from the date of the tenancy to the date possession is claimed.

Condition (c) is deemed to be fulfilled in the following instances:

(a) Where the landlord's interest is vested in trustees on trust (or trust for sale) for a beneficiary or beneficiaries, at least one of whom occupies the dwelling-house as his only or principal home (para. 18(a)).

(b) Where the landlord's interest has been so vested in trustees, and the tenancy has come to an end, during the full duration of any new tenancy of the same (or substantially the same) dwelling-house which the trustees grant to the sitting tenant (para. 19).

(c) For a period, not exceeding two years, throughout which the landlord's interest is vested in personal representatives (i.e., the persons who, following the death of the resident landlord, have his estate vested in them by his will or on his intestacy) (para. 20).

The effect of condition (c) being deemed to be fulfilled is that the tenancy is not assured, and it can at any time be terminated and possession obtained by reference to the general principles of landlord and tenant law: the landlord will not need to satisfy Part I of the Housing Act 1988.

Example 2.3 The house is settled on trust by settlor S. The trustees are A and B, the beneficiaries C, D and E. E occupies a room in the house as his dwelling. The tenants who live in other rooms in the house will not be assured tenants so long as E continues to live there and, during his occupation, the trustees will be able to obtain possession of any of the rooms occupied by the tenants by giving them the notice to which they are entitled under the terms of their contracts of tenancy,

The following periods are to be 'disregarded' in determining whether condition (c) has been fulfilled:

(a) A period of 28 days following the vesting of the landlord's interest in an individual who does not occupy the dwelling-house as his only or principal home (e.g., on a purchase of the landlord's interest) para. 17(1)(a)).

(b) A further period of six months following the vesting of the landlord's interest in such an individual, *provided that* the individual has notified the tenant in writing of his intention to occupy the dwelling-house as his only or principal home during the initial period of 28 days. The six months will run from the date the landlord's interest was vested in the individual concerned (*not* the date of the written notice) (para. 17(1)(b)).

(c) A period of two years following the vesting of the landlord's interest in trustees or the Probate Judge (i.e., on death intestate) (para. 17(1)(c)).

(d) A period of two years following the death of a beneficiary behind a trust, whose occupation of the dwelling-house has until then caused condition (c) to be deemed to be fulfilled by virtue of para. 20(2) (para. 18(2)).

In each of these cases, the period of disregard will end on condition (c) being once more fulfilled, whether by the individual owning the landlord's interest commencing to occupy the dwelling-house as his only or principal home or by the deeming provisions of paras 18(1), 19 or 20.

The effect of a period being disregarded is that when condition (c) is once more fulfilled, possession can be obtained of the dwelling-house let to the tenant by reference to general principles of landlord and tenant law: the tenancy not being assured, the landlord will not have to satisfy Part I of the 1988 Act. However, during a period of disregard, no order for possession of the dwelling-house shall be made other than an order which might be made were the tenancy an assured tenancy (para. 21).

Example 2.4   L, the landlord, lives in the basement flat of a house of which he owns the freehold and which has been converted into several one-bedroom flats, T lives in the ground-floor flat which was let to him under a weekly tenancy on 1 February 1989. L has satisfied the condition of residence throughout the period of T's tenancy. On 1 December 1989, L sells the freehold in the house to P, who becomes T's landlord. On 22 December 1989, P serves notice on T stating that he intends to occupy the basement in the six-month period which began on 1 December, the day he completed the purchase. Until he goes into occupation, P cannot obtain possession of T's flat unless he can show that were T an assured tenant a possession order would be made.

On 1 April 1990, P goes into occupation of the basement. He can now end T's tenancy by terminating the contract, i.e., by giving four weeks' notice. If, however, P goes into occupation on or after 1 June 1990, it will be too late. The period of disregard has ended, and so, unless condition (c) is otherwise satisfied, the tenancy will no longer be excluded from being an assured tenancy by the resident landlord provisions.

2.3.11   Tenancies held of certain landlords

Paragraphs 11 and 12 of sch. 1 state that tenancies under which the interest of the landlord belongs to certain bodies cannot be assured tenancies. Both paragraphs require the court to consider the ownership of the landlord's interest at the time the status of the tenancy has to be ascertained, rather than the time the tenancy is granted. Thus if the landlord's interest is assigned to or from the exempted body subsequent to the grant of the tenancy, that tenancy will cease to be, or become, an assured tenancy as the case may be.

Paragraph 11 excludes tenancies where the landlord's interest belongs to Her

Majesty in right of the Crown (save for interests under the management of the Crown Estate Commissioners), a government department, or is held in trust for Her Majesty for the purposes of a government department.

Paragraph 12 overlaps considerably with para. 13(3). whereby secure tenancies are excluded from assured status. This leads to complications, exacerbated by s. 35(3): see further 6.7.

A tenancy can only be secure if the interest of the landlord belongs to a particular body, listed in the Housing Act 1985, s. 80(1), but that is only one of the statutory conditions it must satisfy. In the following list, it is presumed that in each case, all other necessary conditions are fulfilled.

(a)   If the landlord's interest belongs to one of the following, the tenancy will be secure, and cannot be assured (para. 12):

    (i)   a local authority, defined in para. 12(2);
    (ii)   the Development Board for Rural Wales;
    (iii)   an urban development corporation;
    (iv)   a housing action trust (see chapter 9).

(b)   If the landlord's interest belongs to one of the following, the tenancy will be secure, and cannot be assured (para. 13(3)):

    (i)   a new town corporation;
    (ii)   a housing cooperative, as defined in the Housing Act 1985, s. 27B.

(c)   If the landlord's interest belongs to one of the following, the tenancy will not be secure or assured (para. 12):

    (i)   the Commission for the New Towns;
    (ii)   a development corporation;
    (iii)   a waste disposal authority;
    (iv)   a residuary body.

(d)   If the landlord's interest belongs to one of the following, the tenancy will be secure if entered into on or before the commencement of the 1988 Act or if within s. 35(3)(d) or (e).

    (i)   the Housing Corporation;
    (ii)   a housing trust which is a charity;
    (iii)   a housing association within the Housing Act 1985, s. 80(2).

If so, it cannot be assured (para. 13(3)). If not secure, the tenancy may be assured: paras 12 and 13(3) will not prevent it.

(e)   If the landlord's interest belongs to a fully mutual housing association, as defined in the Housing Associations Act 1985, s. 1(2), the tenancy may or may not be secure, depending on the type of housing association (see Housing Act 1985, s. 80(2)) and whether the tenancy was entered into on or before the commencement of the Act. The tenancy cannot in any event be assured (para. 12).

2.3.12 *'Transitional cases'*

Of the four tenures listed in sch. 1, para. 13, three are phased out by Part I of the Housing Act 1988, and the effect of the Act on existing tenancies of these types is outlined in chapter 6. The exception is the secure tenancy, which will remain a significant feature after the Act, albeit with major changes to the kinds of landlord who can let on such a tenancy. Thus para. 14 in referring to secure tenancies is dealing with more than just 'transitional cases': see further 2.3.11 and chapter 6.

2.4   Terms of assured tenancies

2.4.1   *Types of assured tenancy*
An assured tenancy may be:

    (a)   a periodic tenancy
    (b)   a fixed-term tenancy
    (c)   a statutory periodic tenancy.

A periodic tenancy is not defined in the Housing Act 1988. It is a tenancy the maximum duration of which is not ascertainable at its commencement. If created by the parties' express agreement, it will be stated in the lease that the tenancy is 'weekly', 'monthly' or 'yearly' as the case may be. It may also be created by implication from the parties' conduct, the tenant being let into possession and paying rent to the landlord on a periodic basis. A periodic tenancy will be terminable by notice given by either party to it, but unless and until notice is given the tenancy will continue from period to period.

A fixed-term tenancy is defined for the purposes of the Housing Act 1988 by s. 45 as 'any tenancy other than a periodic tenancy'. A fixed-term tenancy will not, generally speaking, be terminable by notice. It will terminate on the expiry of the term agreed between the parties ('expiry by effluxion of time'): for example, if the tenancy is for three years, and the three years have now elapsed. On general principles, a fixed term will also terminate if there is express provision in the lease for the landlord to terminate it before it has run its course in the event of the tenant being in breach of a covenant or condition in the lease, and following such breach of covenant the landlord does so terminate it ('forfeiture' or 're-entry', a process fraught with legal and procedural complexities). It is also possible for the lease to provide for termination before it has run its course on notice given by one party to another at given intervals during its currency (e.g., in a lease for 21 years, that either party may terminate on notice at seven-year intervals): such a provision, which again must be expressed in the lease, is referred to as a 'break clause'.

A statutory periodic tenancy arises where a fixed-term tenancy which is an assured tenancy comes to an end, and the tenant under that fixed-term tenancy is not expressly granted another tenancy of the dwelling-house (or 'substantially the same dwelling-house') (s. 5(2) and (4)). However, a statutory periodic tenancy will not arise if the fixed-term tenancy comes to an end by the tenant's own action, such as surrendering the lease, or if it comes to an end by order of the court (s. 5(2); see chapter 3). (It will be only rarely that the court will order possession of a dwelling-house let on a fixed-term tenancy which has not yet expired by effluxion of time.) The statutory periodic tenancy, although it is the creation of the Housing Act 1988, need not necessarily be an assured tenancy itself. Section 5(2) requires only that the fixed-term tenancy from which it evolves is an assured tenancy.

Example 2.5 A dwelling-house is let on a fixed term of three years. The fixed term is within s. 1 and the tenancy is not excluded from assured tenancy status by any of the categories in sch. 1. On its expiry by effluxion of time, the tenant continues in possession as a statutory periodic tenant. He then starts to use the premises for the purposes of his import-export business. Although the tenancy will cease to be assured (by virtue of sch. 1, para. 4), it will continue to be a statutory periodic tenancy.

2.4.1.1 Establishing the terms of tenancies The periodic tenancy and the fixed-term tenancy are based on the agreement of landlord and tenant, and to ascertain the terms of such tenancies one must apply the normal rules of the law of contract to construe the agreements in question. The statutory periodic tenancy, on the other hand, is the creature of statute, and the terms of the statutory periodic tenancy are to be determined by an application of the Housing Act 1988.

2.4.2 Statutory periodic tenancy
The statutory periodic tenancy will (s. 5(3)):

(a) take effect in possession immediately the fixed-term tenancy comes to an end;
(b) have as its landlord and tenant those persons who were landlord and tenant under the fixed term immediately before it came to an end;
(c) be of the dwelling-house let under the fixed term;
(d) have as its periods those by which rent was last payable under the fixed term (e.g., if rent paid was £2,000 per annum payable monthly, the statutory periodic tenancy will be a monthly tenancy);
(e) have as its terms those of the fixed term immediately before it came to an end, except that any term allowing landlord or tenant to terminate is not to have effect while the tenancy remains an assured tenancy.

Section 5(3) attempts to preserve the rights and obligations agreed by the parties in the contract of tenancy save in one respect: the termination of their relationship and the landlord's ability to recover possession. The termination of the statutory periodic tenancy, as long as it is an assured tenancy, and the recovery of possession by the landlord, are matters for the court, which must apply the principles of Part I of the Housing Act 1988. If, however, a statutory periodic tenancy is *not* an assured tenancy any more (and has not become, for example, a business tenancy), it will be determinable on the landlord giving the notice appropriate for the periods of the tenancy (e.g., if a monthly tenancy, one month's notice; there is a statutory minimum of four weeks' notice where premises are let as a dwelling: Protection from Eviction Act 1977, s. 5(1) as amended by Housing Act 1988, s. 32; see chapter 7).

2.4.2.1 *Section 6 procedure* The landlord and the tenant to a statutory periodic tenancy may agree to vary the terms of the tenancy, and they will be free to do so, although any term making provision for determination by either of them will have no effect while the tenancy remains an assured tenancy (ss. 6(7) and 5(3)(e)). The parties cannot unilaterally vary the terms of the tenancy, but s. 6 provides a procedure whereby a proposal of either party to vary the terms can be made and, in the event of opposition by the other, may be referred to a rent assessment committee which will make a determination on the merits of the proposal which will be binding on the parties.

The s. 6 procedure can be used in relation to any statutory periodic tenancy, whether or not it is an assured tenancy. However, the procedure cannot be used if the tenancy is not an assured tenancy by virtue of sch. 1, paras 11 or 12 (interest of landlord now belonging to Crown or local authority etc.). The s. 6 procedure cannot be used to vary the rent payable under the tenancy, although the rent assessment committee are empowered to adjust the rent to take account of other terms they have determined. For the procedure for securing an increase in rent, see chapter 3.

The s. 6 procedure will take the following course:

(a) The fixed term ends, and a statutory periodic tenancy takes effect.

(b) Not later than the first anniversary of the ending of the fixed term, the landlord (or tenant) serves a notice proposing varied terms.

(c) Within three months of notice being served, the tenant (or landlord) refers the notice to the rent assessment committee.

(d) The committee consider the proposed terms and make a 'determination'.

(e) The committee specify an adjustment to the rent to take account of their determination.

(f) The committee direct the date (no earlier than the date specified in the notice proposing variation) from which the terms they have determined shall become terms of the statutory periodic tenancy, and the adjustment in rent, if any, takes effect.

If a tenant fails to refer the landlord's notice (or vice versa) to a rent assessment committee within three months of service, the variation, and any adjustment of rent, proposed will take effect (s. 6(3)(b)).

The committee must determine whether the terms proposed in the notice are such as might reasonably be expected to be found in an assured periodic tenancy of the dwelling-house concerned. This tenancy must be viewed as one beginning on the termination of the fixed-term tenancy, granted by a willing landlord, and having the same terms as the statutory periodic tenancy before them except for those terms which relate to the subject-matter of the terms proposed (s. 6(4)). The committee are not bound either to accept the proposed terms or to reject them. They may devise terms of their own in place of the terms presently implied, as long as the terms they devise deal with the same subject-matter as the proposal which is before them (s. 6(4)).

If the committee consider it appropriate, they shall specify a rent adjustment, even though the initial landlord's (or tenant's) notice did not propose such an adjustment (s. 6(5)). In making their determination and specifying a rent adjustment, the committee must disregard any effect on the terms or rent attributable to the tenancy being granted to a sitting tenant (s. 6(6)).

The committee may require the landlord or the tenant to provide such information as they may reasonably require for the performance of their functions, and a failure to comply may result in the imposition of a fine on conviction in the magistrates' court (s. 41). The initial landlord's (or tenant's) notice, the reference by the tenant (or landlord) to the committee, and a request by the committee for information must be in prescribed form, (see SI 1988 No. 2203, Forms No. 1, 2 and 9 respectively).

The committee may find that an application under the s. 6 procedure and an application to determine the market rent have been referred to it with respect to the same dwelling-house. In such circumstances, although they are under no statutory duty to do so, it will usually be desirable (and economical) to hear the two applications at the same time, before the same persons. If the committee do decide to 'consolidate' applications in this way, they must determine the s. 6 reference first (s. 14(6)). This is common sense: the committee will be able to fix the market rent only when the terms of the tenancy have been properly established.

The s. 6 procedure requires rent assessment committees to perform a function which will be wholly foreign to them: to compose the terms of a lease. It is a task which they will find particularly difficult to begin with, as they will have no 'comparable' tenancies to refer to. Yet there is no right of appeal from their determination: only where they have misdirected themselves in law will there be remedy, and that will be by way of judicial review: see 3.5.6.

2.4.3 Terms implied by law

2.4.3.1 *Assignment and subletting* In the case of a statutory periodic tenancy (which is still an assured tenancy), s. 15(1) implies a term that the tenant shall not assign the tenancy (in whole or in part) or sublet or part with possession of the whole or part of the dwelling-house without the landlord's consent. A similar term will be implied into assured tenancies which are non-statutory (i.e., contractual) periodic tenancies unless the parties have themselves made express provision about assignment or subletting in the lease (s. 15(3)). If a covenant against assignment or subletting is implied by virtue of s. 15(1), the tenant will not be able to question the refusal of the landlord to give his consent to a proposed assignment, as the operation of the Landlord and Tenant Act 1927, s. 19, whereby consent to assign is not to be unreasonably withheld, is expressly excluded. Moreover, as the statutory covenant against assignment is not qualified by a provision that the landlord's consent is not to be unreasonably withheld, the landlord will not be under a statutory duty to make his decision whether or not to consent within a reasonable time of one tenant's application to assign (see Landlord and Tenant Act 1988, s. 1(1)). For security of tenure of subtenants, see 3.4.

2.4.3.2   Transfer on divorce   Despite the general antipathy to assignment of assured tenancies, the court has jurisdiction to order the transfer of an assured tenancy from one spouse (or former spouse) to the other on or after a decree of divorce (sch. 17, para. 34(1), amending Matrimonial Homes Act 1983, sch. 1, para. 1). For the effect of such a transfer on succession rights, see 2.5.

2.4.3.3   Access for repairs   It is an implied term of every assured tenancy that the tenant shall afford the landlord access (and 'all reasonable facilities') to execute such repairs as he is entitled to execute (s. 16). The most important statutory repairing obligation is that contained in the Landlord and Tenant Act 1985, s. 11 (as amended by the Housing Act 1988, s. 116, see chapter 11). By s. 11(6) of the 1985 Act, a tenant to whose dwelling-house such a covenant applies is contractually obliged to allow the landlord, at reasonable times and on 24 hours' notice, to enter the dwelling-house for the purpose of viewing its condition and state of repair. If the tenancy is an assured tenancy, the tenant is also obliged to allow the landlord to do the work necessary to put the premises into repair.

2.4.3.4   Rent books   If the rent under an assured tenancy is payable weekly, the landlord is under a statutory duty to provide the tenant with a rent book (Landlord and Tenant Act 1985, s. 4). The rent book must contain notice of such matters as are prescribed (Landlord and Tenant Act 1985, s. 5(1)(b), as amended by Housing Act 1988, sch 17, para. 67). These 'matters' are prescribed in SI 1982 No. 1474, as amended by SI 1988 No. 2198. The latter instrument provides the statutory form of notice appropriate for a rent book of an assured tenant.

2.5   Statutory succession to assured tenancies

Succession to an assured tenancy is strictly limited to one successor, and that successor must be the spouse, or common law spouse, of the tenant. The statutory rules are to be found in s. 17. They take precedence over any will of the tenant, or the normal operation of the intestacy rules. Section 17 only operates in relation to an assured periodic tenancy (i.e., a 'contractual' periodic tenancy or a statutory periodic tenancy). If the assured tenancy is for a fixed term which has not yet expired at the time of the tenant's death, the remainder of the fixed term will devolve on whoever is entitled to it under the terms of the tenant's will or on intestacy.

An assured periodic tenancy will vest in the spouse of a tenant on his death, provided three conditions are satisfied: (a) the tenant must have been the sole tenant; (b) the spouse must have been occupying the house as her only or principal home immediately before the tenant's death; and (c) the tenant must not himself have been a 'successor', a term widely defined in s. 17(2) and (3).

(a)   Where the tenancy was held jointly with another, the succession provisions of s. 17 do not apply. They would be either unnecessary or unworkable in such a situation. If the tenant and his spouse are themselves joint tenants, the spouse will succeed to the tenancy by right of survivorship. If the tenant is joint tenant with someone else, that person will be entitled to the tenancy by survivorship, and to grant the spouse succession rights would be to ignore the interest of the surviving joint tenant.

(b)   Whether the spouse was occupying the dwelling-house as her only or principal home is the same question as that asked when considering whether a tenancy is at any given time assured, and the same principles will no doubt apply: see 2.2.5.1. The tenant must also have continued to occupy the house as his only or principal home until his death, for if he ceased to occupy, his assured tenancy would terminate (s. 1(1)(b)). Does the spouse have to have been 'living with' the tenant at the time of his death, or would it suffice that they lived separate lives under the same roof? The statute is not clear, but it may well depend on whether the tenant and his 'spouse' were lawfully married or just 'common law' man and wife. This is because to qualify as a spouse, a person who is not lawfully married must show that she 'was living with the tenant as his . . . wife' (s. 17(4)). The statute does not say when this condition must be satisfied, but if one states the possibilities (at any time during the tenant's life, within a reasonable time of the tenant's death, immediately before the tenant's death), the final one would appear to be both the most workable and the one which is most compatible with s. 17(1)(b). Where the tenant was lawfully married, there is no requirement that she was 'living with the tenant' at any time, and it would be wrong to limit arbitrarily the circumstances in which she could succeed.

(c)   A surviving spouse cannot succeed to a person who is himself a successor. A tenant will be a successor if the tenancy came to be vested in him by virtue of the will or intestacy of a previous tenant, or by survivorship. He will be a successor if the tenancy devolved on him by a previous 'statutory succession', whether under the Rent Act 1977, sch. 1, or under s. 17 itself. He will still be a successor even though the landlord has granted him a new tenancy of the dwelling-house (or substantially the same dwelling-house) since the succession took place (see s. 17(2) and (3). Where a successor to an assured tenancy transfers the tenancy to his spouse or former spouse on or after a decree of divorce, the transferee will be deemed to be a successor also, and on her death, no further statutory succession will be possible (sch. 17, para. 34(2), amending Matrimonial Homes Act 1983, sch. 1, para. 2(3)).

If an assured periodic tenancy does not go, by virtue of s. 17, to a surviving spouse, it will devolve on somebody else by the tenant's will or the intestacy rules. In those circumstances, the landlord will have 12 months in which to decide whether to exercise the mandatory ground for possession contained in Ground 7 of sch. 2.

Chapter Three
Assured Tenancies: Security of Tenure and Rents

3.1 Security of tenure: introduction

Although the assured tenancy regime of security of tenure introduced by Part I of the Housing Act 1988 has many similarities, in terms of excluded tenancies and grounds for possession, to that of the Rent Act 1977, it is entirely different in its central concept, being more akin to the 'secure tenancy' code contained in Part IV of the Housing Act 1985 which applies to residential tenancies in the public sector. The Rent Act regime was based upon the notion of a contract followed by a status. The contractual 'protected' tenancy was terminable by the landlord in accordance with the ordinary principles of leasehold law: if periodic, it could be terminated by notice to quit, if a fixed term, it would be more likely to terminate by effluxion of time or forfeiture. However, terminating the protected tenancy did not entitle the landlord to possession: far from it. On termination, the tenant would, if and so long as he occupied the dwelling-house as his residence, remain a 'statutory tenant', and possession could only be obtained by the landlord on proof of statutorily prescribed grounds.

The dichotomy between protected and statutory tenancy made the law unnecessarily complex and conceptually convoluted. The solution adopted in 1980 when the code for public sector tenants was promulgated was to have one species of tenancy only (the secure tenancy), provide that such a tenancy is terminable only by obtaining an order of the court, and restrict the grounds on which the court may order possession. In practical effect, there is no substantial difference between the two methods, but the secure tenancy model has the attraction of relative simplicity. The Housing Act 1988 in turn adopts the same concept, but it must be admitted that in the course of its legislative execution much of that essential simplicity has been lost.

The one species of tenancy which is to apply in the private sector is of course the assured tenancy. Thus, before a tenant can claim the protection of the Housing Act 1988, he must first come within the definition of assured tenant. It was explained in chapter 2 that there are three subspecies of assured tenancy: the fixed-term tenancy, the 'contractual' periodic tenancy and the statutory periodic tenancy. One of these, the statutory periodic tenancy, will not necessarily be an assured tenancy. However, although a statutory periodic tenant may not necessarily be assured, the tenant will only be able to claim security of tenure if he is an assured tenant. For the purposes of security of tenure, there is no distinction made between assured 'contractual' periodic tenancies and assured statutory periodic tenancies. Where mention is made in this chapter of 'periodic tenancies', it will include statutory periodic tenancies too.

Where a tenancy is assured, there are four routes by which possession can be obtained:

(a) the tenant surrenders the tenancy, or ceases to occupy the dwelling-house;

(b) the court makes an order for possession;

(c) the tenancy ceases to be an assured tenancy;

(d) other statutory powers, which can override assured tenancies, are exercised.

3.1.1 Termination of tenancy by tenant

The Housing Act 1988 does not stand in the way of the tenant who surrenders his lease and gives up possession. From the time he gives up possession, he will have ceased to occupy the dwelling-house as his home, and the assured tenancy will have thereby terminated (s. 1(1)(b)). If, when or before the tenancy is entered into, the tenant agrees, in whatever fashion, to give up possession at a time in the future when the tenancy will be assured, the agreement will be of no effect (s. 5(5)). A landlord who seeks to enforce such an agreement, whether by specific performance or by order for possession, will fail. If such an agreement is made after the date of the tenancy, s. 5(5) will not vitiate it, but the agreement will probably be unenforceable by the landlord. Section 7(1) restricts the jurisdiction of the court to order possession of dwelling-houses which are let on assured tenancy, and so if the tenancy remains assured, the existence of an agreement to give up possession will be of no avail to the landlord (*Barton* v *Fincham* [1921] KB 291).

Another possibility is that the tenant and landlord have come to an agreement varying the terms on which the tenant holds in such a way that he is no longer a tenant at all, but a mere licensee. When this agreement takes effect, the tenancy will be surrendered 'by operation of law', and the licence will be outside the provisions of the Housing Act 1988 altogether (see *Foster* v *Robinson* [1951] 1 KB 149).

3.1.2 Termination of tenancy by landlord

The landlord who wishes to initiate proceedings for possession of a dwelling-house held by an assured tenant will not find s. 5 an immediately comprehensible provision: yet it is to s. 5 that he must turn. To consider the alternative courses of action open to him, the landlord must first identify the subspecies of assured tenancy with which he is dealing: is it a fixed term, a 'contractual' periodic tenancy, or a statutory periodic tenancy? (The meaning of these terms is stated in 2.4.1.)

If the assured tenancy is a periodic tenancy (whether contractual or statutory), the position is straightforward. Such a tenancy cannot be brought to an end by the landlord except by obtaining an order of the court (s. 5(1)). A notice to quit by the landlord in relation to such a tenancy will be of no effect.

If the assured tenancy is a fixed-term tenancy, the position is more complicated. The statement in s. 5(1) that a fixed-term tenancy can be brought to an end by a landlord who exercises a power contained in the lease to determine it in certain circumstances is true but misleading. First, the exercise of such a power will not entitle the landlord to possession: it will merely end the fixed term, and a statutory periodic tenancy will immediately arise protecting the right of the tenant to remain in possession. A court order will, of course, be required to terminate the statutory periodic tenancy (unless it ceases to be an assured tenancy: see 2.4.1). Secondly, the 'power to determine' referred to in s. 5(1) is *not* a right of re-entry or proviso for forfeiture (see s. 45(4)). It is presumably a reference to a 'break clause' (see 2.4.1), under which the landlord at one of the prescribed intervals exercises his option to terminate the fixed term. What, then, of the landlord who discovers that his tenant is in breach of covenant and who wishes to forfeit the tenancy, as the lease entitles him to do? His proper course of action will be to take possession proceedings. The landlord may seek possession of a dwelling-house let on an assured fixed-term tenancy, but the court has a restricted number of grounds on which a possession order may be made. In particular, the landlord must have been entitled under the terms of the tenancy to bring the tenancy to an end on the ground in question by forfeiture, re-entry or notice (s. 7(6)).

A fixed-term tenancy will, of course, also come to an end 'by effluxion of time' when the term expires. This will not entitle the landlord to possession either: by s. 5(2), a statutory periodic tenancy will come into being to protect the tenant. Note, however, that if the tenant accepts a grant of a new tenancy of the same or substantially the same dwelling-house then the tenancy will take effect under the contract and will not be a statutory periodic tenancy (s. 5(4)).

The court is restricted in the granting of a possession order in relation to dwellings let on assured tenancy. It must not make a possession order unless it is satisfied that certain grounds, listed in sch. 2, have been established. Where the assured tenancy is a fixed-term tenancy which has not yet come to an end, the number of grounds on which possession may be ordered is fewer than usual (Grounds 2, 8 and 10 to 15 inclusive are available) and there must also be provision in the terms of the tenancy for it to be brought to an end on the ground in question (s. 7(6)). Where the assured tenancy is a periodic tenancy, the landlord may seek possession on any of the grounds in sch. 2.

Proof of any one of Grounds 1 to 8 entitles the landlord to an order for possession, and the court does not even have a discretion to adjourn proceedings or suspend the operation of the possession order once it is satisfied that such a ground has been established (ss. 7(3) and 9(6)). These grounds will be referred to as the 'mandatory grounds'. Proof of any one of Grounds 9 to 16 does not entitle the landlord to possession as of right: the court may only make an order for possession if it considers it reasonable to do so, and has wide powers to adjourn proceedings or suspend the operation of a possession order (ss. 7(4) and 9). These grounds will be referred to as the 'discretionary grounds'.

3.2   Grounds for possession

Many of the statements of ground for possession set out in sch. 2 are intricate and lengthy. It is not intended here to repeat the provisions verbatim, but merely to comment on their likely practical uses, and to identify difficulties which may arise in their practical application.

3.2.1   Ground 1 (mandatory ground)

This ground contains two quite distinct alternatives. The landlord may rely on his past occupation of the dwelling-house as his only or principal home (which need not have been immediately before the grant of the tenancy), and he does not have to show any intention to reoccupy in the future: he may simply want to sell with vacant possession. Alternatively, he may rely on his present requirement for the dwelling-house as his (or his spouse's: note the possible use of this ground in ancillary relief proceedings if the parties are still married) only or principal home, and need not show any past use of it as such. In the latter, but not the former, situation, the landlord will be prohibited from using the ground if he (or any predecessor in title of his) is a 'landlord by purchase', having bought the reversion to the dwelling-house while the present tenancy was in existence: an important exception, as it would otherwise be open to entrepreneurs to buy up any property let on assured tenancy and seek possession on the basis of a relatively short-term intention to occupy. The exception only applies where the reversion was acquired 'for money or money's worth'. If the landlord now seeking possession inherited the dwelling-house concerned from the landlord who gave the notice, he will not be precluded from using this ground.

3.2.2   Ground 2 (mandatory ground)

Although the Rent Act 1977 did not contain a ground approximating to Ground 2, the Court of Appeal had established that where a mortgagor let a dwelling-house on protected tenancy, in breach of a term in the mortgage deed, the mortgagee's right to possession would prevail over the tenant (*Dudley and District Benefit Building Society* v *Emerson* [1949] Ch 707). This ground gives statutory recognition to the primacy of the mortgagee's rights in such a situation. It comes into operation only if a written notice was served before the beginning of the tenancy, and mortgagees would be wise to insert a clause in mortgage deeds which contemplate lettings requiring the service of such a notice on any assured tenant. If no notice was served, and the court refused to exercise its dispensation powers (see 3.2.6.1), it is arguable that the mortgagee could fall back on his common law rights and rely on *Dudley and District Benefit Building Society* v *Emerson* to assert his right to possession. Note that Ground 2 preserves the rights of the mortgagee who has a mortgage over the interest of the landlord or a superior landlord. The rights of a mortgagee who has a mortgage over the interest of the tenant in the assured tenancy (for example, where the tenancy in question is a long lease) will not be affected by the Housing Act 1988 (s. 7(1)). His position is merely approximated to that of a mortgagee of a Rent Act tenant (see Emmet on Title, 25. 004).

3.2.3   Ground 3 (mandatory ground)

Out-of-season lets of holiday accommodation are covered by Ground 3. It will frequently be the case that during the holiday season the occupier will hold on a tenancy which is excluded from assured status by sch. 1, para. 9, but it is not necessary to activate Ground 3 for this to be so: for example, the so-called 'holiday let' may be a licence only. The fixed term of the out-of-season let must not exceed eight months, and if the landlord wished to let for six months or over, the assured shorthold may be a viable alternative.

3.2.4   Ground 4 (mandatory ground)

This ground is intended to cover vacation lets of student accommodation, although in contrast to Ground 3 the accommodation must have been let in the previous 12 months on a tenancy excluded from assured status by sch. 1, in this case para. 8. It is not necessary that the vacation let is by a specified educational institution, although that will normally be the case.

3.2.5   Ground 5 (mandatory ground)

This ground enables the recovery of accommodation which is 'held for the purpose of being available' as a residence for a minister of religion. Such accommodation may be presently occupied by such a person, who is coming to the end of his term of office. Ground 5 would also seem to allow recovery where the dwelling-house had been let out temporarily, perhaps during an interregnum between two incumbents. When the property is once more required, the court will be compelled to make a possession order.

3.2.6   Notice in writing

All five grounds so far considered require the landlord to give notice in writing to the tenant, no later than the beginning of the tenancy, that possession might be recovered on the ground in question. This is a mandatory requirement as far as Grounds 3, 4, and 5 are concerned: if no notice is served, the ground in question cannot be used. Grounds 1 and 2 give the court discretion to dispense with the notice requirement, a discretion which will be considered below.

Where the tenant is now holding under a different tenancy to that before which written notice was given, the notice will comply with sch. 2 if the present tenancy took effect immediately on the other coming to an end, with the same tenant and substantially the same dwelling-house as under the earlier tenancy (sch. 2, para. 8(2)). For the purposes of these provisions, 'the beginning of the tenancy' means the date the tenancy is entered into, and so if the notice is served after the lease is signed but before the tenant goes into possession, it will be too late (sch. 2, para. 11).

3.2.6.1   Dispensation power

The court may be invited to apply its discretion to dispense with the requirement for notice in writing in all kinds of circumstances. The landlord, ignorant of the finer points of sch. 2 to the Housing Act 1988 and rushing off abroad on business for a few months, may tell the tenant that the property he is about to rent is his home, but not put the information in writing. The landlord may send the tenant written notice, but it is delayed in the post and arrives after he has executed the lease. Or the landlord may not think about recovering the house at all at the time of the initial letting, but two years later when he wants to reclaim possession so that he can live there he reads Ground 1 and regales the court with tales of the hardships he is now under.

On a literal reading of Grounds 1 and 2, the court's discretion appears to be unlimited, and when the Court of Appeal had to consider a dispensation power which was couched in identical terms in Case 11 of the Rent Act 1977 it held that the judge must look at all the circumstances of the case:

> Those would embrace the circumstances affecting the landlord, or his successors in title, the circumstances of the tenant and, of course, the circumstances in which the failure to give written notice arose. It is only if, having considered all those circumstances, the court considers that it would be just and equitable to give possession that it should do so, because it must be borne in mind that, by failing to give the written notice, the tenant may well have been led into a wholly false position. (Per Griffiths LJ in *Bradshaw* v *Baldwin-Wiseman* (1985) 49 P & CR 382, 388.)

To return to our hypotheses, the landlord who gives the tenant oral notice and the landlord whose notice is delayed by the post may argue strongly, and possibly with some success, that the dispensation power should be exercised in their favour: see *Fernandes* v *Parvardin* (1982) 5 HLR 33, and *Minay* v *Sentongo* (1983) 45 P & CR 190. Where the landlord himself did not at the outset envisage that recovery of possession could be attained by the use of these grounds, it is submitted that the courts should take a strong line and refuse to dispense with the requirement of written notice. In *Bradshaw* v *Baldwin-Wiseman,* Griffiths LJ stated that it could not be 'just and equitable' to dispense where there was no initial intention to create a 'Case 11' tenancy, and the same can be said in relation to Grounds 1 and 2 of the new code.

3.2.7   Ground 6 (mandatory ground)
This ground had no counterpart in the Rent Act 1977, but it has a familiar look to it, the likenesses being a ground for possession existing in relation to secure tenancies (Housing Act 1985, sch. 2, para. 10) and a ground for opposition to the tenant's application for a new business tenancy (Landlord and Tenant Act 1954, s. 30(1)(f)). The landlord must not be a landlord by purchase. He must intend to demolish or reconstruct, or carry out substantial works on, the dwelling-house or a substantial part of it. The ground does not say how immediate the implementation of these intentions must be. Two statements from business tenancy cases may be of application in this context:

> An 'intention' . . . connotes a state of affairs which the party 'intending' . . . does more than merely contemplate: it connotes a state of affairs which, on the contrary, he decides, so far as in him lies, to bring about, and which, in point of possibility, he has a reasonable prospect of being able to bring about, by his own act of volition (per Asquith LJ in *Cunliffe* v *Goodman* [1950] 2 KB 237).

> . . . the court must be satisfied that the intention to reconstruct is genuine and

not colourable; that it is a firm and settled intention, not likely to be changed; that the reconstruction is of a substantial part of the premises, indeed so substantial that it cannot be thought to be a device to get possession; that the work is so extensive that it is necessary to get possession of the holding in order to do it; and that it is intended to do the work at once and not after a time (per Denning LJ in *Fisher* v *Taylors Furnishing Stores Ltd* [1956] 2 QB 78, 84).

Ground 6 puts before the court possible alternatives it must consider before finding that the landlord is entitled to possession: variation of terms of the tenancy, the grant of an assured tenancy of part only of the dwelling-house while the works are carried out. In seeking to establish that he has an intention within the ground, the landlord should come to court armed with the planning permission (if necessary), proof of ability to finance the operation and sufficient details of the intended works to convince the court that the plan is not merely colourable. If the landlord is a company, its intention is best shown by a resolution of the directors as recorded in the minutes or, if the matter is beyond their powers, by a resolution of the company in general meeting. Where the landlord seeking possession is a registered housing association or a charitable housing trust, the intention of their superior landlord will suffice: otherwise, Ground 6 is only made out if it is the tenant's immediate landlord who has the intention.

The two further conditions which the landlord must satisfy are as follows. First, the landlord's interest must either have been acquired before the grant of the tenancy or have been in existence at the time of the grant and not acquired since then by any landlord for money or money's worth. This provision, designed to discourage property developers from buying up dwelling-houses let on assured tenancies and then using Ground 6 to obtain vacant possession, may give a protection which is illusory. The tenant must be particularly on his guard against the new landlord who offers him a new tenancy agreement on attractive terms. If he accepts a new tenancy at any time, he is giving to his landlord the right to use Ground 6, because from then onwards the 'landlord seeking possession' will have acquired his interest before the grant of the tenancy. The second condition is that the assured tenancy concerned did not come into being as a result of succession to a Rent Act protected or statutory tenancy. For the circumstances where this might occur, see 6.1.5.

It is considered likely that many landlords will seek to use Ground 6, obtaining possession and then doing as they wish with the property. Unfortunately, the protections which the ground purports to give the tenant are relatively lightweight, and the determined landlord may be able to bluster his way through them. The courts must be on their guard against landlords who form an intention to demolish or reconstruct as a means to an end, and must insist on compelling evidence of a firm, settled and genuine state of mind. Where the court orders possession on Ground 6, the tenant is entitled to be paid his reasonable removal expenses by the landlord, and if the landlord fails to pay them, the tenant can sue him for the debt owed to him (s. 11).

3.2.8   Ground 7 (mandatory ground)
This ground has no Rent Act equivalent. It gives the landlord a 12-month period

of grace following the death of a periodic tenant to assess the character and financial viability of the person who has inherited the tenancy under the general law. If the landlord does not wish him to remain tenant, he need not justify his decision to seek possession, and if proceedings are commenced within the 12-month period the court must make the order sought. The landlord may, at the court's discretion, have longer than 12 months if he did not become immediately aware of the tenant's death, the period then running from the date of knowledge. Such a landlord may feel safer claiming possession within the initial 12 months, as he will otherwise be putting himself at the mercy of the court.

If a court were to imply that a new periodic tenancy had been created during the 12-month period from the tender and acceptance of rent, the policy of the ground would be frustrated. The tenancy would not any longer be the periodic tenancy which had devolved under the will or intestacy of the former tenant, and Ground 7 would not apply. A rider therefore provides that the court must not make such an implication, unless the landlord agrees in writing to a change in one of the terms of the tenancy. *Quaere* whether the court could find that the parties had during the 12-month period entered into a new periodic tenancy by express oral agreement.

Ground 7 does not affect the rights of the one statutory successor to an assured tenancy, namely the surviving spouse. It is expressly stated that her tenancy vests by virtue of the operation of the statute and does not devolve under the tenant's will or intestacy (s. 17(1)).

3.2.9 Ground 8 (mandatory ground)

This is the first of three grounds for possession which may be available in the event of non-payment of rent, the others being Grounds 10 and 11. Ground 8, being mandatory, is obviously the most attractive to a landlord seeking possession. He must first ensure that when he serves his 's. 8 notice' (and the court has no discretion to dispense with service: s. 8(5)) there is sufficient rent which is lawfully due but unpaid. Ground 8 then clearly contemplates the recalcitrant tenant paying the arrears and frustrating the landlord's attempts to obtain possession. If, by the date of the hearing, the tenant does pay the arrears, or enough arrears to reduce the amount unpaid to below the levels necessary for possession to be granted under Ground 8, the landlord will no longer be able to rely on the mandatory ground. A landlord will be well advised, in order to mitigate his position in such circumstances, to have included Grounds 10 and 11 as alternatives in his s. 8 notice, leaving open the possibility of obtaining possession on those discretionary grounds, or at last obtaining a suspended order whilst the tenant pays off the arrears, if any, that remain.

Note that Grounds 8, 10 and 11 will be the landlord's most effective remedy for non-payment of rent. The statutory restrictions on levying distress contained in the Rent Act 1977 are carried over to assured tenancies as well (s. 19).

3.2.10 The discretionary grounds

Grounds 9 to 16, if satisfied, empower the court to order possession if it considers it reasonable to do so. The classic statement of the duty of the court in such a case is that of Lord Greene MR in *Cumming v Danson* [1942] 2 All ER 653, 655, a Rent Acts authority, where the county court judge was instructed to take into account:

all relevant circumstances as they exist at the date of the hearing. That he must do in what I venture to call a broad, common-sense way as a man of the world, and come to his conclusion giving such weight as he thinks right to the various factors in the situation. Some factors may have little or no weight, others may be decisive, but it is quite wrong for him to exclude from his consideration matters which he ought to take into account.

The judge who has to decide whether it is reasonable to order possession of a dwelling-house let on an assured tenancy will be expected to carry out a similar exercise. The matter being one for the discretion of the judge, an appeal will only succeed if the appellant can show that the judge has misdirected himself (*Cresswell* v *Hodgson* [1951] 2 KB 92).

3.2.11   Ground 9

'Suitable alternative accommodation' is defined in Part III of sch. 2. The landlord has two primary options open to him in establishing this ground. He may produce a certificate of the local housing authority stating that the authority will provide suitable alternative accommodation, and such a certificate will be conclusive evidence that such accommodation will be provided by the date there specified. Alternatively, he may pursue the more difficult course of satisfying the court (without any certificate) that the accommodation he is suggesting is suitable. Whichever option he chooses, the court will ultimately have to decide the question whether it is reasonable to order possession independently of the question whether the accommodation offered is suitable (see *Battlespring Ltd* v *Gates* (1983) 268 EG 355).

Where the landlord does not produce a certificate from the local authority and attempts to show that the accommodation is suitable, the accommodation will be deemed to be suitable if it satisfies two requirements, one concerning the security of tenure of the premises concerned, the other concerning the suitability of the accommodation itself. The premises must be let on assured tenancy, but not assured shorthold or subject to one of the mandatory grounds dependent on service of a notice (i.e., Grounds 1 to 5), or alternatively on terms affording the tenant reasonably equivalent security to that offered by an assured tenancy. Thus, a public sector letting to the tenant might satisfy this, if the tenancy was secure and therefore within Part IV of the Housing Act 1985.

The accommodation offered must in any case be reasonably suitable to the needs of the tenant and his family as regards proximity to place of work, and must either satisfy the comparison with local authority accommodation in the area which is provided for persons with similar needs to the tenant and his family as regards extent (see sch. 2, part III, para. 3(1)(a)) or be otherwise reasonably suitable to their needs as regards extent and character. The 'character' of the accommodation is only significant if the accommodation is not being compared with the local authority accommodation. 'Character' may include the physical environs of the property concerned (*Redspring* v *Francis* [1973] 1 WLR 134), but not the provision of on-site recreations (e.g., a pony: *Hill* v *Rochard* [1983] 1 WLR 478).

The accommodation must be furnished if that under the assured tenancy was furnished, and the furniture provided must be either similar to that in the present house or reasonably suitable to the needs of the tenant and his family (sch. 2, part III, 3(1)). There is no reason why part of the dwelling-house presently let to the tenant should not constitute suitable alternative accommodation in an appropriate case (*Mykolyshin* v *Noah* [1970] 1 WLR 1271).

Where the landlord obtains an order for possession on Ground 9, the tenant is entitled to his reasonable removal expenses from the landlord, and can sue the landlord if he fails to pay them (s. 11).

3.2.12　Ground 10

Some rent must be due at the date of commencement of proceedings. There must also have been rent due at the time of service of the s. 8 notice, although (in contrast to Ground 8) the court can in its discretion waive the necessity for service of such a notice. The tenant who pays off all arrears by the date of the hearing will not deny the court jurisdiction to order possession, but the court is extremely unlikely to make such an order unless there is a particularly bad record of non-payment in the tenant's case.

3.2.13　Ground 11

To satisfy Ground 11, the landlord need not show that any rent is in arrears at any particular time. However, that is not to say that his task will be any the easier. To prove persistent delay, he will need to show a long record of tardy payment by the tenant, and he may be expected to furnish the court with quite detailed particulars of the dates of payment and non-payment. Even if satisfied that Ground 11 is made out, the court may be reluctant to hold that it is reasonable to order possession when the landlord has been paid all the rent which is due to him under the tenancy.

3.2.14　Ground 12

This covers apparently any breach of covenant by the tenant, but, the ordering of possession being discretionary, the landlord is only likely to succeed if the breach is serious or continuing despite repeated requests to remedy. Note the terms specifically implied into assured tenancies by ss. 15 and 16.

3.2.15　Ground 13

This ground, like the following two, does not require the tenant to be in breach of covenant. It does require him (or someone residing with him) to be guilty of an act of waste or some 'neglect or default' which causes the condition of the dwelling-house to deteriorate. An act of waste is, technically, any act which alters the nature of the land let to the tenant (see Megarry and Wade, *The Law of Real Property*, 5th ed., p. 96); the expression here is presumably intended to cover the tenant whose action, as opposed to inaction (neglect) causes the deterioration. It adds little to 'default'. As the assured tenancy will include land let together with the dwelling-house (s. 2(1)), the failure of the tenant to attend to the garden may fall within this ground (cf. *Holloway* v *Povey* (1984) 15 HLR 104).

3.2.16　Ground 14

This ground is based either on conduct or on a criminal conviction. If the complaint is conduct, it must amount to a nuisance or annoyance to adjoining occupiers: 'annoyance' is wider, less technical, and easier to prove, the definition still used being the rather archaic one in *Tod-Heatley* v *Benham* (1888) 40 ChD 80, 98: it is something which 'reasonably troubles the mind and pleasure, not of a fanciful person . . . but of the ordinary sensible English inhabitant of a house'. Nuisance is in this context given its ordinary everyday meaning: it is not necessary for the elements of the tort of nuisance to be proved. 'Adjoining' has been held to mean 'neighbouring' rather than 'contiguous': all that is required is that the premises of the adjoining occupiers should be near enough to be affected by the conduct of the tenant or his co-occupier (*Cobstone Investments Ltd* v *Maxim* [1985] QB 140).

If the landlord seeks possession following a conviction, it is essential that he prove that the premises have been 'used': the fact that a crime was committed there is not on its own enough. The receipt of stolen goods on the premises, the possession of a controlled drug there, will not suffice unless there is an additional factor of, perhaps, storage or concealment of the property on the premises (*S. Schneiders and Sons* v *Abrahams* [1925] 1 KB 301; *Abrahams* v *Wilson* [1971] QB 88). The premises will have been used for immoral purposes where the conviction relates to an offence involving unlawful sexual intercourse such as living on the earnings of prostitution or keeping a brothel (Sexual Offences Act 1956, ss. 30 and 33). Using the premises for immoral purposes may in itself cause nuisance or annoyance to adjoining occupiers, and in those circumstances it will not be necessary for there to be a conviction. The courts are less prepared to take a high moral stance on these matters than was once the case: see, for example, *Heglibiston Establishment* v *Heyman* (1977) 36 P & CR 351.

3.2.17   Ground 15
'Ill-treatment' can arguably cover both positive action by the tenant and mere neglect: the case of the landlord to obtain possession in the exercise of the court's discretion will not be strong in the face of neglect to furniture and nothing else.

3.2.18   Ground 16
It is not necessary for the landlord to show that the dwelling-house is now required for the occupation of another employee (cf. Case 8 in the Rent Act 1977). If that is the case, however, the court may be more likely to decide that it is reasonable to order possession of the premises. Ground 16 is not available as a ground for possession of dwelling-houses let on assured agricultural occupancies (s. 25(2)).

3.2.19   Termination of tenancy outside the Housing Act 1988
Although s. 7(1) deprives the court of jurisdiction to make an order for possession of a dwelling-house let on an assured tenancy except on proof of statutory grounds, there remain certain instances where the claim to possession is not based on rights under the assured tenancy itself where the scheme of security of tenure contained in the Housing Act 1988 will not apply. Obviously, if the tenant has ceased to be an assured tenant, by going out of occupation, or by the tenancy falling within one of the paragraphs in sch. 1 to the Act, s. 7(1) will not be applicable, and possession can then be obtained under the general principles of landlord and tenant law. Possession proceedings may be brought by a mortgagee

who wishes to obtain his security. If he is the mortgagee of the landlord's interest, he can force the landlord to make use of Ground 2 in sch. 2. If he is the mortgagee of the tenant's interest, he can pursue possession proceedings despite the fact that the tenant is an assured tenant: see rider to s. 7(1).

The Housing Act 1985 contains many of the statutory duties owed by local authorities with regard to housing, and it is provided by s. 612 of that Act (as amended by sch. 17, para. 63 of the 1988 Act) that where in the exercise of their powers 'under any enactment in relation to housing' possession is required, nothing in Part I of the 1988 Act will prevent possession being obtained. Specific provisions contained in the 1985 Act which exempt the effect of assured tenants' security are as follows (the relevant amendments are contained in sch. 17, paras 47 and 50):

(a) s. 264(5) (enforcement of undertaking that premises will not be used for human habitation),
(b) s. 270(3) (demolition order),
(c) s. 276 (closing order),
(d) s. 286(3) (obstructive building order),
(e) s. 368 (as s. 264 above).

3.3 Proceedings for possession

Before proceedings are commenced, the landlord must serve on the tenant an 's. 8 notice'. The notice, which must be in the prescribed form (see SI 1988 No. 2203, Form No. 3), must inform the tenant of the ground or grounds on which possession is to be sought, and further set out the time-scale of the action (s. 8(3)). If the landlord fails to serve such a notice, the court 'shall not entertain' the proceedings, although it may dispense with the notice requirement if it considers it just and equitable to do so and hear the action provided that possession is not sought on Ground 8 (s. 8(1) and (5)).

Proceedings will be commenced in the county court in almost all cases: if proceedings are taken in the High Court, the plaintiff will recover county court costs only (s. 40(1) and (4); see, however, s. 40(5)). If an s. 8 notice is served, the plaintiff must begin proceedings within the time-limits set out in s. 8(3). Proceedings should not commence earlier than two weeks from the service of the s. 8 notice, unless possession is sought under Grounds 1, 2, 5 to 7, 9 and 16, in which case proceedings should not commence earlier than two months from service and, if the tenancy is periodic, the date on which the tenancy could be terminated by notice to quit given on the date of service of the notice (s. 8(3)(b) and (4)). The proceedings should not commence later than 12 months after service of the notice (s. 8(3)(c)).

The action commenced by the landlord should be by plaint, and the particulars of claim should comply with the County Court Rules 1981, Ord. 6, r. 3.

Where the court is not satisfied that the plaintiff is entitled to possession of the dwelling-house by the establishment of a mandatory ground for possession, or on the termination of an assured shorthold, it has wide powers to adjourn proceedings, stay or suspend execution of a possession order, or postpone the date for the delivery up of possession (s. 9(1) and (2)). Where it exercises these powers it must, however, impose conditions on the tenant with regard to payment of rent arrears (if rent is in arrears), unless to do so would cause exceptional hardship to the tenant or be otherwise unreasonable (s. 9(3)). By s. 9(5), the occupying spouse or former spouse who has statutory rights of occupation under the Matrimonial Homes Act 1983 is given the same right to apply in the action for the court to exercise these discretionary powers as the tenant. Once the court is satisfied that the landlord is entitled to possession by virtue of a mandatory ground or the effective termination of an assured shorthold, it must order possession (s. 9(6)).

There is provision in s. 12 for the tenant to be compensated by the landlord where the order for possession is obtained by misrepresentation or concealment of material facts (cf. Rent Act 1977, s. 102 considered in Megarry, *The Rent Acts,* 11th ed, pp. 440–2).

3.4   Subtenancies

3.4.1   *Security of tenure of subtenants*
The provisions of the Rent Act 1977 concerning the security of tenure applicable to subtenants are notoriously complicated: see, for example, J. E. Martin, *Security of Tenure under the Rent Act* (1986), ch. 9. Part I of the Housing Act 1988 does appear to advance a scheme of protection which is, at least in theory, relatively straightforward.

The landlord (L) lets a dwelling-house on assured tenancy to a tenant (T), who then sublets the property to a subtenant (ST). What rights does the subtenant have? In particular, can the landlord who obtains a possession order against the tenant enforce it against the subtenant too? The answers are to be found in s. 18, which has the following effect.

If the subtenancy is (a) lawful and (b) assured, ST will, on termination of the head lease, hold directly from L. T will 'drop out of the picture'. As long as L is a landlord who can let on assured tenancy (i.e., he is not within sch. 1, paras 11 or 12), ST will hold as assured tenant and grounds for possession will need to be proved to obtain possession against him. It is not necessary that the head lease (between L and T) was assured, although it probably will have been.

A subtenancy will be 'lawful' unless it is in breach of a covenant in the head lease. If, however, such a breach is waived by the landlord (the best evidence of waiver being the acceptance of rent knowing that the tenant has sublet), the subletting will be 'lawful' again (*Oak Property Co. Ltd* v *Chapman* [1947] KB 886).

There is no specific ground for possession available to the landlord whose assured tenant has assigned or sublet the whole of the dwelling-house without the landlord's consent (cf. Rent Act 1977, sch. 15, Case 6). Where there is a covenant against assignment or subletting in the lease, however (and there will be in most assured tenancies, see s. 15), the landlord will be able to bring possession proceedings based on the general allegation that an obligation of the tenancy has been broken (sch. 2, Ground 12). If the court considers that it is reasonable to do so, it may order possession on such a ground. It is arguable, following the reasoning of Slade LJ in *Leith Properties Ltd* v *Byrne* [1983] QB 433, that the landlord could claim possession against both tenant and subtenant based on the unlawful subletting.

3.4.2 Reversionary leases

A guide to the Housing Act 1988 would not be complete without an explanation of its most obscure provisions, and that accolade can be bestowed with some confidence on s. 18(3) and (4). Paraphrase is impossible: perhaps an example may give an indication of their practical effect.

Example 3.1 In June 1989, L lets a dwelling-house to T1 on assured tenancy, a fixed term due to expire on 31 December 1990. In June 1990, L enters into a lease with T2 granting T2 exclusive possession of the same dwelling-house as from 1 January 1991. When the fixed term expires on 31 December 1990, a statutory periodic tenancy will arise, by reason of s. 5(2), in favour of T1. In these circumstances, T2 will not be able to take possession of the dwelling-house, as by s. 18(3) his 'reversionary' tenancy will be bound by the rights of T1.

In effect, what s. 18(3) and (4) are attempting to convey is the notion that an assured periodic tenancy has priority over a reversionary lease which is granted to take effect in possession after the expiry of the first period of the tenancy. It does not matter whether the reversionary lease is granted before or after the periodic tenancy in question: it can even be granted before the commencement of the Housing Act 1988.

3.5 Rents under assured tenancies

When landlord and tenant enter into a leasehold agreement, they will agree upon the rent to be paid, and the dates on which payment is to be made. The policy of the Housing Act 1988 is to allow the parties to enjoy freedom of contract to stipulate the level of the rent, to agree upon a rent review clause in appropriate cases, and to limit the degree of statutory intervention. It is important when considering the rights conferred by the Housing Act 1988 in this area to identify the type of assured tenancy in question, as the law applicable is by no means the same. The subject of rents in relation to assured shorthold tenancies and assured agricultural occupancies is dealt with in the chapters on those tenures.

3.5.1 Fixed-term tenancies

While a fixed-term tenancy is continuing, the parties will be held to the contract which they have entered into. If the tenant has agreed to pay the landlord £x per month for the term of y years, the landlord will not be able to increase the rent unilaterally, and if he purports to do so, the tenant can simply refuse to pay. Nor will the landlord be able to go before the rent assessment committee and ask for the rent to be increased: he will be bound by the contract he has made (see s. 13(1)). Of course, there may be a rent review clause in the lease, and if there is such express provision, the parties will be bound by it. The timing and frame of reference of the rent review will be as agreed by the landlord and tenant, and any legal challenge to the review procedure will be conducted through the courts: the Housing Act 1988 will have no bearing upon it. Save in the case of an assured shorthold tenancy, the tenant has no right to apply during the fixed term to have the rent reduced: he, too, is bound by the agreement of the parties.

3.5.2   Statutory periodic tenancies

A statutory periodic tenancy will arise when an assured fixed-term tenancy comes to an end, generally by expiry of the term (s. 5(2)). The initial agreement of the parties to the lease was for the term which has now expired, but under the tenancy which the statute imposes, the rent payable will continue at the same level as before (s. 5(3)). However, the landlord will now have the right to propose a rent increase. It is argued that to allow the landlord to increase the rent is not an interference with the sanctity of the parties' contract: under a periodic tenancy the landlord would normally be free to obtain an increase, terminating the tenancy by notice to quit if the tenant refuses to agree. Where the tenancy is assured, the option of recovering possession is not freely available in view of the security-of-tenure provisions, and so the landlord is given the right to propose an increase in rent at the earliest opportunity following the coming to an end of the fixed term. He will have the same right where the statutory periodic tenancy has just come into being following the tenant's succession to a previously Rent Act protected or statutory tenancy (see s. 39(6)(f)). The tenant is given no corresponding right to propose that the rent be reduced. The rent increase provisions apply to all statutory periodic tenancies, even where they are no longer assured, as long as the reason they are not assured is not that the landlord's interest belongs to the Crown or one of the public bodies listed in sch. 1, paras 11 and 12.

3.5.3   'Contractual' periodic tenancies

Where the periodic tenancy has been created by agreement, express or implied, of the parties, the landlord would again normally be able to obtain an increase in rent by serving, or threatening to serve, notice to quit on the tenant. Once again, the availability of this course of action is curtailed by the security-of-tenure provisions contained in Part I of the Housing Act 1988, and so it is necessary to enable the landlord to seek a rent increase by some other method. The rent proposal provisions are therefore open to all landlords letting on periodic tenancy as long as the tenancy is an assured tenancy. There is one exception: if, in the lease, there is provision for the rent to be greater (or to be made greater) for a particular (later) period of the tenancy, then s. 13 cannot be used for as long as such a provision is binding on the tenant. Freedom of contract will there prevail.

3.5.4   Rent increase procedure

The landlord serves on the tenant a notice in prescribed form (SI 1988 No. 2203, Form No. 5).The notice proposes the new rent and the date it is to take effect (see below). The notice will have to inform the tenant of the rights he has in relation to the procedure. If the tenant wishes to contest the rent proposed, he must refer the notice to a rent assessment committee (SI 1988 No. 2203, Form No. 6) before the date on which the proposed rent is to take effect. If he fails to do so, the rent as proposed will take effect on the date shown in the notice.

The procedure for the increase of rent, which may be initiated only by the landlord, is quite distinct from the procedure whereby the terms of a statutory periodic tenancy may be varied (at the behest of either landlord or tenant). The latter procedure (the s. 6 procedure) may only increase rent in the sense of 'adjusting' it to take account of the terms which have been determined. The increase of rent procedure contained in ss. 13 and 14 does not entitle the rent assessment committee to vary any terms other than rent. As the rent assessment committee are the tribunal in both cases, it is possible that the committee will have two references pending which relate to the same tenancy. The committee are not obliged to hear the two references together, but it would seem to be common sense to do so. If they do, the s. 6 reference should be heard first: once the terms of the tenancy have been determined, the committee can go on to consider what the appropriate rent should be for an assured tenancy having those terms (s. 14(6)).

The date on which the rent is proposed to take effect must comply with s. 13(2) and (3), provisions which are at first sight complex, but not perhaps difficult in application. Two examples follow, relating to the different kinds of tenancy in relation to which a rent increase may be sought.

Example 3.2   Landlord lets house on a weekly tenancy (i.e., a contractual periodic tenancy) commencing on 1 July 1989. The earliest date for a rent increase will be 1 July 1990 (s. 13(2)(b)). If the landlord wants to propose an increased rent from that date, he must serve his notice no later than one month before (i.e., 1 June 1990), as the period of the tenancy is less than a month (s. 13(3)(b)). Let us say that the tenant does not refer the notice to a rent assessment committee and the rent is therefore increased as from 1 July 1990 (s. 13(4)). The landlord will next be able to propose an increase effective from 1 July 1991 (s. 13(2)(c)), notice to be served no later than 1 June 1991.

Example 3.3   Landlord lets house on fixed term of 12 months, which expires by effluxion of time on 22 April 1990. A statutory periodic tenancy then takes effect, the rent being the same as under the old fixed term, and the periods of the tenancy being those for which rent was payable (s. 5(2)). The rent was payable monthly, so the new tenancy is a monthly tenancy. In principle, the landlord can propose an increased rent to take effect on 22 May 1990 (s. 13(3)(c)), but it is unclear from the statute whether the landlord can serve the one month's notice which will be necessary (s. 13(3)(b)) before the fixed term has in fact expired. Although s. 13 only 'applies' to periodic tenancies, there seems no good reason why the service of notice may not pre-date the coming into being of the statutory periodic tenancy. However, the cautious landlord will wait until the fixed term has ended, and serve his notice then.

3.5.5   Market rent

Where the tenant refers the notice to the rent assessment committee, the committee must determine the rent at which they consider the dwelling-house concerned might reasonably be expected to be let in the open market by a willing landlord under an assured tenancy having the same terms as the tenancy in question (s. 14(1)). In making the determination, the committee must disregard any effect on the rent attributable to the granting of a tenancy to a sitting tenant, any increase in value of the dwelling-house attributable to certain tenant's improvements (defined s. 14(3)), and any reduction in value of the house attributable to the tenant's breach of covenant (s. 14(2)).

By ss. 18 to 30 of the Landlord and Tenant Act 1985, the tenant of a flat is given protection against the landlord who seeks to recover a service charge from him.

Where a service charge would fall within those sections of the 1985 Act, the committee must not incorporate it in any determination of the rent. Otherwise (i.e., in particular where the tenant rents a house rather than a flat), services, repairs, maintenance, insurance and management costs are to be included in the sum the committee arrive at as the rent for the property (s. 14(4)). The determination of the committee should be on the basis that the landlord (or superior landlord) does not bear the rates for the property, even if he does (s. 14(5)).

The formula adopted by s. 14 of the Housing Act 1988 is, of course, radically different from that which prevailed in relation to Rent Act regulated tenancies, and the provision is central to the ideology guiding this Part of the Act. In its attempt to free the private landlord from the shackles of letting at a 'fair rent', which, by definition, was less than the market rent, and thereby revitalise the private rented sector, the Housing Act 1988 places the responsibility in the hands of the rent assessment committees rather than the rent officers. These committees will be expected in each case to consider the local 'market', the number of potential tenants for this particular property, and then assess the sum at which a 'willing landlord', i.e., someone who wants to let, given a reasonable return on his property, being apprised of the market conditions, would reasonably expect the house to be rented for. The committee are not being asked to determine what is a reasonable rent for this tenant to pay or, indeed, what a reasonable rent for the property would be. Their task is to determine what the landlord's reasonable expectation for the rent for this property should be, if it is let on an assured tenancy with the same terms on which the tenant presently holds.

The committee may, in determining the rent under s. 14, wish to refer to comparable assured tenancy rents in the vicinity, and the president of each rent assessment panel is placed under a duty to keep and make publicly available certain information with respect to rents under assured tenancies (including assured shortholds) and assured agricultual occupancies: it is expected that this will provide a ready source of comparables for those appearing before rent assessment committees (see s. 42 and SI 1988 No. 2199 which indicates how the president should collect the information concerned).

It is very difficult to predict how the rent assessment committees will go about their task. There is a potentially important role to be played here by surveyors and valuers who will be singularly well placed to give an expert opinion on the market rent for a particular property. Section 14 is attractively concise in its direction to the committees, but it has been questioned whether the legislation proffers enough guidance: 'It provides a definition and then leaves it completely to the imagination and to speculation as to how rents are to be fixed' (Mr Simon Hughes, Standing Committee G, 26 January 1988, col. 412). It may be up to the Court of Appeal to lead the way.

3.5.6 Effect of the 'determination'
When the rent assessment committee have made their determination of the rent, the rent thus determined will be the rent under the tenancy with effect from the date specified in the landlord's initial notice proposing the increase. Only if the committee form the view that this would cause undue hardship to the tenant may they specify a later date, and that date may not be later than the date of the

committee's determination in any circumstances (s. 14(7)). The effect of this provision is that where there is a substantial delay between the landlord's notice and the decision of the rent assessment committee, and the rent is then increased, the tenant may find himself with a substantial amount of back rent to pay off.

At all stages of the proceedings (including after the determination by the rent assessment committee), the parties may come to an agreement about the rent to be charged, and withdraw the reference to the committee or vary the decision which the committee has reached (s. 14(7) and (8)). The tenant is not usually in an equal bargaining position with the landlord, and may agree a rent higher than that which the committee has determined or is likely to determine. Although to a certain extent the tenant is protected by the security of tenure afforded him by his assured tenancy, it may be a notional security, particularly if the landlord has served him with valid notices under Grounds 1 to 5 of sch. 2. Paying the rent demanded by the landlord may in certain circumstances be the only practical option open to the tenant.

By s. 74 of the Rent Act 1977, the Secretary of State may make regulations regulating the procedure to be followed by rent assessment committees under Part I of the Housing Act 1988 as well as the Rent Act itself (Housing Act 1988, s. 41(1)). The regulations are to be found in SI 1971 No. 1065 as amended by SI 1988 No. 2200. Appeals from the decision of the rent assessment committee are governed by the Tribunals and Inquiries Act 1971, s. 13(1): appeal is on a point of law and is to the High Court. Unlike the Rent Act 'two-tier' system of rent officer and rent assessment committee, neither party may appeal on a question of fact, such as the quantum of the market rent. Only if the committee have misdirected themselves in law will an appeal be tenable. For a full treatment of review of decisions of rent assessment committees, see Megarry *The Rent Acts,* 11th ed, chapters 24 and 33.

Chapter Four
Assured Shorthold Tenancies

4.1 Introduction

From 1980 onwards, the Rent Act regime allowed landlords to enter into short-term lettings known as protected shorthold tenancies, whereby the tenant obtained no security of tenure over and above that afforded by the contract. The landlord in turn had to ensure that the rent was registered or the subject of a fair rent certificate, a condition which was relaxed by subsequent legislation, and serve the tenant with written notice of the fact that the tenancy was protected shorthold. The protected shorthold was, perhaps surprisingly, unpopular. The minimum term which was tenable was 12 months, and so a strong commitment to let was necessary on the part of the landlord. The greatest disincentive, though, was the procedure for recovering possession of protected shortholds, a procedure which was veritably riddled with pitfalls for the unwary. If the landlord mistimed service of notice, he could well find his action dismissed and no further action possible for another 12 months or so. It was clear to the proponents of the Housing Act 1988 that if short-term letting was to be encouraged, it was necessary to make the recovery of possession much less complicated and therefore make the venture of letting a less hazardous and more attractive proposition. Whether the 'assured shorthold tenancy' which is introduced by Chapter II of Part I of the Housing Act 1988 succeeds in these aims time alone will tell. As it is, it is one of the most politically contentious measures in the entire statute, described in Committee as 'a charter for housing sharks . . . who will be able to get their properties back every six months and to increase rents twice a year' (Mr Richard Livsey, Standing Committee G, 26 January 1988, col. 430).

4.2 Definition

An assured shorthold tenancy is defined in s. 20. It must be an assured tenancy: s. 1 must be satisfied and the tenancy not be excluded from assured tenancy status by sch. 1. In particular, the tenancy must be entered into on or after the date of commencement of the Act (sch. 1, para. 1). An assured shorthold must be a fixed-term tenancy of no less than six months, and the landlord must not have reserved for himself the power to determine the tenancy at any time earlier than six months from its beginning except by exercise of a right of re-entry or forfeiture for breach of covenant or condition (ss. 20(1)(b) and 45(4)). The landlord must serve on the tenant before the tenancy is entered into a notice in prescribed form stating that the tenancy is to be a shorthold tenancy (s. 20(2); SI 1988 No. 2203, Form No. 7). There is no power in the court to dispense with the requirement for such a notice, and so if none is served, or it is served late, the tenancy will not be an assured shorthold.

The above conditions must be met where the landlord has not previously let this dwelling-house to this tenant. If he has, there are other factors to be considered. Where there has been an assured shorthold of these premises, or substantially the same premises, and on that tenancy coming to an end, a new assured tenancy comes into being (probably a statutory periodic tenancy by virtue of s. 5(2)), that new tenancy will also be an assured shorthold, even though it does not satisfy all or any of the conditions in s. 20(1) (s. 20(4)). The landlord may serve notice on the tenant stating that the new tenancy is not to be an assured shorthold, and in that (unlikely) eventuality the tenancy will not be an assured shorthold (s. 20(5)). Where the previous letting was on assured tenancy which was not an assured shorthold, and the previous tenancy was 'immediately before' the new one, then the new tenancy cannot be assured shorthold either (s. 20(3)). Where the previous letting was entered into prior to the commencement of the Housing Act 1988, and comprised a *protected* shorthold, the new letting will be an assured shorthold whether or not s. 20(1) is otherwise satisfied (unless, again, the landlord serves notice on the tenant that it is not to be shorthold) (see s. 34(1)(b) as qualified by s. 34(3)). Note also that an assured shorthold may arise on a succession to a *protected* shorthold tenant (s. 39(7)).

4.3   Security of tenure

Once the fixed term has expired by effluxion of time, the landlord can obtain possession of the dwelling-house let on assured shorthold. He must give the tenant two months' notice, but this notice may be given before the fixed term has expired, as long as it is to take effect at a time when it has (s. 21(1) and (2)). By the time the action comes to court, the tenant may well be holding as a statutory periodic tenant 'by virtue of s. 5(2), but this will not prejudice the landlord (s. 21(3)). The court, on being satisfied of the above conditions, must order possession of the dwelling-house.

The right of the landlord to recover possession by virtue of the provisions in s. 21 is 'without prejudice' to his rights to use the provisions in Part I for the recovery of possession of assured tenancies generally. It will, however, be only rarely that the landlord of an assured shorthold tenant will wish to use them: perhaps during a long fixed term, he may wish to utilise statutory grounds for possession, but they are limited in number where a fixed term is continuing and has not yet expired (s. 7(6)). More likely is the recovery of possession where the tenant has surrendered the tenancy, or has ceased to occupy the dwelling-house as his only or principal home (s. 5(2)).

The recovery of possession appears to be free of obvious pitfalls. A problem which may arise, however, and which landlords should guard against, is the creation of a periodic tenancy by agreement following the expiry of the assured shorthold. Normally, as stated above, the expiry of the term will lead to the implication of a statutory periodic tenancy. If, however, the tenant can point to the grant of another tenancy on the coming to an end of the fixed term, that tenancy will not be a statutory periodic tenancy (s. 5(4)). It will almost certainly be an assured tenancy (unless, that is, it no longer satisfies s. 1), and the court will no longer be able to be satisfied as required by s. 21(1) ('no further assured tenancy (*whether shorthold or not*) is for the time being in existence'). The new 'contractual' periodic tenancy will almost inevitably be an assured shorthold (see s. 20(4)), but the landlord, having failed to satisfy s. 21(1) in relation to that tenancy, will have to start back at square one.

Where the landlord has conferred on the assured shorthold tenant a contractual periodic tenancy, he may have to give the tenant more than two months' notice. If the periodic tenancy requires by its terms a longer notice than the two months (e.g., a yearly tenancy, which requires six months' notice at common law), that is the notice which the landlord must give (s. 21(4)).

4.4   Rents

The rent provisions applicable to assured shorthold tenancies are not immediately easy to comprehend. During the fixed term which the parties initially agree upon, the landlord has no right to seek an increase in rent. He has contracted with the tenant that the rent will be a specified sum for the term, and he will not be permitted to renege upon his agreement. During that same fixed term, however, the assured shorthold tenant is given the right to apply to the rent assessment committee for a reduction in rent (SI 1988 No. 2203, Form No. 8). On such an application, the committee are to determine 'the rent which, in the committee's opinion, the landlord might reasonably be expected to obtain under the assured shorthold tenancy' (s. 22(1)). If the tenant's application is successful, he may not apply again (s. 22(2)(a)). Once that initial fixed term has ended, the tenant no longer has the right to apply, even if he has not applied before and even if landlord and tenant enter into a new fixed-term assured shorthold (s. 22(2)). The rationale for this restriction is that once the initial fixed term has expired, the landlord has chosen not to exercise his right to repossession of the property and so should not be liable to have his commercial return diminished.

Under the s. 22 procedure, the committee must determine the rent the landlord might be reasonably expected to obtain under an assured shorthold. The committee are directed not to make a determination at all unless they consider that there is a sufficient number of similar dwelling-houses in the locality let on assured tenancies (shorthold or not), presumably enabling the committee to compare the applicant's rent to those in a like position (s. 22(3)(a)). There will in time be lists of comparables publicly available (see s. 42). The committee are not expected to tamper with the rent payable by the tenant: unless they consider that the rent he pays is 'significantly higher' than those with comparable tenancies, they should not make any determination at all (s. 22(3)(b)).

Where the committee make a determination under s. 22, it will take effect on the date they specify, not being earlier than the date of the application, and the rent which exceeds the rent so determined will thereafter be irrecoverable from the tenant (s. 22(4)). The Secretary of State has powers to order that the s. 22 procedure will no longer apply in certain areas or in certain circumstances (s. 23).

When the initial fixed term of the assured shorthold has expired, the landlord may propose an increase in rent under s. 13. However, if the committee has made a determination under s. 22 on the tenant's application, the landlord will have to wait 12 months before he can make a proposal (s. 22(4)(c)). As it is a condition of making a proposal to increase rent under s. 13 that the tenancy is periodic, the landlord will lose this power during the currency of a fixed term. If he makes a new grant of a fixed term to the tenant, he will once more be prevented from proposing an increase in rent. When the landlord is free to propose an increased rent, the procedure to be followed will be the same as for any other assured tenancy (s. 20(7)). The committee will have to determine the rent at which the dwelling-house might reasonably be expected to be let in the open market by a willing landlord under an assured shorthold tenancy.

Although there is no provision which says as much, the inference is that a landlord who lets on assured shorthold should not reasonably expect to obtain as much as a landlord who lets on an assured tenancy which is not shorthold. The price to the landlord of conferring no security of tenure is a return on the property lower than that otherwise obtainable. All will depend on the way the market operates. If there are more potential tenants than available properties the level of rents under assured shortholds will not be substantially lower than that for assured tenancies with security of tenure.

The right of the tenant under an assured shorthold to apply for a reduction in rent is unique in the Housing Act 1988, and its shortcomings should be noted. Although at the time of application, the tenant may have the protection of a fixed-term tenancy, the tenant's continued occupation of the property after the expiry of the fixed term will depend entirely on the goodwill of the landlord, who has up his sleeve an unassailable right to recover possession. If the tenant wishes to stay beyond the term, then, it is in his interests not to apply for a rent reduction. Moreover, the landlord who wishes to increase the rent is not in any real sense 'bound' by the determination made by the rent assessment committee: it is open to landlord and tenant to agree a new rent at any time, before, during or after committee proceedings. The fixed term having expired, the tenant will be in an extremely weak negotiating position, the landlord being able to recover possession as of right, subject only to two months' notice, in the event of the tenant refusing to agree to a rent acceptable to him.

The assured shorthold tenant is in a similarly invidious position as far as repair of the property is concerned. The landlord has a very simple answer to the insistent shorthold tenant who is continually complaining about the terrible state his house or flat is in: he commences possession proceedings. The 'security' afforded by the contractual fixed term will normally be so minimal (because of its shortness) that a tenant who pursued his contractual remedies in court would be out of the premises well before his case comes on for trial. In brief, the assured shorthold tenant, save in the situation where the fixed term initially agreed is lengthy and has some considerable time still to run, is given little support by the provisions of the Housing Act 1988, and there can be little doubt that private sector landlords will soon come to appreciate the position of dominance they can achieve by employing this new device.

Chapter Five
Assured Agricultural Occupancies

5.1 Introduction

The Rent (Agriculture) Act 1976 ('the 1976 Act') conferred on agricultural workers a security of tenure and a considerable degree of rent protection with respect to their tied cottages. Largely modelled on the provisions of the Rent Act, the 1976 Act was necessary as many agricultural workers would be excluded from being Rent Act protected tenants, their tenancies either being at a low rent or being within the agricultural holding exemption: many, indeed, would not be tenants at all. Chapter III of Part I of the Housing Act 1988 phases out the statutory scheme of the 1976 Act. It seeks to retain security of tenure for agricultural workers, whilst allowing the landlord to charge a market rent. The new tenure which is introduced to cater for these persons is the assured agricultural occupancy. Although the consequences of an assured agricultural occupancy differ from those of protection under the 1976 Act, the conditions which must be satisfied in order to come within the statutory code are in substance the same: in defining the new tenure, the Housing Act 1988 makes ready use of the definitions contained in the earlier statute.

5.2 Definition

The conditions necessary for an assured agricultural occupancy of a dwelling-house are as follows:

(a)   There must be a tenancy or licence within s. 24(2) of the Housing Act 1988 (unhelpfully referred to as a 'relevant tenancy or licence', the same terminology as the 1976 Act). To satisfy s. 24(2), the tenancy must be assured (but *not* an assured shorthold), or only miss out on being assured because it is a tenancy at a low rent and/or a tenancy of an agricultural holding (sch. 1, paras 3 and 7 respectively). A licence will be relevant if the licensee has exclusive occupation of a dwelling-house as a separate dwelling and, if it were a tenancy, would be assured or miss out for the above reasons. The tenancy or licence must not have been entered into before, or pursuant to a contract made before, 15 January

1989: if such were the case, the interest would be a relevant tenancy or licence within the 1976 Act, and, the conditions below being satisfied, a 'protected occupancy' within that Act (see Housing Act 1988, s. 34(4)).

(b)   The 'agricultural worker condition', defined in sch. 3, is for the time being fulfilled with respect to the dwelling-house. The definition is complicated, requiring extensive reference back to the 1976 Act. The rules on statutory succession of assured agricultural occupancies are incorporated into the schedule, the agricultural worker condition being capable of fulfilment by a successor as well as by a worker himself. The summary of these provisions which follows must be supplemented by a careful reading of the statutory provisions themselves.

5.2.1   *'Agricultural worker condition': the worker*

(a)   The dwelling-house subject to the tenancy or licence within s. 24(2) must have as its tenant or licensee ('occupier') either a 'qualifying worker' or someone who is incapable of work in agriculture in consequence of a 'qualifying injury or disease'. 'Qualifying worker' is defined in sch. 3, para. 1 of the 1976 Act, and looks to the worker working whole-time for 91 out of the last 104 weeks in agriculture. Whether someone is incapable of whole-time work in agriculture requires reference to para. 2 of the same schedule, which also defines 'qualifying injury or disease': for example, an injury will qualify if it was caused by an accident arising out of and in the course of his employment in agriculture.

(b)   The dwelling-house must be in 'qualifying ownership', defined in sch. 3, para. 3 of the 1976 Act. The occupier must at the time be employed in agriculture, and the house must be owned by his employer (or at least provided by his arranging with the owner for it to be used as housing accommodation for his agricultural workers). 'Agriculture' has the definition given it by s. 1(1) of the 1976 Act.

The agricultural worker condition will also be fulfilled if the tenancy or licence of the house was granted to him in consideration of his giving up possession of a dwelling-house of which he was an assured agricultural occupier (Housing Act 1988, sch. 3, para. 4).

5.2.2   *'Agricultural worker condition': the successor*

Succession to an assured agricultural occupancy depends on there having been an occupier who fulfilled the above conditions, but who has since died. If there is now a 'qualifying widow or widower' or a qualifying member of the previous occupier's family, then that person will fulfil the agricultural worker condition by virtue of the Housing Act 1988, (sch. 3, para. 3), and will effectively succeed to the occupancy. If, however, any of these potential successors themselves satisfied the agricultural worker condition pursuant to para. 2, then they would not take as successor, but as an occupier in their own right.

To be a 'qualifying widow or widower', the spouse must have been residing in the dwelling-house immediately before the death of the previous occupier (sch. 3, para. 3(2)). A person who was living with the previous occupier as his wife (or her husband) is to be treated as his widow or her widower (sch. 3, para. 3(5)). A qualifying widow or widower will take precedence over qualifying members of the family. To be a 'qualifying member of the family', the person concerned must have been residing in the dwelling-house with the previous occupier at the time of, and for a period of two years before, the occupier's death (para. 3(3)). For the meaning of 'member of the family', see 6.1.4.2. In the event of dispute between rival qualifiers, the county court is to choose one (para. 3(4)). The policy of the Housing Act 1988, as with the Rent (Agriculture) Act 1976, is that only one succession is possible. Where a successor is granted a new tenancy or licence by the landlord, the rights of the landlord to recover possession on his death will not be affected thereby (para. 5(3)).

5.3   Security of tenure

The policy of Chapter III of Part I is to bring the regime for agricultural workers occupying tied cottages into line with the code for all other private sector lettings. Accordingly, for all security-of-tenure purposes, the assured agricultural occupancy is treated as if it were an assured tenancy (even though it may not be a tenancy at all) (s. 24(3)). If the assured agricultural occupancy was a fixed-term tenancy, it would therefore become a statutory periodic tenancy once the fixed term came to an end: s. 25(1)(b) states how the periods are to be defined where, as will frequently be the case, no rent was payable under the agreement. That statutory periodic tenancy would, however, remain an assured agricultural occupancy as long as the agricultural worker condition was fulfilled (s. 25(1)(a)).

The recovery of possession of an assured agricultural occupancy differs only in two respects from other assured tenancies. The discretionary ground of possession in Ground 16 of sch. 2 (tenant having ceased to be in the landlord's employment, the dwelling-house having been let in consequence of his employment) would, if available, drive a coach and horses through the protective code. The landlord cannot therefore use it (s. 25(2)).

Secondly, the rehousing provisions of Part IV of the Rent (Agriculture) Act 1976 will apply to dwelling-houses let on assured agricultural occupancies. Under these provisions, if the landlord requires vacant possession of a dwelling-house so let in order to house a person employed in agriculture, being unable to provide, by any reasonable means, suitable alternative accommodation for the present occupier, the local authority, if satisfied of the above, and that it ought, in the interests of efficient agriculture, to provide that alternative accommodation, will be under a statutory duty, enforceable by a damages action, to use its best endeavours to provide the accommodation (Rent (Agriculture) Act 1976, s. 27). If the landlord is able to use this procedure to secure suitable alternative accommodation for the occupier, he will be able to argue that it is reasonable for the court to order possession of the dwelling-house, producing a certificate from the local authority as conclusive evidence of the availability of suitable alternative accommodation for the tenant when the order takes effect (Housing Act 1988, s. 7(4); sch. 2, Ground 9; part III, para 1).

5.4   Rents

As the assured agricultural occupancy is to be treated as if it were an assured tenancy (s. 24(3)), the rent payable will be governed by ss. 13 and 14. The rent assessment committee must determine the rent at which they consider the dwelling-house concerned might be let in the open market by a willing landlord under an assured agricultural occupancy (ss. 14(1) and 24(4). It is anticipated that the market rent for an assured agricultural occupancy will be somewhat lower, as a general rule, than the market rent for other assured tenancies, but there is no express statement to this effect in the Housing Act 1988. Many landlords letting on assured agricultural occupancies will presumably carry on their old practice of charging a low rent, or no rent at all.

Chapter Six
Existing Tenancies: The Transitional Provisions

The Housing Act 1988 does not, by and large, make significant changes to rights of existing tenants which have accrued prior to the commencement of the Act. It is necessary, however, to look at each type of tenure in turn to consider the effect of the Act, and to outline the inroads which are made into the codes of protection presently affecting existing tenants. The effect of the Housing Act 1988 on existing tenancies is summarised in the table which appears on pp. 138–9.

6.1 Rent Act protected and statutory tenancies

The Rent Act code of protection, previously dominant in the private housing sector, is, of course, one of the main casualties of Part I of the Housing Act 1988. Under the Rent Act 1977, a tenant of a dwelling-house let to him as a separate dwelling would (subject to exceptions) enjoy a protected tenancy and, on termination of that contractual tenancy, such a tenant would, if and so long as he occupied it as his residence, be a statutory tenant of it (Rent Act 1977, ss. 1 and 2). A landlord cannot obtain possession of a dwelling-house let on a protected or statutory tenancy save on proof of statutory grounds of possession, set out in the Rent Act 1977, sch. 15, and the tenant is entitled to the benefit of the fair rent provisions of Parts III and IV of that Act. On the death of a protected or statutory tenant, there may be a statutory succession, under which a successor will be entitled to the tenancy enjoyed by the deceased tenant together with the privileges of security of tenure and a below-market rent. For a full treatment of the rights conferred by the Rent Act 1977, see J. E. Martin, *Security of Tenure under the Rent Act* (1986) and, for reference, see Megarry, *The Rent Acts,* 11th ed. (1988). A protected shorthold tenancy is a form of protected tenancy but, as the transitional provisions of the Housing Act 1988 deal with protected shortholds differently from protected tenancies which are not shortholds, they must be distinguished. Protected tenancies which are not shortholds are dealt with in 6.1.1. to 6.1.5. Protected shortholds are dealt with in 6.2.

6.1.1   Tenancies entered into before 15 January 1989
Where a dwelling-house was let as a separate dwelling under a tenancy entered

into prior to 15 January 1989, that tenancy, if protected under the Rent Act 1977, will remain a protected tenancy. If a protected tenancy terminated prior to 15 January 1989, and the tenant held over as statutory tenant, his tenancy will remain a statutory tenancy if and so long as he continues to occupy the dwelling-house as his residence. If a protected tenancy, entered into before 15 January 1989 terminates after that day, the tenant will nevertheless hold over as statutory tenant and the statutory tenancy will continue as before. In short, if a tenant is a protected tenant, nothing in the Housing Act 1988 can 'convert' *him* (as opposed to certain of his statutory successors) into an assured tenant, and when his tenancy terminates a statutory tenancy will arise if and so long as the Rent Act 1977, s. 2(1), is satisfied.

Where a tenancy is transferred from the public sector (local authorities etc.) to the private sector on or after 15 January 1989, it will not become a protected tenancy on transfer, even though the tenancy was entered into prior to that date (s. 38(3); see 2.3.1). The policy of the Act is to give such tenancies assured tenancy status. The one exception to this arises where the public sector landlord is a new town corporation (s. 38(4)).

6.1.2   Tenancies entered into on or after 15 January 1989

There are certain instances where a tenancy may be protected under the Rent Act 1977 even though it was entered into on or after the date of the commencement of Part I of the Housing Act (15 January 1989):

(a)   If the parties make a contract prior to 15 January 1989 for a tenancy beginning after that date, the tenancy will be protected if it otherwise satisfies the Rent Act 1977 (s. 34(1)(a)).

(b)   If the tenant was a protected or statutory tenant immediately before the grant (i.e., under an earlier tenancy), and the grant is by the same landlord as before, the tenancy will again be protected (s. 34(1)(b)).

(c)   If the tenant previously enjoyed a protected or statutory tenancy of a dwelling-house of which the landlord obtained possession on the ground that the present premises constituted suitable alternative accommodation, the court may direct, even after 15 January 1989, that the property is to be held on a protected tenancy (Rent Act 1977, sch. 15, part IV, para. 4). If so, the tenancy of the property will be protected as ordered by the court (s. 34(1)(c)). Note that in making such a direction, the court must have considered that 'in the circumstances the grant of an assured tenancy would not afford the required security'. A protected or statutory tenant who is the defendant in possession proceedings based on the availability of suitable alternative accommodation should ensure that the attention of the court is drawn to this provision so that the appropriate direction can be made.

(d)   A tenancy under which the landlord's interest has passed from a new town corporation into the private sector may be a protected tenancy if the transfer took effect before 15 November 1990 (ss. 34(1)(d) and 38).

Subject to the exceptions outlined above, a tenancy entered into on or after 15 January 1989 cannot be a protected tenancy (s. 34(1)). In the main, tenancies entered into from now on, which would have been protected under the Rent Acts, will now be assured tenancies, will enjoy the security of tenure conferred by Part I of the Housing Act 1988 and will be subject to its rent increase provisions.

6.1.3   Amendments to the Rent Act 1977

The Housing Act 1988 makes several amendments to the Rent Act 1977 which will affect existing protected and statutory tenants. The powers of a local authority to apply of its own motion to the rent officer for him to determine a fair rent for a regulated tenancy or to refer a restricted contract to the rent tribunal (Rent Act 1977, ss. 68 and 77) are removed. The system whereby a potential landlord may apply for a certificate of fair rent (Rent Act 1977, s. 69) is abolished, it being otiose as future lettings will not attract a fair rent any more (see Housing Act 1988, sch. 17, paras 22 and 23). The Act also reforms the administration of rent assessment committees and the appointment of rent officers, all of which will affect applications for a fair rent (see ss. 120 and 121; sch. 14 and 11.5).

A further amendment is made relating to sublettings. Section 137(1) of the 1977 Act was the subject of rather careless consolidation. As drafted, it indicated that a possession order would not of itself affect the right of a lawful subtenant to retain possession 'by virtue of this Part of this Act'. Unfortunately, Part XI of the Rent Act, in which s. 137 appears, did not confer any rights to retain possession: such rights were granted by Part I. This anomaly has been glossed over by the courts: now the Housing Act 1988, sch. 17, para. 25, cures it by removing the words 'this Part of' from s. 137. It may be that the effect of this amendment is to give some protection in transitional cases to subtenants who hold on restricted contract (e.g., with a resident immediate landlord), as well as those who hold on protected or statutory tenancy, from the mesne landlord: see J. E. Martin, *Security of Tenure under the Rent Act* (1986), pp. 123-4.

The most important amendments to the Rent Act 1977 concern statutory succession, and are effective where a protected or statutory tenant (or a 'first successor') dies after the commencement of the Housing Act 1988: the amendments are made by sch. 4, para. 1 (see also s. 39(2) and (3)). Note that where the person concerned dies before the commencement of the Act, the rules applicable for statutory succession remain those in part I of sch. 1 to the Rent Act 1977, in its unamended form.

6.1.4   Succession to protected or statutory tenancies

Under the Rent Act regime, the death of the protected or statutory tenant does not by itself enable the landlord to obtain possession of the demised premises. Quite apart from the possibility that a protected (i.e., contractual) tenancy may be disposed of by will, or would otherwise be transmitted in accordance with the intestacy rules, there is provision in sch. 1 to the Rent Act 1977 for a 'statutory succession' to the protected or statutory tenant by which a successor will become statutory tenant of the dwelling-house in the place of the deceased tenant. In certain circumstances, two successions are possible, so the death of a successor will not necessarily enable the landlord to regain possession.

The Housing Act 1988 introduces restrictions on the circumstances in which a statutory succession can take place, and also dictates that following certain successions the new tenant will not be a statutory tenant under the Rent Act regime, but will instead become an assured tenant within the meaning of Part I of the Housing Act 1988 itself. The most important consequence of this is, of course, that such a successor would not be entitled to the benefit of the fair rent provisions, and the landlord could once more recover a market rent.

6.1.4.1   Death of an original tenant after 15 January 1989: surviving spouse   If a protected or statutory tenant dies leaving a widow (or widower), then that person will generally become statutory tenant of the dwelling-house, and so long as she continues to occupy it as her residence she will enjoy the benefits of the protection of the Rent Act 1977. She must have been residing in the dwelling-house immediately before the death of her husband, although it is not essential that she was living *with him* there (Rent Act 1977, sch. 1, para. 2).

An important amendment made here by the Housing Act 1988 is to include within the definition of 'spouse' a person who was living with the tenant as his or her wife or husband (and, by inference, was not in fact married to him) (sch. 4, para. 2). Under the previous law, there was considerable litigation on the question of whether a 'common-law spouse' could be a member of the tenant's family. This amendment deems such a person to be a spouse: and therefore not only entitled to succeed but in a stronger position than other 'members of the family'. There will still no doubt be dispute in particular cases about whether a potential successor was living with the tenant as his wife, but the case law, although of some assistance, will be distinguishable on the basis that a different question was being asked in all the previous authorities (i.e., whether the common-law wife was a member of the tenant's family).

In *Harrogate Borough Council* v *Simpson* (1984) 17 HLR 205, construing the more closely analogous, although still not identical, provision relating to succession to secure tenancies (now Housing Act 1985, s. 113(1)), it was held that a lesbian couple could not come within the ordinary meaning of persons living together as husband and wife. There is little doubt that this case would be followed in the context of this amendment to sch. 1 to the Rent Act 1977.

Where a common-law spouse is concerned, it will be necessary for her to have been living *with* the tenant at the time of his death. The arguments have already been considered in relation to the succession provisions applicable to assured tenancies: see 2.5.

In the (presumably uncommon) eventuality of a tenant leaving more than one 'spouse' who qualifies to succeed him as statutory tenant, the county court is empowered to determine who should in fact succeed if the protagonists are unable to agree (Rent Act 1977, sch. 1, para. 2(3)). There is no provision made for more than one successor to hold on joint tenancy.

6.1.4.2   Death of an original tenant after 15 January 1989: other members of the tenant's family   Where there is no surviving spouse or common-law spouse on the death of the original tenant after 15 January 1989, a member of the tenant's family may be entitled to succeed if he satisfies the Rent Act 1977, sch. 1, para. 3, as amended. However, if he does qualify, he will become an assured tenant rather than a statutory tenant.

No amendment or addition is made to the words 'member of the original tenant's family': there is still no statutory definition of the term. Much of the old case law concerned attempts by common-law spouses to bring themselves within the tenant's family unit, and in the future no such claims need be made: the common-law spouse will have the greater reward of Rent Act protection for showing that she was living with the tenant as his wife within para. 2.

Whether a claimant was a member of the tenant's family at the time of the tenant's death requires 'at least a broadly recognisable *de facto* familial nexus', a nexus 'capable of being found and recognised as such by the ordinary man — where the link would be strictly familial had there been a marriage, or where the link is through adoption of a minor, *de iure* or *de facto,* or where the link is "step-", or where the link is "in-law" or by marriage' (per Russell LJ in *Ross* v *Collins* [1964] 1 WLR 425, 432). Courts have, however, drawn the line at two strangers who attempt to establish artificially such a familial nexus, for example, by calling themselves sisters (*Sefton Holdings Ltd* v *Cairns* (1988) 20 HLR 124) or aunt and nephew (*Carega Properties SA* v *Sharratt* [1979] 1 WLR 928).

Once a claimant can show he was a member of the tenant's family within para. 3, he must go on to show (save in transitional cases) that he was residing with him *in the dwelling-house* for the period of *two years* immediately before the tenant's death. Whether the claimant was residing with the tenant for the requisite period is a question of fact and degree, the claimant having to show that he had a home with the tenant, and was 'in a true sense' part of the tenant's household (*Swanbrae Ltd* v *Elliott* 1987) 19 HLR 86). This element will not be proved if the tenant was not himself residing in the property during part of the relevant time (see *Foreman* v *Beagley* [1969] 1 WLR 1387).

The residence must have been in the dwelling-house to which the claimant now wishes to succeed. The addition of the words 'in the dwelling-house' resolves the ambiguity present on a reading of the old paragraph in the way the Court of Appeal had interpreted it in *Edmunds* v *Jones* [1957] WLR 1118, a case recently brought to light by the Court of Appeal in *South Northamptonshire District Council* v *Power* [1987] 1 WLR 1433.

The period of residence is increased to two years from six months by the Housing Act 1988, sch. 4, para. 3(b). In accordance with the general policy that rights which have accrued prior to commencement of the Act are not to be affected by it, a claimant who was on 15 January 1989 entitled to succeed, having resided with the tenant in the dwelling-house for six months, will remain qualified to succeed as long as he continues to so reside (para. 3(2)). However, this provision only assists the claimant who has completed his six-month period of residence as at 15 January 1989.

If there is more than one qualifying member of the tenant's family then, in default of agreement, the county court has jurisdiction to choose, and in doing so it should take account of all the circumstances (*Williams* v *Williams* [1971] 1 WLR 1530). Joint successors are not permitted.

6.1.4.3   Death of 'first successor' after 15 January 1989   The provisions of the Rent Act 1977, sch. 1 in their amended form will apply not only where the original tenant dies after 15 January 1989 (to establish his first successor and the successor to that successor) but also where the original tenant died before, and the first successor after, 15 January 1989 (in this case to establish the second successor). If, on the death of a first successor, he or she was still statutory tenant of the dwelling-house, there may be a further succession by virtue of para. 6

(sch. 4, para. 6). However, the second successor will take as assured tenant rather than as statutory tenant, and the conditions for succession under para. 6 are onerous. To qualify, the claimant must have been a member of the original tenant's family and a member of the first successor's family, in each case looking at the position immediately before the death of the respective tenants. The claimant must have resided in the dwelling-house with the first successor for the period of two years immediately before the first successor's death. This provision will be satisfied in many cases by the child of statutory tenants who have succeeded each other to the tenancy. The increased period required for succession is again offset where the claimant has, prior to 15 January 1989, resided with the first successor for six months (see para. 6(2)).

6.1.4.4 Assured tenancy by succession Schedule 1 to the Rent Act 1977, as amended, allows certain Rent Act protected or statutory tenancies to undergo a metamorphosis on a succession occurring, and be thereafter Housing Act 1988 assured tenancies. Questions therefore arise concerning the terms on which the successor will hold, and the routes to a possession order available to a landlord who may have acted at the beginning of the tenancy, on the basis of the then existing law, by serving certain notices on the tenant.

Where a successor becomes an assured tenant of a dwelling-house which was previously let on a protected or statutory tenancy, the tenancy will be periodic (s. 39(5)). The periods for the tenancy will be the same as those for which rent was payable by the predecessor under the Rent Act tenancy, and the other terms will be ascertained by reference to s. 39(6).

Where, immediately before his death, the predecessor was a tenant under a fixed-term tenancy, the tenancy to which the successor will succeed will nevertheless be periodic, and the terms of that tenancy will be determined by s. 39(6). However, the landlord, or the succeeding tenant, may not agree with the terms imposed by statute. Either can, in those circumstances, use the 's. 6 procedure' in an attempt to vary the terms of the contract (s. 39(9)).

Where the landlord, at the beginning of the original tenancy, served notices on the tenant giving himself the right to regain possession on grounds in the Rent Act, his position will be preserved on the tenancy becoming assured following a succession. Section 7, as modified for these purposes by s. 39(10), together with sch. 4, para. 13, provides that the court 'shall make an order for possession' of the dwelling-house if it is satisfied that the circumstances are as specified in any of Cases 11, 12, 16, 17, 18 and 20 in sch. 15 to the Rent Act 1977. If a notice was given for the purposes of Cases 13, 14 or 15 in the same schedule, the court will be in the same position, albeit by a different route. These three Cases have exact parallels among grounds of possession in the Housing Act 1988: notices given for Rent Act purposes to the predecessor shall be treated as having been given for the equivalent ground in the Housing Act 1988 (sch. 4, para. 15). Finally, if a protected shorthold tenancy is on succession converted into an assured tenancy, it will be treated as an assured shorthold tenancy, whether or not s. 20(1) is otherwise fulfilled (s. 39(7)).

Paragraph 10 of sch. 1 to the Rent Act 1977, whereby a landlord who grants a new tenancy to a successor is not prejudiced in terms of recovering possession, is not amended by the Housing Act 1988.

6.1.5   Surrender of Rent Act tenancies

The deregulation of rents which the Housing Act 1988 occasions will provide a strong incentive for landlords to negotiate the surrender of tenancies currently held under the Rent Act regime, and relet the properties thus recovered on assured tenancies. A reletting to a previously protected or statutory tenant may not be effective to do this if the reletting immediately follows the termination of the Rent Act tenancy (s. 34(1)(b)). Landlords should also be cautious of the way the surrender is arrived at. An executory agreement to surrender a protected or statutory tenancy will be unenforceable by the landlord (*Barton* v *Fincham* [1921] 2 KB 291). Only if the tenant actually delivers up possession of the premises will the landlord be safe, the statutory tenancy ending on the tenant ceasing to occupy the house as his residence.

6.2   Protected shorthold tenancies

The protected shorthold is the form of temporary letting first introduced in the Housing Act 1980 (see 4.1). Its place is taken in the new regime by the assured shorthold, by which fixed-term agreements for six months or more can be entered into without conferring a security of tenure. As with protected tenancies (of which it is a subspecies), a protected shorthold entered into before 15 January 1989 will remain a protected shorthold. So too, a protected shorthold entered into on or after 15 January 1989 will remain a protected shorthold if entered into pursuant to a contract made before that day, or if (as is extremely unlikely) it constitutes suitable alternative accommodation according to an order of the court (s. 34(1)(a) and (c)).

There is, however, a major difference between protected shortholds and other protected tenancies where the landlord makes a grant of a new tenancy to a former protected shorthold tenant after 15 January 1989. If, on or after 15 January 1989, a landlord grants a tenancy to a tenant who was, immediately before the grant, a protected shorthold tenant, and the landlord and the tenant under the tenancy are the same as under the protected shorthold, the new tenancy will be an *assured* shorthold tenancy. This will be so even if s. 20(1) (which states the conditions for the creation of an assured shorthold) is not satisfied (s. 34(3)). Only if the landlord serves notice on the tenant to the effect that the tenancy is not an assured shorthold (a somewhat unlikely state of affairs) will this not be the case. The same result will follow if the tenant was not a protected shorthold tenant as at 15 January 1989, but had been at some time earlier and was, at 15 January, 'holding over' or holding under a new protected or statutory tenancy (s. 34(2)(b); and see Rent Act 1977, sch. 15, Case 19).

6.3   Housing Act 1980 assured tenancies

Sections 56 to 58 of the Housing Act 1980 created another form of tenure in the assured tenancy, a tenure which bears few similarities to its namesake which the 1988 Act promotes. While the protected shorthold, to begin with at least, conferred no security of tenure at the price of rent control, the assured tenancy allowed landlords a commercial return on their properties while giving their tenants a security based loosely on the provisions of Part II of the Landlord and

Tenant Act 1954. 1980 Act assured tenancies could only be granted in the case of newly erected buildings or (later) where substantial works had been carried out on the dwelling-house, and the landlord had to be 'approved' by the Secretary of State in a statutory instrument.

The Housing Act 1988 converts all 1980 Act assured tenancies into 1988 Act assured tenancies, whether or not they would otherwise satisfy the provisions of section 1. (Being by definition created before the 1988 Act, they would fall foul of sch. 1, para. 1, without more.) Only where the landlord's interest now belongs to the Crown or a local authority (i.e., a landlord within sch. 1, paras 11 and 12) will they not become 1988 Act assured tenancies (s. 1(4)). No 1980 Act assured tenancies can be created on or after 15 January 1989 (s. 37(1)). A contract made before that date for the grant of a 1980 Act assured tenancy will have effect after that date as a contract for the grant of a 1988 Act assured tenancy instead. On grant, the only exceptions from assured tenancy status which may operate are those in sch. 1, paras 11 and 12 (s. 37(4)).

There are two further cases to watch:

(a) Where the 1980 Act assured tenant has, prior to 15 January 1989, applied to the court for a new tenancy and the old tenancy is continuing pending the determination of that application. Until the court makes its decision, the tenancy will remain under the 1980 Act. If the court refuses to grant him a new tenancy, the tenant will deliver up possession. If it does grant him one, that tenancy will be an assured tenancy for the purposes of the 1988 Act, unless the tenancy cannot be assured by virtue of paras 11 or 12 of sch. 1 (s. 37(3) and (5)).

(b) Where the 1980 Act assured tenant has as his landlord a fully mutual housing association immediately prior to 15 January 1989. Although such landlords are not generally capable of letting on assured tenancy under Part I of the 1988 Act (sch. 1, para. 12(1)(h)), the tenancy will become assured under that Act and remain so despite the landlord (s. 1(5)).

6.4 Housing association tenancies

Most lettings by housing associations were denied Rent Act security of tenure by the Rent Act 1977, ss. 15 and 16, but were allowed the benefit of the fair rent provisions by Part VI of the same Act. Where a letting by a housing association is entered into before 15 January 1989, or pursuant to a contract made before that day, it will be a 'housing association tenancy' so-called, and will be entitled to the rent protection afforded by Part VI of the Rent Act 1977 (s. 35(2)). A grant to a tenant who immediately before the grant was holding such a housing association tenancy will take effect as a housing association tenancy although entered into on or after 15 January 1989, and the same will apply if the tenancy granted to the tenant constituted suitable alternative accommodation under a court order (s. 35(2)(b) and (c)). The only other possibility of a letting by a housing association being subject to rent control if made after 15 January 1989 is where the landlord's interest under a tenancy is transferred to the housing association from a new town corporation in the two-year period following 15 November 1988 (ss. 35(2)(d) and 38(4)). For lettings by housing associations generally, see 8.7.

6.5   Restricted contracts

This form of tenure imposed some rent control and, at least in days gone by, some security. The holder of the restricted contract would have either a tenancy, excluded from being a protected or statutory tenancy for a particular reason (e.g., the presence of a resident landlord), or a right to occupy a dwelling as a residence falling short of a tenancy (see Rent Act 1977, s. 19(1), J. E. Martin, *Security of Tenure under the Rent Act* (1986), ch. 8 and Megarry, *The Rent Acts,* 11th ed. (1988), Part 6).

The Housing Act 1988 abolishes the status of restricted contract, but again allows for the preservation of accrued rights. If the restricted contract were entered into before, or pursuant to a contract made before, 15 January 1989, it will continue to be a restricted contract with the same rights under the Rent Act as before. However, as from 15 January 1989, the holder of the restricted contract must beware of entering into an agreement to vary the terms under which he holds: if the variation affects the level of rent, a new contract will be automatically inferred, a contract which will not be restricted as before (s. 36(2)(a)). If the rent is unaffected by the variation, it will remain a matter of construction whether a new contract has been entered into. If it is found that there is a new contract then that contract will no longer be a restricted contract (s. 36(2)(b)). Contractual variations consequent upon the decision of a rent tribunal regarding the level of the rent will not count for these purposes (s. 36(3)).

By s. 81A of the Rent Act 1977 (itself added by the Housing Act 1980, s. 71), the rent tribunal must cancel an entry on the register of rents under restricted contracts on application by the landlord if the dwelling is no longer subject to a restricted contract. The requirement that two years must elapse from the date of entry of a rent upon the register before cancellation can take place is now deleted, enabling landlords to remove their properties from the register as quickly as those restricted contracts existing at the commencement of the Act come to an end (s. 36(4)).

6.6   Rent (Agriculture) Act 1976 tenancies and licences

As explained in chapter 5, it is the policy of the legislation to phase out these tenures in favour of assured agricultural occupancies. Thus, a tenancy or licence entered into on or after 15 January 1989 cannot be a 'relevant licence or relevant tenancy for the purpose of the Rent (Agriculture) Act 1976', unless it falls within the transitional provisions (s. 34(4)). (These subject new tenancies which are granted to old tenants and pre 15 January 1989 contracts for a tenancy or licence to the regime of the 1976 Act.) As the conditions to be satisfied for an assured agricultural occupancy are practically identical to those for a 1976 Act protected occupancy, the date of the tenancy or licence will be all-important.

Part II of sch. 4 to the Housing Act 1988 makes several amendments to the succession provisions contained in the 1976 Act, such amendments applying where the original occupier dies after 15 January 1989 (s. 39(4)). References in the following discussion to the 1976 Act are to that Act as amended. Common-law spouses are now entitled to succeed, and will have priority over other members of the occupier's family (1976 Act, s. 4(5A)). Other members of the family must now have resided with the original occupier in the dwelling-house for a period of two years immediately before his death (1976 Act, s. 4(4)), subject to certain transitional cases (1976 Act, s. 4(5C)). If more than one family member qualifies, the county court is to choose one in default of agreement (1976 Act, s. 4(5B)).

Where succession to a protected occupier or statutory tenant is by a member of the original occupier's family, the successor will become an assured tenant of the dwelling-house rather than a statutory tenant under the 1976 Act (1976 Act, s. 4(4)). This assured tenancy will be an assured periodic tenancy, the terms being determined in accordance with s. 39(6) of the 1988 Act, and it will also be an assured agricultural occupancy even if the conditions in s. 24(1) are not fulfilled (s. 39(4) and (8)). The effect of it being treated as an assured agricultural occupancy is that recovery of possession will be restricted (and facilitated) as outlined in 5.3 and a market rent will be chargeable.

An amendment is made to s. 28 of the 1976 Act extending the time-limit in which any information must be laid in respect of a prosecution for an offence under that section: see sch. 17, para. 21.

6.7 Secure tenancies

The secure tenancy, first introduced by the Housing Act 1980, and now governed by the provisions of Part IV of the Housing Act 1985, is largely unaffected by Part I of the Housing Act 1988. The most important changes are those consequent upon the transfer of housing associations from the public to the private sector. Tenancies entered into by housing associations will in future be assured and subject to the 1988 Act code, rather than secure and within the 1985 Act. The effect of this is considered in 8.7. Lettings by local authorities, new town corporations, urban development corporations, housing cooperatives, or the newly created housing action trusts, will continue to be on secure tenancy (s. 35(4)(a)).

The two provisions in Part I which have some implications for secure tenancies are considered elsewhere: s. 35 in 8.7.1 and s. 38 in 2.3.1. Parts III and IV have major implications for secure tenants: see chapters 9 and 10 respectively.

Chapter Seven
Protection from Eviction

7.1 Introduction

From the outset, the government recognised that its proposals to deregulate the privately rented sector would be greeted with accusations from its opponents of pandering to Rachmanism and sought to negate their concerns by strengthening the existing laws against unlawful eviction. There is no doubt that the abolition of rent control from new lettings will provide landlords with a considerable financial incentive to repossess properties let to tenants protected by the Rent Acts, and it takes little imagination to perceive that some will be prepared to use fair means or foul. The most difficult time will be the period of transition, as once landlords are obtaining an open market rent for their properties, they may not be as keen to recover possession for reletting or selling the freehold. The Act gives recognition to these transitional problems by providing that the new 'statutory tort' of unlawful eviction can be committed at any time after 9 June 1988 (the first day of the report stage of the Bill in the Commons).

7.2 Criminal liability for eviction

The Protection from Eviction Act 1977 (which is set out in its amended form on pp. 364–74) creates two offences which may be committed by 'any person'. By s. 1(2), a person who unlawfully deprives the residential occupier of any premises of his occupation thereof (or attempts to do so) shall be guilty of the offence known as unlawful eviction. It is a defence for the defendant to prove that he believed, with reasonable cause, that the occupier had ceased to reside. The residential occupier as the 'victim' of the eviction must be 'a person occupying the premises as a residence, whether under a contract or by virtue of any enactment or rule of law giving him the right to remain in occupation or restricting the right of any other person to recover possession of the premises' (s. 1(1)). This offence is not amended in any way by the Housing Act 1988.

The Protection from Eviction Act 1977, s. 1(3) ('unlawful harassment'), makes it an offence for 'any person' to do acts (cf. omission: *R* v *Zafar Ahmed* (1986) 18 HLR 416) 'calculated' (see below) to interfere with the peace or comfort of the residential occupier or members of his household, or persistently to withdraw or withhold services reasonably required for the occupation of the premises as a residence. The defendant must *intend* to cause the residential occupier *either* to give up occupation (permanently: *Schon* v *Camden London Borough Council* (1986) 279 EG 859) *or* to refrain from exercising any right or pursuing any remedy in respect of the premises. If the defendant honestly believed, on reasonable grounds, that the persons he harassed were not residential occupiers (as being, for example, squatters), he is not guilty of the offence under s. 1(3): *R* v *Phekoo* [1981] 1 WLR 1117.

The offence under s. 1(3) has in practice caused difficulties. In particular, many defendants escape conviction because the prosecution is unable to prove that they specifically intended to cause the occupier to leave, rather than merely to make things less pleasant for him in the hope that he might decide to go. The Housing Act 1988 seeks to facilitate conviction for unlawful harassment, not by widening the ambit of the present s. 1(3), but by creating another offence which will sit, somewhat uneasily, next to s. 1(3) on the statute book. The one amendment to s. 1(3) is cosmetic but worthwhile: the word 'calculated', archaic and with undertones of deliberate machination, is replaced by 'likely' (Housing Act 1988, s. 29(1)), which is what 'calculated' means in this context anyway.

The new s. 1(3A) creates an offence which can be committed only by certain individuals. The defendant must be either the landlord of the residential occupier concerned, 'landlord' being defined as including any superior landlord (s. 1(3C)), or an agent of the landlord. The *actus reus* of s. 1(3A) is identical to that for s. 1(3); the only difference is the *mens rea*. The defendant must know, or have reasonable cause to believe, that his conduct is likely to cause the residential occupier to give up occupation, or refrain from exercising any right or pursuing any remedy in respect of the premises. The stupid landlord loses his protection: if he has reasonable cause to believe that the occupier is likely to go, that is enough. It remains open to the landlord to argue that he did not know that the 'victim' was a residential occupier at all, and nothing in s. 1(3A) appears to derogate from the principle, stated in *R* v *Phekoo,* that such belief of the defendant must be held on reasonable grounds. It is a defence, as under s. 1(3), for the defendant to prove (the onus being on him) that he had reasonable grounds for doing the acts or withdrawing or withholding the services in question (s. 1(3B)). However, a mistake about his legal rights to repossess will not constitute such a defence.

There are now, therefore, three offences in the amended s. 1 of the Protection from Eviction Act 1977. Although it might be thought that the offence of unlawful eviction was the most serious, all three attract the same maximum penalties: on summary conviction, a fine of 'the prescribed sum' (currently £2,000) and/or six months' imprisonment; on indictment, an unlimited fine and/or two years' imprisonment.

7.3 Civil liability for eviction

The occupier who was evicted from his dwelling-house by the actions of his landlord had two main remedies available to him under the civil law as it stood prior to 10 June 1988. The most immediately effective would be an injunction, perhaps *ex parte,* ordering the landlord to allow him back into occupation at once, the sanction for the landlord being committal for contempt. The occupier would probably also have a claim in damages, based on the loss he had suffered as a result of the landlord's actions, but the size of damages awards has not notably deterred landlords from taking the law into their own hands. The Housing Act 1988 sets out to make the prospect of a civil action for damages against the landlord more of a deterrent than it has been in the past, but to comprehend fully the scope of the reforms, it is necessary first to give a brief outline of the existing law.

7.3.1 The existing law

The occupier evicted on or before 9 June 1988 who seeks damages may have one or more cause of action. He may sue the landlord for breach of contract, the term in question being, usually, the landlord's implied covenant for quiet enjoyment. He may sue the landlord in tort, the landlord having committed trespass, and, possibly, assault and/or nuisance. In practice, the occupier will probably plead in both contract and tort. In tort, the damages recoverable may include sums in respect of any personal injury sustained by the plaintiff and compensation for loss of, or damage to, personal property. There may also be a head of 'aggravated damages', compensating the plaintiff for the suffering, feelings of outrage and indignation, and distress, which he incurred as a result of the eviction. On top of all this, the court may award a sum of 'exemplary damages', where 'the defendant's conduct has been calculated by him to make a profit for himself which may well exceed the compensation payable to the plaintiff' (per Lord Devlin in *Rookes* v *Barnard* [1964] AC 1129, 1226). This item, which is essentially a punitive measure 'to teach a wrongdoer that tort does not pay' is particularly appropriate to eviction cases, as the landlord may well have made a calculation of the kind contemplated in *Rookes* v *Barnard,* assessing whether the advantages consequent upon obtaining vacant possession outweigh the disadvantages of liability to the evicted occupier in a civil action (and the possibility of prosecution before the criminal courts).

> How, it may be asked, about the late Mr Rachman, who is alleged to have used hired bullies to intimidate statutory tenants by violence or threats of violence into giving vacant possession of their residences and so placing a valuable asset in the hands of the landlord? My answer must be that if this is not a cynical calculation of profit and cold-blooded disregard of a plaintiff's rights [and therefore incurring liability to an award of exemplary damages], I do not know what is. (Per Lord Hailsham of St Marylebone LC in *Broome* v *Cassell and Co. Ltd* [1972] AC 1027, 1079.)

Awards of exemplary damages have been upheld in several eviction cases: see, for example, *Drane* v *Evangelou* [1978] 1 WLR 455; *Asghar* v *Ahmed* (1984) 17 HLR 25; *McMillan* v *Singh* (1984) 17 HLR 120. However, exemplary damages (or, for that matter, aggravated damages) are not available where the allegation is one of breach of contract alone, and, if the evicted occupier brings proceedings in the county court, his total damages award will be limited to £5,000,

In *McCall* v *Abelesz* [1976] QB 585, the Court of Appeal held that an evicted occupier could not base a civil action against the landlord on what is now s. 1 of the Protection from Eviction Act 1977. Sections 27 and 28 of the Housing Act

1988 effectively overturn that decision, conferring on the evicted occupier a right to sue his landlord for damages for committing the conduct which s. 1 renders criminal. The damages available will be substantial, and although the new remedy will not replace the traditional causes of action for unlawful eviction, it will become the most lucrative of the remedies available.

7.3.2 Liability (section 27)

The plaintiff in an action under s. 27 must be a 'residential occupier', as defined in the Protection from Eviction Act 1977, s. 1(1). The defendant must be his landlord, or any superior landlord under whom that landlord derives title (s. 27(9)(c)). The plaintiff must show that the defendant, or any person acting on his behalf, committed acts which amounted to criminal offences under the Protection from Eviction Act 1977, s. 1. It may be that the landlord actually evicted the plaintiff, or it may be that he caused the plaintiff to leave the premises as a result of his conduct (a sort of 'constructive eviction'): either will do to satisfy s. 27, the vital precondition of liability being the departure of the plaintiff from the premises in question. While the ingredients of the statutory tort are identical to those for the criminal offences, it will not be necessary for there to have been a conviction, or indeed a prosecution: indeed, it will only be in a minority of cases where criminal proceedings have been initiated. It will be open to the plaintiff to use a conviction of the defendant under the Protection from Eviction Act 1977 as evidence in subsequent civil proceedings for unlawful eviction (Civil Evidence Act 1968, s. 11; RSC, Ord. 18, r. 7A). The standard of proof in s. 27 proceedings will, of course, be the civil standard.

Two defences are made available to the landlord by s. 27(8), and both are based, almost word for word, on the defences which are available to the criminal offences in the Protection from Eviction Act 1977, s. 1. The landlord who believed, and had reasonable cause to believe, that the occupier had ceased to reside in the premises, or that he had reasonable grounds for withdrawing or withholding services, will have a defence to the statutory tort. The burden of proof, on the balance of probabilities, will be upon the landlord.

Liability under s. 27 is to be in addition to any liability otherwise arising. Thus, it will be open to the plaintiff to sue in trespass, nuisance, assault and breach of contract as before. However, the plaintiff cannot be awarded damages twice over in respect of the same loss (s. 27(5)). This provision is difficult to interpret, as it is arguable that the statutory tort does not compensate for loss at all: the award of damages to which the plaintiff may be entitled may bear no relation to his actual financial loss, and if it does, the correlation will be coincidental. Damages as calculated under s. 28 are punitive: they are intended to deprive the defendant of the fruits of his illegal actions, and whether the plaintiff has suffered any loss which can be quantifed in money terms is irrelevant. The award of damages available at common law which the statutory s. 28 award most closely resembles is the award of exemplary damages, in that they both seek to 'teach a wrongdoer that tort does not pay'. This is therefore probably the only 'common law' head of damages which will be unavailable to the plaintiff who has obtained a statutory award. Such a plaintiff should also be able to recover, at common law, damages for personal injury and for damage to property, and, arguably, aggravated damages.

Section 27(6) will relieve from liability a landlord who can show that its provisions are applicable. First, if, before proceedings are 'finally disposed of' (as defined in s. 27(6)), the plaintiff has been reinstated in the premises, so that he becomes again residential occupier, no liability will arise. However, the occupier is not obliged to accept an offer of reinstatement by the landlord. If such an offer is made before proceedings are *commenced,* then an unreasonable refusal of the offer by the occupier may result in a reduction in the damages award (s. 27(7)(b), see 7.3.3). However, once the proceedings have been commenced, the plaintiff is in a position of strength. He is no longer liable to have his damages award reduced, however unreasonable his refusal of the defenant's offer to reinstate: only if he accepts such an offer and is reinstated in consequence does he prejudice his position. The moral is clear: issue the summons promptly and refuse all overtures by the landlord thereafter.

The second defence provided by s. 27(6) overlaps to a considerable degree with the first, as a result of their Parliamentary history rather than anything else. The plaintiff must have requested the court to reinstate him, and the court must have acceded to his request so that he has been reinstated in the premises in question and become residential occupier of them once more. It will often be the case that the occupier will issue proceedings at the same time for remedies at common law and by virtue of the statute, and the court is able in an appropriate case to order the reinstatement of the plaintiff into the premises from which he has been evicted as an alternative to making the statutory award of damages. An undertaking to the court given by the defendant will constitute an order of the court (see, e.g., *Neath Canal Co.* v *Ynisarwed Resolven Colliery Co.* (1875) LR 10 Ch App 450). Once again, the matter is in the plaintiff's hands: if he does not wish to be reinstated, or simply wants the money available under s. 27, he can insist on the award. Only where the occupier has requested reinstatement will a court order having that practical effect exonerate the landlord from liability under s. 27.

7.3.3   The measure of damages (section 28)
As has been already noted, the damages award is not calculated by reference to any loss which the occupier has suffered as a result of the eviction. If he has sustained loss, he should proceed with an action in trespass, assault or nuisance, as well as proceeding with his action under s. 27, and the actions could and should be consolidated. The measure of damages for the statutory tort is relatively straightforward: it is the difference in value between the property with the occupier in it and the property with vacant possession. In other words, it is the profit which the landlord stood to make by acting unlawfully, whether or not he in fact makes it. In assessing the value of the land (or to be technically correct the landlord's interest in the land, covering the position where he has a leasehold interest himself), certain assumptions must be made. The landlord is deemed to be selling his interest on the open market to a willing buyer, neither the occupier nor a member of his family (as defined in Housing Act 1985, s. 113) want to buy, and it is unlawful to carry out any substantial development of the land or demolish buildings upon it. The 'development value' of the land is therefore generally disregarded, subject only to the exceptions in s. 28(6). The values are to be assessed as at the time of the eviction (s. 28(1)).

It is clear from this that the level of damages available to evicted occupiers who pursue the new statutory remedy is potentially very high indeed. It will, of course, be necessary for each side to instruct its own surveyor to value the landlord's interest, and the usual procedure of disclosing reports will have to be anticipated in any directions made during the course of the action. A particularly attractive feature of the way the damages award is to be assessed is that the occupier who has most to lose will get more money, or, looking at it from the point of view of the landlord, it will cost him more to evict an occupier with substantial security of tenure than an occupier who has little or no such protection. There will be a strong incentive to landlords who have let properties on Rent Act protected tenancies to obtain possession at the earliest possible opportunity. Some will succumb to the temptation of using illegal methods, and they are the ones who will be penalised the most heavily by the statutory tort. There is a very considerable difference between the value of a house subject to a Rent Act tenancy and the value of the same house with vacant possession. It is that difference which an evicting landlord would be liable to pay under s. 28. A landlord who anticipated the effect of the new provisions and sought to evict prior to 15 January 1989 will find his efforts wasted too, as the new remedy will apply to any eviction taking place after 9 June 1988.

Section 27(7) imposes on the plaintiff a statutory duty to mitigate his loss. It is, however, extremely specific, and, the tort of unlawful eviction being a creature entirely of statute, there is no residual 'common law' duty to mitigate in the event of the plaintiff not being caught by its provisions. The plaintiff's damages may be reduced in two instances only. As mentioned above, the landlord may offer to reinstate the occupier in the premises from which he has been evicted. If this offer was made before the commencement of proceedings, and it was unreasonable of the occupier to refuse it or would have been had the occupier not already obtained other accommodation, damages may be reduced (s. 27(7)(b)). It is not necessary for the occupier to have actually refused the offer: thus the plaintiff who never communicates his decision to the landlord may fall within the section. If he accepts the offer and is reinstated, then the landlord will not be liable under s. 27 (s. 27(6)). Reduction of damages may also be ordered where the conduct of the occupier or any person living with him in the premises in question was such that it is reasonable to 'mitigate' the damages payable (s. 27(7)(a)).

It is to be hoped that the courts will be slow to use their power to reduce damages. The statutory tort of unlawful eviction has been provided with a very clear motive: deterrence. The damages payable are not assessed so as to compensate the plaintiff, but to punish the defendant: they are penal. The purpose of s. 27(7) is on the one hand to give the plaintiff an incentive to come to terms with his landlord if that is a reasonable thing to do, and on the other to prevent the plaintiff whose conduct has been such as to drive the defendant to evict him from enjoying a windfall at the landlord's expense. In many cases, the manner of the eviction will be such as to make any refusal by the occupier of an offer to go back perfectly understandable. 'Conduct' which might provide a ground for possession under the Rent Act 1977, (sch. 15, Case 2) or under Part I of the Housing Act 1988 (sch. 2, Ground 14), should not automatically result in a reduction in damages. The landlord in those circumstances has a lawful means of obtaining possession available to him: his election not to use those means and to evict unlawfully should not result in an automatic reduction in damages. It is precisely that sort of calculated self-help which the statutory tort is seeking to deter.

7.4 Recovery of possession

Sections 3 and 5 of the Protection from Eviction Act 1977 were intended to prohibit landlords from resorting to self-help in their efforts to recover possession of their properties. The Housing Act 1988 first widens the ambit of these provisions by including licences as well as tenancies, then narrows it by creating a new category of 'excluded' tenancies and licences which do not enjoy the protection of ss. 3 and 5. The general effect of these provisions will be considered first and then the tenancies and licences which are excluded by the new legislation.

The only lawful method of recovering possession of premises to which s. 3 applies is by court proceedings. Section 3 applies where the premises have been let as a dwelling under a tenancy (or licence: s. 3(2B)) which is neither 'statutorily protected' nor 'excluded', and in which premises the occupier is still residing. A tenancy is statutorily protected if it is a Rent Act, or Rent (Agriculture) Act, protected or statutory tenancy, a long tenancy, a business tenancy, a tenancy of an agricultural holding or (the Housing Act 1988 addition) an assured tenancy (including an assured shorthold) or an assured agricultural occupancy (Protection from Eviction Act 1977, s. 8(1)). In each of these cases, the protection given by s. 3 would be superfluous, as the statutes which confer protection on these individuals prohibit recovery of possession without reference to the court.

Section 5(1) invalidates certain notices to quit which may be given by the landlord (or tenant). Broadly speaking, a notice to quit any dwelling will be valid only if it is in writing, contains such information as the Secretary of State has prescribed (see SI 1988 No. 2201), and is given not less than four weeks before the date on which it is to take effect. These requirements are extended by s. 5(1A) to a 'periodic licence', a term which is not defined in the legislation, but which presumably indicates a licence to occupy, where the maximum duration of the licensee's right to occupy is not specified at the outset.

Neither s. 3 nor s. 5 applies where the premises are occupied pursuant to an excluded tenancy or an excluded licence. To be 'excluded', a tenancy must have been entered into on or after 15 January 1989 (and not pursuant to a contract made before that date) (ss. 3(2C) and (5(1B)). An 'excluded licence' may have been entered into at any time. Note, however, that a variation of an existing contract affecting the amount of rent payable may cause the tenancy or licence as varied to be deemed to be a new tenancy or licence, taking effect on the date of variation (s. 8(5)).

There are five categories of excluded interest for these purposes: shared accommodation, temporary accommodation for trespassers, holiday lets, rent-free accommodation, and hostel accommodation. If the tenancy or licence comes within any of these categories, the landlord will be free to re-enter upon the premises and retake possession once the contract between the occupier and himself has been terminated. It will not be necessary for a landlord to give four weeks' notice unless that is the provision made in the contract, nor will he need to obtain a possession order from the court. He must, however, take care that he does not commit the criminal offence under the Criminal Law Act 1977, s. 6, of securing entry to premises by violence.

Accommodation is 'shared' where the occupier has the use of it in common with another person. That person must be either the landlord or a member of his family (as defined in the Housing Act 1985, s. 113), one of whom must occupy premises as his only or principal home (see 2.2.5.1) of which the shared accommodation formed part: see s. 3A(2) and (3) for details of the times at which the landlord or member of the landlord's family must have been sharing the accommodation concerned. These provisions are obviously aimed at the occupier who is either a 'lodger', in colloquial terms, or someone not far removed from a lodger. However, the landlord does have a fair amount of leeway. 'Accommodation' is given a broad part definition in s. 3A(5)(a), such that the occupier who shares merely a cupboard or a staircase or corridor will not be excluded from the provisions of the Protection from Eviction Act 1977. This apart, as long as the tenant has the right to use some shared accommodation, it is not necessary for the accommodation concerned to be an integral part of the tenant's premises.

Example 7.1   The landlord owns a boarding-house containing three floors each with two rooms on them, and a basement with a self-contained flat. Each occupier has exclusive occupation of his own room, and the landlord occupies the flat in the basement. There are a kitchen and bathroom on each floor to which the tenants have access. In the terms of the written agreements which the landlord imposes on his tenants, the landlord reserves to himself the right to use the bathrooms. Although the occupiers are tenants of their rooms, having exclusive possession of them, they are not assured tenants nor are they protected by the Protection from Eviction Act 1977, ss. 3 or 5. The tenancies are not assured because there is no letting of the room as a separate dwelling, and the Housing Act 1988, s. 3, does not assist as the tenant shares with the landlord, who is in any event probably 'resident' within sch. 1, para. 10. They are not protected by the Protection from Eviction Act 1977 because the tenant has the use of accommodation, namely the bathroom, in common with his landlord. The landlord will therefore be able to retake possession without the necessity of going to court once he has effectively terminated the tenancy: if the tenancy is weekly, a week's notice will do.

A tenancy or licence will be excluded if it was granted as a temporary expedient to a person who *entered* the premises or other premises as a trespasser (s. 3A(6)). This may be relevant more to landlords such as local authorities and housing associations than to individual private landlords, who are less likely to take a sympathetic view of squatters and accommodate them. The tenancy or licence will be excluded even if the occupier in question had been granted a tenancy or licence to occupy by the landlord at some earlier time. However, the occupier who 'holds over' following the termination of his interest in the premises by the landlord will not be excluded, as he will not have entered the premises as a trespasser.

Holiday lets are excluded tenancies or licences: the definition is identical to that in the Housing Act 1988, sch. 1, para. 9, on which see 2.3.9. Also excluded are tenancies or licences which are granted other than for money or money's worth, covering the position of non-paying house guests who overstay their welcome. It does not follow that if no rent is paid the tenancy or licence in question will therefore be excluded: for example, agricultural employees may not pay for their accommodation as such, but they will give 'money's worth', accepting lower wages in lieu of their 'free' accommodation.

A licence (*not* a tenancy) is excluded if it confers rights of occupation in a hostel provided by one of the bodies (public sector landlords and housing associations) listed in s. 3A(8). 'Hostel' is defined in the Housing Act 1985, s. 622, as:

> a building in which is provided, for persons generally or for a class or classes of persons—
>
> (a) residential accommodation otherwise than in separate and self-contained sets of premises, and
> (b) either board or facilities for the preparation of food adequate to the needs of those persons, or both.

The Secretary of State has the power to add to the list of bodies who can provide excluded hostel accommodation (s. 3A(8)).

Chapter Eight
Housing Associations

8.1 Introduction

The voluntary housing movement, as embodied by the housing associations, has provided for many years an alternative to tenants who seek well managed, relatively cheap, accommodation with the security which the public sector generally affords. There is an infinite variety of housing associations, but the common factor which they share is that they are essentially non-profit-making bodies. Associations may build properties, improve them, let them, sell them, and many will do all of these. In the conduct of their affairs, they are supervised by the autonomous statutory body known as the Housing Corporation, which acts both as policeman and financier to the voluntary movement. Funding is partly by rental (and other) income, partly by central and local government subsidy. Prior to Part II of the Housing Act 1988 coming into force, the law governing housing associations was to be found in several statutes, the most important being the Housing Associations Act 1985. The leading work is J. Alder and C. R. Handy, *Housing Association Law* (1987).

The Housing Act 1988 heralds an important turning-point in the history of housing associations. Until now, they have been viewed in terms of finance, public duty and tenant security as being closer to the public than the private sector. The 1988 Act pushes them firmly out into the more dangerous waters of the open market, of the private sector, 'encouraging' them to seek finance independent of government, and enabling them to maximise their rental income by deregulating the tenancies under which their properties are held. It is hoped that by these, and other associated, reforms, the movement will be strengthened, and will be ready to take on the responsibilities of being a 'social landlord' in the new regime:

> The whole purpose of [Part II of the Act] is to try to enable housing associations to meet the needs of their traditional client groups, while being freed to some extent from the inevitable government constraints of being fully within the public sector when it comes to the national accounts. Its purpose is to get more housing association property that meets the needs of the people. (Mr William Waldegrave, HC Deb., 13 June 1988, col. 243.)

Housing associations are less conspicuously enthusiastic about the provisions, their national federation stating its concerns thus:

Housing associations wish to concentrate on helping those people for whom market forces are not producing the answer. They want to help a mix of households; they do not see their role either as providing welfare housing entirely for the destitute, or becoming like commercial landlords charging market rents.

The pushing of housing associations 'a little further from government' is achieved by devolving the major powers to fund from the Secretary of State for the Environment to the Housing Corporation. New tenancies from associations will cease to be secure tenancies (the public sector regime) and become assured tenancies instead. The Housing Corporation and a new equivalent entity in Wales called Housing for Wales are given powers to issue 'management guidance' to associations, and the overall picture of the voluntary movement changes so that the Housing Corporation and Housing for Wales ('the Corporations") are placed in a more influential position than before, assuming a role previously played by the Secretary of State himself. Whether the new structure will succeed in attracting private sector finance, or lead to an escalation in rents for the tenants which the associations exist to serve, will be seen in the fullness of time. Part II of the Housing Act 1988, which this chapter considers, is in many respects setting housing associations up to acquire more properties, to play a more forward role in housing policy, and Parts III and IV give Corporations the important function of approving purchasers of local authority and housing action trust housing stock. It is anticipated that it will be the housing associations themselves which will take the most advantage from Parts III and IV of the Act.

8.2   Housing for Wales

The establishment of a separate independent Corporation to deal specifically with the difficult housing problems faced in Wales, was first mooted by Mr Peter Walker, Secretary of State for Wales, in a speech in December 1987. Following an indication in the committee stage of the Housing Bill that the government was contemplating this possibility, provisions were introduced by amendment at the report stage in the Commons by the Parliamentary Under-Secretary of State for Wales (Mr Ian Grist):

Against the background of the new opportunities that the Bill will herald for associations, the government have decided that the time is now right for the work of associations in Wales to be supervised by a body that has its roots based in Wales, can develop a depth of understanding about the housing problems that we face in the principality, and is fully capable of leading the development of strategies to meet problems within a policy framework set by the Secretary of State for Wales (HC Deb., 13 June 1988, col. 108).

Sections 46 and 47 place the newly constituted Housing for Wales (in Welsh, Tai Cymru) in the shoes of the Housing Corporation. All property held by the

Housing Corporation in Wales will be transferred to Housing for Wales on the day s. 46 comes into effect. Any housing association registered with the Housing Corporation which has its registered office (or, in the case of a charity, its registered address) in Wales will have its registration transferred to Housing for Wales. All rights, liabilities and obligations of the Housing Corporation in relation to such associations or to land in Wales held by unregistered associations will likewise be transferred. The constitution of Housing for Wales is set out in sch. 5, the provisions of which are identical to those in the Housing Associations Act 1985, sch. 6, stating the constitution of the Housing Corporation, with the exception of paras 7 to 11, which provide for the appointment of staff for the new body and which, *inter alia,* preserve the statutory rights of employees transferred from the Housing Corporation. Schedule 6 to the Housing Act 1988 amends the legislation affecting the Housing Corporation in the light of the establishment of Housing for Wales. Particular note should be taken of the new s. 2A(2) of the Housing Associations Act 1985, whereby, in relation to a housing association which has its registered office in Wales, any references to 'the Corporation' in that Act (and the Housing Act 1988 too) will refer to Housing for Wales. In the text which follows, the same terminology will be used.

The effect of these provisions is that Housing for Wales will be given the identical role in Wales to that previously undertaken by the Housing Corporation in both England and Wales. The object is to ensure that there is a more sympathetic and informed institution with final responsibility for the rejuvenation of the voluntary housing movement in Wales. Housing associations which have dealings with Housing for Wales may see a change in emphasis, and the Corporations are free to follow their own registration criteria, issue their own management guidance and make their own general determinations (see sch. 6, paras 1 and 4). However, the legal relationships between associations and their financing corporation will not differ between England and Wales. There are now in effect three 'Housing Corporations', Scotland having recently had its own Corporation (Scottish Homes) established by the Housing (Scotland) Act 1988.

8.3 Financing housing associations

Before Part II of the Housing Act 1988 comes into force, the complicated procedure of housing association finance is governed by Part II of the Housing Associations Act 1985. The provisions dealing with housing association grant (HAG), revenue deficit grant (RDG), hostel deficit grant, surplus rental income and tax reliefs are all repealed by sch. 18 to the 1988 Act and are replaced by ss. 50 to 55. The new code which these sections introduce transfers primary responsibility for the allocation of HAG and RDG from the Secretary of State to the Corporations, subsumes hostel deficit grant under RDG, and enables the administration of tax reliefs and the recovery of surplus income to be delegated to the Corporations. It is consistent with the policy which the Act is hoping to advance of loosening the reins of the voluntary movement and distancing the associations from central government by enlarging the powers of the Corporations.

8.3.1 *Grants administered by the Corporations*
Under the previous regime, HAG was the most important source of government

finance for housing associations, and was the responsibility of the Secretary of State, who would, however, use the Housing Corporation as his agent to make payments. The Housing Associations Act 1985 set out a list of instances in which HAG would be payable, and the Secretary of State had, therefore, to comply with the statutory qualifying conditions. Section 50 of the 1988 Act now gives the power to make grants to the Corporations, and they are not subjected to narrowly prescribed statutory conditions. Not only may the Corporations make grants in respect of expenditure incurred or to be incurred by registered housing associations 'in connection with housing activities' (a definition which is widened by sch. 6, para. 36, to include all activities in pursuance of the housing association's purposes, objects and powers), but they are to make their own rules about procedure, qualifying conditions, calculation of the grant and manner of payment (s. 50(1) and (2)). The freedom to administer HAG will be notional, however, unless the Corporations are given adequate sums by central government to allocate to the associations, and there is behind the provisions of Part II of the 1988 Act a cost-cutting exercise. According to the Minister of Housing and Planning, the government envisaged that HAG would, on average, account for 'about 50%' of the income of housing associations, a substantial fall from the present level of approximately 80%.

Revenue deficit grant also becomes payable at the discretion of the Corporations, in circumstances where the expenditure of the association concerned has exceeded its income. The precise conditions are, again, as the Corporations themselves determine (s. 51). Although hostel deficit grant ceases as an independent head of finance, payments can still be made for revenue deficits which occur in relation to hostels as they would be covered as 'housing activities of the association of a particular description': in effect, hostel deficit grant will become a species of RDG.

The Corporations are given wide powers to reduce grant once it has been made, suspend or cancel any instalment, or direct an association to pay back grant, with interest if appropriate (s. 52). In exercising these powers, the Corporations must act in accordance with the principles which they have determined, and in particular they will only become exercisable on the occurrence of a 'relevant event': a failure to do so would leave them open to a challenge by way of judicial review. What is a relevant event has again to be decided by reference to the principles which the Corporations have themselves determined, s. 52 departing from the previous practice of stating expressly in the statute the conditions which need to be fulfilled for the powers to become applicable.

Payment of HAG may be made conditional on the association complying with specified conditions (s. 50(3)), and the Corporations will almost certainly make a failure to comply with such conditions (e.g., that the money is used for a particular purpose) a relevant event activating the claw-back provisions. The Corporations may also be guided by the repealed s. 52 of the Housing Associations Act 1985, which specified the circumstances under the old system in which the Secretary of State could reduce, suspend or claw back grant. It is not easy to anticipate what other relevant events might be:

I do not envisage that the Corporation would introduce a plethora of new circumstances giving rise to recovery, but novel situations may arise in which recovery may be merited (Mr William Waldegrave, Standing Committee G, 4 February 1988, col. 705).

Housing associations are under a statutory duty to notify the Corporation of the occurrence of a relevant event, and may be required to furnish further particulars of the event by the Corporation (s. 52(3)). The Land Registry may provide information too, a power which will no longer be necessary once Lord Templeman's Land Registration Act 1988, opening up the Registry to public scrutiny, comes into force (s. 52(4)).

There is an entirely new power to levy interest on HAG or RDG clawed back by the Corporation. Interest can only run from the date of the relevant event and, as an incentive to settle expeditiously, the Corporation may direct that interest is 'suspended' so that if it is paid before a certain date the interest claimed will be waived (see generally s. 52(7) to (9)).

In their new role as administrators of HAG and RDG, the Corporations are made responsible for formulating their own principles, as part of the policy of slackening the constraints of central government on the voluntary movement in general. Until these principles are formulated, the picture will not be complete. Two types of statement of principle may be made: a 'general determination', and a determination which relates solely to a particular case (s. 53(4)). Before making a general determination, the Corporation must consult with representative bodies of housing associations, traditionally the National Federation of Housing Associations. The terms of the general determination must then be approved by the Secretary of State and accorded the consent of the Treasury. The general determination having been made, it must be published in such a way as to bring it to the notice of the associations concerned. Where a determination is not 'general', there is no need for prior consultation or subsequent publication. The Corporation must, however, obtain the approval of the Secretary of State (see generally s. 53).

Under the old system of financing housing associations, local authorities played an important role. They would often prepare the 'approved development programme', or suggest housing projects, and would be the chief administrators of HAG. The new Act puts them in a much less influential position, being allowed (with the specific consent of the Secretary of State and the Treasury) to act as agent of the Corporations in connection with the assessment and payment of HAG (s. 50(4)). What the Act envisages is that the local authority which itself sponsors a particular project may be given the job of scrutinising the claim for grant and certifying to the Corporation that the work has been satisfactorily completed.

8.3.2 Tax relief grants

By the Housing Associations Act 1985, s. 62 (formerly Finance Act 1965 s. 93), the Secretary of State was enabled to reimburse payments of income tax and corporation tax made by a registered housing association which did not trade for profit, provided that during the relevant taxation period the association was concerned wholly or mainly with letting houses and hostels for housing accommodation. Although s. 62 is repealed by the Housing Act 1988, sch. 18, it is substantially re-enacted by s. 54 with no significant differences. It should, however, be noted that, by s. 57, the Secretary of State is empowered to delegate his functions under s. 54 to the Corporation.

8.3.3   Surplus rental income

Housing associations being essentially non-profit-making bodies, there was provision under the Housing Associations Act 1985 for the Secretary of State to recoup 'surplus rental income' from associations to which payments of HAG had been made and which had, according to the Secretary of State's calculations, made a surplus of income (including unrealised income) over expenditure. There is little change to the existing law: s. 53 of the 1985 Act is repealed and replaced by s. 55 of the Housing Act 1988. Under the new provisions, a registered association which has been in receipt of HAG must show separately in its accounts the surpluses arising from increased rental income accruing from housing activities to which the grant relates. Any surplus will be represented by a notional fund known as the rent surplus fund, and sums standing in that fund at the end of a period of account may on notice be appropriated by the Secretary of State, together with interest. The Secretary of State is given powers to demand information from the associations which he reasonably requires in connection with the exercise of his functions in relation to surplus rental income, and failure to supply information so demanded will constitute an offence (see s. 55(9); sch. 6, para. 18, amending Housing Associations Act 1985, s. 27(2)). The provisions will apply with respect to any accounting period which ends after s. 55 comes into force, so as to ensure that the new arrangements can operate in relation to accounting periods which 'straddle' the date of commencement.

The surplus rental income provisions will not be fully comprehensible until the Secretary of State makes the various determinations required of him by s. 55. Thus, the manner of calculating the surplus, and the housing activities which are to be considered in making that calculation, will be for the Secretary of State to determine, after the appropriate consultation, and once made the determination must be published so as to bring it to the notice of the associations concerned. As with tax relief grants, the Secretary of State may delegate his functions regarding surplus rental income (and, in transitional cases, those regarding the old 'grant redemption fund') to the Corporations (s. 57).

8.4   The Corporations

Whilst the creation of Housing for Wales is the most radical reform of the Housing Corporation contained in Part II of the Housing Act 1988, and both Corporations will assume the important role of approving private sector landlords who can take over property on an acquisition from local authorities and HATs (Parts III and IV), there are other significant changes to the powers and duties of the Corporations. By s. 49 (adding s. 36A to the Housing Associations Act 1985), the Corporations are empowered to issue management guidance to registered housing associations on a variety of matters such as allocation policies, rent levels, repair strategies and tenant consultation. Whilst the associations are not statutorily bound to follow every word of such guidance, they will ignore it at their peril. By s. 30 of the Housing Associations Act 1985, the

Corporations have powers to remove or suspend committee members, officers, agents and/or employees of associations the affairs of which have been misconducted or mismanaged, and they may also freeze the assets of such associations. In adjudicating whether an association has been guilty of misconduct or mismanagement, the Corporations may have regard to the extent to which management guidance has been followed. Prior to issuing management guidance, the Corporations must consult representative bodies and must also obtain the approval of the Secretary of State.

The issue of management guidance is indicative of the central role the Corporations are now required to play in the voluntary housing movement. It will be imperative for any well managed housing association to keep abreast of the papers emanating from the Corporations from time to time and adjust its policies accordingly.

The Corporations are, by sundry amendments to the Housing Associations Act 1985 contained in sch. 6 to the Housing Act 1988, granted greater powers than before over registered housing associations. The power to petition for the winding up of a housing association is extended by adding a second ground: that the association is unable to pay its debts (sch. 6, para. 16, amending Housing Associations Act 1985, s. 22). The appointment of new committee members and trustees to associations by the Corporations is no longer restricted to the numerical limit set out in the association's constitution (sch. 6, paras 12 and 13(2), amending Housing Associations Act 1985, ss. 17 and 18), The powers of the Corporations to inquire into the activities of associations are widened by sch. 6, para. 19, amending Housing Associations Act 1985, s. 28. Where it is necessary for the purposes of an inquiry into the affairs of an association, the person appointed to inquire may look into the business not only of the association itself, but also that of any subsidiary or associate (terms which are defined in sch. 6). He may now make interim reports to the Corporation, on the faith of which the Corporation may exercise its powers under Housing Associations Act 1985, s. 30 (Housing Act 1988, sch. 6, para 21).

There is a small variation in the grounds on which the Secretary of State may remove a member of a Corporation from office. He can no longer remove him on the ground of being 'incapacitated by physical or mental illness' (Housing Associations Act 1985, sch. 6, para. 3(3)(b) repealed by Housing Act 1988, sch. 6, para. 37), a power which is probably unnecessary anyway, as the member concerned will be almost certainly 'unable or unfit' to discharge his functions, and removable under Housing Associations Act 1985, sch. 6, para. 3(3)(d)).

The Housing Act 1988, s. 56, imposes on the Corporations the statutory duty imposed on local authorities under the Race Relations Act 1976, s. 71, to make appropriate arragements with a view to securing that their various functions are carried out with due regard to the need to eliminate racial discrimination and to promote equality of opportunity and good relations between persons of different racial groups.

8.5 Registration of housing associations

Registration of a housing association with a Corporation remains the precondition for assistance by way of grant, and it will therefore continue to be a status which associations will cherish. Section 48 of the Housing Act 1988 enables non-charitable registered associations to have more widely drafted purposes and objects than before, and allows them to have powers under their constitutions which would previously have been considered incompatible with registration. The conditions that the association does not trade for profit and is established for the purpose of the provision, construction, improvement or management of houses for letting, or for occupation of association members, or of hostels are unchanged. However, the category of permissible additional purposes or objects is widened: in particular, an association which seeks to develop the community by providing amenities or services in the area where its tenants live will be able to do so if its constitution allows, and yet remain eligible for registration. The powers which an association seeking to be registered may have are also broadened: now, the association may acquire commercial premises and even carry on businesses for a limited period, as long as it is part of a project undertaken for purposes or objects which are permissible. The association which enters into such activities must beware that it does not 'trade for profit' (as defined in *Goodman* v *Dolphin Square Trust Ltd* (1979) 38 P & CR 257): that would render the association ineligible for registration, and Housing Associations Act 1985, s. 4(4), would be of no avail. The Secretary of State is empowered to amend the new s. 4(3) and (4), of the Housing Associations Act 1985 but not so as to restrict or limit the permissible purposes, objects or powers (Housing Act 1988, s. 48(2)). In other words, he can add further permissible additional purposes objects or powers, or widen the purposes, objects or powers a registered association may have: he cannot take away or narrow them.

8.6 The 'HOTCHA' scheme

The 'Home Ownership Scheme for Tenants of Charitable Housing Associations' ('HOTCHA') was introduced by the Housing and Building Control Act 1984, consolidated in Housing Act 1985, and is now preserved, with amendments, by Housing Act 1988, s. 58. The scheme is complex, and for a detailed description, reference should be made to J. Alder and C. R. Handy, *Housing Association Law* (1987), pp. 292–5. Briefly, secure tenants of charitable housing trusts and housing associations are denied the right to buy (Housing Act 1985, sch. 5, para. 1). However, in an attempt to free their accommodation for other needy individuals, the scheme allowed the purchase of alternative accommodation and onward disposal to the tenant in question on discounted terms analogous to the right to buy. By Housing Associations Act 1985, s. 45, the purchase of the alternative accommodation qualified as a housing project and could therefore be financed by HAG. However, as participation in a HOTCHA arrangement was not a charitable purpose, a non-charitable association had to be engaged to buy the alternative accommodation on behalf of the charitable association.

Under the new legislation, the qualification of projects for HAG is a matter for the Corporations to determine, and is no longer set out specifically in the statute. Section 58 of the Housing Act 1988 is necessary, however, to ensure that a sale under the HOTCHA scheme will continue to be on 'right-to-buy terms'. If, therefore, the (usually non-charitable) association disposes of its interest in a house without first taking the conveyance, it will nevertheless be treated as having acquired the house prior to its transmission to the tenant, as long as that disposal is at a discount. The tenant will covenant to repay the discount or a proportion of it in the usual way and, if he sells on within three years, the association will be entitled to the return of the discount or some part of it.

8.7 Housing association as landlord

Before considering the changes made by Part I of the Housing Act 1988 to the status of tenancies granted by housing associations, a brief résumé of the position prior to the commencement of that Part of the Act (15 January 1989) is called for. The position is complex. The majority of tenancies granted by housing associations are neither secure tenancies (within Part IV of the Housing Act 1985) nor protected tenancies (within the Rent Act 1977), but are subject to a fair rent regime modelled on that applicable to regulated tenancies, the provisions being contained in Part VI of the 1977 Act. It is possible for a tenant of a housing association to have security of tenure as a secure tenant and still enjoy the benefit of rent controls under Part VI. The question of which code is applicable to a given tenancy is to be answered primarily by discovering what type of housing association is the landlord. Note that a reference in the 1988 Act to a 'housing association tenancy' has a restricted meaning: it is a tenancy to which Part VI of the Rent Act 1977 applies.

The general effect of the Housing Act 1988 on lettings by housing associations is to move them out of the public sector and into the private sector. Most (but not all) lettings which are entered into on or after 15 January 1989 will be assured tenancies. As before, much will depend on the legal status of the housing association concerned. The principles to be applied can be broken down as follows.

8.7.1 Secure tenancies
Save in the transitional circumstances mentioned below, a tenancy or licence entered into by a housing association will not be a secure tenancy. The relevant parts of Housing Act 1985, s. 80, are repealed accordingly by sch. 18 (note the provision at the end of the schedule).

A tenancy entered into before 15 January 1989 will (if Housing Act 1985, s. 79 is satisfied and the tenancy is not otherwise excluded by Housing Act 1985, sch. 1) be a secure tenancy if the landlord's interest belongs to:

(a)   the Housing Corporation;
(b)   a housing trust (defined Housing Act 1985, s. 6) which is a charity;
(c)   a housing association (Housing Act 1985, s. 5) registered with the Housing Corporation (Housing Associations Act 1985, ss. 3 to 7) which is *not* a cooperative housing association;
(d)   a cooperative housing association which is not registered with the Housing Corporation.

(A cooperative housing association is a 'fully mutual' housing association which is registered under the Industrial and Provident Societies Act 1965. A housing association is fully mutual when its rules restrict membership of the association to tenants or prospective tenants, and the grant of tenancies will be to members only: Housing Act 1985, s. 5.)

If a tenancy fulfils the above conditions, it will continue to be a secure tenancy after 15 January 1989 (s. 35(4)).

A tenancy entered into on or after 15 January 1989, fulfilling all the other conditions listed above, will be a secure tenancy in any of the following situations (s. 35(2)):

(a)   It is entered into pursuant to a contract made before that date.

(b)   It is a grant to a tenant who was, immediately before the tenancy, a secure tenant holding under a lease from the same landlord. (Note that as long as tenant and landlord are the same as under the old lease — and one of two or more joint tenants will suffice — it does not matter that the premises are different.)

(c)   Prior to the grant of the tenancy a possession order had been made against the tenant on the court being satisfied, *inter alia,* that suitable alternative accommodation was available to the tenant, this dwelling-house being the accommodation in question, and the court directed that the tenancy of the dwelling-house would be secure. (Note that the court must have considered that, in the circumstances, the grant of an assured tenancy would not afford the required security: see also sch. 17, para. 65.)

(d)   If the tenancy is granted pursuant to an obligation under the Housing Act 1985, s. 554(2A). By Part XVI of the Housing Act 1985 (formerly the Housing Defects Act 1984), a person who purchased a dwelling (perhaps but not necessarily under the right to buy) which has since been designated as defective may be eligible to demand that the house be repurchased by the vendor, which may be a registered housing association. The unlucky purchaser may also be entitled to be granted a secure tenancy of the house once repurchased. Section 554(2A) (added by Housing Act 1988, sch. 17, para. 61) provides that in these circumstances, the tenancy to be granted will be secure, even though the tenancy is entered into after the commencement of the Act. (For other amendments to Part XVI of the Housing Act 1985, see sch. 17, paras 59, 60 and 62.)

A tenancy from a housing association entered into on or after 15 January 1989 may also be secure if the landlord's interest in the dwelling-house (i.e., the reversion) has been transferred to the housing association from a landlord who was previously letting the dwelling-house under a Rent Act protected or statutory tenancy (s. 35(5)). Where a housing association is letting on a secure tenancy subsequent to the 1988 Act, the tenancy cannot also be assured: the two codes are mutually exclusive (sch. 1, para. 13).

Example 8.1
In December 1988, L agrees to let a dwelling-house to T from March 1989, The tenancy, although entered into after the 1988 Act, is protected (s. 34(1)(b)). In July 1989, a housing association purchases L's reversion, and becomes landlord of T. The tenancy will be converted from a protected tenancy to a secure tenancy.

8.7.2   Rent Act tenancies
Very few housing association lettings have constituted protected or statutory

tenancies under the Rent Act 1977. Sections 15 and 16 of that Act exclude from protection tenancies held directly of the following bodies:

(a) the Housing Corporation;
(b) a housing trust (defined in Rent Act 1977, s. 15(5)) which is a charity;
(c) any housing association registered with the Housing Corporation;
(d) any other housing association which is a cooperative housing association (see 8.7.1).

The only housing associations which are therefore capable of letting on protected tenancies are non-mutual associations which have not been registered with the Housing Corporation, or fully mutual associations which are constituted under the Companies Act 1985 (i.e., not within the Industrial and Provident Societies Act 1965).

In the rare circumstances where a housing association has let on protected tenancy, the transitional provisions applicable will be no different from those for other protected tenancies (see chapter 6).

8.7.3 'Housing association tenancies'

Many tenants of housing associations enjoy the benefit of the fair rent provisions of the Rent Acts by virtue of having 'housing association tenancies' or 'Part VI tenancies', as they are sometimes called. A tenancy entered into prior to 15 January 1989 will be a 'housing association tenancy' if the landlord is a housing association, housing trust or the Housing Corporation, and the tenancy would be protected but for Rent Act 1977, ss. 15 and 16 (Rent Act 1977, s. 86). ('Co-ownership tenancies' are excluded from Part VI: Rent Act 1977, s. 86(3A).)

'Housing association tenancies' are phased out by Part I of the Housing Act 1988. If a tenancy is entered into on or after 15 January 1989, it cannot be a housing association tenancy unless it is within the (usual) transitional provisions (s. 35(2)). If the tenancy is within these provisions, it cannot be an assured tenancy (sch. 1, para. 13).

If a tenancy entered into prior to 15 January 1989 (or pursuant to a contract made before then) is a housing association tenancy within Part VI of the Rent Act, 1977, and it ceases to be a housing association tenancy (e.g., the housing association transfers the reversion, and Rent Act 1977, s. 86, is no longer satisfied), it may then become an assured tenancy even though it is prima facie incapable of assured status as it falls within sch. 1, para. 1 (s. 38(2) and (3); see 2.3.1).

8.7.4 Restricted contracts

Some tenancies and licences granted by housing associations prior to 15 January 1989 may be restricted contracts. (A 'housing association tenancy' within Rent Act 1977, Part VI, cannot be a restricted contract: Rent Act 1977, s. 19(5)(e).) Save in transitional circumstances, restricted contracts cannot be created on or after 15 January 1989: for an outline of the effect of the Act on existing restricted contracts, see 6.5.

8.7.5 Assured tenancies

The government's policy of pushing housing associations from the public to the private sector is carried through to the regime which will now affect their tenants. Instead of being equated with tenants of local authorities and other public bodies, which are subject to the secure tenancy regime contained in the Housing Act 1985, tenants of housing associations are now placed in the same position as tenants of private landlords, the code generally applicable to them being that of the assured tenancy.

There is only one kind of housing association which cannot generally let on assured tenancy: the fully mutual housing association, which is on the list of bodies excluded by sch. 1, para. 12. The nature of these associations is such that it is felt that the tenant does not require a statutory security over and above that provided by his contract of membership. Certain fully mutual associations were approved for letting on '1980 Act assured tenancies', and the effect of the 1988 Act on such tenancies which these associations may have granted is dealt with in s. 1(5). The tenancy will be translated into a 1988 Act assured tenancy, and the fact that the landlord remains a fully mutual association will not in itself exclude it from assured status. If, however, the tenancy ends and is replaced by a new contract (as opposed to a statutory periodic tenancy arising on its termination under s. 5(2)), the new tenancy will not be assured.

Transfers of tenancies from the public sector to housing associations are dealt with by s. 38. Where, for example, a property is let by a 'public body' (see s. 38(5)) before 15 January 1989 and, on or after that date, the freehold is purchased by a housing association, the tenancy cannot be secure, nor can it be a 'housing association tenancy' within Part VI of the Rent Act 1977. Instead, the tenancy will be capable of being an assured tenancy, and the fact that it was entered into prior to 15 January 1989 is to be disregarded in determining whether it is assured. A variation on this general rule is made in the case of transfers from new town corporations into the private sector (s. 38(4); see further 2.3.1).

8.7.6   Housing association rents

What rent may be charged by housing associations now they will be letting, by and large, generally on assured tenancies? Previously, housing associations have been subject to rent controls, and where they have not been, they have nevertheless kept rents to a reasonable level, being subsidised to a considerable extent by housing association grant and other income. Can housing associations now let at a full market rent, like any other private sector landlord, or is there still some, more subtle, control being exercised? There is very little on the face of the Act to appease tenants of housing associations. Prima facie, the associations appear to be given a much greater discretion than before. However, although rents will increase as housing associations balance their books following the drop in HAG payments, it is not anticipated that rents will be on a par with those for dwellings held of private landlords.

As mentioned above, the Corporations have wide powers to issue guidance to associations, and one of the matters specifically mentioned in the new s. 36A of the Housing Associations Act 1985 is 'the terms of tenancies and the principles on which the levels of rent should be determined'. Under this head, the Corporations will be expected to instruct associations on the way in which rents should be calculated, and if an association refused to comply with the directions of a Corporation, its registered status (together with eligibility for government funding) could be removed (Housing Associations Act 1985, ss. 5 and 6). The position was summarised by the Minister for Housing and Planning in the committee stage of the Housing Bill:

... rents should be negotiated by the housing association with the Housing Corporation depending on the client group that it wishes to help. That has to be the fundamental principle of what we are doing in this part of the Bill, and we reiterate that the purpose is to produce accommodation which helps the client groups. The importation of rent controls, and probably of an implicit government guarantee by the back door, would negate what we are doing. (Standing Committee G, 9 February 1988, col. 747.)

8.7.7 Housing cooperatives

The term 'housing cooperative' is distinct from the cooperative housing association, defined in 8.7.1. A housing cooperative is 'a society, company or body of trustees' approved by the Secretary of State for the purposes of entering into agreements with local housing authorities by which the cooperative will exercise certain of the authority's powers and perform certain of its duties. A housing cooperative may or may not be a housing association. The so-called 'housing cooperative agreements' were superseded by the more widely based 'management agreements' made possible by the new ss. 27, 27A and 27B of the Housing Act 1985 substituted by s. 10 of the Housing and Planning Act 1986. Where the landlord's interest under a tenancy belonged to a housing cooperative, and the dwelling-house was comprised in a housing cooperative agreement, the 'landlord condition' required for a secure tenancy was satisfied (Housing Act 1985, s. 80). Tenancies entered into on or after 15 January 1989 which are within this provision will remain secure tenancies (Housing Act 1988, s. 35(4)(b)).

Chapter Nine
Housing Action Trusts

9.1 Introduction

The Conservative Party was returned to government by the 1987 general election having pledged in its manifesto to revive the fortunes of the inner cities. There had been earlier attempts to target certain underprivileged geographical areas, notably the introduction of the urban development corporations in London and Merseyside and elsewhere, and the enterprise zone authorities. None of these entities was considered suitable for an intensive, high-expenditure revitalisation of chosen estates in the inner cities for the benefit of their inhabitants: the urban development corporations were devised to tackle largely derelict industrial areas in need of regeneration, while enterprise zones aimed to encourage private sector commercial and industrial expansion rather than the improvement of living conditions. Accordingly, the White Paper, *Housing: the Government's Proposals* (Cm 214), published shortly after the election victory in September 1987, proposed the creation of entirely new bodies, broadly modelled on the urban development corporation, which would tackle the social problems and housing disrepair endemic in certain estates.

> The government . . . proposes to take powers to establish analogous bodies [to urban development corporations] in designated areas to take over responsibility for local authority housing, renovate it and pass it on to different forms of management and ownership including housing associations, tenants' cooperatives, and approved private landlords. The new bodies, to be known as housing action trusts (HATs), will provide scope for tenants in these areas to have a diversity of landlord and ownership. And as well as improving housing conditions, they will act as enablers and facilitators for provision of other community needs such as shops, workshops and advice centres, and for encouraging local enterprise. (Cm 214, para. 6.3.)

This statement of intent cast a thin veil over the political controversy which was bound to greet the advocacy of HATs. Central to the philosophy which underpins Part III of the Housing Act 1988 is the notion that local authorities have not done a very good job in the inner cities, that they bear some responsibility for their decline, and that the first step necessary in any rejuvenation process is to remove the areas of greatest concern out of their hands altogether. The transfer of control is to be achieved by exercise of statutory powers by the Secretary of State for the Environment, and it almost goes without saying that certain local authorities will adopt a hostile attitude towards HATs in consequence. Once the homes are out of public sector control, they are not expected to return. The 'diversity of landlord and ownership' sought by the White Paper is not so eagerly sought as to allow local authorities freely to regain ownership of one-time council properties when the HAT has finished its work on them.

The precise number of dwellings which will be initially subjected to a HAT regime will not be known until the first tenants' ballots have been conducted, but it will be something below 100,000 homes, a minute proportion of the housing in this country. Whether the Secretary of State seeks to make further designations will no doubt depend on the success of these opening projects, but it is important not to overestimate the significance of the HAT provisions in relation to the law of housing as a whole.

The HATs are not seen as being providers of housing and housing repair for the indefinite future. Each HAT is required to use its best endeavours to secure that its objects are achieved as soon as practicable, and when they have been, the trust will be dissolved by the Secretary of State. In the words of the Secretary of State (Hansard, vol. 140, col. 627), 'The trusts are intended to be short-life bodies which will take over large areas of run-down council housing — perhaps up to 5,000 or 6,000 homes — and refurbish and improve them before passing them on to new forms of ownership and management'. The HATs will not be short of money, at least at the outset: the government has pledged that £192 million will be provided for HATs over the first three years.

'Housing action trust' is not the most fortunate or unambiguous term which the proponents of these new bodies could have seized upon, and it may lead to initial confusion. Care must therefore be taken to distinguish HATs from 'housing trusts', a type of (generally charitable) housing association (defined in Housing Associations Act 1985, s. 2), and 'housing action areas', a method of designation of run-down inner city areas by the local authority entitling the authority to grant aid and conferring wide powers with a view to the overall improvement of the area concerned (see Housing Act 1985, Part VIII).

Part III of the Housing Act 1988, together with schs 7 to 11, provides a comprehensive code governing the formation, constitution, functions, powers and duties of HATs. However, much is left to the directions and policy of the Secretary of State; in particular, he will provide the HATs with detailed 'management guidance' which will become the code by which they will operate on a day-to-day basis, and which will instruct HATs in matters of management of the housing stock, transfer of estates and interaction with other agencies such as local authorities and housing associations. This chapter gives a basic outline to the structure of Part III of the Act, but, as always, for a detailed knowledge of the law of HATs, reference must be made to the Act itself and to the regulations and directions issued.

9.2   Formation of housing action trusts

The initiative to establish a HAT over a particular area comes from the Secretary of State. First of all, he considers whether to 'designate' an area, i.e., earmark it for a HAT. In deciding whether an area should be designated, he shall have regard to any matters he thinks fit, but he is particularly prompted to have regard to areas with a large proportion of local authority housing, which housing is in a poor state of repair and which is in need of better management, and where the inhabitants do not enjoy good living conditions (see s. 60(4) and (5)). In deciding whether or not to establish a HAT over a given area, the Secretary of State will be entitled to demand that a local authority supply him with information (s. 90(1)), and may also use any information obtained in connection with his functions under the Housing Act 1985 or any other enactment (s. 90(5)). The sort of information he may require may concern the present contractual arrangements between the local authority and its tenants, as well as a sight of the agreements the authority has with suppliers of services to the estate being contemplated for designation.

A particularly controversial issue has been the extent to which the tenants who live in the chosen area have a right to choose their landlord. As originally laid before Parliament, the Housing Bill gave the tenants no more than the right to be consulted. However, a rare government defeat in the House of Lords resulted in an amendment providing for tenants' ballots, Lord McIntosh of Haringey arguing successfully that 'there should be a proper basis of consent established for the taking over of a particular estate in order that the long-term policy can be safeguarded'.

As a result, the Act requires that before the Secretary of State can make any order creating a HAT, he must do two things. He must consult every local housing authority any part of whose district is to be included in the area to be designated for the HAT (s. 61(1)). Even though a local authority has no properties let to tenants in the area concerned, it must still be consulted. And he must make arrangements for a ballot or poll of tenants in the area. A 'ballot' is intended to indicate postal voting, a 'poll' voting in person at polling booths (see *Hansard,* vol. 140, col. 691). (Reference will be made hereafter to 'ballots' as indicating ballots or polls.) Only where such a ballot is conducted, the proposal to form a HAT is not opposed by a majority of the tenants voting, can the Secretary of State go on to exercise his statutory powers (s. 61(4)). Eligibility to vote will be conferred on those to whom the Secretary of State has given notice of the proposal in pursuance of his statutory duty to use his best endeavours to let them know. They must be either secure tenants or tenants of a prescribed description (s. 61(2)). Ballots may be conducted under the auspices of an independent person, or in such other manner as appears to the Secretary of State best suited to establish the tenants' opinions (s. 61(3)). The Secretary of State has in fact indicated that the conduct of ballots will be entrusted to the Electoral Reform Society.

The ballot is conducted to establish the tenants' opinions about the proposal to make the designation order, and although the question is not expressed in the statute, it will be phrased in such a way as to indicate whether tenants want a HAT as landlord or not. In marked contrast to the ballots under Part IV, the proposal will be defeated by a simple majority of tenants voting against it. If the ballot rejects designation, the Secretary of State cannot make the order. If the ballot approves the Secretary of State's proposal, he will establish a HAT over the area concerned by making a 'designation order' (s. 60(1)). This order will designate an area of land (which may consist of two or more different pieces of land) for which he deems it expedient that a HAT be established. In the same order, or by a separate, subsequent order, he must provide for the establishment of a HAT over the designated area (s. 62(1)). The HAT may be newly formed for this particular urban area, or it may be an already existing HAT which has been carrying out functions in relation to another designated area.

The defeat of the government in the Lords on tenants' ballots had substantial repercussions. Having previously announced the first six areas to be designated (three in the Greater London area, and one each in Leeds, Sandwell and Sunderland) the Secretary of State was not free to designate them immediately on royal assent as had been originally intended.

9.3 Constitution of housing action trusts

A HAT is a body corporate, and will therefore be capable of suing and being sued in its own name (s. 62(3)). It is not an agent of the Crown (s. 62(6)). Schedule 7 contains provisions providing for the constitution of HATs. Each HAT will consist of a chairman and between five and 11 other members. Appointment and removal of HAT members is a matter for the Secretary of State. In appointing, he must have regard to the desirability of having 'local people' in control, although he may appoint no local people at all. A HAT member must not have a financial interest likely to prejudice the exercise of his functions, but he may be a tenant of the HAT: indeed, it may be that it will prove desirable to have tenants on each HAT. Before appointing members of a HAT, all local housing authorities in the designated area must be consulted.

The HAT must appoint one employee, namely the 'chief officer', who will be responsible for the general exercise of the HAT's functions, and who must be approved by the Secretary of State. It may then appoint such number of other employees as the Secretary of State approves, although he cannot veto particular employees. The remuneration of HAT members will be fixed by the Secretary of State (though the HAT will itself be responsible for paying). The rate of pay of HAT employees will be decided by the HAT, subject to the approval of the Secretary of State. In either case, the Treasury must consent to the Secretary of State's decision. The HAT is largely self-governing as far as the conduct of its meetings is concerned, although it must abide by any directions given by the Secretary of State.

The financing of HATs is governed by sch. 8. HATs are to be financed in part by grants and loans from central government, and in part by loans from the private sector, such loans being guaranteed in appropriate cases by the Treasury. The financial position was summarised by Mrs Marion Roe for the government as follows:

The financial arrangements for HATs will be closely modelled on those of the UDCs [urban development corporations]. There will be various sources of finance. In addition to income from rents and sales, HATs will be expected to maximise resource input from the private sector. However, it will be essential for government borrowing and grant to be available to cover start-up costs and to begin the expensive refurbishment task. Because we believe the approach to be right, we are prepared to make available additional resources for those areas. (Standing Committee G, 11 February 1988, col. 835.)

HATs are not intended to be profit-making bodies, and if a surplus does arise on either capital or revenue account, the Secretary of State may direct that the surplus, or part of it, be paid over to him, in a similar way to the exercise of his power under s. 55 to recoup surplus rental income from housing associations (sch. 8, para. 7). If the HAT is at that time still indebted to the Secretary of State as a result of its earlier borrowings, the sum so paid will normally be treated as being a repayment of that debt. The Secretary of State must prepare an annual account of grants and loans made to HATs and sums received as repayment of loans and accounting for surpluses, and the account, together with a report of the Comptroller and Auditor General upon it, will be laid before Parliament (sch. 8, para. 9).

A HAT is under an obligation to keep proper accounts, and must prepare an annual statement of account: both accounts and the annual statement will then be audited, the auditor's report being sent to the Secretary of State with the annual statement (sch. 8, para. 10). The Secretary of State must also be supplied with an annual report 'dealing generally with the trust's operations during the year' (para. 13). He is entitled to be supplied with such information relating to the HAT's activities as he may require, including access to any of its papers (para. 14).

9.4   Objects and functions of housing action trusts

The primary objects of a HAT relate not only to the housing accommodation held by the HAT itself, but also to the other housing accommodation and general environment of its designated area (s. 63). As far as its own accommodation is concerned, the HAT's role is to secure its repair and its proper and effective management and use. With respect to its wider objects in the area as a whole, the HAT is 'to encourage diversity' in land holdings, in other words, seek to enable local authority tenants to choose alternative forms of tenure, whether by purchasing their freeholds under the right to buy, or by having their reversions transferred to a private sector landlord. The HAT should have wider aims too: the improvement of living conditions, social conditions and the general environment: it may, for example, bring about the provision of shops, advice centres and any 'other facilities', a very wide remit indeed, including perhaps the initiation and support of sports centres, health centres and social centres.

The HAT must as soon as practicable after its establishment, and after consulting with the local housing authorities, prepare a statement of its proposals for the area (s. 64). This statement should be given 'adequate publicity' (sending a copy to every resident is probably not necessary, but may be advisable), and the residents of the area should then be given the opportunity to make representations with respect to the proposals. A public meeting, well advertised throughout the area, with HAT members present, would satisfy the statutory requirements. Following this, the HAT must consider the representations made and report to the Secretary of State with a copy of its proposals. The purpose of reporting to the Secretary of State is so that he can have a record of the proposals and can confirm that the correct procedure has been complied with. His consent to the HAT's proposals is not required, and if he does not agree with them, he has no power of veto.

Once established over a particular area, a HAT will be expected to take over the ownership and management of local authority dwellings, and the Secretary of State will provide for their transfer to the HAT by statutory instrument (see 9.5.1). It will also be a matter for the Secretary of State whether other 'functions' previously of the local authority in the designated area should now become functions of the HAT or, possibly, shared between the local authority and the HAT. In carrying out all its functions, the HAT must comply with the directions issued and published from time to time by the Secretary of State (s. 72).

By s. 65(2), the Secretary of State is empowered to grant to the HAT a number of what may loosely be described as functions relating to housing. It is not made clear exactly what 'function' means in this context, but what is envisaged is the conferment on the HAT of various statutory powers and duties (or such of them as the Secretary of State provides by his order) presently held by the local authority.

These powers and duties relate to:

(a)   The provision of housing accommodation (Housing Act 1985, Part II), e.g., duty to consider housing needs in the area, duty to give reasonable preference to certain persons in the allocation of housing (Housing Act 1985, ss. 8 and 22): these may include a duty to have regard to the special needs of chronically sick and disabled persons (Chronically Sick and Disabled Persons Act 1970, s. 3(1)).

(b)   Service of repair notices in respect of unfit houses or houses in substantial disrepair (Housing Act 1985, Part VI as amended by Housing Act 1988, sch. 15).

(c)   Service of improvement notices in respect of dwellings (Housing Act 1985, Part VII).

(d)   Slum clearance, by means of demolition or closing orders (Housing Act 1985, Part IX).

(e)   Prevention of overcrowding (Housing Act 1985, Part X).

(f)   Registration and control of houses in multiple occupation (Housing Act 1985, Part XI).

(g)   Provision of assistance to owners of defective dwellings (Housing Act 1985, Part XVI).

(h)   Promotion of and assistance to housing associations (Housing Associations Act 1985, Part II).

(i)   Rehousing residents displaced by certain types of public action (Land Compensation Act 1973, ss. 39 to 41).

The Secretary of State may also give a HAT powers and duties under the Housing Act 1985, Part XVII (compulsory purchase and land acquisition powers ancillary to slum clearance etc.), and such of the miscellaneous provisions in Part

XVIII of that Act will apply to the HAT as he prescribed in the order (s. 65(6)). Where functions to be reposed in the HAT include any of those at (b), (c), (d) and (f) above, the HAT will, by s. 65(5), be able to recover establishment charges under Local Government Act 1974, s. 36.

The Secretary of State has no power to impose on HATs the general duties in relation to housing homeless persons which are contained in Housing Act 1985, Part III: such duties will remain with the local authorities, and no doubt will become even more difficult to satisfy as their housing stock dwindles (less so as a result of HATs than by the operation of Part IV of the new Act). However, where a local authority requests a HAT to assist it in the discharge of such functions, the HAT must cooperate in rendering such assistance as is reasonable in the circumstances (Housing Act 1985, s. 72 as amended by Housing Act 1988, s. 70). In appropriate cases (for example where the HAT has some vacant accommodation), this might involve housing particular homeless persons, and it is envisaged that HATs may enter into formal agreements with local authorities for the placing of nominated persons on the authority's housing list. The duty to cooperate is not restricted to requests from local authorities whose districts are within the HAT's designated area.

The Secretary of State may order that a HAT become the local planning authority for its designated area, or part of it, in relation to such kinds of development (e.g., dwelling-houses only) as he may specify (s. 67(1)). He has very wide powers in terms of the functions of a local planning authority which he may confer on the HAT, and the enactments which will be applicable to it. Where a HAT has by order become the local planning authority and it then wishes to develop its own land, Town and Country Planning Act 1971, s. 270, will apply with appropriate modifications (s. 67(5)). This will in turn impose on the HAT the obligations on local authorities set out in the Town and Country Planning Regulations 1976 (SI 1976 No. 1419), obligations with which the courts have in the past demanded strict compliance (see Victor Moore, *A Practical Approach to Planning Law,* pp. 163–9).

In cases where the HAT does not become the local planning authority, it may submit its development proposals direct to the Secretary of State, who may approve them following consultation with the local planning authority (s. 66(1)). Alternatively, the Secretary of State may make a special development scheme for the designated area, which may incorporate the development proposals submitted by the HAT (s. 66(2)). Where the designated area contains features of special architectural or historical interest, and/or listed buildings, the Secretary of State must give directions to the HAT with regard to the disposal and development of its land so as to secure their preservation (s. 66(3)). The HATs are not to be given power to deal with listed building consents themselves 'because as short-life organisations they will not develop the expertise to do the work' (Mr William Waldegrave, Standing Committee G, 16 February 1988, col. 914).

The Secretary of State may by order transfer to a HAT the environmental health functions conferred on a local authority under the Public Health Acts of 1936 and 1961, and the Prevention of Damage by Pests Act 1949 (s. 68). However, this is seen by the government as a 'reserve power' only: local authority environmental health departments have expertise based on years of experience in what is often a sensitive and difficult area of public relations, and it will be only in cases where the local authority is failing to cooperate with the HAT that this power is likely to be exercised.

A HAT is given certain powers in relation to highways (s. 69). It may serve notice on a street works authority when works have been executed in a private street within the designated area requiring the authority to declare the street to be a highway maintainable at the public expense. The authority may appeal against the notice to the Secretary of State, but if the notice is confirmed (or the street works authority does not appeal within two months of service of the notice), the street will become a highway maintainable at public expense.

The various functions imposed on HATs by ministerial regulation or by the Housing Act 1988 itself are in turn delegable by the HAT which may, with ministerial approval, enter into an agreement with another body whereby that body will exercise the functions concerned as agent of the HAT (s. 87). There are no statutory restrictions on the 'persons' who might act as agents of HATs, but directions issued under s. 72 may indicate policy in granting consents.

A HAT is given wide powers, subject to the Secretary of State's approval, to give financial assistance in any form 'to any person', on such terms as it thinks appropriate (s. 71). It must in its annual report give full particulars of financial assistance rendered under s. 71 (sch. 8, para. 13(2)). In giving financial assistance, the HAT should, of course, keep within its objects, and particularly relevant in deciding whether a particular applicant should be given financial assistance may be the powers listed in s. 63(2). Therefore, it may be appropriate for the HAT to assist a trader in setting up a shop which will benefit the community, and it may see fit to lend him capital to do so. It will also be open to a HAT to make grants to housing associations or other 'social landlords' in the area with a view to the improvement of living conditions. It is unlikely that a HAT will transgress in this exercise of its powers as long as it obtains the approval of the Secretary of State.

9.5 Acquisition of property by housing action trusts

A HAT may acquire land in one of five ways: by transfer order, by vesting order, by compulsory purchase, by agreement, or on a take-over of another HAT's functions in respect of that HAT's designated area. The type of property which may be acquired, and the consequences of acquisition, will depend on the method used.

9.5.1 Transfer order
A transfer order, whereby housing or land may be transferred from a local authority (as defined in s. 74(8)) to the HAT at the whim of the Secretary of State, will frequently be the first step to be taken following the establishment of the HAT. It is envisaged that in most cases, the transfer order will see all the local authority's housing situated within the designated area going to the HAT. However, the Secretary of State may decide that certain accommodation, for example, special housing for the disabled, is best left in the hands of the local authority. Section 74, by referring to 'all or any' of the housing accommodation, leaves the identity of the housing to be transferred a matter for the Secretary of State's discretion. The scope of the transfer order to be made will be an important feature of the preliminary consultation exercise, and as well as consulting the

local authority from which the property concerned is proposed to be transferred, the Secretary of State must take 'such steps as appear to him to be appropriate' to bring the proposal to the attention of tenants, and others with an interest in the property, such as mortgagees (s. 75(2) and (3)).

As well as transfer of housing, the Secretary of State may also provide for the transfer of any other land held or provided in connection with the housing (s. 74(1)(b)). This land need not be situated within the designated area, although it usually will be. He may also transfer any land which is situated in the designated area and which the HAT requires for the purposes of its functions (s. 74(2)) and any 'property' which is held or used in connection with its housing or other land being transferred to the HAT.

These wide powers lead one to ask what the local authority is to obtain in return for the loss of its housing, land or property as the case may be. Section 74(4) tells only half the tale in stating that the transfer shall be on such terms as the Secretary of State shall think fit. It is open to him to order that the local authority pay the HAT (a 'dowry') at the time of transfer (s. 74(5)).

Where the local authority is ordered to transfer property which is profit-making and income-generating, the authority can expect to receive a sum equal to the market value of that property in its let condition:

> . . . the local authority will receive the real market value which will enable it to subsidise, or cross-subsidise, other operations within its borough. The only difference will be that instead of having a flow of revenue from that estate the authority will have a lump sum that will represent that flow of income. (Mr William Waldegrave, Standing Committee G, 18 February 1988, col. 962.)

Where the property concerned is in a less happy condition (which one would imagine would be more likely to be the case), then the terms which the Secretary of State will stipulate will include a 'dowry' payment from local authority to HAT:

> . . . some estates, through no fault of the borough, have some very unattractive tower blocks which in some cases, the borough has rightly emptied because people feel they are unsafe. . . . Such estates have a negative value now insofar as the borough has to undertake any expense incurred. Therefore, a flow of money is going into those estates from rents and other ratepayers in the borough. Therefore, the equal and opposite to my previous argument applies. Instead of that obligation for expenditure running into the future, it might be right for the borough to make a once-and-for-all payment to get rid of it. (Mr William Waldegrave, loc. cit.)

The 'dowry' would be calculated by reference to the value to the local authority of ridding itself of such an estate. In committee, the government indicated that the local authority would receive sufficient Housing Investment Programme allocation to make the necessary capital payment (Standing Committee G, 18 February 1988, col. 964). However, only 20% of sums received from a HAT will be available to the authority to supplement capital expenditure, as they will be treated as capital receipts (s. 74(6)).

9.5.2   Vesting orders

By s. 76, the Secretary of State is empowered to vest land, which is presently vested in statutory undertakers (defined in sch. 9, para. 4) or any other public body or wholly owned subsidiary of a public body and which is situated in the designated area, in the HAT for that area. If the land is vested in statutory undertakers, it must not be held for operational purposes, and the Minister responsible for the statutory undertaker concerned must join in the vesting order proposed. The effect of the vesting order will be that the HAT will be deemed to have conveyed the property to itself (s. 76(5); Compulsory Purchase (Vesting Declarations) Act 1981, s. 8). The statutory undertaker or other body will be entitled to compensation under the Land Compensation Act 1961, the date of the s. 76 order coming into force being treated as the date of service of the notice to treat (s. 76(6); sch. 9, para. 7). The valuation exercise will therefore be based on the value of the land at the date of the s. 76 order in question.

9.5.3   Compulsory purchase

A HAT has, by s. 77(1) and (2), compulsory purchase powers, exercisable with the authority of the Secretary of State, to acquire land:

(a)   within the designated area;

(b)   adjacent to the designated area, required for purposes connected with the discharge of the HAT's functions within the area; and

(c)   outside the area, required for the provision of services connected with the discharge of its functions within the area.

A HAT may also acquire compulsorily certain rights over land, both within and outside the designated area (s. 77(5)). Where land is to be acquired by compulsory purchase, the HAT must follow the procedures laid down in the Acquisition of Land Act 1981 (subject to the cosmetic modifications in Housing Act 1988, sch. 10, part I) and the owner of the land will be entitled to compensation pursuant to the Land Compensation Act 1961. Where rights are compulsorily acquired, the Acquisition of Land Act 1981, sch. 3, will be applicable.

9.5.4   Agreement

A HAT may agree to purchase any land which it has power to purchase compulsorily, although it will not need the authority of the Secretary of State to do so. Where land is acquired by agreement, Part I of the Compulsory Purchase Act 1965 will apply (s. 77(7)). In one situation, a HAT may purchase land which it does not require for the discharge of its functions: where the land it wishes to acquire (or has acquired) forms part of a common, open space or fuel or field garden allotment and other land is purchased to give in exchange for it (s. 77(3)).

9.5.5   Transfer of functions

The Secretary of State is empowered to transfer the functions of a HAT over an area to another HAT, which may or may not be newly created (s. 73(1)). He must first consult with the HAT(s) concerned (s. 73(3)). In such a case, the dissolution of the transferor HAT will be followed by the transfer of its 'functions, property, rights and liabilities' (s. 73(2)).

9.6   Disposals by housing action trusts

HATs are, by s. 63(3), given the legal capacity to dispose of any land and other property which they own, and s. 79(1) dictates how and when they can make a disposal. The disposal must be in accordance with any directions issued by the Secretary of State and be with his consent. Disposals of houses and flats which are subject to secure tenancies are governed by special rules, dealt with in 9.7.3 to 9.7.5. If a disposal is made without the Secretary of State's consent, its effect will be governed by s. 80. A distinction is made between the disposal of a *house* (part defined in s. 92(1)(b)) and the disposal of *land*. The disposal of land without consent will take effect unless there is some other vitiating factor, and the purchaser will not be concerned to see that the consent has been given (s. 80(2)). The disposal of one house or flat without consent will be effective insofar as it is a disposal to individuals (i.e., not a company or other institution) (s. 80(1)). Any other disposal of a house, or a disposal of more than one house, without consent, will be void. These provisions (which are modelled on Housing Act 1985, s. 44) protect the individual who wishes to purchase a house in accordance with a 'voluntary sale' (no consent being required where sale is pursuant to the right to buy). The entrepreneur who is seeking to buy a number of HAT houses, no doubt with a view to letting or selling on, will, however, be at risk.

The consent of the Secretary of State may be general or specific (s. 79(4)). In particular, consent may be given conditionally, 'including conditions as to the amount by which, on the disposal of a house by way of sale or by the grant or assignment of a lease at a premium, the price or premium is to be, or may be, discounted by the housing action trust' (s. 79(5)). Where sale is at a discount in accordance with the Secretary of State's consent, the provisions of sch. 11 will apply unless the consent specifically excludes its operation (s. 79(13); sch. 11, para. 1). The essence of these provisions is the imposition on the purchaser of a covenant to repay the discount, or part of it, in the event of his selling the house within three years of purchase. In other words, if the Secretary of State directs that a discount be made for the benefit of the purchaser, that purchaser will be in the same position as a purchaser under the right to buy. The paragraphs of sch. 11 set out, almost word for word, ss. 35, 36 and 38 to 42 of the Housing Act 1985 (as amended by the Housing and Planning Act 1986), applying the provisions for disposals at a discount applicable to local authority voluntary sales to disposals at a discount by HATs.

9.7   Housing action trust as landlord

9.7.1   *Rights and obligations*
A tenant whose landlord is a HAT cannot be an assured tenant within Part I of the 1988 Act (sch. 1, para. 12). Nor can he be a protected or statutory tenant under the Rent Act 1977 (s. 62(7), amending Rent Act 1977, s. 14). A HAT will satisfy the 'landlord condition' in Housing Act 1985, s. 80, and so when a HAT lets a dwelling-house as a separate dwelling (or creates a licence to occupy it) to an individual who occupies it as his only or principal home, the interest created will be a secure tenancy unless the agreement is specifically excluded from secure tenancy status by sch. 1 of that Act (s. 83(2)). Note that where the premises have been let to the occupier in consequence of his employment with the HAT, he may

be excluded by Housing Act 1985, sch. 1, para. 2(1) as amended by Housing Act 1988, s. 83(6)(a). As a secure tenant, the occupier will be entitled to the security of tenure conferred by Part IV of the 1985 Act (note amendments to grounds for possession to accommodate certain HAT employees and former employees: s. 83(6)(b)). He will also be prima facie entitled to the right to buy the freehold (or the landlord's leasehold interest where that is all the landlord has) pursuant to Part V of the Housing Act 1985 (there are amendments to exceptions to right to buy in s. 83(6)(d)). There are no other provisions governing the security of tenure, or exercise of the right to buy, specific to tenants of HAT properties, and so the reader is referred to Parts IV and V of the Housing Act 1985, as amended by the Housing and Planning Act 1986 and the Housing Act 1988. The 1988 amendments are contained in s. 83 and Part V. Part V is dealt with in chapter 11.

The HAT is treated as a 'landlord authority' for the purposes of Part IV of the Housing Act 1985 (Housing Act 1988, s. 83(4)), the consequences of which are twofold. First, it must make and maintain arrangements to inform and consult those of its secure tenants who may be substantially affected by certain matters of housing management (Housing Act 1985, s. 105). It need not, however, inform and consult under this provision where its reversion is to be disposed of (Housing Act 1988, s. 84(8): see, however, 9.7.4.) Secondly, it must publish a summary of its rules governing allocation priorities and exchanges and transfers, and make available to any applicant for housing accommodation details of the particulars given by him to the HAT which the HAT has recorded as being relevant to his application (Housing Act 1985, s. 106).

9.7.2   Rents

HATs are put on a similar footing to local authorities as far as fixing rents is concerned. By s. 85, a HAT may make such reasonable charges for its housing accommodation as it may determine, and it shall review rents from time to time, making such changes as circumstances may require. This provision, modelled on Housing Act 1985, s. 24, gives the HAT the same breadth of discretion already enjoyed by local authorities. There is no formal mechanism available to tenants to challenge rents fixed by HATs, and any legal challenge must therefore be made on the basis that the HAT has acted in a manner in which no reasonable HAT fixing rents would act. The discretion vested in the HAT by s. 85 is considerable.

The considerations which a HAT must look towards will, however, differ from those relevant where a local authority fixes the appropriate level of rents. In particular, the courts have on many occasions stressed the importance of the local authority performing a balancing exercise between the interests of its tenants and the interests of its ratepayers, necessary as any shortfall in the housing account will fall to be met out of the general rate fund (see, for example, *Belcher* v *Reading Corporation* [1950] Ch 380; *Luby* v *Newcastle-under-Lyme Corporation* [1964] 2 QB 64). This will not be a relevant consideration in the rent-fixing exercise as far as HATs are concerned, as any deficit will not be met by the ratepayers of the designated area. The HAT, as a body which may be made to account for its profits to the Secretary of State, and as a landlord which is expected to be reasonably benevolent (a 'social landlord', to use the government's terminology), is more closely akin to the housing associations than the local authorities in these respects.

An attempt was made in committee to amend the Bill so as to prevent HATs from increasing rents until they had put the premises let into good repair. It failed, but the Minister for Housing and Planning assured the opposition that the management guidance to be issued under s. 72 would prohibit HATs from increasing rents until there had been improvements to the properties concerned. It was further stated that HATs would not promote a market regime for rents: the 'funding arrangements and the rent policy pursued by the HATs must be such as to keep them firmly in the social landlord sector' (Mr William Waldegrave, Standing Committee G, 23 February 1988, col. 1043). These words are not given any legal force by the terms of the Act, but it can be expected that management guidance to HATs will cover the proper principles for rent fixing.

Where a HAT has reviewed rents in accordance with s. 84, and determines that an increase is to be made, the procedure it should then follow will depend on whether a given tenancy is or is not secure. In the case of secure tenancies, the provisions relevant for rent increases are those of Housing Act 1985, ss. 102 and 103. In the case of periodic tenancies other than secure tenancies, Housing Act 1988, s. 86 (modelled on Housing Act 1985, s. 25), enables the HAT to increase rent by written notice, there being no need to terminate the tenancy. The proposed increase must take effect at the beginning of a rental period. At least four weeks' notice of an increase must be given, and the tenant must be informed of his right to refuse to pay the increased rent and terminate the tenancy. If the tenant serves notice to quit within 15 days of service of the notice to increase rent, his notice to quit expiring no later than the last day of the rental period from the beginning of which the rent increase was intended to take effect, he will not be liable to pay the increased rent during his period of notice (s. 86(4)). Where a HAT grants a fixed-term tenancy (whether secure or not), it will not be able to increase the rent unless the contract expressly so provides.

The statutory code limiting the amount which can be claimed as a service charge by a landlord who lets a flat will only be applicable to HATs where the tenancy in question is a long tenancy (see Housing Act 1988, s. 79(12); Landlord and Tenant Act 1985, s. 26). However, the provisions of Housing Act 1985, ss. 45 to 51, protecting purchasers and long lessees of *houses* (not flats) from public sector landlords who have covenanted to pay service charges will apply to disposals by HATs (Housing Act 1988, s. 79(11)).

9.7.3   Disposals of reversions on secure tenants' leases

Elaborate provisions, contained in ss. 79 and 84, dictate the manner in which HATs can dispose of houses (or flats, treated as houses for the purposes of Part III: s. 92(1)(b)) which are let to secure tenants. Disposals can only be made to a limited category of persons, and considerable care is taken to confer certain rights upon the individual secure tenants. Disposals of houses subject to secure tenancies must be with the Secretary of State's consent, and in accordance with any directions he may give. However, the general mandate to a HAT that it may dispose to 'such persons, in such manner and on such terms as it considers expedient for the purpose of achieving its objects' (s. 79(1)) is heavily qualified where houses subject to secure tenancies are concerned. There are only two categories of person to whom the HAT may dispose of such houses: 'approved persons' and local authorities, the latter only in tightly prescribed circumstances.

And before a HAT can proceed to dispose of such houses, it must satisfy the procedure set out in s. 84.

9.7.4 Section 84 procedure

In any case where a HAT is proposing to make a disposal of houses subject to secure tenancies, it must satisfy s. 84 before it applies to the Secretary of State for the necessary consent. The procedure contained in s. 84 gives to local authorities the right to express their wishes to acquire the house or houses concerned and, in the event of the secure tenant intimating that he would like to have the local authority as landlord rather than the assignee being proposed by the HAT, the HAT is under a duty to consider again the proposed disposal and it may, in an appropriate case, decide to dispose to the local authority after all. This procedure is the only way in which a local authority can purchase houses subject to secure tenancies from a HAT. It has no right to purchase, simply a right to air its views. Nor has the secure tenant the right to choose his landlord, merely the right to make representations in the hope that the HAT may change its mind. If the HAT does agree to sell back to the local authority, it will be on the basis of the market value of the house in question at the time of the sale, the HAT therefore obtaining credit for the improvement works which it will probably have carried out. The procedure is:

(a)   HAT serves notice on (i) any local housing authority in whose area houses to be disposed of are situated, and (ii) any local authority from which any of these houses had been acquired by s. 74 vesting order (s. 84(2)).

(b)   Within the period specified by HAT (no less than 28 days), LA must serve notice on HAT informing it whether LA wishes to acquire houses concerned; if so, which houses (s. 84(3)). LA notice must give information of likely consequences for the tenant of acquisition by LA.

(c)   HAT serves notice on tenant informing him of initial proposed disposal, its likely consequences to him, the wishes of any LA, the likely consequences if the house were to be acquired by that LA, and the tenant's right to make representations to HAT within the period specified (not less than 28 days) (s. 84(4)).

(d)   HAT must then consider tenant's representations, and may amend its proposals if it considers it appropriate, having regard to the representations and any other information provided by LA.

The HAT is under no duty to dispose to a local authority merely because that is the tenant's wish. It is under a duty to give due consideration to his representations, and a failure to do so, or the apparent existence of a policy in the HAT not to allow transfers to local authorities whatever the individual merits of the case, will be susceptible to judicial review. Once the s. 84 procedure has been concluded, the HAT should apply to the Secretary of State for consent under s. 79, furnishing him with the s. 84 papers (s. 84(6)). It will, of course, be open to the Secretary of State to refuse his consent to a disposal to a local authority, even though the HAT has taken the view that it corresponds to the wishes and interests of the secure tenants. Alternatively, the Secretary of State may require the HAT to carry out further consultation, or furnish him with further information (s. 84(7)).

9.7.5 'Approved persons'

Which persons are to be approved for these purposes is left to the discretion of the Corporations which must establish their own criteria to be satisfied by a person seeking approval: the Secretary of State for the Environment has indicated that: 'Landlords will have to demonstrate stability, viability and a commitment to the long-term provision of rented housing at rents within reach of those in lower-paid jobs' (HC Deb., 11 November 1988, col. 674). The Corporations will keep registers of approved persons, which will be available to public inspection (s. 79(10)). In making a decision on whether to approve in any given case, the Corporation must then 'have regard' to whether the person satisfies the criteria (s. 79(8)). It would seem that the Corporation may remain reasonably flexible and depart from the criteria if it considers it right to do so, as long as it has had regard to them. The Corporation may make approval conditional on certain undertakings being given, and approval may be revoked by notice in writing. Revocation of approved status will have serious consequences to the person concerned (although it will not operate retroactively), and the Corporation must pay heed to the reason for revoking: it may be 'by reason of a failure to honour an undertaking or to meet any criteria or for any other reason' (s. 79(9)(c)). The Corporation must be able to identify the reason for its decision, or risk a challenge by judicial review.

There are certain bodies which the Corporations cannot approve: 'public' sector landlords' (local housing authorities, as defined in Housing Act 1985, s. 4, new town corporations and the Development Board for Rural Wales), county councils and any other body which a Corporation has reason to believe might not be independent of public sector landlords or county councils (s. 79(6) and (7)). A Corporation must ask itself whether such 'other body' is, or appears likely to be, under the control of, or subject to influence from, such a landlord or council or particular members or officers of such a landlord or council (s. 79(6)). This provision is very widely drawn. Its purpose is clear — to ensure that houses which may well have come into the hands of a HAT by a vesting order, in the teeth of determined opposition by the local authority, do not on a disposal by the HAT (and the HAT, being a 'short-life body' will of necessity dispose of such houses sooner or later) fall back into the public sector, unless and until the local authority has satisfied the s. 84 procedure.

A tenant transferred from a HAT to an 'approved person' will cease to be a secure tenant (as Housing Act 1985, s. 80, will no longer be satisfied on a transfer to the private sector), but he will become, in all likelihood, an assured tenant. This will be the case even if he is tenant under a tenancy which was entered into before 15 January 1989, as s. 38 will come into play (see 2.3.1). However, although his tenancy is not secure any more, the tenant will retain his right to buy, as it will be preserved by Housing Act 1985, ss. 171A to 171H. He will also be entitled to apply to the Housing Corporation (or Housing for Wales) for legal assistance (s. 82).

9.7.6 Subsequent disposals

It would defeat the object of protecting the tenants in a designated area (or former designated area) if the purchaser of their landlord's reversion from the HAT were able to dispose of the property freely on the open market, and force upon the tenants a landlord they did not want and who may well not be a person approved by the Corporations. In the words of the Earl of Caithness, for the government:

> We are looking for a commitment from those who buy from HATs to provide long-term rented housing for those who need it. We do not expect landlords taking over HAT housing to sell it in normal circumstances because they have that long-term commitment. (HL Deb., 25 October 1988, col. 1584.)

Section 81, introduced at report stage in the House of Lords, places restraints upon the onward disposal of tenanted property which has been purchased from HATs by approved persons. The approved person must covenant in the conveyance to him of the property concerned that he will not transfer the freehold, transfer an existing lease or grant a new lease without the consent of the Secretary of State. Consent can only be given by the Secretary of State if he is satisfied that full consultation with the tenants has been carried out and, in deciding whether to give consent, he must have regard to the views of the tenants (s. 81(5)). If the approved person is a registered housing association (or an unregistered association disposing of grant-aided land), the consent of the Corporation would normally be required for a disposal (Housing Associations Act 1985, s. 9 as amended by Housing Act 1988, sch. 6, para. 7). As long as the Secretary of State consults with the Corporation in these circumstances, the consent of the Corporation is not also necessary (s. 81(7)). Exempt from the requirement of Ministerial consent are disposals set out in s. 81(8). Particularly important here are the disposal of a dwelling-house pursuant to the right to buy, and the grant of secure (or almost secure) tenancies, assured tenancies or assured agricultural occupancies.

There is a point which will be of some concern to the tenant of an 'approved' landlord. If, after it has purchased the HAT's reversion, the new landlord has its approval revoked by the Corporation, the tenant has no remedy on the face of the statute, and it will be left to Ministerial directions to protect his position. The conveyance of the reversion cannot be set aside, as the transaction was completed before revocation took place (s. 79(9)(c)), and the Secretary of State has no powers to bring the property back into HAT control. The s. 81 covenant in the conveyance will still bind, however, and so control will be exercisable over the disposal of the purchaser's interest.

9.8 Dissolution of housing action trusts

A HAT, as a short-life body, is statutorily bound to use its best endeavours to secure the expeditious achievement of its objects (s. 88(1)). Dissolution of the HAT will take place by order of the Secretary of State. Once the HAT considers that its objects have been substantially achieved, it must commence to wind up its affairs, selling off such of its property as it can (respecting, of course, its statutory duties to tenants and others), and then submitting proposals to the Secretary of State for the dissolution of the trust (s. 88(2)). The Secretary of State may then make the dissolution order which will provide for the disposal of any property which the HAT has not been able to rid itself of. His powers ancillary to dissolution are wide (s. 88(4)).

Chapter Ten
Change of Landlord

10.1 Introduction

This chapter deals with the provisions of Part IV of the Housing Act 1988, which in its passage through Parliament proved the most politically controversial and potentially divisive part of the entire statute. Indeed, such was the opposition to Part IV that attention was diverted away, at least as far as the media were concerned, from the serious consequences to tenants of the other Parts of the Act. Its background is as follows.

In 1980, the Conservative government introduced the celebrated 'right to buy', under which public sector tenants became legally entitled to purchase the freehold of their dwelling-houses from their landlords at a discount. Whilst the initial take-up was good, sales slowed down and recent figures suggest that of those tenants who obtained the right to buy in 1980, some 80% remain tenants of the State. Should a public sector landlord sell the reversion of a tenanted property to a private sector purchaser, the tenant will remain entitled to his right to buy: it will be 'preserved' by virtue of ss. 171A to 171H of the Housing Act 1985 (added by Housing and Planning Act 1986, s. 8). Despite these attempts by central government to facilitate the disposal of properties by the public sector, that sector remains relatively large: a combination of tenant ignorance, tenant poverty and tenant disinclination being the likely cause.

Part IV intends to open up the vast realm of public sector rented properties to private sector landlords, by giving to 'approved persons' the right to purchase at market price the freeholds of tenanted properties. Local authorities have had the *power* to dispose of their housing stock (subject to Ministerial consent) for many a year, a power now enshrined in the Housing Act 1985, ss. 32 and 43 (on which see 11.10). The 1988 Act imposes a *duty* on them to sell in certain circumstances. Of particular relevance in considering whether the duty arises will be the identity of the prospective purchaser ('the applicant'), the properties which the applicant is seeking to acquire, and the satisfaction of the relatively intricate procedure which must be followed. Concealed in the detailed provisions of Part IV is reference to the interests of the tenants, whose houses are, of course, to be sold over their heads. The extent to which they are to be consulted, and their powers to veto particular applicants, were the fiercest areas of political contention as the Bill wended its way through Parliament. Referred to by its proponents as 'tenants' choice', it soon became clear that Part IV gave tenants very little choice indeed; their rights are no more than to reject given applicants, and the effective exercise of even those rights will require an extraordinarily high degree of organised resistance to the proposals concerned.

In outline, the applicant, who must be approved by the Housing Corporation or Housing for Wales ('the Corporations'), applies to acquire dwelling-houses let to secure tenants which are owned by a public sector landlord. A lengthy procedure ensues, establishing the extent of the property which is to be acquired, any ancillary rights and the consideration for the transfer, at the end of which the tenants are entitled to vote on the proposed acquisition. If a majority of those eligible to vote reject the proposal, the collective will prevails and the acquisition may not go ahead. If, however, the majority do not reject the proposal, the acquisition will proceed, and all tenants will be transferred to the new landlord with the exception of those who opposed opting out: they will retain individual rights to remain tenants of the local authority.

10.2   The vendor: 'public sector landlords'

Part IV confers a right to acquire the freehold in buildings and property which belong to a public sector landlord at the date the application to purchase is made. Section 93(2) defines 'public sector landlord' as a local housing authority (i.e., a district council, a London borough council, the Common Council of the City of London, or the Council of the Isles of Scilly), a new town corporation, a housing action trust, or the Development Board for Rural Wales. A county council is not within the definition of 'local housing authority' provided by Housing Act 1985, s. 1, and it cannot therefore be a public sector landlord for the purposes of Housing Act 1988, Part IV.

Part IV does not grant any rights whatsoever to acquire any property which is owned by any person other than a 'public sector landlord'.

10.3   The applicant: 'approved persons'

The person who seeks to exercise the right conferred by Part IV must first have been approved by the Corporations (i.e., the Housing Corporation or Housing for Wales, whichever is appropriate: see s. 114(1)). Each Corporation is to maintain a register of persons currently approved, and the list must be open to public inspection at all reasonable times (s. 94(7)). Thus, it is in principle open to public sector tenants who are dissatisfied with their landlord to initiate a Part IV acquisition by inspecting the register and approaching one of the bodies which have been approved by the Corporation. In practice, it is the approved persons themselves who will target particular properties or even estates and make their move with the greatest possible speed.

An application to the Corporation for approval will have to be accompanied by a fee, and the procedure of making application may be the subject of directions to be given by the Secretary of State to the Corporations pursuant to his statutory power to do so under Housing Associations Act 1985, s. 76. The

Corporations must set their own criteria to be regarded when considering an application for approval (s. 94(3)), and although the Act is silent on this, it is anticipated that the Corporations will only approve what the government would call, rather loosely, 'social landlords'. Most housing associations can expect to be approved for the purposes of Part IV: how much further the Corporations will go is a matter for conjecture. (It has been intimated to the Department of the Environment by the Charity Commissioners that charitable housing associations will be barred from Part IV acquisitions as such action would not fall within the ambit of a charitable purpose: see *The Independent,* 7 October 1988.) The Corporations cannot approve public sector landlords themselves, the whole purpose of the provisions being to facilitate the transfer of property out of the hands of local authorities, and although county councils are not themselves liable to Part IV acquisitions, they are barred from obtaining approval as well (s. 94(1)). The Corporations are also prohibited from approving any body which they have reason to believe might not be independent of a public sector landlord or county council, in the sense of being, or being likely to be, under the control of, or subject to influence from, such a landlord or council or members or officers thereof (s. 94(1) and (2); cf. s. 79(6)).

Approval may be made conditional on the body in question entering into certain undertakings (s. 94(4)(d)). The Secretary of State is expected to make directions which will govern such matters as management of properties, tenant allocation, rent levels, repairing obligations, disposals and so forth (the 'tenants' guarantee'), and it will be a condition of obtaining approval that the body concerned undertakes to comply with these directions. In the event of non-compliance, the Corporation will have two sanctions. In the case of approved persons which are housing associations, breach of an undertaking may be 'misconduct or mismanagement', entitling the Corporation to exercise its powers under the Housing Associations Act 1985 to remove committee members, officers, trustees, agents or employees of the association, or to direct the transfer of its land (Housing Associations Act 1985, ss. 28 and 30 as amended by Housing Act 1988, sch. 6). In all cases, the Corporation will have the power to revoke its approval.

Revocation of approval is a Draconian power which the Corporations will no doubt exercise with great circumspection, as service of notice of revocation has the effect of 'freezing' any application to acquire property under Part IV (s. 94(5)(c)). In revoking, a Corporation must heed any directions which the Secretary of State has made under Housing Associations Act 1985, s. 76, and it must satisfy itself that there is good reason: the examples given in s. 94(5) are breach of undertaking or failure to meet the Corporation's criteria, but these are not exhaustive. A clear case where the Corporation would be duty bound to revoke would be where it discovered that an approved person was no longer independent of a public sector landlord. Having said this, there is no statutory right to a hearing, nor indeed to make written representations: it may be such matters will be dealt with by s. 76 directions. Revocation is in all cases provisional for an initial period (to be specified by the Corporation) of at least 14 days (s. 94(5)(a)) and, during that period, any application to acquire which is pending will not be prejudiced (see s. 110(3)). If the Corporation withdraws the notice of revocation within the specified period, the approval is to be treated as though it had never been revoked (s. 94(5)(b)).

10.4   Property which can be acquired

10.4.1   Definition

As stated above, the only property which can be acquired by an approved person under Part IV is property the freehold of which is owned by a public sector landlord. That said, the property must be *either* buildings each of which comprises or contains one or more dwelling-houses which on the date of the application to purchase are occupied by 'qualifying tenants' of the public sector landlord concerned *or* other property (defined as 'land with or without buildings': s. 114(1)) which is reasonably required for occupation with such buildings (s. 93(1)).

It is essential for the applicant to be able to identify precisely, at the outset, which 'buildings' he intends to acquire. Only buildings which contain dwelling-houses (which may be houses or flats) occupied by qualifying tenants will be capable of acquisition. Take as an example a pair of semi-detached houses, owned by the local authority, one of which is occupied by a qualifying tenant and one of which is not. If the houses are to be treated as one building, both can be acquired under Part IV. If they are treated as being two buildings, only the house occupied by the qualifying tenant can be the subject of acquisition. A more extreme case would be a terrace of houses, only some of which are occupied by qualifying tenants. A block of flats may normally be classed as a single building, but what if the block is subdivided in such a way that access from one part to another can only be attained by going outside? The correct analysis of what constitutes the building will also affect what property can be excluded from the acquisition (s. 95).

'Building' is not defined in the Act: nor, indeed, is it defined in the Housing Act 1985 (where it is a frequently used term). It is a word which has featured in a multitude of previous statutory contexts, and the courts have with a fair degree of consistency baulked at the challenge of definition. The comments of Cairns LJ in *Bardrick* v *Haycock* (1976) 31 P & CR 420, 425, a decision on whether an extension was part of the same building as a flat (for the purposes of the resident landlord exclusion to the Rent Acts), are, however, helpful:

> When an Act of Parliament uses the word 'building' without defining it there must be some structures or pairs of structures which as a matter of law could be said to be two buildings within the meaning of the Act and some which as a matter of law could be said to be one building. If a judge held, for example, that two quite separate houses constituted one building, he might be said to have erred in law. On the other hand, if a judge held that two floors in the same house constituted separate buildings that might be said to be erroneous in law. There must, however, be some borderline cases as to which it is a question of fact whether there is one building or two. . . . Some guidance as to what Parliament meant by 'building' in the particular Act may be gained by considering the context in which the word is used.

The context of Part IV of the Housing Act 1988 does not give a great deal of assistance. It is clear that in certain instances a building may consist of two 'houses'; in some instances, it will be a one-house building. Obviously, a building may contain any number of flats. 'House' and 'flat' are defined, by reference to Housing Act 1985, s. 183 (see Housing Act 1988, s. 114(2)):

(2) A dwelling-house is a house if, and only if, it . . . is a structure reasonably so-called; so that —

(a) where a building is divided horizontally, the flats or other units into which it is divided are not houses;
(b) where a building is divided vertically, the units into which it is divided may be houses;
(c) where a building is not structurally detached, it is not a house if a material part of it lies above or below the remainder of the structure.

(3) A dwelling-house which is not a house is a flat.

The basic difference between houses and flats, therefore, is the way in which the building which contains them is subdivided. If the divisions are horizontal, so that units are one on top of another, they will be flats. If the divisions are vertical, so that units are side by side, they will be houses, as long as they can 'reasonably' be called houses: back once more to giving a word its ordinary everyday meaning. The term 'dwelling-house' in Part IV is used both for houses and flats.

It may be that the building has only one dwelling-house in it (e.g., a detached house, or a semi-detached which is a single 'building'): in that case, the position is straightforward. If the dwelling-house is occupied by a 'qualifying tenant', who holds directly of the public sector landlord, the building can be the subject of an acquisition under Part IV. If the building consists of more than one dwelling-house (e.g., a block of flats), the matter is more complicated. The number of dwelling-houses (i.e., flats) occupied by 'qualifying tenants' must be ascertained. If none of the dwelling-houses is occupied by a qualifying tenant, then the building cannot be acquired under Part IV (s. 93(1)(a)). If one or more are occupied by qualifying tenants, then Part IV acquisition is prima facie legitimate. However, if the number of dwelling-houses in the building occupied by secure tenants who are not qualifying tenants exceeds 50% of the total number of dwelling-houses in the building (and there are at least two dwelling-houses in the building), then the building cannot be acquired under Part IV (s. 95(3)).

Example 10.1 A block of flats contains 30 dwelling-houses (i.e., flats). 12 of these flats are occupied by qualifying tenants. 15 are occupied by secure tenants who are not qualifying tenants. Three flats are not occupied at all. The building can still be acquired by an approved person under Part IV. Although, of the dwelling-houses which are occupied, more are occupied by non-qualifying tenants than by qualifying tenants, the number occupied by non-qualifying secure tenants does not exceed 50% of the total number of dwelling-houses in the building.

On a Part IV acquisition, the applicant may obtain with the buildings any other property reasonably required for occupation with the buildings (s. 93(1)(b)). This could include the forecourt of a block of flats, used by the tenants for parking their vehicles, gardens which are enjoyed with houses or flats, or outhouses, garages, boiler sheds and so forth. The applicant who does not initially specify such property in his application may find that the public sector landlord insists he has it anyway, on the ground that it cannot otherwise be reasonably managed or maintained (s. 98(1)(d)).

10.4.2   Excluded property
Section 95 sets out property which is excluded from an acquisition under Part IV. A building which is substantially occupied for non-residential purposes will be excluded by s. 95(1). A statutory equation is to be applied. First, one ascertains the (cumulative) internal floor area of any part or parts of the building which are occupied otherwise than for residential purposes. Secondly, one ascertains the internal floor area of the entire building. In each of these calculations, the common parts or common facilities are disregarded. If the first figure exceeds 50% of the second figure, the building as a whole cannot be acquired. (Note that the Secretary of State is empowered to vary the percentage applied in this equation: s. 95(7).) It can be seen from this that many small shops with living accommodation on the floors above may not be excluded property, and therefore potentially subject to acquisition under Part IV.

A building may (albeit rarely) consist of more than one house (see 10.4.1). If a house in such a building is occupied on the date of the Part IV application by a tenant who is not a secure tenant (and *a fortiori* not a qualifying tenant), or who is a secure tenant but is not a qualifying tenant by virtue of s. 93(4)(b) (tenant excluded from right to buy because of type of accommodation), then that dwelling-house (but not the entire building) will be excluded from acquisition under Part IV (s. 95(4)). Note that s. 95(3) is not necessary to exclude a house which is a building on its own. In such a situation, the building would not contain a dwelling-house occupied by a qualifying tenant, and the applicant would not even overcome s. 93(1).

Pleasure grounds, open spaces and burial grounds are also excluded from acquisition (as property within s. 93(1)(b)) except to the extent that they comprise or are let together with a dwelling-house (s. 95(6)). For the effect of a transfer under Part IV on such property, see s. 109. Treated as excluded too is a building or other property which is the subject of an earlier application to acquire under Part IV, which application is still pending (s. 95(5)).

10.4.3   'Qualifying tenant'
A qualifying tenant must be a secure tenant. He must hold directly from a public sector landlord, as defined in s. 93(2), in the sense that there must be no intervening interests (s. 93(3)). The subtenant whose immediate landlord is a public sector landlord will not be a qualifying tenant, even if the head landlord is a public sector landlord too. By s. 93(4), a secure tenant will not be a qualifying tenant:

(a)   If a court has, by the date the application to acquire the freehold is made, ordered him to give up possession of the dwelling-house (whether immediately or at some future fixed date) he cannot be a qualifying tenant. The existence of a suspended order of possesson is not sufficient to disqualify the tenant, as he will only be obliged to give up possession if he fails to fulfil a particular condition in the possession order (see *R* v *Ilkeston County Court, ex parte Kruza* (1985) 17 HLR 539, and cf. Housing Act 1985, s. 121).

(b) If the secure tenant does not have the right to buy by virtue of Housing Act 1985, sch. 5, paras 5 to 11. These paragraphs ensure that certain accommodation for which the local authority has a specific purpose are not lost to the authority. However, by the Housing Act 1988, s. 123 (a late amendment at the report stage in the Lords: see 11.6.1) paras 6 and 8 of sch. 5 are repealed, thereby conferring the right to buy on secure tenants of accommodation designed with certain features or the subject of certain alterations making it suitable for physically disabled persons. Although s. 93(4) was not consequentially amended, it must surely be read as 'disqualifying' only those tenants who now fall within those paragraphs of sch. 5 which are still in force, i.e., paras 5, 7, 9, 10 and 11. A tenant of any accommodation within these paragraphs will not be a qualifying tenant. Such accommodation must be excluded from an acquisition under Part IV: s. 95(4)(a).

10.4.4   Cooperative management agreements
It is government policy to encourage the formation of housing management cooperatives, and special provisions in s. 96 attempt to ensure that agreements once formed are not prejudiced by a private sector acquisition of the houses or flats which are within the scope of the agreement. The Act does not exempt such dwelling-houses from acquisition, but it requires any applicant to take all the dwelling-houses within a particular agreement or none of them, and it may not combine in its application acquisitions of any buildings which do not contain dwelling-houses within a management agreement. The government recognised, in debate in the Lords, that these provisions did not protect cooperatives which were still in the process of reaching agreement with the local authority. It is likely that the directions issued to the Corporations will go some way towards remedying the situation, perhaps by requiring applicants to satisfy s. 96(2) where the negotiations for a management agreement have reached the stage of the local authority resolving to consult the tenants affected (see HL Deb., 26 October 1988, col. 1647 to 1649).

10.5   Acquisition procedure

10.5.1   'Preselection'
Although the statute is silent, it has been made clear in the Parliamentary debates that the Corporations will conduct a 'preselection procedure' before any applications under Part IV will be accepted. Approved persons will be required to undertake, as a condition of obtaining approval, that they will take part in such procedure before making formal application. The procedure will ensure, wherever possible, that there is competition for the right to acquire, and it will include some informal consultation with tenants, giving them the opportunity to assess the attractions of alternative potential applicants:

An applicant must in any event be able to demonstrate that he has the support of at least 10% of tenants consulted at this stage before he can put in a formal application. Where there are two or more applicants, the one with most support will be able to put in a formal application. (Earl of Caithness, HL Deb., 27 October 1988, col. 1635–6.)

The preselection procedure is intended to ensure that there is a reasonable level of support among the tenants for opting out of local authority control, and that there is not a rush of frivolous or hopeless applications. It is not an auction, as the consideration for the properties in question is set by statute, and not the subject of negotiation and agreement between the local authority and the applicant.

Application must be in prescribed form, that is, in the form prescribed by the Secretary of State in regulations made by statutory instrument (ss. 111 and 112). The forms are not available at the time of writing, but s. 96(1)(b) indicates that the applicant must provide with the form a plan showing the buildings and property which it is proposed to acquire. It is obviously important that the plan is accurate: if, for example, it omitted to specify certain property which the applicant was in fact seeking, it would not have the desired effect of preventing another applicant from proposing to purchase that property. The date of the application is the 'relevant date' referred to throughout Part IV (s. 93(5)).

10.5.2 Initial procedure

Within four weeks of making the application, the landlord must serve a notice on the applicant giving him information about the tenants and licensees who occupy the buildings which the applicant is seeking to acquire (s. 97(1)). It must include their names and addresses, and state 'the general nature' of their tenures, presumably whether the tenants concerned are secure tenants and, perhaps, giving details of the period of notice required to terminate their interests. At this stage, the applicant will be entitled to various rights connected with obtaining information about the property he proposes to acquire (s. 97(2)). He will be entitled to be shown the documents which record the rent arrears of individual tenants, as they are matters which a vendor would be expected to make available to a purchaser on a proposed sale (s. 97(3)). (A likely condition of approval will be an undertaking that the applicant does not divulge information obtained in the course of a Part IV application.) The applicant will have the right of access, at any reasonable time, and on giving reasonable notice, to any property which is *not* subject to a tenancy. Nothing in the Act compels a tenant to permit a representative of the applicant to enter his property for any reason.

Within 12 weeks of making the application, the landlord must serve another notice on the applicant, this time containing much more information concerning the reaction of the landlord to the proposal being made (s. 98). This document is, to adopt the language of court pleadings, the landlord's 'defence' to the applicant's 'claim'. The landlord puts across in this document its side of the story: it must detail which buildings and property it contends should be excluded from the acquisition, stating its grounds for such a contention. It may also argue that the applicant should be compelled to acquire other property (not being excluded by ss. 95 or 96(2)(b)) belonging to the landlord on the ground that it cannot otherwise be reasonably managed or maintained, and that the acquisition should be subject to the retention of rights in the landlord (e.g., easements) over the land to be acquired, again on the ground of proper management or maintenance. This notice should go on to set out the other proposed terms of the conveyance, and anything else which is prescribed by the Secretary of State by regulations. However, this notice is not expected to deal with the price to be paid for the acquisition of the property: the ascertainment of the price (or 'disposal cost') is a separate, later procedure.

Within four weeks of the 'defence' of the landlord, the applicant must make a 'reply' if he wishes to contest anything in the landlord's 'defence' (s. 98(4)). It is presumably open to landlord and applicant to come together and settle their differences, although the Act is silent on the possibility of compromise. If they do not, the claim is then resolved by arbitration, in accordance with provisions which have yet to be prescribed, the person adjudicating being agreed between the parties, in default of agreement by the Secretary of State (s. 98(5)). It must again be stressed that this procedure may not resolve the price to be paid, over which the arbitrator has no jurisdiction.

10.5.3   Consideration

Having defined the property which is to be acquired, the rights which the landlord is to retain over that property, and the other terms of the conveyance, the consideration for the acquisition (the price or 'disposal cost') is the next matter to be resolved. The landlord must 'start the bidding': within eight weeks of the resolution of any argument over terms of the acquisition or, in the event of no argument, within eight weeks of its 'defence' under s. 98, the landlord must serve notice on the applicant putting a price upon the property to be acquired and giving the applicant details of how the figure proposed has been arrived at (s. 99(1) and (4)).

The price is determined by an application of the principles set out in s. 99(2). It is to be assessed on the basis of what the property would realise if sold on the open market by a willing vendor on the date the application to acquire was made. Accordingly, in the event of an inflationary property market, the applicant will not suffer financially through delays in the acquisition procedure. Certain assumptions are to be made. Sale is assumed to be subject to tenancies but otherwise with vacant possession; the terms of the conveyance are to be those already determined. and the applicant is not given any benefit by reason of the likelihood of his having to grant leases back to the landlord in respect of those tenants of flats who wish to continue to be tenants of the landlord (by s. 100(2)). Although the sale is 'on the open market', it is rather inconsistently assumed that the only bidders in that market are persons approved by the Corporation to acquire properties under Part IV or persons approved to purchase houses let to secure tenants of HATs. Finally, it must also be assumed that the applicant will fulfil the landlord's repairing obligations 'within a reasonable period', presumably of completion of the acquisition. The most important repairing obligations implied by law are of course those contained in Landlord and Tenant Act 1985, s. 11.

It may be that the repairing liability is so substantial that the property to be acquired would not realise any price at all on the basis of the s. 99(2) calculation. In such a case, not only will there be no charge for the acquisition of the property, but the landlord may be liable to pay to the applicant, on completion of the acquisition, a 'dowry', referred to in s. 99(3) as a 'disposal cost'. In effect, the landlord which has failed to comply with its legal obligations has to suffer the consequences. The 'disposal cost' is calculated by assessing the market value of the property on the assumption that it is in a state of repair such that the landlord's obligations have (for the time being at least) been fulfilled, but otherwise with the same assumptions as before. This sum is then subtracted from the cost of repairs necessary to put the property into that condition.

Once the landlord's notice specifying the price (or disposal cost) which it considers should be payable on acquisition has been served, the applicant has four weeks in which to notify the landlord in writing of any matters stated in the notice which he does not accept (s. 99(5)). If there is no such notice forthcoming from the applicant, the next stage is consultation with the tenants affected by the proposed acquisition. If the applicant does contest the landlord's notice then the dispute is to be settled by the district valuer in accordance with such provisions as the Secretary of State may prescribe (s. 99(6)).

10.5.4   Consultation with tenants: ballots
The rights of tenants to object to the acquisition of the reversion by approved persons has been the most contentious issue in the whole of Part IV, arguably in the whole of the Act. In the normally calm environment of the House of Lords, the enactment of the ballot provisions was seen as 'more akin to the actions of some Stalinist clique than of a responsible government' (Lord Stoddart of Swindon, HL Deb., 26 October 1988, col. 1619). The first point to note is how late in the acquisition procedure the applicant is placed under a statutory duty to consult with tenants (as opposed to the non-statutory informal preselection procedure). Application has been made, the buildings to be acquired have been defined, the terms of the conveyance have been identified and the price has been fixed. Only then do the tenants have a statutory right to be consulted. It may be that, by that time, many tenants will feel that things have gone so far that consultation is nothing more than a token gesture. Apathy is the greatest enemy of those who wish to oppose an acquisition of their landlord's interest. Despite the lateness, and despite the difficulties which an effective opposition will encounter, the tenants can nevertheless succeed in their campaign, if that is what it is, because a ballot which goes against the applicant will subvert the acquisition entirely.

Consultation is mandatory (s. 101(1)). It must take place within a period (to be prescribed) following the determination of the purchase price, and the applicant must consult (in accordance with provisions to be prescribed) all those tenants to whom s.102 applies. These tenants are qualifying tenants (see 10.4.2) or tenants under long leases (over 21 years: Housing Act 1985, s. 115) who occupied a dwelling-house proposed to be acquired both at the date of the application and throughout the period (to be prescribed) beginning with the determination of the purchase price. Further categories of tenants may be added by statutory instrument: it has been indicated that these may include lawful successors to qualifying tenants, and tenants whose homes are added to the acquisition by the landlord on the ground that they cannot otherwise be reasonably managed or maintained (s. 98(1)(d); see HL Deb., 26 October 1988, col. 1679–80).

The word 'ballot' does not appear anywhere in Part IV of the Act, but it is accepted that the conduct of a ballot, organised by an independent teller instructed (and financed) by the applicant will be the proper mode of consultation as prescribed in the regulations. By s. 103(2), which is the provision to which objection has been made, the applicant's acquisition will be prevented if more than 50% of the tenants eligible to vote intimate that they wish to remain tenants of the public sector landlord. This contrasts sharply with the ballot concerning designation for HAT purposes which will require a simple majority of those voting to block the proposal made by the Secretary of State (s. 61), and it is argued by the opposition that it is an affront to the most basic of democratic principles. To take a frequently quoted example: if 100 tenants are to be consulted, 49 may state that they wish to remain tenants of the local authority, and one tenant may vote in favour of the proposed transfer. The acquisition can go ahead. Only if the figure in favour of the status quo exceeds 50% of the tenants entitled to vote will the tenants' wishes prevail. Looking at the ballot in a slightly different way, an abstention implies agreement with the acquisition proposed and is treated as a yes vote.

Only one vote per household is permitted. Where a house is held on joint tenancy, the tenants are regarded as one, and a 'notice' under s. 102 (i.e., vote) is of no effect unless given by or on behalf of all joint tenants (s. 103(3)). Where a couple are estranged, or one is out of the country and cannot be contacted, this provision has the apparent effect of disenfranchising both tenants, as the vote is not made 'on behalf of all joint tenants'. It can only be hoped that the practical difficulties of applying this provision strictly will lead to a sympathetic attitude on the part of the tellers concerned.

One minor amendment which was successfully urged upon the government was a requirement that at least 50% of the tenants concerned must vote to give the ballot its true effect. If the turn-out is less than 50%, then the acquisition is vetoed. While this may add some degree of fairness to the system, it may have rather odd results. Taking the example above, the 49 who voted against would have achieved their object by not voting at all. The final one of their number, who voted to reject the proposal, will by his act of voting have turned an overall rejection of the proposal into an acceptance!

A rather lame government reply to the criticisms of the ballot provisions has been that similar ballots are already conducted in an analogous statutory context. The Housing and Planning Act 1986 requires consultation with secure tenants prior to the *voluntary* disposal of their landlord's reversion to a private sector purchaser. Ministerial consent is required for such disposals and, by Housing Act 1985, sch. 3A (inserted by Housing and Planning Act 1986, s. 6 and sch. 1), the Secretary of State shall not give his consent 'if it appears to him that a majority of the tenants of the dwelling-houses to which the application relates do not wish the disposal to proceed'. With the apparent encouragement of the Department of the Environment, certain local authorities have sought to consult tenants by means of ballots and have used the terminology of sch. 3A to legitimise ballots conducted on the same lines as ballots under the 1988 Act will be conducted. By a remarkable irony, the first of these ballots to be publicised took place the week after the Housing Act 1988 received royal assent. On 21 November 1988, *The Independent* reported that Torbay Borough Council had sought to consult with its tenants over the transfer of its entire housing stock to two housing associations. In a ballot supervised by the Electoral Reform Society,

2,210 tenants voted against the proposed sale, and 787 voted in favour. The turn-out was 57%, some 2,200 tenants not voting at all. Although three out of four of those voting voted against the sale of their homes to the housing associations, the council treated the ballot as supporting the disposal they had proposed. As the proven opponents of the sale did not comprise a majority of the tenants, the Secretary of State was asked to give his consent. Defeat by 1,423 votes became victory by 777.

The 'undemocratic deceit' (as an *Independent* editorial on 22 November referred to it) manifested in the Torbay experience is one with which tenants will have to come to terms. In the context of the Housing and Planning Act 1986, the inequity is mitigated to some small extent by the fact that the Secretary of State may decide that the majority (including some of those who did not vote) was probably opposed to the proposal. (At the time of writing the Secretary of State had refused to give consent to Torbay, requiring the council to hold a new postal ballot: *The Independent*, 12 January 1989.) The Housing Act 1988 procedure does not vest such a residual discretion in the Minister. Once the ballot is 'in favour' of the proposal, the acquisition must go ahead. The only compensation for the aggrieved tenants is that if they voted against, they will be entitled to remain tenants of the local authority.

It is extremely difficult for tenants who object to opting out to organise a coherent and effective resistance, as there are two methods available, each diametrically opposed. One is to encourage total apathy, in the knowledge that if the turn-out fails to reach 50% the acquisition will fail. The other is to be activist and attempt to ensure that more than 50% of the electorate vote against the proposal. It would be necessary to discover exactly who is entitled to vote, paying heed to any additions to the categories of eligible tenants under s. 102(2) by statutory instrument, and drawing up a list for canvassing purposes. Joint occupiers may particularly require an explanation of their rights. The emphasis must then be on the importance of voting. The most important decision for tenants opposing the acquisition will be the initial policy to adopt, bearing in mind that the applicant is likely to do everything possible to ensure a turn-out of 50%. The danger of apathy is that, in the event of the applicant succeeding, a tenant who fails to vote will lose his individual right to remain a council tenant, and will be deemed to accept the terms being offered by the applicant for continued occupation (see 10.6 and 10.8). The activist who fails may find that the act of encouraging tenants to vote has pushed the turn-out to 50%, but has not achieved the vital figure of 50% of the electorate voting against.

10.5.5 Final procedures

If the ballot does not veto the application, the applicant has two weeks in which to serve notice of his intention to proceed on the landlord (s. 103). This is an important document, finalising many matters which were previously unresolved. It must contain a list of those tenants who expressed a wish in the consultation process to continue as tenants of the landlord: their reward for opposing the acquisition is to remain with their present landlord. It must also contain the price or disposal cost of the property, which will have required recalculation in the light of the consultation process. The applicant may inform the landlord that it wishes to enter into a 'claw-back' arrangement. This is based on the fact that the secure tenants which the applicant is taking over will have their right to buy preserved. The prospect of future receipts for the purchaser represented by these rights would normally be taken account of in the valuation process, increasing the price payable for the property as a whole. The claw-back arrangement allows the valuer to disregard these 'hope values', on the basis that the purchaser covenants to pay a proportion of the receipts it gets from future sales under the right to buy to the disposing landlord. The practical workings of claw-back will not be apparent until the appropriate regulations are promulgated (s. 103(7)).

Following receipt of the notice of intention to proceed, the landlord has two weeks in which to notify the applicant in writing of any matters stated in the notice of intention to proceed which he does not accept (s. 103(5)). Any dispute at this stage will be resolved by the county court on application being made to it (s. 113(1)). Once any disputes have been resolved, the landlord is then obliged to complete the transfer to the applicant, granting to him an estate in fee simple absolute in the property, subject to any rights which the landlord sought to have reserved under s. 98(1) and which have not been denied to the landlord in the course of the arbitration process (s. 104(1)). The duty to complete is enforceable by injunction (s. 104(3)). At the same time, the applicant must grant to the landlord any leases of flats which it is obliged to grant by virtue of regulations made under s. 100(1)(b), a duty which is also enforceable by injunction.

10.6   Tenants who wish to remain public sector tenants

It is anticipated that some, perhaps many, tenants of public sector landlords will not wish to be transferred into the private sector. If they are in the majority of the tenants affected by attempted acquisition, they may succeed in preventing the acquisition altogether, as we have seen, by dint of meticulous planning, forceful campaigning and careful organisation. If they fail to prevent the acquisition going ahead, those who voted against the acquisition will be free to remain tenants of the public sector landlord. The Secretary of State is, by s. 100, under a duty to make regulations excluding such tenants from the transfer.

The tenant must give notice of his wish to continue as a tenant of the public sector landlord, within the time allowed (to be prescribed under s. 102). In other words, he must vote against the proposal. If he votes in favour of the acquisition, or fails to vote at all, he will not be able to insist on remaining a tenant of his current landlord. The practical effect on the individual who holds out in this way will depend on whether the dwelling-house occupied by the tenant in question is a house or a flat. If it is a house, the house will be excluded from the acquisition altogether (s. 100(1)(a)). If it is a flat, the freehold will be transferred to the applicant, but it will be bound to make a lease-back of the flat to the landlord immediately after the acquisition, the landlord then subletting the flat to the tenant (s. 100(1)(b)).

The views of the tenants only being consulted at a very late stage, the price (or disposal cost) of the property will have already been determined. In the light of certain tenants rejecting the opportunity to escape into the private sector, and some of the houses being now excluded from the purchase, a readjustment of the price will be necessary. This is governed by a pair of remarkably convoluted provisions, subsections (3) and (4) of s. 100. Their effect can best be understood by reference to practical examples.

Example 10.2   An applicant is proposing to acquire 26 houses and a block of 14 flats which belong to a district council. It has been determined that the applicant should pay a price of £350,000, the houses being valued at £260,000 and the flats at £90,000. Each house is three-bedroomed, with a through dining-room/lounge, a kitchen, bathroom and WC. In the consultation stage, 10 tenants of the houses indicate that they wish to continue as tenants of the district council; they are all within s. 100(2). In accordance with the regulations under s.100, the houses which these 10 tenants occupy are excluded from the acquisition. The purchase price to be paid must now be adjusted.

The 'amount attributable to houses' is £260,000: the price payable for the property if there were excluded all property 'other than dwelling-houses which are houses' (s. 100(4)). The flats are therefore excluded, and that leaves the houses, valued at £260,000.

The 'sum referable to excluded houses' is then to be deducted from the price as determined. It is the proportion of that £260,000 which the number of habitable rooms in the houses excluded bears to the number of habitable rooms in all the houses comprised in the property to which the application relates (s. 100(3)). It is suggested this should be applied as follows. Each of the houses has five habitable rooms (see s. 114(1)). The number of habitable rooms in the excluded houses is 50 (10 × 5). The number of habitable rooms in all the houses is 130 (26 × 5). The fraction 5/13 is then applied to the amount attributable to houses: £260,000 × 5/13 = £100,000. This sum, the 'sum referable to excluded houses' is then deducted from the price payable for the property to be acquired: £350,000 − £100,000 = £250,000 (s. 100(3)(b)). This is the adjusted price which the applicant must pay for the property as a whole.

Example 10.3   An applicant is proposing to acquire 10 houses and 25 flats which belong to a district council. It has been determined that the applicant should pay a purchase price of £150,000; the flats are valued at £200,000, but there is a disposal cost in relation to the houses, which are in a poor state of repair, of £50,000. Four tenants of the houses do not want to be transferred; they have given notice accordingly and they fall within s. 100(2). Each of the houses has five habitable rooms.

The 'amount attributable to houses' is a disposal cost of £50,000 (s. 100(4)).

The number of habitable rooms in the houses to be excluded is 20 (4 × 5). The number of habitable rooms in all the houses is 50 (10 × 5). The fraction 2/5 is applied to the amount attributable to houses: £50,000 × 2/5 = £20,000. As this 'sum referable to excluded houses' is based on an 'amount attributable to houses' which is a disposal cost, it must be added to the price which had been fixed: £150,000 + £20,000 = £170,000 (s. 100(3)(c)). The adjusted price which the applicant must pay is £170,000, increased because his repairing liability is less than was originally the case.

10.7   Tenancies granted after the date of application

The landlord faced with an application to acquire property under Part IV could make the prospect of acquisition considerably less attractive by letting out all empty dwelling-houses between the date of application and the likely completion date. The applicant who had made his calculations on the basis of a certain number of properties being vacant and therefore either available to let on the applicant's own terms, or free to redevelop could be placed in a difficult position. The Act operates so as to save him from his embarrassment by freezing the properties as at the date of the application ('the relevant date').

Any tenancy or licence which commences after the relevant date will be deprived of any statutory security of tenure, whether under Housing Act 1985, Part IV, Housing Act 1988, Part I, Landlord and Tenant Act 1954, Part II, or Agricultural Holdings Act 1986, Parts III to VI (s. 101(2)). Instead, any such tenancy or licence will be terminable on four weeks' notice expiring at any time (s. 101(3)). Section 101 is strongly worded and it may work injustice. A tenant may enter into a contract prior to the application to take a tenancy of property to which the acquisition relates, having no idea that an application is on the cards. If the tenancy commences after the application it will be subjected to s. 101. Another tenant who will be in an invidious position will be the sitting tenant who enters into a new tenancy agreement with his landlord after an application has been made. Again, on the wording of s. 101, he would lose his secure tenancy, and his new tenancy would be determinable on four weeks' notice to quit.

By s. 101(4), the Secretary of State is empowered to make regulations which, if made, might mitigate the effect of the remainder of the section. In particular, he might require the landlord to give notice to any potential tenant of the lack of security of tenure, enabling the tenant to make at least an informed decision whether to accept the tenancy on offer or not. If the application were to fall through, the regulations might make provision for the tenants or licensees to become secure tenants from that time onwards: it would certainly seem inequitable for the landlord to take advantage of s. 101, which is demonstrably for the protection of the applicant. The Secretary of State may also exclude certain tenancies from the effect of s. 101, and the Earl of Caithness, moving this amendment in the House of Lords, indicated that the government was minded to exclude leases where, after the relevant date, the tenant either completes under the right to buy or enters into a shared ownership lease (HL Deb., 26 October 1988, col. 1676).

10.8   Tenants who are transferred

The position of the tenant who is transferred from a public sector landlord to a new private sector landlord pursuant to Part IV will be very similar to that of a tenant whose house has been sold by a HAT to an 'approved person' (see 9.7.5). He will cease to be a secure tenant, and will probably become an assured tenant, even if his tenancy was entered into prior to 15 January 1989 (s. 38; see 2.3.1). He will have his right to buy the freehold preserved. He may apply to the Corporation for legal advice and assistance (s. 107(2)). Section 103(2) has no equivalent with regard to purchases from HATs. By this provision, the tenant who is transferred will be deemed to have accepted, and to have given consideration for, any offer made by the applicant in the course of the consultation procedure. This may be to the tenant's advantage if the applicant, in an attempt to obtain tenant support for its proposal, made wild promises about rent levels and the like. It could on the other hand work against the tenant if the applicant had indicated the likelihood of rent increases. This is an area which will require close policing by the Corporations, and directions are likely to be issued which will require all applicants to provide the tenants concerned with a legally binding offer of the terms on which the tenant will hold after the transfer. This offer would be made before the ballot. In view of the serious consequences of inertia by the tenants concerned, such documents should, of course, be carefully studied.

10.9 Subsequent disposals

As with purchasers from HATs, the approved status of those who acquire under Part IV will mean little if they are free to dispose of the reversions they acquire and thereby confer on the tenants a landlord they are not even consulted about, let alone have a however nebulous right to reject. To allow this would be to derogate from the commitment which is expected from approved persons towards their tenants. Accordingly, s. 105 makes similar provision in relation to Part IV as does s. 81 in relation to Part III (see 9.7.6).

Disposals, save for exempt disposals, are to be subject to Ministerial consent. 'Disposal' is widely defined to include, for example, the disposal of an interest in land and entering into contracts or option agreements to sell the property or an interest in it (s. 105(8)). Consent can be conditional and there must be tenant consultation (s. 105(4)). Where the landlord is a housing association, requiring consent of the Corporation under Housing Associations Act 1985, s. 9, the Secretary of State must consult the relevant Corporation and, having done that, there is no additional need for the Corporation to consent (s. 105(5) and (6)). Numerous disposals are exempt from the requirement for Ministerial consent, most notably sales under the right to buy, lease-backs to public sector landlords under s. 100 and grants of secure or assured tenancies (s. 105(7)).

Chapter Eleven
Miscellaneous Provisions

Part V of the Housing Act is titled 'Miscellaneous and general', which is a fairly accurate description of what follows. There is no identifiable theme, and it is a veritable pot-pourri of amendments to existing statutes which the occasion of a new Housing Act gives the opportunity to effect. The following commentary takes the sections in an order approximating to that in the Act itself, save with respect to those applying to Scotland, which are dealt with in summary form at the end.

11.1   Premiums on long leases

By Part IX of the Rent Act 1977, the payment of premiums or the making of loans as a condition of the grant, renewal, continuance or assignment of a Rent Act protected tenancy is rendered unlawful, and the person who requires or receives such a premium or a loan commits a criminal offence (ss. 119 and 120). An established exception to this general rule applies to long tenancies (defined in Landlord and Tenant Act 1954, s. 2(4), as terms certain exceeding 21 years). Most long tenancies will be excluded from Rent Act protection by virtue of being at a low rent (see Rent Act 1977, s. 5(1): rent less than two thirds rateable value on appropriate day), but where the rent payable is sufficiently high so that the tenancy is protected, premiums and loans will be lawful as long as the conditions listed in Rent Act 1977, s. 127 are satisfied.

The Housing Act 1988, s. 115, relaxes and simplifies the conditions which have to be satisfied for a premium or loan to be lawful. First, the landlord must have no power to determine the tenancy within the 20 years beginning with the date of grant, save in exercise of a right of re-entry for breach of covenant or condition, i.e., there must be no 'break clause' (see 2.4.1) exercisable by the landlord in the 20-year period. Secondly, the terms of the tenancy must not 'inhibit' (defined in Rent Act 1977, s. 127(5)) assignment or subletting of the whole of the premises, except within the final seven years of the fixed term. The fact that the tenancy permits variation of its rent within the 20-year period will no longer render premiums or loans unlawful, and the inhibition on assignment and subletting need not apply throughout the whole term.

These amendments will apply to any premium received or required to be paid, or any loan required to be made, after 15 January 1989. As there will be very few protected tenancies entered into subsequent to the Act, the greatest relevance of s. 115 will be in relation to assignments after 15 January 1989 of long tenancies which were entered into before then. The effect of these reforms in practice will be that premiums will be legitimatised on the assignment of almost all long tenancies.

11.2 Covenants to repair

The most important repairing obligation imposed by statute is that contained in Landlord and Tenant Act 1985, s. 11, which applies, subject to certain exceptions, to any lease of a dwelling-house granted on or after 24 October 1961 for a term of less than seven years (Landlord and Tenant Act 1985, s. 13, subject to the exceptions in s. 14). In outline, the covenant is to keep in repair the structure and exterior of the dwelling-house, and to keep in repair and proper working order the installations in the dwelling-house for the supply of water, gas and electricity and for space heating and heating water. Section 11 (and its predecessor, Housing Act 1961, s. 32) has been found wanting as far as the protection of tenants of flats have been concerned, and the amendments now made in Housing Act 1988, s. 116 have been prompted by decisions of the courts.

As the covenant is to keep in repair the structure and exterior of the dwelling-house, in the case of flats the dwelling-house being the individual flat occupied by the tenant in question rather than the building as a whole, landlords have escaped liability by showing that the individual flat was in fact in repair and the conditions of which the tenant complained were caused by disrepair to some other part of the building which was not part of the flat itself. Thus in *Campden Hill Towers Ltd* v *Gardner* [1977] QB 823, a tenant of a third-floor flat (not on the top floor of the block) could not allege that the structure or exterior of her flat was in disrepair where the defect of which she complained was in the roof to the block: the roof was not part of the structure or exterior of her flat (cf. *Douglas-Scott* v *Scorgie* [1984] 1 WLR 716). The same principle would apply to installations, which, according to s. 11, have to be 'in the dwelling-house' for the covenant to apply: a defect to a central-heating boiler serving several flats and situated in the common parts would not fall within the ambit of the statutory covenant.

Section 116 seeks to remedy the situation. It amends s. 11 in its application to leases entered into on or after 15 January 1989 (except for those entered into pursuant to a contract made before that date) (s. 116(4)). It modifies the statutory covenant where the lease in question is of a dwelling-house which forms part of a building (i.e., usually a flat). The landlord in such cases will now be held to covenant:

(a) That he will keep in repair the structure and exterior of any part of the building in which he has an estate or interest.

(b) That he will keep in repair and proper working order installations (as listed in s. 11) which directly or indirectly serve the flat and which either form part of any part of a building in which the landlord has an estate or interest or which are owned by the landlord or under his control. The landlord's liability is by no means absolute. He is only responsible for repairs to a part of the building in which he has an interest (e.g., as owner or tenant) or which is under his control.

There are two further riders to the above. First, the tenant must 'mind his own business'. He will only be able to complain of disrepair to the structure and exterior of a part of the building other than his own flat or of disrepair or malfunctioning of an installation outside his own flat where he can show that his enjoyment of the flat or the common parts of the building has been affected as a result. Secondly, the landlord has a statutory defence to an action where he needs to carry out repairs or works outside the flat if he does not have sufficient right in the part of the building or the installation concerned to enable him to carry them out. He must prove (the onus is on him) that he used all reasonable endeavours to obtain the rights he required to do the works, but that he was unable to obtain them. This will protect from liability those landlords who let out flats in buildings which they do not own exclusively, where the cause of the tenant's complaint relates to a part of the building which they do not own and the owner of which refuses them the access required.

11.3 Bankruptcy of tenant

Section 117 amends Insolvency Act 1986, s. 283, so that certain types of residential tenancy are prima facie excluded from the estate of a bankrupt at the commencement of the bankruptcy. However, by s. 308A (inserted by Housing Act 1988, s. 117(2)), the trustee in bankruptcy may, within 42 days of the tenancy coming to his knowledge (or with leave of the court subsequently), serve written notice on the bankrupt vesting such a tenancy in the trustee as part of the bankrupt's estate (see also s. 309). Once notice is served within s. 308A, the trustee's title relates back to the commencement of the bankruptcy (with the usual protection for the bona fide purchaser), and the trustee can only disclaim the tenancy with leave of the court (s. 315). The effect of s. 117 is that the tenant does not lose his tenancy on becoming bankrupt where the tenancy is of no value to his trustee.

11.4 Landlord and Tenant Act 1987

The Landlord and Tenant Act 1987 implemented the main recommendations of the Nugee Committee which had reported on the management of privately owned blocks of flats. It came into force during 1988 and the Housing Act 1988, sch. 13, makes several amendments to its provisions of varying degrees of importance. The 1987 Act is complex in its aims and in its operation and only the briefest outline of the amendments can be given.

Part I of the 1987 Act grants to 'qualifying tenants' rights of first refusal on certain disposals which affect their premises. The Housing Act 1988, sch. 13:

(a) excludes assured tenants (including assured shorthold tenants) and assured agricultural occupiers from the status of 'qualifying tenant' (para. 2(1));
(b) excludes tenants who are tenants not only of the flat in question but also

of two or more other flats in the premises (para. 2(2): a further attempt to exclude tenants who are sub-letting);

(c) provides that a disposal by a mortgagee in possession (whether or not made in the name of the landlord) will be a 'relevant disposal' for the purposes of Part I (para. 3(1)).

Part III of the 1987 Act provides for the compulsory acquisition of the landlord's interest by 'qualifying tenants' on application to court for an 'acquisition order'. The Housing Act 1988, sch. 13, redefines 'qualifying tenants' for these purposes, again excluding those who hold tenancies of the flat in question plus two others (para. 4(1)). If an associated company of a corporate tenant of a flat, it will be treated as being the same entity (para. 4(2)).

Part IV of the 1987 Act enables parties to a long lease to apply to the court for variation of its terms. However, by Housing Act 1988, sch. 13, para. 5, if the premises consist of or include three or more flats in the same building, Part IV will not apply. A similar provision (Landlord and Tenant Act 1987, s. 40), concerning applications to vary the insurance provisions of a lease of a dwelling other than a flat, is amended in a like manner (para. 6).

There is considerable scope for avoiding the application of the Landlord and Tenant Act 1987 (see, for example, the schemes promoted by Lightman (1988) 19 EG 21 and Adams (1988) 32 EG 40). The Housing Act 1988 does not affect the potential of the 'associated company' and 'intermediate landlord' schemes propounded by these authors. Their efficacy remains untested and statutory amendments in their light must await another opportunity.

The definition of disposals which are exempt from the right of first refusal contained in Part I of the 1987 Act is clarified. It is now relatively clear from sch. 13, para. 3, that a disposal by a mortgagee in possession should activate the right of first refusal, whereas a grant by the landlord of a mortgage should not.

11.5 Rent officers and housing benefit

The regime for the determination of rents under assured tenancies has as its sole tribunal the rent assessment committee (RAC). Whereas the assessment of Rent Act fair rents had, and will still have, a 'two-tier' process, of rent officer followed by appeal to the RAC, the new system has only one. Rent officers will continue to assess fair rents for those premises which have regulated tenancies, and they will continue to carry out their role in relation to housing benefit of assessing what rent a tenant should be paying for particular premises and setting the level of housing benefit accordingly. There is a risk that the rent officer will set a lower level of rent under an assured tenancy for the purposes of housing benefit than that dictated by the RAC under Part I. The Minister for Housing and Planning stated:

> The tenant in receipt of housing benefit should not be placed in financial difficulties because the rent assessment committee determine a higher rent than the rent officer in making an assessment of a reasonable market rent for housing benefit purposes. (Standing Committee G, 21 January 1988, col. 401).

He went on to say that this would be dealt with in the rules setting out the detailed procedures for calculating housing benefit.

Section 121 empowers the Secretary of State to make regulations requiring rent officers to carry out such functions as may be specified in connection with housing benefit and rent allowance subsidy. It is anticipated that these regulations will provide for a rent officer to determine that a particular dwelling-house occupied by a person in receipt of housing benefit is more extensive than that person or his family reasonably requires, and that the housing benefit payable should be reduced accordingly. Further provision may be made for the Secretary of State to reduce any amount he pays to the local authority by way of rent allowance subsidy in the light of determinations to this effect made by rent officers (s. 121(5)). The regulations under s. 121 are likely to come into effect once adequate evidence of open market rents for residential lettings is available. Reference must, of course, be made to them for further details of the effect of these provisions.

The Housing Act 1988 takes the opportunity of rationalising and streamlining the rent officer service. The relevant provisions are set out in sch. 14 to the Act, which makes amendments to ss. 63 and 64 of the Rent Act 1977. The schedule grants to the Secretary of State wide regulatory powers to make schemes shifting the balance of power from the local authorities to central government. The most radical power is that contained in the new s. 64B, whereby the Secretary of State may take the appointment, remuneration and administration of rent officers out of the hands of the local authorities, or a particular local authority, altogether. In those circumstances, he would be empowered to make such alternative provision for a rent officer service as appeared to him to be appropriate. Somewhat less Draconian are the powers devolved on him by s. 64A, enabling him to amalgamate rent officer services for two (or more) registration areas, powers which would be exercised most effectively with regard to adjoining areas (but which are not so restricted in the statute). The hierarchy of rent officers is liable to be changed: the Act itself abolishes the role of deputy rent officers, and the powers of the Secretary of State under the new s. 63(2A) include the right to delegate to 'a proper officer of the local authority' the right to appoint a chief rent officer, and to designate one or more officers as senior rent officers.

11.6   Right to buy

The tenant's 'right to buy', i.e., the right to purchase the freehold owned by a public sector landlord (and in some circumstances to take out a long lease or 'shared ownership lease') was introduced in the first major piece of housing legislation enacted by the Conservative government, the Housing Act 1980, and, following consolidation, the provisions are now to be found in Part V of the Housing Act 1985. Important amendments were made by the Housing and Planning Act 1986, in particular to the quantum of discount available to purchasers, the circumstances in which the discount might become repayable to the vendor, and the 'preservation' of the right to buy on a transfer of the landlord's interest from the public to the private sector. The last of these is, of course, especially relevant to sales of the reversion of secure tenancies under Parts III and IV of the present statute. Part V of the Housing Act 1988 makes several important changes to the law affecting tenants' right to buy. Two exceptions to the right to buy are repealed. A new sanction is given to tenants in the event of their landlords delaying in following the statutory procedure. The 'cost-floor' provision, dictating the minimum price at which a dwelling-house can be sold under the right to buy, is amended. Further restrictions are made on the disposal of dwelling-houses in National Parks, both in relation to right-to-buy sales and 'voluntary' sales, and there are amendments to the preserved right-to-buy provisions consequential upon Part I of the Housing Act 1988.

11.6.1   The disabled and the right to buy

Paragraphs 6 to 9 of sch. 5 to the Housing Act 1985 exclude the right to buy in the case of secure tenants who occupy certain dwelling-houses which are provided by the landlord essentially for disabled persons. By Housing Act 1988, s. 123, paras 6 and 8 are repealed. The only such accommodation which is now excluded from the right to buy is sheltered accommodation, i.e., where the house or flat is one of a group of dwelling-houses which it is the practice of the landlord to let for occupation by physically disabled persons, or by persons who are suffering from a mental disorder and where a social service or special facility is provided wholly or partly for the purpose of assisting those persons. Where those persons are physically disabled, the dwelling-house itself must have features substantially different from those of ordinary dwelling-houses, designed to make it suitable for occupation by the physically disabled *and* the service or facility concerned must be in close proximity to the group of dwelling-houses (see Housing Act 1985, sch. 5, paras 7 and 9). The repeal of paras 6 and 8 will only have effect where the tenant's notice claiming to exercise the right to buy is served on or after 15 January 1989, or if it was served before that date but no notice in response had been served by the landlord under Housing Act 1985, s. 124, before that date (s. 123(3)).

11.6.2   The cost floor

The 'cost floor' provision of Housing Act 1985, s. 131, is amended by Housing Act 1988, s. 122. Secure tenants who are exercising the right to buy are entitled to a discount based on the length of time that they have been public sector tenants. However, the discount must not take the purchase price of the dwelling-house below the amount of costs incurred in respect of the dwelling-house since a certain time. By the 1985 Act, all costs incurred since 31 March 1974 (the date of local government reorganisation) counted in calculating the cost floor below which the purchase price must not fall. As from the coming into force of s. 122 (on a date to be appointed: s. 141(2)) only those costs incurred in the eight-year period prior to the date of the tenant's notice claiming to exercise the right to buy will be aggregated to provide the cost floor. The time will in fact run from the beginning of the landlord's period of account in which the date eight years prior to the tenant's notice falls.

Example 11.1   Tenant serves notice on 12 June 1990. Landlord's accounting year runs from 1 January to 31 December. All works incurred on the dwelling-house on or after 1 January 1982 will be counted in calculating the cost floor.

Section 122 will have effect where the tenant serves his notice claiming to exercise the right to buy on or after the date on which s. 122 comes into force. As an incentive to landlords to expedite their dealings with tenants seeking to exercise the right to buy, s. 122 will also have effect where the tenant's notice pre-dates the new section coming into force, but the landlord has not yet served an s. 125 notice, an s. 147 notice, or a notice under Housing Act, sch. 8, para. 3, as the case might be (s. 122(4)). The Secretary of State may by order vary the eight-year period (s. 122(2)).

11.6.3   Sanctions for delay

The Housing Act 1988, s. 124, adds two new sections to Part V of the Housing Act 1985, ss. 153A and 153B. They create a new sanction for the public sector landlord which is dragging its feet over the statutory procedure. Until now, the only effective sanction for the tenant has been to complain to the Secretary of State, who might threaten to intervene and use his powers under Housing Act 1985, ss. 164 to 166, on which see *R v Secretary of State for the Environment, ex parte Norwich City Council* [1982] QB 808.

The precondition for the tenant using the new sanctions is *either* that the landlord has failed to serve a notice under ss. 124, 125, 146 or 147 within the period laid down by statute *or* that the tenant considers that the landlord's delays are preventing him from exercising expeditiously the right to buy (or to be granted a shared ownership lease: s. 153A(1)). The tenant may then serve a notice on the landlord (the 'initial notice of delay') specifying the landlord's most recent action, and giving the landlord a period of not less than one month in which to serve a counter-notice (s. 153A(2)). If the landlord does not serve an effective counter-notice, at the end of the period, the tenant may then serve a second notice (the 'operative notice of delay'). If, however, the landlord serves an effective counter-notice, the procedure will be aborted. It will be effective if (in the event of the tenant making a specific complaint of failure to serve a particular notice in the right-to-buy procedure) the landlord serves the notice in question together with (or before) the counter-notice or if (in the event of the tenant pursuing the more general allegation of delays) the landlord takes the action he had to take to allow the tenant expeditiously to exercise the right to buy (s. 153A(3)).

The landlord should be stirred into action once the tenant has served him with an operative notice of delay. From that date onwards, all payments of rent made by the tenant are to be treated as payments towards the purchase price of the dwelling-house he is in the course of acquiring, making due deduction for payments which are attributable to rates and service charges. Moreover, if more than 12 months' rent is paid on this basis, the tenant will obtain extra credit: the punitive provision of s. 153B(3) states that a further sum of 50% of the rent payments made is to be added as having been made towards the purchase price. The tenant is entitled to off-set all payments made from the 'default date' (i.e., the date the landlord's notice should have been served if complaint is made of a failure to serve a specific notice) or otherwise the date of service of the operative notice of delay. In transitional cases, where the landlord should have served the notice before the date s. 124 comes into force (to be appointed: s. 141(2)) the date it comes into force is the default date.

Example 11.2 Landlord was obliged to serve a s. 124 notice by 1 June 1989, but fails to do so. Tenant serves initial notice of delay on 1 July 1989, giving the landlord one month in which to respond. Landlord fails to serve counter-notice within the month. Tenant serves operative notice of delay on 1 September 1989. From that date his payments of rent (£200 per month exclusive of rates and service charge) made since 1 June are treated as payments towards the purchase price. Landlord has still failed to serve s. 124 notice by 1 June 1990. Once rent paid by tenant exceeds 12 months' rent (i.e., exceeds £2,400), the contribution he is treated as having made to the purchase price will be increased by 50%. By September 1990, he has made £3,000 in rent payments, and still no s. 124 notice. He will be treated as having paid £4,500 towards the eventual purchase price of the house.

The tenant is in effect given an 'account' into which payments or rent made after the default date (or the operative notice of delay where s. 153A(1)(e) is applicable) are fed. Thus, if the landlord transgresses on several occasions throughout the right-to-buy procedure, and more than one operative notice of delay is served, the tenant may still leap over the 12-month barrier and claim his 50% bonus even though no one delay has been of the order of 12 months.

What does the landlord do to obviate the Draconian consequences of an operative notice of delay? He serves the counter-notice which he should have served in reply to the initial notice of delay as soon as he can, with whatever other notice the tenant requires (s. 153B(1)). If no such counter-notice is served, the attribution of rent payments to the purchase price will stop on the day of conveyance of the dwelling-house to the tenant, the day the tenant serves notice claiming he is entitled to defer completion, the day the tenant withdraws his notice claiming to exercise the right to buy, or the day the tenant ceases to be entitled to the right to buy (s. 153B(1)).

What if the tenant does not buy the house after all, despite having made rent payments which are to be treated as going towards the purchase price? He cannot recover the payments which he has made, as they are still treated as payments of rent (s. 153B(2)).

11.6.4 *Restrictions on disposals in National Parks*
Sections 37 and 157 of the Housing Act 1985 empower local authorities, on a conveyance (or grant or assignment: for exposition purposes a conveyance of the freehold will be considered) of a house situated in a National Park, a designated area of outstanding natural beauty or a designated rural area (i.e., an area designated under s. 157: SI 1980 No. 1375; 1980 No. 1345; 1981 No. 397; 1981 No. 940; 1982 No. 21; 1982 No. 187; 1986 No. 1695; 1988 No. 2057), to include a covenant in the conveyance to the effect that the purchaser (and his successors in title) shall not convey the freehold or grant a long lease of the house except with the authority's written consent. Certain disposals are exempted from the prohibition (ss. 39 and 160), and the authority's consent must be given where the person to whom the disposal is made has had his place of work or only or principal home in a designated region throughout the three-year period preceding the application for consent (ss. 37(3) and 157(3)).

Sections 125 and 126 of the Housing Act 1988 extend the scope of the covenant which can be extracted. Whereas the earlier provisions discouraged the onward transmission of former public sector housing to outsiders for 'second homes', these sections are aimed at the speculator who buys such property from the council to let as holiday homes. The authority on a sale, whether a 'voluntary sale' (s. 125) or a sale under the right to buy (s. 126), may include a covenant to the effect that the purchaser (or his successors in title etc.) shall not dispose of the house by way of tenancy or licence unless:

    (a)   the authority gives its written consent; or
    (b)   the tenant or licensee is a person who has had his place of work or only or principal home in a designated region throughout the three-year period preceding the grant of the tenancy or licence (a designated region is a region designated by order under Housing Act 1985 s. 157(3): see SI 1980 No. 1375; 1980 No. 1345; 1981 No. 397; 1982 No. 21; 1982 No. 187; 1986 No. 1695; 1988 No. 2057); or
    (c)   the house remains the only or principal home of the person making the disposal throughout the period of the tenancy or licence.

In other words, the covenant would seek to restrict occupation of the house to those who have worked for some time in the local area, or in a similar area elsewhere, or to those who take an interest in the house which is of an essentially temporary nature, their landlord still treating the house as his only or principal home. Note that the covenant is not to the effect that the landlord must occupy the house as his home; merely that the house is and remains his only or principal home. The covenant is registrable as a local land charge, and is enforceable by the vendor of the land (ss. 125(4) and 126(4)). It may be included in conveyances or grants made on or after 15 January 1989: it is, of course, up to the disposing landlord concerned whether it chooses to extract such covenants, and they must be expressed in the conveyance. All ss. 125 and 126 do is to empower the landlord to include, and thereafter to enforce, such covenants.

11.6.5 'Preserved' right to buy

Sections 171A to 171H of the Housing Act 1985 were added by the Housing and Planning Act 1986 and 'preserve' the right to buy of a tenant on the transfer of his landlord's reversion from the public to the private sector. The Housing Act 1988, s. 127 makes amendments to ss. 171B and 171C which are consequential on the changes in the law governing private sector tenancies effected by Part I of the new Act. The right to buy will be preserved where the person seeking to exercise it is a 'qualifying successor'. By s. 171B(4) in its unamended form, this term included a first successor, within the meaning of the Rent Acts, of the person who, before the transfer of the reversion, was secure tenant of the dwelling-house. This is now amended with the following effect.

On the transfer of the landlord's reversion to the private sector, the secure tenancy under which the tenant held will be translated into an assured tenancy (even though the tenancy was entered into before 15 January 1989: s. 38; see 2.3.1). If that asssured tenant had the preserved right to buy in relation to that dwelling-house, the preserved right to buy will be transmitted to:

(a) a member of the assured tenant's family who acquires the assured tenancy under the assured tenant's will or on his intestacy (*not* by virtue of statutory succession under s. 17);

(b) a member of the assured tenant's family to whom the assured tenant assigned his tenancy.

'Member of the family' is defined in Housing Act 1985, s. 186.

There is a serious, and probably unintended, restriction on succession to the preserved right to buy which was not present in the old s. 171B. If on the death of the assured tenant (who was not a joint tenant), his spouse (including common-law spouse) is entitled to succeed him to the tenancy under Housing Act 1988, s. 17, she will not have the preserved right to buy. She will not have acquired the tenancy under the will or on the intestacy of her husband: s. 17 expressly states that where it applies, the tenancy will vest by virtue of that section, and will not devolve under the tenant's will or intestacy. Section 127 seems, therefore, to exclude spouses who succeed to assured tenancies from the benefit of the preserved right to buy.

The power in the Secretary of State to provide that certain exceptions to the right to buy do not apply where the preserved right to buy is concerned (i.e., after a transfer of the reversion out of the public sector) is extended to include two more exceptions: Housing Act 1985, sch. 1, paras 1 and 3 (landlord a charitable housing trust or housing association, or a housing association which has never received a public grant) (s. 127(2)). Charitable housing trusts or housing associations are not, however, free to take action which conflicts with their objects, and if sale of the houses in question does so conflict, they will be able to resist an attempt to exercise the preserved right to buy (s. 127(3)).

11.6.6 Application of capital moneys
By s. 136, capital money received by a local authority in respect of disposals under the right to buy, or disposals of its housing stock, may be applied to meet the administrative costs of and incidental to such disposals.

11.7 Schemes for house purchase and improvement

In an attempt to secure vacancies of local authority rented accommodation, the local housing authority (defined in Housing Act 1985, s. 1) is given power by s. 129 to devise a scheme (approved by the Secretary of State) for the payment of grants to 'qualifying tenants' to obtain accommodation other than as tenants or licensees of the authority. The grant may be towards the purchase of a house (e.g., a contribution to the mortgage deposit) or towards works the tenant wishes to carry out to a house with a view to providing additional accommodation. The ambit of the schemes is wide, and it is left to the Secretary of State to work out the details by statutory instrument. The provision as it stands goes much further than the present power of the local authority to pay removal, and other, expenses incurred by a tenant on moving or in connection with the purchase of a house (Housing Act 1985, s. 26). Section 129 received the muted approval of the opposition in the House of Lords:

> Anything which the Ministry does which is designed to be of practical help to
> local authorities to fulfil their wretched role in the housing field in 1988 to 1989
> in trying to get a quart out of a pint pot would be sensible. (Lord Graham of
> Edmonton, HL Deb., 27 October 1988, col. 1765).

Practitioners advising landlords or potential landlords should also be aware of
the powers recently granted to local housing authorities to provide financial
assistance 'for the purposes of, or in connection with, the acquisition, construction, conversion, rehabilitation, improvement, maintenance or management . . .
of any property which is or is intended to be privately let as housing
accommodation (Local Government Act 1988, s. 24(1) and see also ss. 25 and 26
thereof).

11.8   Repair notices

A repair notice may be served by a local housing authority on its being satisfied
either that a house (or flat) is unfit for human habitation (as defined by Housing
Act 1985, s. 604), or that a house (or flat), although fit, is in need of substantial
repair to bring it up to a reasonable standard having regard to its age, character
or locality or is in such a state of disrepair that its condition interferes materially
with the personal comfort of the occupying tenant (Housing Act 1985, ss. 189
and 190). In either case the authority must not serve a notice if it is satisfied that
the property in question is not repairable at a reasonable expense. Notice is to be
served on the 'person having control' of the property (defined in Housing Act
1985, s. 206) and, in the event of the repairs not being carried out, the authority
has power to execute the works itself and charge the cost of repairs to the person
in receipt of the repairs notice. This apart, there is no penalty as such which can
be extracted as a result of a failure to comply with a repairs notice.

Section 130 of the Housing Act 1988 amends Part VI of the Housing Act 1985,
the amendments (set out in sch. 15) having effect in relation to repair notices
served on or after 15 January 1989 (s. 141(3)). The amendments seek to ensure
that the person responsible for disrepair to flats, who might not necessarily be the
landlord, is the person whom the repair notice will require to do the works; to
expedite the works required by repair notices and introduce penalties for
non-compliance with repair notices; and to prevent tenants from recovering the
cost of complying with repair notices from their landlords. The prescribed forms
of repair notes, amended to take account of sch. 15, are to be found in SI 1988
No. 2189.

The rationale behind s. 130 (see similarly s. 116 on repairing covenants) is that
a flat is frequently in a state of disrepair, or even unfit for human habitation, as a
result of the defective condition or disrepair of parts of the building outside the
flat itself: the corridors or staircases may be dangerous, the pipes in the flat above
may leak causing water to enter, the roof of the building may be in poor condition
and so forth. The tenant's landlord will in many cases own the freehold of the
entire building, and so a repair notice served on him would be proper: he can
reasonably be expected to perform the works of repair. This will not always be
the case, however, and, particularly with present government policy to encourage
'diversity of tenures', the tenant may find (for example) that the common parts

have a different landlord altogether, and the adjacent flats may be owner-occupied. Schedule 15 responds to this problem by attempting to ensure that the repair notice finds its way to the person having control of the part of the building from which the tenant's difficulties emanate.

Sections 189 and 190 of the Housing Act 1985 are amended so that the authority may serve a repair notice on the person having control of the part of the building concerned where the authority is satisfied:

(a)   that a flat is unfit for human habitation by reason of the defective condition of a part of the building outside the flat (unless the works required exceed a reasonable expense);

(b)   that the flat (although fit) is in such a state of disrepair that substantial repairs are necessary to a part of the building outside the flat to bring the flat up to a reasonable standard; or

(c)   that the building containing the flat is in such a state of disrepair that the condition of a part of the building outside the flat is such as to interfere materially with the occupying tenant's personal comfort.

It would be a relatively easy defence for the person in receipt of a repair notice served pursuant to s. 189 to argue that if the complaint concerns, say, common parts, the flat would not itself be 'unfit for human habitation' so as to activate that provision. However, Housing Act 1988, s. 130(2) provides (amending Housing Act 1985, s. 604) that, in considering whether a flat is unfit, regard must be had to the condition of any part of the building which affects the flat, and the defective condition of a part of the building outside the flat, although perhaps not itself a dwelling (e.g., common parts), may lead to a finding of unfitness.

The repair notice must be served on the person having control of the part of the building concerned. In the case of a repair notice served under these new provisions, the person having control of the part of the building will be 'a person who is an owner in relation to that part of the building', and who in the opinion of the authority ought to execute the works (sch. 15, para. 12). This is a far more straightforward and flexible definition than that which has applied in the past, and which will continue to apply in all cases except where notices are served pursuant to ss. 189(1A) and 190(1A) (see Housing Act 1985, s. 207(1)(a), and *Pollway Nominees Ltd* v *Croydon London Borough Council* [1987] AC 79). The authority simply has to find an 'owner', who may be the freeholder or a long leaseholder, and as long as it is of the opinion that he ought to execute the works it may serve the repair notice on him. The authority is now under a duty (as opposed to having the power) to serve a copy of any repair notice on a freeholder, mortgagee or lessee who has an interest in the house or flat concerned (sch. 15, paras 1(4) and 2(4)). The notice, once operative, is a local land charge and registrable under the Local Land Charges Act 1975 (sch. 15, paras 1(5) and 2(5)).

What happens if the local authority serves a repair notice under s. 189(1) or s. 190(1), and the person in receipt of the notice wishes to contend that the unfitness or disrepair of the flat is attributable to the defective condition or disrepair of a part of the building of which he does not have control? That person may appeal against the repair notice on this ground, and, if he does so, he must serve a copy of the repair notice on the person(s) he claims ought to execute the works (sch. 15, para. 3). The court, on hearing the appeal, will then have wide powers to vary the repair notice and make orders for monetary payment, and must take into account a range of factors (para. 3(3)). This procedure is in practical effect a method of joining another party to the repair notice proceedings at the instance of the person originally served with the notice.

The local authority retains the power to do the work required to be done under the notice where the repair notice has not been complied with (Housing Act 1985, s. 193). However, it is now under a duty in all cases to serve notice of intention to enter the house or flat and execute the works in question (sch. 15, para. 6(1)(b)). If, having served such notice, the person having control carries out the works, the authority may nevertheless claim its administrative and other expenses incurred with a view to itself doing the works (para. 5(2)). Moreover, any expenses which the authority claims under Housing Act 1985, sch. 10, will now be the liability of the person having control of the dwelling-house or part of the building to which the repair notice relates (para. 13(1)). Thus, the person on whom the notice is originally served who succeeds in his contention that some other person who has control of the building ought to do the works will be acquitted of liability under sch. 10.

Schedule 15 to the 1988 Act strengthens the powers of local housing authorities to compel compliance with repair notices. Until now, the period in which the works were to be done was specified in the notice, but there was no duty imposed to begin the works in a given time. By paras 1(3) and 2(3), the authority must specify in the repair notice the date by which the works must have begun. This date must be 'reasonable', and not earlier than the seventh day after the notice becomes operative. The notice must also specify (as is the case under the present law) the date by which the works must be completed, although this date no longer has to be at least 21 days from the notice becoming operative. The advantage of these amendments is that the authority does not have to wait for the entire period which was given under the repair notice to elapse before taking steps to enforce the notice. A notice will not be complied with if the works are not commenced within the period specified in the notice (subject to special provisions concerning appeals), and the authority will be empowered to do the work itself under Housing Act 1985, s. 193 (para. 5(1)). If the works are commenced within that period, the authority need not wait until the completion date: if it appears to the authority that reasonable progress is not being made towards compliance with the notice, it may (it does not have to) step in and do the works (para. 5(1)). If it does this, and then demands the recovery of its expenses from the person having control it will be a ground of appeal that reasonable progress was in fact being made at the time the authority served notice under s. 194 of its intention to enter and do the works (para. 13(3)).

The penalties for non-compliance with a repair notice are increased. The maximum fine for obstructing someone authorised to enter premises when exercising a power of entry under Housing Act 1985, Part VI, has been increased to level 3 (currently £400) (para. 7). It is now an offence, punishable summarily with a fine not exceeding level 4 (currently £1,000), for a person having control of premises to which a repair notice relates to intentionally fail to comply with the notice, s. 193(2) (as amended by sch. 15, para. 5) determining what constitutes non-compliance (para. 8).

Section 199 to 201 of the Housing Act 1985 are repealed (para. 9). A tenant who carries out the work required under a repair notice will not be able to recover that expenditure from the landlord if the repair notice was served on or after 15 January 1989. However, if there is a contract between them to do the works the repeal of s. 199 will not prevent the tenant from claiming the sum due under the contract. The repeal of ss. 200 and 201 deprives the local housing authority of its jurisdiction to make a charging order over the house or flat where the owner has executed works of repair under a repair notice.

11.9 Improvement grants

Section 131 makes amendments to the provisions governing improvement grants which are set out in Part XV of the Housing Act 1985. With respect to applications for grants approved after 15 January 1989, the applicant will have to state in his certificate of availability for letting that he does not intend to grant a long tenancy of the dwelling concerned. A similar condition will be imposed on the recipient of grant as a condition of that grant. These amendments are required to promote the policy that the State should not subsidise those who will gain a considerable premium as a result of the occupation for which improvements are being made. It will no longer be sufficient to rely on the authority to impose a condition under Housing Act 1985, s. 504(1), that the dwelling will be let or available for letting on a regulated tenancy or restricted contract to ensure that long tenancies at a premium are not created following the payment of grant, as such lettings are phased out by Part I of this Act and there is no prohibition on premiums affecting the new assured tenancies. 'Long tenancy' is defined in Housing Act 1985, s. 115. Where an application for grant is pending as at 15 January 1989, the transitional provisions contained in s. 131(7) and (8) apply.

11.10 Disposals of housing stock

Section 32 of the Housing Act 1985 confers power on a local authority to dispose of its housing stock, but the consent of the Secretary of State is generally required (s. 32(2)). Ministerial consent is also required for the disposal of houses (other than right-to-buy disposals) which are not held specifically for housing purposes but which are let on secure tenancy or under a lease granted pursuant to Part V of that Act (Housing Act 1985, s. 43). By ss. 34 and 43, Ministerial consent may be particular to one piece of land or description of land, or may be general to all or particular authorities, and it may be conditional. By ss. 34(4A) and 43(4A), now inserted by Housing Act 1988, s. 132, the Secretary of State is placed under a statutory duty to have regard, in determining whether to give consent or to impose conditions, to the extent to which the purchaser is free from local authority dependence, control or influence, and to the extent to which the purchaser may become the predominant or substantial owner in the housing area concerned. The policy behind the provision, the first part of which mirrors ss. 79(6) (disposals by HATs) and 94(2) (disposals under tenants' choice) is to obviate or at least to diminish the risk of land alienated by the local authority returning to local authority control, and to ensure a diversity of landholding within a particular area, in an attempt to retain a competitive housing market.

Disposals of one-time local authority houses have until now been subject to little statutory control following the first conveyance away from the local authority ('the original disposal'). Conditions annexed to Ministerial consent have sometimes affected the rights of purchasers to dispose, and where the house has been in a National Park or other similar rural area, the local authority has been empowered to extract restrictive covenants fettering certain subsequent disposals (see Housing Act 1985 ss. 37 and 157, and 11.6.4). Section 133 is therefore an important provision, because it now is the case that where the consent of the Secretary of State has been required for the original disposal, it will be required also for the subsequent disposal (including a sale by a mortgagee in possession), unless (a) it is exempt as falling within Housing Act 1988, s. 81(8) (e.g., sales under the right to buy, grants of assured or secure tenancies) or (b) the consent to the original disposal expressly stated that consent for subsequent disposals would not be necessary. Consent to the subsequent disposal, when required, is on the same basis as before (i.e., it can be conditional, and the Secretary of State must have regard to the matters set out in ss. 34(4A) and 43(4A)), and the Secretary of State must satisfy himself that full tenant consultation has taken place and have regard to the tenants' responses in making his decision (s. 133(5)). Where the disposal is by a housing association and requires Corporation consent by Housing Associations Act 1985, s. 9 (as amended by Housing Act 1988, sch. 6, para. 7), the Corporation must also be consulted. The subsequent disposal will in most cases activate Land Registration Act 1925, s. 123, requiring compulsory registration of the title to the land (s. 133(8)).

11.11   Race relations codes of practice

By s. 137, the Commission for Racial Equality is empowered to issue codes of practice which will be operative in the field of rented housing. If such a code is issued, the failure of a person to observe it must be taken into account in county court proceedings where a provision in the code appears to the court to be relevant to a question rising in the proceedings (Race Relations Act 1976, s. 47(10) as amended by s. 137(5)). It is possible, for example, that the failure of a landlord to comply with such a code could be relevant to the question of whether it is reasonable for a court to order possession on proof of one of the discretionary grounds for possession of a dwelling-house let on assured tenancy.

11.12   Scotland

It is beyond the scope of this book to give a detailed analysis of the effect of the Housing Act 1988 on Scots housing law, which would require a disproportionate amount of detailed reference to the recent Housing (Scotland) Acts 1987 and 1988, disproportionate as only a small portion of the Housing Act 1988 has application north of the border. Part II, including the amendments contained in sch. 6, applies to Scotland, which, like Wales, now has its own separate Housing Corporation ('Scottish Homes'), and certain sections in Part V also apply. Thus, s. 118 makes similar provision to s. 117 in relation to bankruptcy of residential tenants. Section 128 preserves the tenants' right to buy, the detail of the provisions being left to statutory regulations. Section 132(3) and (6) apply to Scotland, and s. 134 provides for ministerial consent on a subsequent disposal in much the same way as s. 133 does for England and Wales. Section 135, adding a new sch. 6A to the Housing (Scotland) Act 1987, governs consultation with tenants on sale of the reversion of dwelling-houses let on secure tenancies (cf. Housing Act 1985, sch. 6A). Codes of practice under the Race Relations Act 1976 will have the same application to Scotland as to England and Wales (s. 137). Finally, there are many 'minor and consequential' amendments contained in sch. 17 which have especial significance to Scotland (see those to the Reserve and Auxiliary Forces (Protection of Civil Interests) Act 1951, Social Security Act 1986, Housing (Scotland) Act 1987, Criminal Justice (Scotland) Act 1987 and Housing (Scotland) Act 1988) and amongst the repeals in sch. 18 are sections of the Housing (Scotland) Acts 1986, 1987 and 1988.

11.13   Amendments and repeals

The minor and consequential amendments and repeals contained in schs 17 and 18 are given effect by s. 140, and come into force on dates to be appointed by Secretary of State by statutory instrument. They are dealt with in the appropriate parts of this book. There are substantial amendments to the protective code applicable to 'service men' (contained in the Reserve and Auxilliary Forces (Protection of Civil Interests) Act 1951) consequential upon Part I of the Housing Act 1988 which it has not proved possible to incorporate into the chapters on assured tenancy, and reference should be made to sch. 17, paras 1 to 14, for those affected.

Table: Existing Tenancies and the Housing Act 1988

Tenure	Statutory basis
1980 Act assured tenancy	Housing Act 1980, ss. 56 to 58
Housing association tenancy	Rent Act 1977, Part VI
Protected shorthold tenancy	Housing Act 1980, ss. 52 to 55 Rent Act 1977, sch. 15, Case 19.
Protected/statutory tenancy.	Rent Act 1977
Protected occupancy/statutory tenancy.	Rent (Agriculture) Act 1976.
Restricted contract	Rent Act 1977, ss. 19 to 21 and Part V.
Secure tenancy.	Housing Act 1985, Part V.

Main statutory rights	Effect of Housing Act 1988
1. Security of tenure based on Landlord and Tenant Act 1954, Part II. 2. Rent as agreed by parties.	No 1980 Act assured tenancies after 14 January 1989, and existing tenancies become 1988 Act assured tenancies (subject to one exception). 6.3
1. Rent control. 2. No security of tenure by virtue of being a housing association tenancy, but may be that tenancy is *also* secure.	No new housing association tenancies can be entered into after 14 January 1989 (subject to exceptions). Existing tenancies unaffected. 6.4.
1. Rent control. 2. No security of tenure, but landlord must comply strictly with procedure laid down in order to obtain possession.	No new protected shorthold tenancies can be entered into after 14 January 1989 (subject to exceptions). Existing tenancies unaffected. 6.2
1. Security of tenure. 2. Rent control. 3. Statutory succession.	No new protected tenancies can be entered into after 14 January 1989 (subject to exceptions). Existing tenancies unaffected but note amendments to Rent Act 1977. 6.1.
1. Security of tenure. 2. Rent control. 3. Statutory succession.	No new protected occupancies can be entered into after 14 January 1989 (subject to exceptions). Existing agreements unaffected. 6.6.
1. Rent control. 2. Very limited security of tenure.	No new restricted contracts can be entered into after 14 January 1989 (subject to exceptions). Existing restricted contracts unaffected. 6.5.
1. Security of tenure. 2. Statutory succession. 3. No rent control. 4. Many tenants will have 'right to buy' freehold.	Secure tenancies generally unaffected, but housing associations letting after 14 January 1989 will not let on secure tenancy (8.7.1) and note amendments to right to buy (11.6.5).

Glossary

This glossary gives a broad outline of each of the terms described. 'Tenure' is used to describe a statutory code superimposed upon the contract between the landlord and tenant which affects such matters as recovery of possession, control of rents and succession on death. For further details of the effect of the Housing Act 1988 on the tenures concerned, reference should be made to the chapter or paragraph indicated and to the table on pages 138–9.

Assured agricultural occupancy. New tenure applicable to certain agricultural workers and their successors in respect of their tied cottages. Chapter 5.

Assured shorthold tenancy. New tenure applicable to private sector fixed-term lettings of at least six months where landlord serves notice stating that tenancy is assured shorthold. Chapter 4.

Assured tenancy. Two possible forms:

(a) The '1980 Act assured tenancy', a tenure applicable to private sector tenants holding from approved landlords dwelling-houses which have been newly erected or recently substantially altered. 6.3.
(b) The '1988 Act assured tenancy' (referred to throughout as the 'assured tenancy'), the major form of private sector tenure under the new regime. Chapters 2 and 3.

Fixed-term tenancy. A tenancy the maximum duration of which can be ascertained from its commencement (e.g., a term of three years). 2.4.1

Housing association tenancy. A tenure whereby residential tenants who are not protected tenants by reason of their landlord being a housing association are entitled to rent control. 6.4; 8.7.3.

Periodic tenancy. A tenancy the maximum duration of which cannot be ascertained from its commencement (e.g., a monthly tenancy). 2.4.1.

Protected shorthold tenancy.   A tenure applicable to private sector fixed-term lettings of between 12 months and five years where the landlord serves notice stating that the tenancy is protected shorthold. 6.2.

Protected occupancy.   A contractual tenancy or licence which falls within the Rent (Agriculture) Act 1976, whereby agricultural workers and their successors are given statutory protection in respect of their tied accommodation. 6.6.

Protected tenancy.   The major form of private sector tenure under the Rent Act regime, protected tenancy is the term used to describe a contractual tenancy which falls within the Rent Act 1977. 6.1.

Restricted contract.   A tenure applicable to certain tenancies or licences of resdential accommodation which do not meet the required criteria for being protected tenancies. 6.5.

Secure tenancy.   The major form of public sector tenure, applicable to residential tenants (and some licensees) both before and after the Housing Act 1988. 6.7; 8.7.1.

Statutory periodic tenancy.   Tenancy which arises by operation of statute (Housing Act 1988, s. 5(2)) on the expiry of a fixed-term assured tenancy. 2.4.1.

Statutory tenancy.   Tenure which arises by operation of statute (Rent Act 1977, s. 2) on the termination of a protected tenancy if and so long as the tenant occupies the dwelling-house as his residence. 6.1. Alternatively, the tenure which arises under the Rent (Agriculture) Act 1976 on the termination of a protected occupancy. 6.6.

Commencement of Housing Act 1988 Provisions

15 November 1988 (royal assent)
Part III
ss. 132 to 134
ss. 138 to 139
s. 141

1 December 1988 (SI 1988 No. 2056)
s. 46(1) and (2)
s. 47(2)
s. 47(6) so far as relating to the provisions of s. 47(2)
s. 140(1) so far as it relates to sch. 17, paras 91 to 96, 98 to 102, 104, 105 and 114 to 116

2 January 1989 (SI 1988 No. 2152)
s. 140(1) so far as it relates to sch. 17, paras 77, 78, 85 to 88 and 90
s. 140(2) so far as it relates to repeal in sch. 18 of words in Housing (Scotland) Act 1988, s. 38

15 January 1989 (by s. 141(3))
Part I
ss. 115 to 118
ss. 120 and 121
s. 123
ss. 125 to 127
ss. 130 and 131
ss. 136 and 137

15 January 1989 (SI 1988 No. 2152)
s. 49
s. 57
s. 59(1)
s. 59(2) and (3) so far as it relates to sch. 6, paras 1 (for restricted purposes), 8(2), 25 and 26

s. 94
s. 106
ss. 111 to 114
s. 119 subject to transitional provisions
s. 140(1) so far as it relates to sch. 17, paras 1 to 16, 17(2), 18 to 37, 40, 42 to 65, 67 to 76 and 80 to 84 (and subject to transitional provision)
s. 140(2) so far as it relates to certain repeals and subject to transitional provisions

On dates yet to be appointed
Part II (apart from provisions mentioned above)
Part IV (apart from provisions mentioned above)
s. 119
s. 122
s. 124
ss. 128 and 129
s. 135
s. 140 (except so far as mentioned above)

Commencement Orders

1988 No. 2056 (C.77)

Housing, England and Wales

The Housing Act 1988 (Commencement No. 1) Order 1988

Made - - - -   *18th November 1988*

The Secretary of State for Wales in exercise of the powers conferred on him by section 141(2) of the Housing Act 1988 hereby makes the following Order:—

Citation and interpretation

1.—(1)   This Order may be cited as the Housing Act 1988 (Commencement No. 1) Order 1988.

(2)   In this Order "the Act" means the Housing Act 1988.

Coming into force of certain provisions of the Act

2.   The provisions of the Act specified in column 1 of the Schedule to this Order (which relate to the matters mentioned in column 2 thereof) shall, except as otherwise provided in the said Column 1, come into force on 1st December 1988.

Peter Walker
Secretary of State for Wales

18th November 1988

Article 2

The Schedule
Provisions of the Housing Act 1988 coming into force on 1st December 1988

Provisions of the Act	Subject matter of provisions
Sections 46(1) and (2)	Housing for Wales.
Section 47(2)	Notification to registered housing associations.
Section 47(6) so far as relating to the provisions of section 47(2)	Meaning of "the appointed day".
Schedule 5	Housing for Wales.
Paragraphs 91, 92, 93, 94, 95, 96, 98, 99, 100, 101, 102, 104, 105, 114, 115 and 116 of Part II of Schedule 17, and section 140(1) so far as relating to those provisions	Amendments consequential on the establishment of Housing for Wales.

Explanatory Note

(This note is not part of the Order)
This Order brings into force on 1st December 1988 the provisions of the Housing Act 1988 which relate to the establishment of Housing for Wales.

1988 No. 2152 (C.81)

Housing, England and Wales
Housing, Scotland

The Housing Act 1988 (Commencement No. 2)
Order 1988

Made - - - - *8th December 1988*

The Secretary of State, in exercise of the powers conferred on him by section 141(2) of the Housing Act 1988, and of all other powers enabling him in that behalf, hereby makes the following Order:

   1. This Order may be cited as the Housing Act 1988 (Commencement No. 2) Order 1988.

   2. The following provisions of the Housing Act 1988 shall come into force on 2nd January 1989 —

     section 140(1) in so far as it relates to paragraphs 77, 78, 85 to 88 and 90 of Schedule 17, section 140(2) in so far as it relates to the repeal by Schedule 18 of words in section 38 of the Housing (Scotland) Act 1988.

3. The following provisions of the Housing Act 1988 shall come into force on 15th January 1989—

section 49,

section 57,

section 59(1),

section 59(2) and (3) in so far as it relates to paragraphs 8(2), 25 and 26 (except paragraphs (b) and (c)) of Schedule 6 and, for the purposes only of section 59(1) of the Act and section 36A of the Housing Associations Act 1985, paragraph 1 of that Schedule,

section 94,

section 106,

sections 111 to 114,

section 119, subject to the transitional provisions in paragraphs 2 and 3 of Schedule 1 to this Order,

section 140(1) in so far as it relates to paragraphs 1 to 16, 17(2), 18 to 37, 40, 42 to 65, 67 to 76 and 80 to 84 of Schedule 17, subject to the transitional provision for paragraph 21 in paragraph 1 of Schedule 1 to this Order,

section 140(2) in so far as it relates to the repeals in the Reserve and Auxiliary Forces (Protection of Civil Interests) Act 1951, the Rent (Agriculture) Act 1976, the Rent Act 1977, the Protection from Eviction Act 1977, the Housing Act 1980, the Local Government Act 1985, the Housing Act 1985 and to the repeals specified in Schedule 2 to this Order, subject, as the case may be, to the transitional provisions in that Schedule.

Nicholas Ridley
One of Her Majesty's
8th December 1988   Principal Secretaries of State

Schedule 1
Transitional Provisions

The Rent (Agriculture) Act 1976
1. The amendment to the Rent (Agriculture) Act 1976 in paragraph 21 of Schedule 17 to the Housing Act 1988 does not have effect in relation to an offence committed more than six months before the 15th January 1989.

The Landlord and Tenant Act 1987
2. The amendments to the Landlord and Tenant Act 1987 ("the 1987 Act") in paragraphs 1, 2(2) and 3 of Schedule 13 to the Housing Act 1988 do not have effect in relation to a disposal (within the meaning of Part I of that Act) made in pursuance of a contract entered into before the 15th January 1989 or made under that Act where the offer notice was served, or treated as served, under section 5 of the 1987 Act before that date.

3. The amendments to the 1987 Act in paragraphs 4 to 6 of that Schedule do not apply in relation to an application made to the court before the 15th January 1989.

Schedule 2
Repeals

Chapter	Short title	Extent of repeal
1986 c.63.	The Housing and Planning Act 1986.	Section 7. Section 12. In section 13, subsections (1) to (3) and (5). In Schedule 4, paragraphs 1(3) and 10.
1987 c.31.	The Landlord and Tenant Act 1987.	In section 3(1) (b) the word "or". Section 4(2)(a)(ii) Section 60(2).
1988 c.43.	The Housing (Scotland) Act 1988.	In Schedule 9, paragraph 6(b).

Transitional Provisions

Rent Act 1977

1. The repeal of section 16A of the Rent Act 1977 ("the 1977 Act") does not apply in the case specified in section 37(2) of the Housing Act 1988.

2. The repeals in whole or in part of the provisions of the 1977 Act specified below do not apply in relation to an application under section 69(1) of the 1977 Act (certificate of fair rent) made before the 15th January 1989 or a certificate of fair rent issued pursuant to such an application-
section 67(7),
section 69,
section 87(2),
Schedule 11, Part II,
Schedule 12,
Schedule 20 paragraph 2(2).

3. The repeal of section 68 of the 1977 Act (application to rent officer by local authority) does not apply in relation to an application under subsection (1) of that section made before the 15th January 1989.

4. The repeals in whole or in part of the provisions of the 1977 Act specified below do not apply in relation to an increase in rent up to, or towards, a registered rent—
(1) in relation to which the relevant date for the purposes of Schedule 8 to the Rent Act 1977 (phasing of rent increases: general provisions) falls before the 15th January 1989, or
(2) pursuant to the first application under section 67 or section 68 of the 1977

Act (applications for registration or consideration of fair rent) relating to a regulated tenancy which has been converted from a controlled tenancy and for which no rent was registered under Part IV of the 1977 Act before 4th May 1987—
section 88(2),
section 89,
Schedule 8.

5. The repeal in section 103(1) of the 1977 Act (notice to quit served after reference of contract to rent tribunal) does not apply in relation to an application under section 77 or 80 of the 1977 Act made before the 15th January 1989.

Local Government Act 1985
6. The repeal in paragraph 21 of Schedule 13 to the Local Government Act 1985 does not apply with respect to any tenancy or licence entered into before the 15th January 1989 or entered into in pursuance of a contract made before then.

The Housing Act 1985
7. The repeal of sections 199 to 201 does not have effect in relation to any repair notice served before the 15th January 1989.

Landlord and Tenant Act 1987
8. The repeals in section 3(1)(b) and of sections 4(2)(a)(ii) and 60(2) do not apply in relation to a disposal made as mentioned in paragraph 2 of Schedule 1 to this Order.

Explanatory Note
(This note is not part of the Order)
This Order brings into force on 2nd January 1989 section 140 of the Housing Act 1988 in relation to certain amendments to the Housing (Scotland) Acts 1987 and 1988. It brings into force on 15th January 1989 provisions of the Housing Act 1988 mentioned below—
in Part II (Housing Associations)—
section 49 which provides for the issue of guidance to registered housing associations,
section 57 which enables the Secretary of State to delegate certain of his functions regarding grants,
section 59(1) (interpretation),
section 59(2) and (3) in relation to certain amendments to the Housing Associations Act 1985;
in Part IV (Change of Landlord: Secure Tenants)
section 94 which provides for the approval of persons by the Housing Corporation and for connected matters,
section 106 which enables the Housing Corporation to provide information, advice and assistance to persons approved or seeking approval and to tenants,
sections 111 to 114 (prescription of forms, making of orders and regulations, jurisdiction of the county court and interpretation);

in Part V (Miscellaneous and General)—
section 119 (and hence Schedule 13) which amends the Landlord and Tenant Act 1987 (subject to transitional provisions in Schedule 1 to the Order),
section 140 in relation to certain minor and consequential amendments in Schedule 17 and repeals in Schedule 18 (subject to the transitional provisions in the Schedules to the Order).

Note as to earlier Commencement Orders
(This note is not part of the Order)

Provision	Date of commencement	S.I. No.
section 46(1) and (2) section 47(2) section 47(6) (partially) section 140(1) (in so far as it relates to paragraphs 91 to 96, 98 to 102, 104, 105 and 114 to 116 of Part II of Schedule 17)	1st December 1988	1988/2056

Housing Act 1988

Arrangement of sections

Part I Rented accommodation

Chapter I Assured tenancies

Meaning of assured tenancy etc.

Chapter II Assured shorthold tenancies

Housing Act 1988

1988, c. 50. An Act to make further provision with respect to dwelling-houses let on tenancies or occupied under licences; to amend the Rent Act 1977 and the Rent (Agriculture) Act 1976; to establish a body, Housing for Wales, having functions relating to housing associations; to amend the Housing Associations Act 1985 and to repeal and re-enact with amendments certain provisions of Part II of that Act; to make provision for the establishment of housing action trusts for areas designated by the Secretary of State; to confer on persons approved for the purpose the right to acquire from public sector landlords certain dwelling-houses occupied by secure tenants; to make further provision about rent officers, the administration of housing benefit and rent allowance subsidy,the right to buy, repair notices and certain disposals of land and the application of capital money arising thereon; to make provision consequential upon the Housing (Scotland) Act 1988; and for connected purposes.

[Royal assent 15 November 1988.]

Be it enacted by the Queen's most Excellent Majesty, by and with the advice and consent of the Lords Spiritual and Temporal, and Commons, in this present Parliament assembled, and by the authority of the same, as follows:—

Part I Rented accommodation

Chapter I Assured tenancies

Meaning of assured tenancy etc.

Assured tenancies
1.—(1)   A tenancy under which a dwelling-house is let as a separate dwelling is for the purposes of this Act an assured tenancy if and so long as—

(a)   the tenant or, as the case may be, each of the joint tenants is an individual; and

(b)   the tenant or, as the case may be, at least one of the joint tenants occupies the dwelling-house as his only or principal home; and

(c)   the tenancy is not one which, by virtue of subsection (2) or subsection (6) below, cannot be an assured tenancy.

(2)   Subject to subsection (3) below, if and so long as a tenancy falls within any paragraph in Part I of Schedule 1 to this Act, it cannot be an assured tenancy; and in that Schedule—

(a)   'tenancy' means a tenancy under which a dwelling-house is let as a separate dwelling;

(b)   Part II has effect for determining the rateable value of a dwelling-house for the purposes of Part I; and

(c)   Part III has effect for supplementing paragraph 10 in Part I.

(3)   Except as provided in Chapter V below, at the commencement of this Act, a tenancy—

(a)   under which a dwelling-house was then let as a separate dwelling, and

(b)   which immediately before that commencement was an assured tenancy for the purposes of sections 56 to 58 of the Housing Act 1980 (tenancies granted by approved bodies),

shall become an assured tenancy for the purposes of this Act.

(4)   In relation to an assured tenancy falling within subsection (3) above—

(a)   Part I of Schedule 1 to this Act shall have effect, subject to subsection (5) below, as if it consisted only of paragraphs 11 and 12; and

(b)   sections 56 to 58 of the Housing Act 1980 (and Schedule 5 to that Act) shall not apply after the commencement of this Act.

(5)   In any case where—

(a)   immediately before the commencement of this Act the landlord under a tenancy is a fully mutual housing association, and

(b)   at the commencement of this Act the tenancy becomes an assured tenancy by virtue of subsection (3) above,

then, so long as that association remains the landlord under that tenancy (and under any statutory periodic tenancy which arises on the coming to an end of that tenancy), paragraph 12 of Schedule 1 to this Act shall have effect in relation to that tenancy with the omission of subparagraph (1)(h).

(6)   If, in pursuance of its duty under—

(a)   section 63 of the Housing Act 1985 (duty to house pending inquiries in case of apparent priority need),

(b)   section 65(3) of that Act (duty to house temporarily person found to have priority need but to have become homeless intentionally), or

(c)   section 68(1) of that Act (duty to house pending determination whether conditions for referral of application are satisfied),

a local housing authority have made arrangements with another person to provide accommodation, a tenancy granted by that other person in pursuance of the arrangements to a person specified by the authority cannot be an assured tenancy before the expiry of the period of twelve months beginning with the date specified in subsection (7) below unless, before the expiry of that period, the tenant is notified by the landlord (or, in the case of joint landlords, at least one of them) that the tenancy is to be regarded as an assured tenancy.

(7) The date referred to in subsection (6) above is the date on which the tenant received the notification required by section 64(1) of the Housing Act 1985 (notification of decision on question of homelessness or threatened homelessness) or, if he received a notification under section 68(3) of that Act (notification of which authority has duty to house), the date on which he received that notification.

Letting of a dwelling-house together with other land
2.—(1) If, under a tenancy, a dwelling-house is let together with other land, then, for the purposes of this Part of this Act,—

(a) if and so long as the main purpose of the letting is the provision of a home for the tenant or, where there are joint tenants, at least one of them, the other land shall be treated as part of the dwelling-house; and

(b) if and so long as the main purpose of the letting is not as mentioned in paragraph (a) above, the tenancy shall be treated as not being one under which a dwelling-house is let as a separate dwelling.

(2) Nothing in subsection (1) above affects any question whether a tenancy is precluded from being an assured tenancy by virtue of any provision of Schedule 1 to this Act.

Tenant sharing accommodation with persons other than landlord
3.—(1) Where a tenant has the exclusive occupation of any accommodation (in this section referred to as 'the separate accommodation') and—

(a) the terms as between the tenant and his landlord on which he holds the separate accommodation include the use of other accommodation (in this section referred to as 'the shared accommodation') in common with another person or other persons, not being or including the landlord, and

(b) by reason only of the circumstances mentioned in paragraph (a) above, the separate accommodation would not, apart from this section, be a dwelling-house let on an assured tenancy,

the separate accommodation shall be deemed to be a dwelling-house let on an assured tenancy and the following provisions of this section shall have effect.

(2) For the avoidance of doubt it is hereby declared that where, for the purpose of determining the rateable value of the separate accommodation, it is necessary to make an apportionment under Part II of Schedule 1 to this Act, regard is to be had to the circumstances mentioned in subsection (1)(a) above.

(3) While the tenant is in possession of the separate accommodation, any term of the tenancy terminating or modifying, or providing for the termination or modification of, his right to the use of any of the shared accommodation which is living accommodation shall be of no effect.

(4) Where the terms of the tenancy are such that, at any time during the tenancy, the persons in common with whom the tenant is entitled to the use of the shared accommodation could be varied or their number could be increased, nothing in subsection (3) above shall prevent those terms from having effect so far as they relate to any such variation or increase.

(5) In this section 'living accommodation' means accommodation of such a nature that the fact that it constitutes or is included in the shared accommodation

is sufficient, apart from this section, to prevent the tenancy from constituting an assured tenancy of a dwelling-house.

Certain sublettings not to exclude any part of sublessor's premises from assured tenancy
4.—(1)   Where the tenant of a dwelling-house has sublet a part but not the whole of the dwelling-house, then, as against his landlord or any superior landlord, no part of the dwelling-house shall be treated as excluded from being a dwelling-house let on an assured tenancy by reason only that the terms on which any person claiming under the tenant holds any part of the dwelling-house include the use of accommodation in common with other persons.

(2)   Nothing in this section affects the rights against, and liabilities to, each other of the tenant and any person claiming under him, or of any two such persons.

Security of tenure

Security of tenure
5.—(1)   An assured tenancy cannot be brought to an end by the landlord except by obtaining an order of the court in accordance with the following provisions of this Chapter or Chapter II below or, in the case of a fixed-term tenancy which contains power for the landlord to determine the tenancy in certain circumstances, by the exercise of that power and, accordingly, the service by the landlord of a notice to quit shall be of no effect in relation to a periodic assured tenancy.

(2)   If an assured tenancy which is a fixed-term tenancy comes to an end otherwise than by virtue of—

(a)   an order of the court, or
(b)   a surrender or other action on the part of the tenant,

then, subject to section 7 and Chapter II below, the tenant shall be entitled to remain in possession of the dwelling-house let under that tenancy and, subject to subsection (4) below, his right to possession shall depend upon a periodic tenancy arising by virtue of this section.

(3)   The periodic tenancy referred to in subsection (2) above is one—

(a)   taking effect in possession immediately on the coming to an end of the fixed-term tenancy;
(b)   deemed to have been granted by the person who was the landlord under the fixed-term tenancy immediately before it came to an end to the person who was then the tenant under that tenancy;
(c)   under which the premises which are let are the same dwelling-house as was let under the fixed-term tenancy;
(d)   under which the periods of the tenancy are the same as those for which rent was last payable under the fixed-term tenancy; and
(e)   under which, subject to the following provisions of this Part of this Act, the other terms are the same as those of the fixed-term tenancy immediately before it came to an end, except that any term which makes provision for determination by the landlord or the tenant shall not have effect while the tenancy remains an assured tenancy.

(4)   The periodic tenancy referred to in subsection (2) above shall not arise if, on the coming to an end of the fixed-term tenancy, the tenant is entitled, by virtue of the grant of another tenancy, to possession of the same or substantially the same dwelling-house as was let to him under the fixed-term tenancy.

(5)   If, on or before the date on which a tenancy is entered into or is deemed to have been granted as mentioned in subsection (3)(b) above, the person who is to be the tenant under that tenancy—

(a)   enters into an obligation to do any act which (apart from this subsection) will cause the tenancy to come to an end at a time when it is an assured tenancy, or

(b)   executes, signs or gives any surrender, notice to quit or other document which (apart from this subsection) has the effect of bringing the tenancy to an end at a time when it is an assured tenancy,

the obligation referred to in paragraph (a) above shall not be enforceable or, as the case may be, the surrender, notice to quit or other document referred to in paragraph (b) above shall be of no effect.

(6)   If, by virtue of any provision of this Part of this Act, Part I of Schedule 1 to this Act has effect in relation to a fixed-term tenancy as if it consisted only of paragraphs 11 and 12, that Part shall have the like effect in relation to any periodic tenancy which arises by virtue of this section on the coming to an end of the fixed-term tenancy.

(7)   Any reference in this Part of this Act to a statutory periodic tenancy is a reference to a periodic tenancy arising by virtue of this section.

Fixing of terms of statutory periodic tenancy
6.—(1)   In this section, in relation to a statutory periodic tenancy,—

(a)   'the former tenancy' means the fixed-term tenancy on the coming to an end of which the statutory periodic tenancy arises; and

(b)   'the implied terms' means the terms of the tenancy which have effect by virtue of section 5(3)(e) above, other than terms as to the amount of the rent;

but nothing in the following provisions of this section applies to a statutory periodic tenancy at a time when, by virtue of paragraph 11 or paragraph 12 in Part 1 of Schedule 1 to this Act, it cannot be an assured tenancy.

(2)   Not later than the first anniversary of the day on which the former tenancy came to an end, the landlord may serve on the tenant, or the tenant may serve on the landlord, a notice in the prescribed form proposing terms of the statutory periodic tenancy different from the implied terms and, if the landlord or the tenant considers it appropriate, proposing an adjustment of the amount of the rent to take account of the proposed terms.

(3)   Where a notice has been served under subsection (2) above,—

(a)   within the period of three months beginning on the date on which the notice was served on him, the landlord or the tenant, as the case may be, may, by an application in the prescribed form, refer the notice to a rent assessment committee under subsection (4) below; and

(b)   if the notice is not so referred, then, with effect from such date, not falling within the period referred to in paragraph (a) above, as may be specified in the notice, the terms proposed in the notice shall become terms of the tenancy in substitution for any of the implied terms dealing with the same subject matter and the amount of the rent shall be varied in accordance with any adjustment so proposed.

(4)   Where a notice under subsection (2) above is referred to a rent assessment committee, the committee shall consider the terms proposed in the notice and shall determine whether those terms, or some other terms (dealing with the same subject-matter as the proposed terms), are such as, in the committee's opinion, might reasonably be expected to be found in an assured periodic tenancy of the dwelling-house concerned, being a tenancy—

(a)   which begins on the coming to an end of the former tenancy; and
(b)   which is granted by a willing landlord on terms which, except in so far as they relate to the subject matter of the proposed terms, are those of the statutory periodic tenancy at the time of the committee's consideration.

(5)   Whether or not a notice under subsection (2) above proposes an adjustment of the amount of the rent under the statutory periodic tenancy, where a rent assessment committee determine any terms under subsection (4) above, they shall, if they consider it appropriate, specify such an adjustment to take account of the terms so determined.

(6)   In making a determination under subsection (4) above, or specifying an adjustment of an amount of rent under subsection (5) above, there shall be disregarded any effect on the terms or the amount of the rent attributable to the granting of a tenancy to a sitting tenant.

(7)   Where a notice under subsection (2) above is referred to a rent assessment committee, then, unless the landlord and the tenant otherwise agree, with effect from such date as the committee may direct—

(a)   the terms determined by the committee shall become terms of the statutory periodic tenancy in substitution for any of the implied terms dealing with the same subject matter; and
(b)   the amount of the rent under the statutory periodic tenancy shall be altered to accord with any adjustment specified by the committee;

but for the purposes of paragraph (b) above the committee shall not direct a date earlier than the date specified, in accordance with subsection (3)(b) above, in the notice referred to them.

(8)   Nothing in this section requires a rent assessment committee to continue with a determination under subsection (4) above if the landlord and tenant give notice in writing that they no longer require such a determination or if the tenancy has come to an end.

Orders for possession
7.—(1)   The court shall not make an order for possession of a dwelling-house let on an assured tenancy except on one or more of the grounds set out in Schedule 2 to this Act; but nothing in this Part of this Act relates to proceedings for possession of such a dwelling-house which are brought by a mortgagee, within the meaning of the Law of Property Act 1925, who has lent money on the security of the assured tenancy.

(2)   The following provisions of this section have effect, subject to section 8 below, in relation to proceedings for the recovery of possession of a dwelling-house let on an assured tenancy.

(3)   If the court is satisfied that any of the grounds in Part I of Schedule 2 to this Act is established then, subject to subsection (6) below, the court shall make an order for possession.

(4)   If the court is satisfied that any of the grounds in Part II of Schedule 2 to this Act is established, then, subject to subsection (6) below, the court may make an order for possession if it considers it reasonable to do so.

(5)   Part III of Schedule 2 to this Act shall have effect for supplementing Ground 9 in that Schedule and Part IV of that Schedule shall have effect in relation to notices given as mentioned in Grounds 1 to 5 of that Schedule.

(6)   The court shall not make an order for possession of a dwelling-house to take effect at a time when it is let on an assured fixed-term tenancy unless—

(a)   the ground for possession is Ground 2 or Ground 8 in Part I of Schedule 2 to this Act or any of the grounds in Part II of that Schedule, other than Ground 9 or Ground 16; and

(b)   the terms of the tenancy make provision for it to be brought to an end on the ground in question (whether that provision takes the form of a provision for re-entry, for forfeiture, for determination by notice or otherwise).

(7)   Subject to the preceding provisions of this section, the court may make an order for possession of a dwelling-house on grounds relating to a fixed-term tenancy which has come to an end; and where an order is made in such circumstances, any statutory periodic tenancy which has arisen on the ending of the fixed-term tenancy shall end (without any notice and regardless of the period) on the day on which the order takes effect.

Notice of proceedings for possession
8.—(1)   The court shall not entertain proceedings for possession of a dwelling-house let on an assured tenancy unless—

(a)   the landlord or, in the case of joint landlords, at least one of them has served on the tenant a notice in accordance with this section and the proceedings are begun within the time-limits stated in the notice in accordance with subsections (3) and (4) below; or

(b)   the court considers it just and equitable to dispense with the requirement of such a notice.

(2)   The court shall not make an order for possession on any of the grounds in Schedule 2 to this Act unless that ground and particulars of it are specified in the notice under this section; but the grounds specified in such a notice may be altered or added to with the leave of the court.

(3)   A notice under this section is one in the prescribed form informing the tenant that—

(a)   the landlord intends to begin proceedings for possession of the dwelling-house on one or more of the grounds specified in the notice; and

(b)   those proceedings will not begin earlier than a date specified in the notice which, without prejudice to any additional limitation under subsection (4) below, shall not be earlier than the expiry of the period of two weeks from the date of service of the notice; and

(c) those proceedings will not begin later than 12 months from the date of service of the notice.

(4) If a notice under this section specifies, in accordance with subsection (3)(a) above, any of Grounds 1, 2, 5 to 7, 9 and 16 in Schedule 2 to this Act (whether with or without other grounds), the date specified in the notice as mentioned in subsection (3)(b) above shall not be earlier than—

(a) two months from the date of service of the notice; and

(b) if the tenancy is a periodic tenancy, the earliest date on which, apart from section 5(1) above, the tenancy could be brought to an end by a notice to quit given by the landlord on the same date as the date of service of the notice under this section.

(5) The court may not exercise the power conferred by subsection (1)(b) above if the landlord seeks to recover possession on Ground 8 in Schedule 2 to this Act.

(6) Where a notice under this section—

(a) is served at a time when the dwelling-house is let on a fixed-term tenancy, or

(b) is served after a fixed-term tenancy has come to an end but relates (in whole or in part) to events occurring during that tenancy,

the notice shall have effect notwithstanding that the tenant becomes or has become tenant under a statutory periodic tenancy arising on the coming to an end of the fixed-term tenancy.

Extended discretion of court in possession claims

9.—(1) Subject to subsection (6) below, the court may adjourn for such period or periods as it thinks fit proceedings for possession of a dwelling-house let on an assured tenancy.

(2) On the making of an order for possession of a dwelling-house let on an assured tenancy or at any time before the execution of such an order, the court, subject to subsection (6) below, may—

(a) stay or suspend execution of the order, or

(b) postpone the date of possession,

for such period or periods as the court thinks just.

(3) On any such adjournment as is referred to in subsection (1) above or on any such stay, suspension or postponement as is referred to in subsection (2) above, the court, unless it considers that to do so would cause exceptional hardship to the tenant or would otherwise be unreasonable, shall impose conditions with regard to payment by the tenant of arrears of rent (if any) and rent or payments in respect of occupation after the termination of the tenancy (mesne profits) and may impose such other conditions as it thinks fit.

(4) If any such conditions as are referred to in subsection (3) above are complied with, the court may, if it thinks fit, discharge or rescind any such order as is referred to in subsection (2) above.

(5) In any case where—

    (a) at a time when proceedings are brought for possession of a dwelling-house let on an assured tenancy, the tenant's spouse or former spouse, having rights of occupation under the Matrimonial Homes Act 1983, is in occupation of the dwelling-house, and

    (b) the assured tenancy is terminated as a result of those proceedings,

the spouse or former spouse, so long as he or she remains in occupation, shall have the same rights in relation to, or in connection with, any such adjournment as is referred to in subsection (1) above or any such stay, suspension or postponement as is referred to in subsection (2) above, as he or she would have if those rights of occupation were not affected by the termination of the tenancy.

(6) This section does not apply if the court is satisfied that the landlord is entitled to possession of the dwelling-house—

    (a) on any of the grounds in Part I of Schedule 2 to this Act; or

    (b) by virtue of subsection (1) or subsection (4) of section 21 below.

Special provisions applicable to shared accommodation

10.—(1) This section applies in a case falling within subsection (1) of section 3 above and expressions used in this section have the same meaning as in that section.

(2) Without prejudice to the enforcement of any order made under subsection (3) below, while the tenant is in possession of the separate accommodation, no order shall be made for possession of any of the shared accommodation, whether on the application of the immediate landlord of the tenant or on the application of any person under whom that landlord derives title, unless a like order has been made, or is made at the same time, in respect of the separate accommodation; and the provisions of section 6 above shall have effect accordingly.

(3) On the application of the landlord, the court may make such order as it thinks just either—

    (a) terminating the right of the tenant to use the whole or any part of the shared accommodation other than living acommodation; or

    (b) modifying his right to use the whole or any part of the shared accommodation, whether by varying the persons or increasing the number of persons entitled to the use of that accommodation or otherwise.

(4) No order shall be made under subsection (3) above so as to effect any termination or modification of the rights of the tenant which, apart from section 3(3) above, could not be effected by or under the terms of the tenancy.

Payment of removal expenses in certain cases

11.—(1) Where a court makes an order for possession of a dwelling-house let on an assured tenancy on Ground 6 or Ground 9 in Schedule 2 to this Act (but not on any other ground), the landlord shall pay to the tenant a sum equal to the reasonable expenses likely to be incurred by the tenant in removing from the dwelling-house.

(2) Any question as to the amount of the sum referred to in subsection (1)

above shall be determined by agreement between the landlord and the tenant or, in default of agreement, by the court.

(3) Any sum payable to a tenant by virtue of this section shall be recoverable as a civil debt due from the landlord.

Compensation for misrepresentation or concealment
12. Where a landlord obtains an order for possession of a dwelling-house let on an assured tenancy on one or more of the grounds in Schedule 2 to this Act and it is subsequently made to appear to the court that the order was obtained by misrepresentation or concealment of material facts, the court may order the landlord to pay to the former tenant such sum as appears sufficient as compensation for damage or loss sustained by that tenant as a result of the order.

Rent and other terms

Increases of rent under assured periodic tenancies
13.—(1) This section applies to—

(a) a statutory periodic tenancy other than one which, by virtue of paragraph 11 or paragraph 12 in Part I of Schedule 1 to this Act, cannot for the time being be an assured tenancy; and

(b) any other periodic tenancy which is an assured tenancy, other than one in relation to which there is a provision, for the time being binding on the tenant, under which the rent for a particular period of the tenancy will or may be greater than the rent for an earlier period.

(2) For the purpose of securing an increase in the rent under a tenancy to which this section applies, the landlord may serve on the tenant a notice in the prescribed form proposing a new rent to take effect at the beginning of a new period of the tenancy specified in the notice, being a period beginning not earlier than—

(a) the minimum period after the date of the service of the notice; and

(b) except in the case of a statutory periodic tenancy, the first anniversary of the date on which the first period of the tenancy began; and

(c) if the rent under the tenancy has previously been increased by virtue of a notice under this subsection or a determination under section 14 below, the first anniversary of the date on which the increased rent took effect.

(3) The minimum period referred to in subsection (2) above is—

(a) in the case of a yearly tenancy, six months;

(b) in the case of a tenancy where the period is less than a month, one month; and

(c) in any other case, a period equal to the period of the tenancy.

(4) Where a notice is served under subsection (2) above, a new rent specified in the notice shall take effect as mentioned in the notice unless, before the beginning of the new period specified in the notice,—

(a) the tenant by an application in the prescribed form refers the notice to a rent assessment committee; or

(b) the landlord and the tenant agree on a variation of the rent which is different from that proposed in the notice or agree that the rent should not be varied.

(5) Nothing in this section (or in section 14 below) affects the right of the landlord and the tenant under an assured tenancy to vary by agreement any term of the tenancy (including a term relating to rent).

Determination of rent by rent assessment committee
14.—(1) Where, under subsection (4)(a) of section 13 above, a tenant refers to a rent assessment committee a notice under subsection (2) of that section, the committee shall determine the rent at which, subject to subsections (2) and (4) below, the committee consider that the dwelling-house concerned might reasonably be expected to be let in the open market by a willing landlord under an assured tenancy—

(a) which is a periodic tenancy having the same periods as those of the tenancy to which the notice relates;

(b) which begins at the beginning of the new period specified in the notice;

(c) the terms of which (other than relating to the amount of the rent) are the same as those of the tenancy to which the notice relates; and

(d) in respect of which the same notices, if any, have been given under any of Grounds 1 to 5 of Schedule 2 to this Act, as have been given (or have effect as if given) in relation to the tenancy to which the notice relates.

(2) In making a determination under this section, there shall be disregarded—

(a) any effect on the rent attributable to the granting of a tenancy to a sitting tenant;

(b) any increase in the value of the dwelling-house attributable to a relevant improvement carried out by a person who at the time it was carried out was the tenant, if the improvement—

(i) was carried out otherwise than in pursuance of an obligation to his immediate landlord, or

(ii) was carried out pursuant to an obligation to his immediate landlord being an obligation which did not relate to the specific improvement concerned but arose by reference to consent given to the carrying out of that improvement; and

(c) any reduction in the value of the dwelling-house attributable to a failure by the tenant to comply with any terms of the tenancy.

(3) For the purposes of subsection (2)(b) above, in relation to a notice which is referred by a tenant as mentioned in subsection (1) above, an improvement is a relevant improvement if either it was carried out during the tenancy to which the notice relates or the following conditions are satisfied, namely—

(a) that it was carried out not more than 21 years before the date of service of the notice; and

(b) that, at all times during the period beginning when the improvement was carried out and ending on the date of service of the notice, the dwelling-house has been let under an assured tenancy; and

(c) that, on the coming to an end of an assured tenancy at any time during that period, the tenant (or, in the case of joint tenants, at least one of them) did not quit.

(4) In this section 'rent' does not include any service charge, within the meaning of section 18 of the Landlord and Tenant Act 1985, but, subject to that, includes any sums payable by the tenant to the landlord on account of the use of furniture or for any of the matters referred to in subsection (1)(a) of that section, whether or not those sums are separate from the sums payable for the occupation of the dwelling-house concerned or are payable under separate agreements.

(5) Where any rates in respect of the dwelling-house concerned are borne by the landlord or a superior landlord, the rent assessment committee shall make their determination under this section as if the rates were not so borne.

(6) In any case where—

(a) a rent assessment committee have before them at the same time the reference of a notice under section 6(2) above relating to a tenancy (in this subsection referred to as 'the section 6 reference') and the reference of a notice under section 13(2) above relating to the same tenancy (in this subsection referred to as 'the section 13 reference'), and

(b) the date specified in the notice under section 6(2) above is not later than the first day of the new period specified in the notice under section 13(2) above, and

(c) the committee propose to hear the two references together,

the committee shall make a determination in relation to the section 6 reference before making their determination in relation to the section 13 reference and, accordingly, in such a case the reference in subsection (1)(c) above to the terms of the tenancy to which the notice relates shall be construed as a reference to those terms as varied by virtue of the determination made in relation to the section 6 reference.

(7) Where a notice under section 13(2) above has been referred to a rent assessment committee, then, unless the landlord and the tenant otherwise agree, the rent determined by the committee (subject, in a case where subsection (5) above applies, to the addition of the appropriate amount in respect of rates) shall be the rent under the tenancy with effect from the beginning of the new period specified in the notice or, if it appears to the rent assessment committee that that would cause undue hardship to the tenant, with effect from such later date (not being later than the date the rent is determined) as the committee may direct.

(8) Nothing in this section requires a rent assessment committee to continue with their determination of a rent for a dwelling-house if the landlord and tenant give notice in writing that they no longer require such a determination or if the tenancy has come to an end.

Limited prohibition on assignment etc. without consent
15.—(1) Subject to subsection (3) below, it shall be an implied term of every assured tenancy which is a periodic tenancy that, except with the consent of the landlord, the tenant shall not—

(a) assign the tenancy (in whole or in part); or

(b) sublet or part with possession of the whole or any part of the dwelling-house let on the tenancy.

(2) Section 19 of the Landlord and Tenant Act 1927 (consents to assign not to be unreasonably withheld etc.) shall not apply to a term which is implied into an assured tenancy by subsection (1) above.

(3) In the case of a periodic tenancy which is not a statutory periodic tenancy subsection (1) above does not apply if—

(a) there is a provision (whether contained in the tenancy or not) under which the tenant is prohibited (whether absolutely or conditionally) from assigning or subletting or parting with possession or is permitted (whether absolutely or conditionally) to assign, sublet or part with possession; or

(b) a premium is required to be paid on the grant or renewal of the tenancy.

(4) In subsection (3)(b) above 'premium' includes—

(a) any fine or other like sum;

(b) any other pecuniary consideration in addition to rent; and

(c) any sum paid by way of deposit, other than one which does not exceed one-sixth of the annual rent payable under the tenancy immediately after the grant or renewal in question.

Access for repairs

16. It shall be an implied term of every assured tenancy that the tenant shall afford to the landlord access to the dwelling-house let on the tenancy and all reasonable facilities for executing therein any repairs which the landlord is entitled to execute.

Miscellaneous

Succession to assured periodic tenancy by spouse

17.—(1) In any case where—

(a) the sole tenant under an assured periodic tenancy dies, and

(b) immediately before the death, the tenant's spouse was occupying the dwelling-house as his or her only or principal home, and

(c) the tenant was not himself a successor, as defined in subsection (2) or subsection (3) below,

then, on the death, the tenancy vests by virtue of this section in the spouse (and, accordingly, does not devolve under the tenant's will or intestacy).

(2) For the purposes of this section, a tenant is a successor in relation to a tenancy if—

(a) the tenancy became vested in him either by virtue of this section or under the will or intestacy of a previous tenant; or

(b) at some time before the tenant's death the tenancy was a joint tenancy held by himself and one or more other persons and, prior to his death, he became the sole tenant by survivorship; or

(c) he became entitled to the tenancy as mentioned in section 39(5) below.

(3) For the purposes of this section, a tenant is also a successor in relation to

a tenancy (in this subsection referred to as 'the new tenancy') which was granted to him (alone or jointly with others) if—

(a)   at some time before the grant of the new tenancy, he was, by virtue of subsection (2) above, a successor in relation to an earlier tenancy of the same or substantially the same dwelling-house as is let under the new tenancy; and

(b)   at all times since he became such a successor he has been a tenant (alone or jointly with others) of the dwelling-house which is let under the new tenancy or of a dwelling-house which is substantially the same as that dwelling-house.

(4)   For the purposes of this section, a person who was living with the tenant as his or her wife or husband shall be treated as the tenant's spouse.

(5)   If, on the death of the tenant, there is, by virtue of subsection (4) above, more than one person who fulfils the condition in subsection (1)(b) above, such one of them as may be decided by agreement or, in default of agreement, by the county court shall be treated as the tenant's spouse for the purposes of this section.

Provisions as to reversions on assured tenancies
18.—(1)   If at any time—

(a)   a dwelling-house is for the time being lawfully let on an assured tenancy, and

(b)   the landlord under the assured tenancy is himself a tenant under a superior tenancy; and

(c)   the superior tenancy comes to an end,

then, subject to subsection (2) below, the assured tenancy shall continue in existence as a tenancy held of the person whose interest would, apart from the continuance of the assured tenancy, entitle him to actual possession of the dwelling-house at that time.

(2)   Subsection (1) above does not apply to an assured tenancy if the interest which, by virtue of that subsection, would become that of the landlord, is such that, by virtue of Schedule 1 to this Act, the tenancy could not be an assured tenancy.

(3)   Where, by virtue of any provision of this Part of this Act, an assured tenancy which is a periodic tenancy (including a statutory periodic tenancy) continues beyond the beginning of a reversionary tenancy which was granted (whether before, on or after the commencement of this Act) so as to begin on or after—

(a)   the date on which the previous contractual assured tenancy came to an end, or

(b)   a date on which, apart from any provision of this Part, the periodic tenancy could have been brought to an end by the landlord by notice to quit,

the reversionary tenancy shall have effect as if it had been granted subject to the periodic tenancy.

(4)   The reference in subsection (3) above to the previous contractual assured tenancy applies only where the periodic tenancy referred to in that subsection is a statutory periodic tenancy and is a reference to the fixed-term tenancy which immediately preceded the statutory periodic tenancy.

Restriction on levy of distress for rent
19.—(1)   Subject to subsection (2) below, no distress for the rent of any dwelling-house let on an assured tenancy shall be levied except with the leave of the county court; and, with respect to any application for such leave, the court shall have the same powers with respect to adjournment, stay, suspension, postponement and otherwise as are conferred by section 9 above in relation to proceedings for possession of such a dwelling-house.

(2)   Nothing in subsection (1) above applies to distress levied under section 102 of the County Courts Act 1984.

Chapter II Assured shorthold tenancies

Assured shorthold tenancies
20.—(1)   Subject to subsection (3) below, an assured shorthold tenancy is an assured tenancy—

(a)   which is a fixed-term tenancy granted for a term certain of not less than six months; and

(b)   in respect of which there is no power for the landlord to determine the tenancy at any time earlier than six months from the beginning of the tenancy; and

(c)   in respect of which a notice is served as mentioned in subsection (2) below.

(2)   The notice referred to in subsection (1)(c) above is one which—

(a)   is in such form as may be prescribed;

(b)   is served before the assured tenancy is entered into;

(c)   is served by the person who is to be the landlord under the assured tenancy on the person who is to be the tenant under that tenancy; and

(d)   states that the assured tenancy to which it relates is to be a shorthold tenancy.

(3)   Notwithstanding anything in subsection (1) above, where—

(a)   immediately before a tenancy (in this subsection referred to as 'the new tenancy') is granted, the person to whom it is granted or, as the case may be, at least one of the persons to whom it is granted was a tenant under an assured tenancy which was not a shorthold tenancy, and

(b)   the new tenancy is granted by the person who, immediately before the beginning of the tenancy, was the landlord under the assured tenancy referred to in paragraph (a) above,

the new tenancy cannot be an assured shorthold tenancy.

(4)   Subject to subsection (5) below, if, on the coming to an end of an assured shorthold tenancy (including a tenancy which was an assured shorthold but ceased to be assured before it came to an end), a new tenancy of the same or substantially the same premises comes into being under which the landlord and the tenant are the same as at the coming to an end of the earlier tenancy, then, if and so long as the new tenancy is an assured tenancy, it shall be an assured

shorthold tenancy, whether or not it fulfils the conditions in paragraphs (a) to (c) of subsection (1) above.

(5)   Subsection (4) above does not apply if, before the new tenancy is entered into (or, in the case of a statutory periodic tenancy, takes effect in possession), the landlord serves notice on the tenant that the new tenancy is not to be a shorthold tenancy.

(6)   In the case of joint landlords—

(a)   the reference in subsection (2)(c) above to the person who is to be the landlord is a reference to at least one of the persons who are to be joint landlords; and

(b)   the reference in subsection (5) above to the landlord is a reference to at least one of the joint landlords.

(7)   Section 14 above shall apply in relation to an assured shorthold tenancy as if in subsection (1) of that section the reference to an assured tenancy were a reference to an assured shorthold tenancy.

Recovery of possession on expiry or termination of assured shorthold tenancy
21.—(1)   Without prejudice to any right of the landlord under an assured shorthold tenancy to recover possession of the dwelling-house let on the tenancy in accordance with Chapter I above, on or after the coming to an end of an assured shorthold tenancy which was a fixed-term tenancy, a court shall make an order for possession of the dwelling-house if it is satisfied—

(a)   that the assured shorthold tenancy has come to an end and no further assured tenancy (whether shorthold or not) is for the time being in existence, other than a statutory periodic tenancy; and

(b)   the landlord or, in the case of joint landlords, at least one of them has given to the tenant not less than two months' notice stating that he requires possession of the dwelling-house.

(2)   A notice under paragraph (b) of subsection (1) above may be given before or on the day on which the tenancy comes to an end; and that subsection shall have effect notwithstanding that on the coming to an end of the fixed-term tenancy a statutory periodic tenancy arises.

(3)   Where a court makes an order for possession of a dwelling-house by virtue of subsection (1) above, any statutory periodic tenancy which has arisen on the coming to an end of the assured shorthold tenancy shall end (without further notice and regardless of the period) on the day on which the order takes effect.

(4)   Without prejudice to any such right as is referred to in subsection (1) above, a court shall make an order for possession of a dwelling-house let on an assured shorthold tenancy which is a periodic tenancy if the court is satisfied—

(a)   that the landlord or, in the case of joint landlords, at least one of them has given to the tenant a notice stating that, after a date specified in the notice, being the last day of a period of the tenancy and not earlier than two months after the date the notice was given, possession of the dwelling-house is required by virtue of this section; and

(b)   that the date specified in the notice under paragraph (a) above is not earlier than the earliest day on which, apart from section 5(1) above, the tenancy could be brought to an end by a notice to quit given by the landlord on the same date as the notice under paragraph (a) above.

Reference of excessive rents to rent assessment committee
22.—(1)   Subject to section 23 and subsection (2) below, the tenant under an assured shorthold tenancy in respect of which a notice was served as mentioned in section 20(2) above may make an application in the prescribed form to a rent assessment committee for a determination of the rent which, in the committee's opinion, the landlord might reasonably be expected to obtain under the assured shorthold tenancy.

(2)   No application may be made under this section if—

(a)   the rent payable under the tenancy is a rent previously determined under this section; or

(b)   the tenancy is an assured shorthold tenancy falling within subsection (4) of section 20 above (and, accordingly, is one in respect of which notice need not have been served as mentioned in subsection (2) of that section).

(3)   Where an application is made to a rent assessment committee under subsection (1) above with respect to the rent under an assured shorthold tenancy, the committee shall not make such a determination as is referred to in that subsection unless they consider—

(a)   that there is a sufficient number of similar dwelling-houses in the locality let on assured tenancies (whether shorthold or not); and

(b)   that the rent payable under the assured shorthold tenancy in question is significantly higher than the rent which the landlord might reasonably be expected to be able to obtain under the tenancy, having regard to the level of rents payable under the tenancies referred to in paragraph (a) above.

(4)   Where, on an application under this section, a rent assessment committee make a determination of a rent for an assured shorthold tenancy—

(a)   the determination shall have effect from such date as the committee may direct, not being earlier than the date of the application;

(b)   if, at any time on or after the determination takes effect, the rent which, apart from this paragraph, would be payable under the tenancy exceeds the rent so determined, the excess shall be irrecoverable from the tenant; and

(c)   no notice may be served under section 13(2) above with respect to a tenancy of the dwelling-house in question until after the first anniversary of the date on which the determination takes effect.

(5)   Subsections (4), (5) and (8) of section 14 above apply in relation to a determination of rent under this section as they apply in relation to a determination under that section and, accordingly, where subsection (5) of that section applies, any reference in subsection (4)(b) above to rent is a reference to rent exclusive of the amount attributable to rates.

Termination of rent assessment committee's functions
23.—(1)   If the Secretary of State by order made by statutory instrument so provides, section 22 above shall not apply in such cases or to tenancies of

dwelling-houses in such areas or in such other circumstances as may be specified in the order.

(2) An order under this section may contain such transitional, incidental and supplementary provisions as appear to the Secretary of State to be desirable.

(3) No order shall be made under this section unless a draft of the order has been laid before, and approved by a resolution of, each House of Parliament.

Chapter III Assured agricultural occupancies

Assured agricultural occupancies

24.—(1) A tenancy or licence of a dwelling-house is for the purposes of this Part of this Act an 'assured agricultural occupancy' if—

(a) it is of a description specified in subsection (2) below; and

(b) by virtue of any provision of Schedule 3 to this Act the agricultural worker condition is for the time being fulfilled with respect to the dwelling-house subject to the tenancy or licence.

(2) The following are the tenancies and licences referred to in subsection (1)(a) above—

(a) an assured tenancy which is not an assured shorthold tenancy;

(b) a tenancy which does not fall within paragraph (a) above by reason only of paragraph 3 or paragraph 7 of Schedule 1 to this Act (or of both of those paragraphs); and

(c) a licence under which a person has the exclusive occupation of a dwelling-house as a separate dwelling and which, if it conferred a sufficient interest in land to be a tenancy, would be a tenancy falling within paragraph (a) or paragraph (b) above.

(3) For the purposes of Chapter I above and the following provisions of this Chapter, every assured agricultural occupancy which is not an assured tenancy shall be treated as if it were such a tenancy and any reference to a tenant, a landlord or any other expression appropriate to a tenancy shall be construed accordingly; but the provisions of Chapter I above shall have effect in relation to every assured agricultural occupancy subject to the provisions of this Chapter.

(4) Section 14 above shall apply in relation to an assured agricultural occupancy as if in subsection (1) of that section the reference to an assured tenancy were a reference to an assured agricultural occupancy.

Security of tenure

25.—(1) If a statutory periodic tenancy arises on the coming to an end of an assured agricultural occupancy—

(a) it shall be an assured agricultural occupancy as long as, by virtue of any provision of Schedule 3 to this Act, the agricultural worker condition is for the time being fulfilled with respect to the dwelling-house in question; and

(b) if no rent was payable under the assured agricultural occupancy which constitutes the fixed-term tenancy referred to in subsection (2) of section 5 above, subsection (3)(d) of that section shall apply as if for the words 'the same as those for which rent was last payable under' there were substituted 'monthly beginning on the day following the coming to an end of'.

(2)   In its application to an assured agricultural occupancy, Part II of Schedule 2 to this Act shall have effect with the omission of Ground 16.

(3)   In its application to an assured agricultural occupancy, Part III of Schedule 2 to this Act shall have effect as if any reference in paragraph 2 to an assured tenancy included a reference to an assured agricultural occupancy.

(4)   If the tenant under an assured agricultural occupancy gives notice to terminate his employment then, notwithstanding anything in any agreement or otherwise, that notice shall not constitute a notice to quit as respects the assured agricultural occupancy.

(5)   Nothing in subsection (4) above affects the operation of an actual notice to quit given in respect of an assured agricultural occupancy.

Rehousing of agricultural workers etc.
26.   In section 27 of the Rent (Agriculture) Act 1976 (rehousing: applications to housing authority)—

(a)   in subsection (1)(a) after 'statutory tenancy' there shall be inserted 'or an assured agricultural occupancy'; and

(b)   at the end of subsection (3) there shall be added 'and assured agricultural occupancy has the same meaning as in Chapter III of Part I of the Housing Act 1988'.

Chapter IV Protection from eviction

Damages for unlawful eviction
27.—(1)   This section applies if, at any time after 9 June 1988, a landlord (in this section referred to as 'the landlord in default') or any person acting on behalf of the landlord in default unlawfully deprives the residential occupier of any premises of his occupation of the whole or part of the premises.

(2)   This section also applies if, at any time after 9 June 1988, a landlord (in this section referred to as 'the landlord in default') or any person acting on behalf of the landlord in default—

(a)   attempts unlawfully to deprive the residential occupier of any premises of his occupation of the whole or part of the premises, or

(b)   knowing or having reasonable cause to believe that the conduct is likely to cause the residential occupier of any premises—

(i)   to give up his occupation of the premises or any part thereof, or

(ii)   to refrain from exercising any right or pursuing any remedy in respect of the premises or any part thereof,

does acts likely to interfere with the peace or comfort of the residential occupier or members of his household, or persistently withdraws or withholds services reasonably required for the occupation of the premises as a residence,

and, as a result, the residential occupier gives up his occupation of the premises as a residence.

(3)   Subject to the following provisions of this section, where this section applies, the landlord in default shall, by virtue of this section, be liable to pay to the former residential occupier, in respect of his loss of the right to occupy the premises in question as his residence, damages assessed on the basis set out in section 28 below.

(4)   Any liability arising by virtue of subsection (3) above—

(a)   shall be in the nature of a liability in tort; and

(b)   subject to subsection (5) below, shall be in addition to any liability arising apart from this section (whether in tort, contract or otherwise).

(5)   Nothing in this section affects the right of a residential occupier to enforce any liability which arises apart from this section in respect of his loss of the right to occupy premises as his residence; but damages shall not be awarded both in respect of such a liability and in respect of a liability arising by virtue of this section on account of the same loss.

(6)   No liability shall arise by virtue of subsection (3) above if—

(a)   before the date on which proceedings to enforce the liability are finally disposed of, the former residential occupier is reinstated in the premises in question in such circumstances that he becomes again the residential occupier of them; or

(b)   at the request of the former residential occupier, a court makes an order (whether in the nature of an injunction or otherwise) as a result of which he is reinstated as mentioned in paragraph (a) above;

and, for the purposes of paragraph (a) above, proceedings to enforce a liability are finally disposed of on the earliest date by which the proceedings (including any proceedings on or in consequence of an appeal) have been determined and any time for appealing or further appealing has expired, except that if any appeal is abandoned, the proceedings shall be taken to be disposed of on the date of the abandonment.

(7)   If, in proceedings to enforce a liability arising by virtue of subsection (3) above, it appears to the court—

(a)   that, prior to the event which gave rise to the liability, the conduct of the former residential occupier or any person living with him in the premises concerned was such that it is reasonable to mitigate the damages for which the landlord in default would otherwise be liable, or

(b)   that, before the proceedings were begun, the landlord in default offered to reinstate the former residential occupier in the premises in question and either it was unreasonable of the former residential occupier to refuse that offer or, if he had obtained alternative accommodation before the offer was made, it would have been unreasonable of him to refuse that offer if he had not obtained that accommodation,

the court may reduce the amount of damages which would otherwise be payable to such amount as it thinks appropriate.

(8)   In proceedings to enforce a liability arising by virtue of subsection (3) above, it shall be a defence for the defendant to prove that he believed, and had reasonable cause to believe—

(a)   that the residential occupier had ceased to reside in the premises in question at the time when he was deprived of occupation as mentioned in subsection (1) above or, as the case may be, when the attempt was made or the acts were done as a result of which he gave up his occupation of those premises; or

(b)   that, where the liability would otherwise arise by virtue only of the doing of acts or the withdrawal or withholding of services, he had reasonable grounds for doing the acts or withdrawing or withholding the services in question.

(9)   In this section—

(a)   'residential occupier', in relation to any premises, has the same meaning as in section 1 of the 1977 Act;

(b)   'the right to occupy', in relation to a residential occupier, includes any restriction on the right of another person to recover possession of the premises in question;

(c)   'landlord', in relation to a residential occupier, means the person who, but for the occupier's right to occupy, would be entitled to occupation of the premises and any superior landlord under whom that person derives title;

(d)   'former residential occupier', in relation to any premises, means the person who was the residential occupier until he was deprived of or gave up his occupation as mentioned in subsection (1) or subsection (2) above (and, in relation to a former residential occupier, 'the right to occupy' and 'landlord' shall be construed accordingly).

The measure of damages
28.—(1)   The basis for the assessment of damages referred to in section 27(3) above is the difference in value, determined as at the time immediately before the residential occupier ceased to occupy the premises in question as his residence, between—

(a)   the value of the interest of the landlord in default determined on the assumption that the residential occupier continues to have the same right to occupy the premises as before that time; and

(b)   the value of that interest determined on the assumption that the residential occupier has ceased to have that right.

(2)   In relation to any premises, any reference in this section to the interest of the landlord in default is a reference to his interest in the building in which the premises in question are comprised (whether or not that building contains any other premises) together with its curtilage.

(3)   For the purposes of the valuations referred to in subsection (1) above, it shall be assumed—

(a)   that the landlord in default is selling his interest on the open market to a willing buyer;

(b)   that neither the residential occupier nor any member of his family wishes to buy; and

(c)   that it is unlawful to carry out any substantial development of any of the land in which the landlord's interest subsists or to demolish the whole or part of any building on that land.

(4)   In this section 'the landlord in default' has the same meaning as in section 27 above and subsection (9) of that section applies in relation to this section as it applies in relation to that.

(5)   Section 113 of the Housing Act 1985 (meaning of 'members of a person's family') applies for the purposes of subsection (3)(b) above.

(6)   The reference in subsection (3)(c) above to substantial development of any of the land in which the landlord's interest subsists is a reference to any development other than—

(a)   development for which planning permission is granted by a general development order for the time being in force and which is carried out so as to comply with any condition or limitation subject to which planning permission is so granted; or

(b)   a change of use resulting in the building referred to in subsection (2) above or any part of it being used as, or as part of, one or more dwelling-houses;

and in this subsection 'general development order' has the same meaning as in section 43(3) of the Town and Country Planning Act 1971 and other expressions have the same meaning as in that Act.

Offences of harassment

29.—(1)   In section 1 of the 1977 Act (unlawful eviction and harassment of occupier), with respect to acts done after the commencement of this Act, subsection (3) shall have effect with the substitution, for the word 'calculated', of the word 'likely'.

(2)   After that subsection there shall be inserted the following subsections—

'(3A)   Subject to subsection (3B) below, the landlord of a residential occupier or an agent of the landlord shall be guilty of an offence if—

(a)   he does acts likely to interfere with the peace or comfort of the residential occupier or members of his household, or

(b)   he persistently withdraws or withholds services reasonably required for the occupation of the premises in question as a residence,

and (in either case) he knows, or has reasonable cause to believe, that that conduct is likely to cause the residential occupier to give up the occupation of the whole or part of the premises or to refrain from exercising any right or pursuing any remedy in respect of the whole or part of the premises.

(3B)   A person shall not be guilty of an offence under subsection (3A) above if he proves that he had reasonable grounds for doing the acts or withdrawing or withholding the services in question.

(3C)   In subsection (3A) above 'landlord', in relation to a residential occupier of any premises, means the person who, but for—

(a)   the residential occupier's right to remain in occupation of the premises, or

(b)   a restriction on the person's right to recover possession of the premises,

would be entitled to occupation of the premises and any superior landlord under whom that person derives title.'

Variation of scope of 1977 ss. 3 and 4

30.—(1) In section 3 of the 1977 Act (prohibition of eviction without due process of law), in subsection (1) for the words 'not a statutorily protected tenancy' there shall be substituted 'neither a statutorily protected tenancy nor an excluded tenancy'.

(2) After subsection (2A) of that section there shall be inserted the following subsections—

'(2B) Subsections (1) and (2) above apply in relation to any premises occupied as a dwelling under a licence, other than an excluded licence, as they apply in relation to premises let as a dwelling under a tenancy, and in those subsections the expressions "let" and "tenancy" shall be construed accordingly.

(2C) References in the preceding provisions of this section and section 4(2A) below to an excluded tenancy do not apply to—

(a) a tenancy entered into before the date on which the Housing Act 1988 came into force, or

(b) a tenancy entered into on or after that date but pursuant to a contract made before that date,

but, subject to that, "excluded tenancy" and "excluded licence" shall be construed in accordance with section 3A below.'

(3) In section 4 of the 1977 Act (special provisions for agricultural employees) after subsection (2) there shall be inserted the following subsection—

'(2A) In accordance with section 3(2B) above, any reference in subsections (1) and (2) above to the tenant under the former tenancy includes a reference to the licensee under a licence (other than an excluded licence) which has come to an end (being a licence to occupy premises as a dwelling); and in the following provisions of this section the expressions "tenancy" and "rent" and any other expressions referable to a tenancy shall be construed accordingly.'

Excluded tenancies and licences

31. After section 3 of the 1977 Act there shall be inserted the following section—

'*Excluded tenancies and licences*

3A.—(1) Any reference in this Act to an excluded tenancy or an excluded licence is a reference to a tenancy or licence which is excluded by virtue of any of the following provisions of this section.

(2) A tenancy or licence is excluded if—

(a) under its terms the occupier shares any accommodation with the landlord or licensor; and

(b) immediately before the tenancy or licence was granted and also at the time it comes to an end, the landlord or licensor occupied as his only or principal home premises of which the whole or part of the shared accommodation formed part.

(3) A tenancy or licence is also excluded if—

(a) under its terms the occupier shares any accommodation with a member of the family of the landlord or licensor;

(b) immediately before the tenancy or licence was granted and also at the time it comes to an end, the member of the family of the landlord or licensor occupied as his only or principal home premises of which the whole or part of the shared accommodation formed part; and

(c) immediately before the tenancy or licence was granted and also at the time it comes to an end, the landlord or licensor occupied as his only or principal home premises in the same building as the shared accommodation and that building is not a purpose-built block of flats.

(4) For the purposes of subsections (2) and (3) above, an occupier shares accommodation with another person if he has the use of it in common with that person (whether or not also in common with others) and any reference in those subsections to shared accommodation shall be construed accordingly, and if, in relation to any tenancy or licence, there is at any time more than one person who is the landlord or licensor, any reference in those subsections to the landlord or licensor shall be construed as a reference to any one of those persons.

(5) In subsections (2) to (4) above—

(a) "accommodation" includes neither an area used for storage nor a staircase, passage, corridor or other means of access;

(b) "occupier" means, in relation to a tenancy, the tenant and, in relation to a licence, the licensee; and

(c) "purpose-built block of flats" has the same meaning as in Part III of Schedule 1 to the Housing Act 1988;

and section 113 of the Housing Act 1985 shall apply to determine whether a person is for the purposes of subsection (3) above a member of another's family as it applies for the purposes of Part IV of that Act.

(6) A tenancy or licence is excluded if it was granted as a temporary expedient to a person who entered the premises in question or any other premises as a trespasser (whether or not, before the beginning of that tenancy or licence, another tenancy or licence to occupy the premises or any other premises had been granted to him).

(7) A tenancy or licence is excluded if—

(a) it confers on the tenant or licensee the right to occupy the premises for a holiday only; or

(b) it is granted otherwise than for money or money's worth.

(8) A licence is excluded if it confers rights of occupation in a hostel, within the meaning of the Housing Act 1985, which is provided by—

(a) the council of a county, district or London Borough, the Common Council of the City of London, the Council of the Isles of Scilly, the Inner London Education Authority, a joint authority within the meaning of the Local Government Act 1985 or a residuary body within the meaning of that Act;

(b) a development corporation within the meaning of the New Towns Act 1981;

(c) the Commission for the New Towns;

(d) an urban development corporation established by an order under section 135 of the Local Government, Planning and Land Act 1980;

(e) a housing action trust established under Part III of the Housing Act 1988;

(f) the Development Board for Rural Wales;

(g) the Housing Corporation or Housing for Wales;

(h) a housing trust which is a charity or a registered housing association, within the meaning of the Housing Associations Act 1985; or

(i) any other person who is, or who belongs to a class of person which is, specified in an order made by the Secretary of State.

(9) The power to make an order under subsection (8)(i) above shall be exercisable by statutory instrument which shall be subject to annulment in pursuance of a resolution of either House of Parliament.'

Notice to quit etc.

32.—(1) In section 5 of the 1977 Act (validity of notices to quit) at the beginning of subsection (1) there shall be inserted the words 'Subject to subsection (1B) below'.

(2) After subsection (1) of that section there shall be inserted the following subsections—

'(1A) Subject to subsection (1B) below, no notice by a licensor or a licensee to determine a periodic licence to occupy premises as a dwelling (whether the licence was granted before or after the passing of this Act) shall be valid unless—

(a) it is in writing and contains such information as may be prescribed, and

(b) it is given not less than four weeks before the date on which it is to take effect.

(1B) Nothing in subsection (1) or subsection (1A) above applies to—

(a) premises let on an excluded tenancy which is entered into on or after the date on which the Housing Act 1988 came into force unless it is entered into pursuant to a contract made before that date; or

(b) premises occupied under an excluded licence.'

Interpretation of Chapter IV and the 1977 Act

33.—(1) In this Chapter 'the 1977 Act' means the Protection from Eviction Act 1977.

(2) In section 8 of the 1977 Act (interpretation) at the end of subsection (1) (statutory protected tenancy) there shall be inserted—

'(e) an assured tenancy or assured agricultural occupancy under Part I of the Housing Act 1988.'

(3) At the end of that section there shall be added the following subsections—

'(4) In this Act "excluded tenancy" and "excluded licence" have the meaning assigned by section 3A of this Act.

(5) If, on or after the date on which the Housing Act 1988 came into force, the terms of an excluded tenancy or excluded licence entered into before that date are varied, then—

(a) if the variation affects the amount of the rent which is payable under the tenancy or licence, the tenancy or licence shall be treated for the purposes of sections 3(2C) and 5(1B) above as a new tenancy or licence entered into at the time of the variation; and

(b) if the variation does not affect the amount of the rent which is so payable, nothing in this Act shall affect the determination of the question whether the variation is such as to give rise to a new tenancy or licence.

(6) Any reference in subsection (5) above to a variation affecting the amount of the rent which is payable under a tenancy or licence does not include a reference to—

(a) a reduction or increase effected under Part III or Part VI of the Rent Act 1977 (rents under regulated tenancies and housing association tenancies), section 78 of that Act (power of rent tribunal in relation to restricted contracts) or sections 11 to 14 of the Rent (Agriculture) Act 1976; or

(b) a variation which is made by the parties and has the effect of making the rent expressed to be payable under the tenancy or licence the same as a rent for the dwelling which is entered in the register under Part IV or section 79 of the Rent Act 1977.'

Chapter V Phasing out of Rent Acts and other transitional provisions

New protected tenancies and agricultural occupancies restricted to special cases
34.—(1) A tenancy which is entered into on or after the commencement of this Act cannot be a protected tenancy, unless—

(a) it is entered into in pursuance of a contract made before the commencement of this Act; or

(b) it is granted to a person (alone or jointly with others) who, immediately before the tenancy was granted, was a protected or statutory tenant and is so granted by the person who at that time was the landlord (or one of the joint landlords) under the protected or statutory tenancy; or

(c) it is granted to a person (alone or jointly with others) in the following circumstances—

(i) prior to the grant of the tenancy, an order for possession of a dwelling-house was made against him (alone or jointly with others) on the court being satisfied as mentioned in section 98(1)(a) of, or Case 1 in Schedule 16 to, the Rent Act 1977 or Case 1 in Schedule 4 to the Rent (Agriculture) Act 1976 (suitable alternative accommodation available); and

(ii) the tenancy is of the premises which constitute the suitable alternative accommodation as to which the court was so satisfied; and

(iii) in the proceedings for possession the court considered that, in the circumstances, the grant of an assured tenancy would not afford the required security and, accordingly, directed that the tenancy would be a protected tenancy; or

(d) it is a tenancy in relation to which subsections (1) and (3) of section 38 below have effect in accordance with subsection (4) of that section.

(2) In subsection (1)(b) above 'protected tenant' and 'statutory tenant' do not include—

(a) a tenant under a protected shorthold tenancy;
(b) a protected or statutory tenant of a dwelling-house which was let under a protected shorthold tenancy which ended before the commencement of this Act and in respect of which at that commencement either there has been no grant of a further tenancy or any grant of a further tenancy has been to the person who, immediately before the grant, was in possession of the dwelling-house as a protected or statutory tenant;

and in this subsection 'protected shorthold tenancy' includes a tenancy which, in proceedings for possession under Case 19 in Schedule 15 to the Rent Act 1977, is treated as a protected shorthold tenancy.

(3) In any case where—

(a) by virtue of subsections (1) and (2) above, a tenancy entered into on or after the commencement of this Act is an assured tenancy, but
(b) apart from subsection (2) above, the effect of subsection (1)(b) above would be that the tenancy would be a protected tenancy, and
(c) the landlord and the tenant under the tenancy are the same as at the coming to an end of the protected or statutory tenancy which, apart from subsection (2) above, would fall within subsection (1)(b) above,

the tenancy shall be an assured shorthold tenancy (whether or not it fulfils the conditions in section 20(1) above) unless, before the tenancy is entered into, the landlord serves notice on the tenant that it is not to be a shorthold tenancy.

(4) A licence or tenancy which is entered into on or after the commencement of this Act cannot be a relevant licence or relevant tenancy for the purposes of the Rent (Agriculture) Act 1976 (in this subsection referred to as 'the 1976 Act') unless—

(a) it is entered into in pursuance of a contract made before the commencement of this Act; or
(b) it is granted to a person (alone or jointly with others) who, immediately before the licence or tenancy was granted, was a protected occupier or statutory tenant, within the meaning of the 1976 Act, and is so granted by the person who at that time was the landlord or licensor (or one of the joint landlords or licensors) under the protected occupancy or statutory tenancy in question.

(5) Except as provided in subsection (4) above, expressions used in this section have the same meaning as in the Rent Act 1977.

Removal of special regimes for tenancies of housing associations etc.

35.—(1)   In this section 'housing association tenancy' has the same meaning as in Part VI of the Rent Act 1977.

(2)   A tenancy which is entered into on or after the commencement of this Act cannot be a housing association tenancy unless—

(a)   it is entered into in pursuance of a contract made before the commencement of this Act; or

(b)   it is granted to a person (alone or jointly with others) who, immediately before the tenancy was granted, was a tenant under a housing association tenancy and is so granted by the person who at that time was the landlord under that housing association tenancy; or

(c)   it is granted to a person (alone or jointly with others) in the following circumstances—

(i)   prior to the grant of the tenancy, an order for possession of a dwelling-house was made against him (alone or jointly with others) on the court being satisfied as mentioned in paragraph (b) or paragraph (c) of subsection (2) of section 84 of the Housing Act 1985; and

(ii)   the tenancy is of the premises which constitute the suitable accommodation as to which the court was so satisfied; and

(iii)   in the proceedings for possession the court directed that the tenancy would be a housing association tenancy; or

(d)   it is a tenancy in relation to which subsections (1) and (3) of section 38 below have effect in accordance with subsection (4) of that section.

(3)   Where, on or after the commencement of this Act, a registered housing association, within the meaning of the Housing Associations Act 1985, grants a secure tenancy pursuant to an obligation under section 554(2A) of the Housing Act 1985 (as set out in Schedule 17 to this Act) then, in determining whether that tenancy is a housing association tenancy, it shall be assumed for the purposes only of section 86(2)(b) of the Rent Act 1977 (tenancy would be a protected tenancy but for section 15 or 16 of that Act) that the tenancy was granted before the commencement of this Act.

(4)   A tenancy or licence which is entered into on or after the commencement of this Act cannot be a secure tenancy unless—

(a)   the interest of the landlord belongs to a local authority, a new town corporation or an urban development corporation, all within the meaning of section 80 of the Housing Act 1985, a housing action trust established under Part III of this Act or the Development Board for Rural Wales; or

(b)   the interest of the landlord belongs to a housing cooperative within the meaning of section 27B of the Housing Act 1985 (agreements between local housing authorities and housing cooperatives) and the tenancy or licence is of a dwelling-house comprised in a housing cooperative agreement falling within that section; or

(c)   it is entered into in pursuance of a contract made before the commencement of this Act; or

(d)   it is granted to a person (alone or jointly with others) who, immediately before it was entered into, was a secure tenant and is so granted by the body which at that time was the landlord or licensor under the secure tenancy; or

(e)　it is granted to a person (alone or jointly with others) in the following circumstances—

(i)　prior to the grant of the tenancy or licence, an order for possession of a dwelling-house was made against him (alone or jointly with others) on the court being satisfied as mentioned in paragraph (b) or paragraph (c) of subsection (2) of section 84 of the Housing Act 1985; and

(ii)　the tenancy or licence is of the premises which constitute the suitable accommodation as to which the court was so satisfied; and

(iii)　in the proceedings for possession the court considered that, in the circumstances, the grant of an assured tenancy would not afford the required security and, accordingly, directed that the tenancy or licence would be a secure tenancy; or

(f)　it is granted pursuant to an obligation under section 554(2A) of the Housing Act 1985 (as set out in Schedule 17 to this Act).

(5)　If, on or after the commencement of this Act, the interest of the landlord under a protected or statutory tenancy becomes held by a housing association, a housing trust, the Housing Corporation or Housing for Wales, nothing in the preceding provisions of this section shall prevent the tenancy from being a housing association tenancy or a secure tenancy and, accordingly, in such a case section 80 of the Housing Act 1985 (and any enactment which refers to that section) shall have effect without regard to the repeal of provisions of that section effected by this Act.

(6)　In subsection (5) above 'housing association' and 'housing trust' have the same meaning as in the Housing Act 1985.

New restricted contracts limited to transitional cases
36.—(1)　A tenancy or other contract entered into after the commencement of this Act cannot be a restricted contract for the purposes of the Rent Act 1977 unless it is entered into in pursuance of a contract made before the commencement of this Act.

(2)　If the terms of a restricted contract are varied after this Act comes into force then, subject to subsection (3) below,—

(a)　if the variation affects the amount of the rent which, under the contract, is payable for the dwelling in question, the contract shall be treated as a new contract entered into at the time of the variation (and subsection (1) above shall have effect accordingly); and

(b)　if the variation does not affect the amount of the rent which, under the contract, is so payable, nothing in this section shall affect the determination of the question whether the variation is such as to give rise to a new contract.

(3)　Any reference in subsection (2) above to a variation affecting the amount of the rent which, under a contract, is payable for a dwelling does not include a reference to—

(a)　a reduction or increase effected under section 78 of the Rent Act 1977 (power of rent tribunal); or

(b)　a variation which is made by the parties and has the effect of making the rent expressed to be payable under the contract the same as the rent for the dwelling which is entered in the register under section 79 of the Rent Act 1977.

(4)　In subsection (1) of section 81A of the Rent Act 1977 (cancellation of registration of rent relating to a restricted contract) paragraph (a) (no cancellation until two years have elapsed since the date of the entry) shall cease to have effect.

(5)　In this section 'rent' has the same meaing as in Part V of the Rent Act 1977.

No further assured tenancies under Housing Act 1980
37.—(1)　A tenancy which is entered into on or after the commencement of this Act cannot be an assured tenancy for the purposes of sections 56 to 58 of the Housing Act 1980 (in this section referred to as a '1980 Act tenancy').

(2)　In any case where—

(a)　before the commencement of this Act, a tenant under a 1980 Act tenancy made an application to the court under section 24 of the Landlord and Tenant Act 1954 (for the grant of a new tenancy), and

(b)　at the commencement of this Act the 1980 Act tenancy is continuing by virtue of that section or of any provision of Part IV of the said Act of 1954,

section 1(3) of this Act shall not apply to the 1980 Act tenancy.

(3)　If, in a case falling within subsection (2) above, the court makes an order for the grant of a new tenancy under section 29 of the Landlord and Tenant Act 1954, that tenancy shall be an assured tenancy for the purposes of this Act.

(4)　In any case where—

(a)　before the commencement of this Act a contract was entered into for the grant of a 1980 Act tenancy, but

(b)　at the commencement of this Act the tenancy had not been granted,

the contract shall have effect as a contract for the grant of an assured tenancy (within the meaning of this Act).

(5)　In relation to an assured tenancy falling within subsection (3) above or granted pursuant to a contract falling within subsection (4) above, Part I of Schedule 1 to this Act shall have effect as if it consisted only of paragraphs 11 and 12; and, if the landlord granting the tenancy is a fully mutual housing association, then, so long as that association remains the landlord under that tenancy (and under any statutory periodic tenancy which arises on the coming to an end of that tenancy), the said paragraph 12 shall have effect in relation to that tenancy with the omission of sub-paragraph (1)(h).

(6)　Any reference in this section to a provision of the Landlord and Tenant Act 1954 is a reference only to that provision as applied by section 58 of the Housing Act 1980.

Transfer of existing tenancies from public to private sector
38.—(1)　The provisions of subsection (3) below apply in relation to a tenancy which was entered into before, or pursuant to a contract made before, the commencement of this Act if,—

(a)　at that commencement or, if it is later, at the time it is entered into, the interest of the landlord is held by a public body (within the meaning of subsection (5) below); and

(b) at some time after that commencement, the interest of the landlord ceases to be so held.

(2) The provisions of subsection (3) below also apply in relation to a tenancy which was entered into before, or pursuant to a contract made before, the commencement of this Act if,—

(a) at the commencement of this Act or, if it is later, at the time it is entered into, it is a housing association tenancy; and

(b) at some time after that commencement, it ceases to be such a tenancy.

(3) On and after the time referred to in subsection (1)(b) or, as the case may be, subsection (2)(b) above—

(a) the tenancy shall not be capable of being a protected tenancy, a protected occupancy or a housing association tenancy;

(b) the tenancy shall not be capable of being a secure tenancy unless (and only at a time when) the interest of the landlord under the tenancy is (or is again) held by a public body; and

(c) paragraph 1 of Schedule 1 to this Act shall not apply in relation to it, and the question whether at any time thereafter it becomes (or remains) an assured tenancy shall be determined accordingly.

(4) In relation to a tenancy under which, at the commencement of this Act or, if it is later, at the time the tenancy is entered into, the interest of the landlord is held by a new town corporation, within the meaning of section 80 of the Housing Act 1985, subsections (1) and (3) above shall have effect as if any reference in subsection (1) above to the commencement of this Act were a reference to—

(a) the date on which expires the period of two years beginning on the day this Act is passed; or

(b) if the Secretary of State by order made by statutory instrument within that period so provides, such other date (whether earlier or later) as may be specified by the order for the purposes of this subsection.

(5) For the purposes of this section, the interest of a landlord under a tenancy is held by a public body at a time when—

(a) it belongs to a local authority, a new town corporation or an urban development corporation, all within the meaning of section 80 of the Housing Act 1985; or

(b) it belongs to a housing action trust established under Part III of this Act; or

(c) it belongs to the Development Board for Rural Wales; or

(d) it belongs to Her Majesty in right of the Crown or to a government department or is held in trust for Her Majesty for the purposes of a government department.

(6) In this section—

(a) 'housing association tenancy' means a tenancy to which Part VI of the Rent Act 1977 applies;

(b) 'protected tenancy' has the same meaning as in that Act; and

(c) 'protected occupancy' has the same meaning as in the Rent (Agriculture) Act 1976.

Statutory tenants: succession

39.—(1) In section 2(1)(b) of the Rent Act 1977 (which introduces the provisions of Part I of Schedule 1 to that Act relating to statutory tenants by succession) after the words 'statutory tenant of a dwelling-house' there shall be inserted 'or, as the case may be, is entitled to an assured tenancy of a dwelling-house by succession'.

(2) Where the person who is the original tenant, within the meaning of Part I of Schedule 1 to the Rent Act 1977, dies after the commencement of this Act, that Part shall have effect subject to the amendments in Part I of Schedule 4 to this Act.

(3) Where subsection (2) above does not apply but the person who is the first successor, within the meaning of Part I of Schedule 1 to the Rent Act 1977, dies after the commencement of this Act, that Part shall have effect subject to the amendments in paragraphs 5 to 9 of Part I of Schedule 4 to this Act.

(4) In any case where the original occupier, within the meaning of section 4 of the Rent (Agriculture) Act 1976 (statutory tenants and tenancies) dies after the commencement of this Act, that section shall have effect subject to the amendments in Part II of Schedule 4 to this Act.

(5) In any case where, by virtue of any provision of—

(a) Part I of Schedule 1 to the Rent Act 1977, as amended in accordance with subsection (2) or subsection (3) above, or

(b) section 4 of the Rent (Agriculture) Act 1976, as amended in accordance with subsection (4) above,

a person (in the following provisions of this section referred to as 'the successor') becomes entitled to an assured tenancy of a dwelling-house by succession, that tenancy shall be a periodic tenancy arising by virtue of this section.

(6) Where, by virtue of subsection (5) above, the successor becomes entitled to an assured periodic tenancy, that tenancy is one—

(a) taking effect in possession immediately after the death of the protected or statutory tenant or protected occupier (in the following provisions of this section referred to as 'the predecessor') on whose death the successor became so entitled;

(b) deemed to have been granted to the successor by the person who, immediately before the death of the predecessor, was the landlord of the predecessor under his tenancy;

(c) under which the premises which are let are the same dwelling-house, as immediately before his death, the predecessor occupied under his tenancy;

(d) under which the periods of the tenancy are the same as those for which rent was last payable by the predecessor under his tenancy;

(e) under which, subject to sections 13 to 15 above, the other terms are the same as those on which, under his tenancy, the predecessor occupied the dwelling-house immediately before his death; and

(f)   which, for the purposes of section 13(2) above, is treated as a statutory periodic tenancy;

and in paragraphs (b) to (e) above 'under his tenancy', in relation to the predecessor, means under his protected tenancy or protected occupancy or in his capacity as a statutory tenant.

(7)   If, immediately before the death of the predecessor, the landlord might have recovered possession of the dwelling-house under Case 19 in Schedule 15 to the Rent Act 1977, the assured periodic tenancy to which the successor becomes entitled shall be an assured shorthold tenancy (whether or not it fulfils the conditions in section 20(1) above).

(8)   If, immediately before his death, the predecessor was a protected occupier or statutory tenant within the meaning of the Rent (Agriculture) Act 1976, the assured periodic tenancy to which the successor becomes entitled shall be an assured agricultural occupancy (whether or not it fulfils the conditions in section 24(1) above).

(9)   Where, immediately before his death, the predecessor was a tenant under a fixed-term tenancy, section 6 above shall apply in relation to the assured periodic tenancy to which the successor becomes entitled on the predecessor's death subject to the following modifications—

(a)   for any reference to a statutory periodic tenancy there shall be substituted a reference to the assured periodic tenancy to which the successor becomes so entitled;

(b)   in subsection (1) of that section, paragraph (a) shall be omitted and the reference in paragraph (b) to section 5(3)(e) above shall be construed as a reference to subsection (6)(e) above; and

(c)   for any reference to the coming to an end of the former tenancy there shall be substituted a reference to the date of the predecessor's death.

(10)   If and so long as a dwelling-house is subject to an assured tenancy to which the successor has become entitled by succession, section 7 above and Schedule 2 to this Act shall have effect subject to the modifications in Part III of Schedule 4 to this Act; and in that Part 'the predecessor' and 'the successor' have the same meaning as in this section.

Chapter VI General provisions

Jurisdiction of county courts
40.—(1)   A county court shall have jurisdiction to hear and determine any question arising under any provision of—

(a)   Chapters I to III and V above, or
(b)   sections 27 and 28 above,

other than a question falling within the jurisdiction of a rent assessment committee by virtue of any such provision.

(2)   Subsection (1) above has effect notwithstanding that the damages claimed in any proceedings may exceed the amount which, for the time being, is the county court limit for the purposes of the County Courts Act 1984.

(3)   Where any proceedings under any provision mentioned in subsection (1) above are being taken in a county court, the court shall have jurisdiction to hear and determine any other proceedings joined with those proceedings, not withstanding that, apart from this subsection, those other proceedings would be outside the court's jurisdiction.

(4)   If any person takes any proceedings under any provision mentioned in subsection (1) above in the High Court, he shall not be entitled to recover any more costs of those proceedings than those to which he would have been entitled if the proceedings had been taken in a county court: and in such a case the taxing master shall have the same power of directing on what county court scale costs are to be allowed, and of allowing any item of costs, as the judge would have had if the proceedings had been taken in a county court.

(5)   Subsection (4) above shall not apply where the purpose of taking the proceedings in the High Court was to enable them to be joined with any proceedings already pending before that court (not being proceedings taken under any provision mentioned in subsection (1) above).

Rent assessment committees: procedure and information powers
41.—(1)   In section 74 of the Rent Act 1977 (regulations made by the Secretary of State) at the end of paragraph (b) of subsection (1) (procedure of rent officers and rent assessment committees) there shall be added the words 'whether under this Act or Part I of the Housing Act 1988'.

(2)   The rent assessment committee to whom a matter is referred under Chapter I or Chapter II above may by notice in the prescribed form served on the landlord or the tenant require him to give to the committee, within such period of not less than fourteen days from the service of the notice as may be specified in the notice, such information as they may reasonably require for the purposes of their functions.

(3)   If any person fails without reasonable excuse to comply with a notice served on him under subsection (2) above, he shall be liable on summary conviction to a fine not exceeding level 3 on the standard scale.

(4)   Where an offence under subsection (3) above committed by a body corporate is proved to have been committed with the consent or connivance of, or to be attributable to any neglect on the part of, any director, manager or secretary or other similar officer of the body corporate or any person who was purporting to act in any such capacity, he as well as the body corporate shall be guilty of that offence and shall be liable to be proceeded against and punished accordingly.

Information as to determinations of rents
42.—(1)   The President of every rent assessment panel shall keep and make publicly available, in such manner as is specified in an order made by the Secretary of State, such information as may be so specified with respect to rents under assured tenancies and assured agricultural occupancies which have been the subject of references or applications to, or determinations by, rent assessment committees.

(2)   A copy of any information certified under the hand of an officer duly authorised by the President of the rent assessment panel concerned shall be receivable in evidence in any court and in any proceedings.

(3)   An order under subsection (1) above—

(a)   may prescribe the fees to be charged for the supply of a copy, including a certified copy, of any of the information kept by virtue of that subsection; and

(b)   may make different provision with respect to different cases or descriptions of case, including different provision for different areas.

(4)   The power to make an order under subsection (1) above shall be exercisable by statutory instrument which shall be subject to annulment in pursuance of a resolution of either House of Parliament.

Powers of local authorities for purposes of giving information
43.   In section 149 of the Rent Act 1977 (which, among other matters, authorises local authorities to publish information for the benefit of landlords and tenants with respect to their rights and duties under certain enactments), in subsection (1)(a) after subparagraph (iv) there shall be inserted—

'(v)   Chapters I to III of Part I of the Housing Act 1988'.

Application to Crown property
44.—(1)   Subject to paragraph 11 of Schedule 1 to this Act and subsection (2) below, Chapters I to IV above apply in relation to premises in which there subsists, or at any material time subsisted, a Crown interest as they apply in relation to premises in relation to which no such interest subsists or ever subsisted.

(2)   In Chapter IV above—

(a)   sections 27 and 28 do not bind the Crown; and

(b)   the remainder binds the Crown to the extent provided for in section 10 of the Protection from Eviction Act 1977.

(3)   In this section 'Crown interest' means an interest which belongs to Her Majesty in right of the Crown or of the Duchy of Lancaster or to the Duchy of Cornwall, or to a government department, or which is held in trust for Her Majesty for the purposes of a government department.

(4)   Where an interest belongs to Her Majesty in right of the Duchy of Lancaster, then, for the purposes of Chapters I to IV above, the Chancellor of the Duchy of Lancaster shall be deemed to be the owner of the interest.

Interpretation of Part I
45.—(1)   In this Part of this Act, except where the context otherwise requires,—

'dwelling-house' may be a house or part of a house;

'fixed-term tenancy' means any tenancy other than a periodic tenancy;

'fully mutual housing association' has the same meaning as in Part I of the Housing Associations Act 1985;

'landlord' includes any person from time to time deriving title under the original landlord and also includes, in relation to a dwelling-house, any person other than a tenant who is, or but for the existence of an assured tenancy would be, entitled to possession of the dwelling-house;

'let' includes 'sublet';

'prescribed' means prescribed by regulations made by the Secretary of State by statutory instrument;

'rates' includes water rates and charges but does not include an owner's drainage rate, as defined in section 63(2)(a) of the Land Drainage Act 1976;

'secure tenancy' has the meaning assigned by section 79 of the Housing Act 1985;

'statutory periodic tenancy' has the meaning assigned by section 5(7) above;

'tenancy' includes a subtenancy and an agreement for a tenancy or subtenancy; and

'tenant' includes a subtenant and any person deriving title under the original tenant or subtenant.

(2)   Subject to paragraph 11 of Schedule 2 to this Act, any reference in this Part of this Act to the beginning of a tenancy is a reference to the day on which the tenancy is entered into or, if it is later, the day on which, under the terms of any lease, agreement or other document, the tenant is entitled to possession under the tenancy.

(3)   Where two or more persons jointly constitute either the landlord or the tenant in relation to a tenancy, then, except where this Part of this Act otherwise provides, any reference to the landlord or to the tenant is a reference to all the persons who jointly constitute the landlord or the tenant, as the case may require.

(4)   For the avoidance of doubt, it is hereby declared that any reference in this Part of this Act (however expressed) to a power for a landlord to determine a tenancy does not include a reference to a power of re-entry or forfeiture for breach of any term or condition of the tenancy.

(5)   Regulations under subsection (1) above may make different provision with respect to different cases or descriptions of case, including different provision for different areas.

Part II Housing associations

Housing for Wales

Housing for Wales

46.—(1)   There shall be a body known as Housing for Wales.

(2)   Schedule 5 to this Act shall have effect with respect to the constitution and proceedings of, and other matters relating to, Housing for Wales.

(3)   Housing for Wales shall have the functions conferred on it by the Housing Associations Act 1985 (in this Part referred to as 'the 1985 Act') as amended in accordance with section 59 below.

(4)   All property in Wales which, immediately before the day appointed for the coming into force of this section, is held by the Housing Corporation shall on that day be transferred to and vest in Housing for Wales.

(5)   Any question whether any property has been transferred to Housing for Wales by virtue of subsection (4) above shall be determined by the Secretary of State.

Transfer to Housing for Wales of regulation etc. of housing associations based in Wales

47.—(1)   Every registered housing association which, immediately before the appointed day,—

(a) is a society registered under the 1965 Act and has its registered office for the purposes of that Act in Wales, or

(b) is a registered charity and has its address for the purposes of registration by the Charity Commissioners in Wales,

shall on the appointed day cease to be registered in the register maintained by the Housing Corporation under section 3 of the 1985 Act and, by virtue of this subsection, be deemed to be registered in the register maintained by Housing for Wales under that section.

(2) Not later than one month before the appointed day, the Secretary of State shall notify every registered housing association which appears to him to be one which on that day will be deemed to be registered as mentioned in subsection (1) above of that fact and of the effect of that subsection.

(3) As soon as may be after the appointed day, Housing for Wales shall give notice of any registration effected by virtue of subsection (1) above,—

(a) if the housing association is a registered charity, to the Charity Commissioners; and

(b) if the housing association is a society registered under the 1965 Act, to the Chief Registrar of friendly societies.

(4) All rights, liabilities and obligations to which, immediately before the appointed day, the Housing Corporation was entitled or subject in relation to—

(a) any registered housing association to which subsection (1) above applies, and

(b) land in Wales held by an unregistered housing association,

shall on that day become rights, liabilities and obligations of Housing for Wales.

(5) Any question whether any rights, liabilities or obligations have become rights, liabilities or obligations of Housing for Wales by virtue of subsection (4) above shall be determined by the Secretary of State.

(6) In this section—

'the 1965 Act' means the Industrial and Provident Societies Act 1965; and 'the appointed day' means the day appointed for the coming into force of this section.

Registration and issue of guidance

Permissible purposes, objects or powers

48.—(1) For subsections (3) and (4) of section 4 (eligibility for registration) of the 1985 Act there shall be substituted the following subsections—

'(3) The permissible additional purposes or objects are—

(a) providing land, amenities or services, or providing, constructing, repairing or improving buildings, for the benefit of the association's residents, either exclusively or together with other persons;

(b) acquiring, or repairing and improving, or creating by the conversion of houses or other property, houses to be disposed of on sale, on lease or on shared ownership terms;

(c) constructing houses to be disposed of on shared ownership terms;

(d)   managing houses which are held on leases or other lettings (not being houses falling within subsection (2)(a) or (b)) or blocks of flats;

(e)   providing services of any description for owners or occupiers of houses in arranging or carrying out works of maintenance, repair or improvement, or encouraging or facilitating the carrying out of such works;

(f)   encouraging and giving advice on the formation of other housing associations or providing services for, and giving advice on the running of, such associations and other voluntary organisations concerned with housing, or matters connected with housing.

(4)   A housing association shall not be ineligible for registration by reason only that its powers include power—

(a)   to acquire commercial premises or businesses as an incidental part of a project or series of projects undertaken for purposes or objects falling within subsection (2) or (3);

(b)   to repair, improve or convert any commercial premises acquired as mentioned in paragraph (a) or to carry on, for a limited period, any business so acquired;

(c)   to repair or improve houses, or buildings in which houses are situated, after the tenants have exercised, or claimed to exercise, acquisition rights;

(d)   to acquire houses to be disposed of at a discount to tenants to whom section 58 of the Housing Act 1988 applies (tenants of charitable housing associations etc.).

(5)   In this section—

"acquisition right" means—

(a)   in England and Wales, the right to buy or the right to be granted a shared ownership lease under Part V of the Housing Act 1985;

(b)   in Scotland, a right to purchase under section 61 of the Housing (Scotland) Act 1987;

"block of flats" means a building—

(a)   containing two or more flats which are held on leases or other lettings; and

(b)   occupied or intended to be occupied wholly or mainly for residential purposes;

"disposed of on shared ownership terms" means—

(a)   in England and Wales, disposed of on a shared ownership lease;

(b)   in Scotland, disposed of under a shared ownership agreement;

"letting" includes the grant—

(a)   in England and Wales, of a licence to occupy;

(b)   in Scotland, of a right or permission to occupy;

"residents", in relation to a housing association, means the persons occupying the houses or hostels provided or managed by the association;
"voluntary organisation" means an organisation whose activities are not carried on for profit.'

(2)   The Secretary of State may by order made by statutory instrument amend the subsections substituted by subsection (1) above, but not so as to restrict or limit the permissible purposes, objects or powers.

(3)   An order under subsection (2) above may contain such incidental, supplemental or transitional provisions as the Secretary of State thinks fit.

(4)   A statutory instrument containing an order under subsection (2) above shall be subject to annulment in pursuance of a resolution of either House of Parliament.

Guidance as to management of accommodation by registered housing associations
49.   After section 36 of the 1985 Act there shall be inserted the following section—

'Issue of guidance by the Corporation
36A.—(1)   In accordance with the provisions of this section, the Corporation may issue guidance with respect to the management of housing accommodation by registered housing associations and, in considering under the preceding provisions of this Part whether action needs to be taken to secure the proper management of an association's affairs or whether there has been mismanagement, the Corporation may have regard (among other matters) to the extent to which any such guidance is being or has been followed.

(2)   Guidance issued under this section may make different provision in relation to different cases and, in particular, in relation to different areas, different descriptions of housing accommodation and different descriptions of registered housing associations.

(3)   Without prejudice to the generality of subsections (1) and (2), guidance issued under this section may relate to—

(a)   the housing demands for which provision should be made and the means of meeting those demands;

(b)   the allocation of housing accommodation between individuals;

(c)   the terms of tenancies and the principles upon which the levels of rent should be determined;

(d)   standards of maintenance and repair and the means of achieving these standards; and

(e)   consultation and communication with tenants.

(4)   Guidance issued under this section may be revised or withdrawn but, before issuing or revising any guidance under this section, the Corporation—

(a)   shall consult such bodies appearing to it to be representative of housing associations as it considers appropriate; and

(b)   shall submit a draft of the proposed guidance or, as the case may be, the proposed revision to the Secretary of State for his approval.

(5)   If the Secretary of State gives his approval to a draft submitted to him under subsection (4)(b), the Corportion shall issue the guidance or, as the case may be, the revision concerned in such manner as the Corporation considers appropriate for bringing it to the notice of the housing associations concerned.'

Grants: functions of Corporation

Housing association grants

50.—(1)   The Housing Corporation and Housing for Wales may make grants to registered housing associations in respect of expenditure incurred or to be incurred by them in connection with housing activities; and any reference in the following provisions of this section to 'the Corporation' shall be construed accordingly.

(2)   As respects grants under this section the following, namely—

(a)   the procedure to be followed in relation to applications for grant;

(b)   the circumstances in which grant is or is not to be payable;

(c)   the method for calculating, and any limitations on, the amount of grant; and

(d)   the manner in which, and time or times at which, grant is to be paid,

shall be such as may be specified by the Corporation, acting in accordance with such principles as it may from time to time determine.

(3)   In making a grant under this section, the Corporation may provide that the grant is conditional on compliance by the association with such conditions as it may specify.

(4)   On such terms as it may, with the appropriate approval, specify, the Corporation may appoint a local housing authority which is willing to do so to act as its agent in connection with the assessment and payment of grant under this section; and, where such an appointment is made, the local housing authority shall act as such an agent in accordance with the terms of their appointment.

(5)   In subsection (4) above, 'the appropriate approval' means the approval of the Secretary of State given with the consent of the Treasury.

(6)   Where—

(a)   a grant under this section is payable to an association, and

(b)   at any time property to which the grant relates becomes vested in, or is leased for a term of years to, or reverts to, some other registered housing association, or trustees for some other such association,

this section (including this subsection) shall have effect after that time as if the grant, or such proportion of it as is specified or determined under subsection (7) below, were payable to that other association.

(7)   The proportion referred to in subsection (6) above is that which, in the circumstances of the particular case—

(a)   the Corporation, acting in accordance with such principles as it may from time to time determine, may specify as being appropriate; or

(b)   the Corporation may determine to be appropriate.

(8)   Where one of the associations mentioned in subsection (6) above is

registered by the Housing Corporation and another is registered by Housing for Wales, the determination mentioned in subsection (7) above shall be such as shall be agreed between the two Corporations.

Revenue deficit grants
51.—(1) The Housing Corporation or, as the case may be, Housing for Wales may make a grant to a registered housing association if—

    (a) in relation to all housing activities of the association,
    (b) in relation to housing activities of the association of a particular description, or
    (c) in relation to particular housing activities of the association,

the association's expenditure as calculated by the Corporation concerned for any period (including a period which is wholly or partly a future period) exceeds its income as so calculated for that period.

    (2) In calculating an association's expenditure or income for the purposes of subsection (1) above, the Housing Corporation or, as the case may be, Housing for Wales—

    (a) shall act in accordance with such principles as it may from time to time determine; and
    (b) may act on such assumptions (whether or not borne out or likely to be borne out by events) as it may from time to time determine.

    (3) Subsections (2) and (3) of section 50 above shall apply for the purposes of this section as they apply for the purposes of that section.

Recovery etc. of grants
52.—(1) Where a grant to which this section applies, that is to say—

    (a) a grant under section 50 or 51 above, or
    (b) a grant under section 41 of the 1985 Act or any enactment replaced by that section, or
    (c) a grant under section 2(2) of the Housing (Scotland) Act 1988,

has been made to a registered housing association, the powers conferred by subsection (2) below are exercisable in such events (including the association not complying with any conditions) as the Corporation may from time to time determine (in this section referred to as 'relevant events').

    (2) The Corporation, acting in accordance with such principles as it may from time to time determine, may—

    (a) reduce the amount of, or of any payment in respect of, the grant;
    (b) suspend or cancel any instalment of the grant; or
    (c) direct the association to pay to it an amount equal to the whole, or such proportion as it may specify, of the amount of any payment made to the association in respect of the grant,

and a direction under paragraph (c) above requiring the payment of any amount may also require the payment of interest on that amount in accordance with subsections (7) to (9) below.

    (3) Where, after a grant to which this section applies has been made to an

association, a relevant event occurs, the association shall notify the Corporation and, if so required by written notice of the Corporation, shall furnish it with such particulars of and information relating to the event as are specified in the notice.

(4)   Where a grant to which this section applies (other than one falling within subsection (1)(c) above) has been made to an association, the Chief Land Registrar may furnish the Corporation with such particulars and information as it may reasonably require for the purpose of ascertaining whether a relevant event has occurred; but this subsection shall cease to have effect on the day appointed under section 3(2) of the Land Registration Act 1988 for the coming into force of that Act.

(5)   Where—

(a)   a grant to which this section applies has been made to an association, and

(b)   at any time property to which the grant relates becomes vested in, or is leased for a term of years to, or reverts to, some other registered housing association, or trustees for some other such association,

this section (including this subsection) shall have effect after that time as if the grant, or such proportion of it as is specified or determined under subsection (6) below, had been made to that other association.

(6)   The proportion referred to in subsection (5) above is that which, in the circumstances of the particular case,—

(a)   the Corporation, acting in accordance with such principles as it may from time to time determine, may specify as being appropriate; or

(b)   the Corporation may determine to be appropriate.

(7)   A direction under subsection (2)(c) above requiring the payment of interest on the amount directed to be paid to the Corporation shall specify, in accordance with subsection (9) below,—

(a)   the rate or rates of interest (whether fixed or variable) which is or are applicable;

(b)   the date from which interest is payable, being not earlier than the date of the relevant event; and

(c)   any provision for suspended or reduced interest which is applicable.

(8)   In subsection (7)(c) above—

(a)   the reference to a provision for suspended interest is a reference to a provision whereby, if the amount which is directed to be paid to the Corporation is paid before a date specified in the direction, no interest will be payable for any period after the date of the direction; and

(b)   the reference to a provision for reduced interest is a reference to a provision whereby, if that amount is so paid, any interest payable will be payable at a rate or rates lower than the rate or rates which would otherwise be applicable.

(9)   The matters specified in a direction as mentioned in paragraphs (a) to (c) of subsection (7) above shall be either—

(a)   such as the Corporation, acting in accordance with such principles as it may from time to time determine, may specify as being appropriate, or

(b) such as the Corporation may determine to be appropriate in the particular case.

Determinations under Part II

53.—(1) A general determination may either—

(a) make the same provision for all cases; or

(b) make different provision for different cases or descriptions of cases, including different provision for different areas or for different descriptions of housing associations or housing activities;

and for the purposes of this subsection descriptions may be framed by reference to any matters whatever, including in particular, in the case of housing activities, the manner in which they are financed.

(2) The Corporation shall not make a determination under the foregoing provisions of this Part except with the approval of the Secretary of State given, in the case of a general determination, with the consent of the Treasury.

(3) Before making a general determination, the Corporation shall consult such bodies appearing to it to be representative of housing associations as it considers appropriate; and after making such a determination, the Corporation shall publish the determination in such manner as it considers appropriate for bringing the determination to the notice of the associations concerned.

(4) In this section 'general determination' means a determination under any provision of sections 50 to 52 above, other than a determination relating solely to a particular case.

Grants: functions of Secretary of State

Tax relief grants

54.—(1) If a housing association makes a claim to the Secretary of State in respect of a period and satisfies him that throughout the period it was a housing association to which this section applies and its functions either—

(a) consisted exclusively of the function of providing or maintaining housing accommodation for letting or hostels and activities incidental to that function, or

(b) included that function and activities incidental to that function,

the Secretary of State may make grants to the association for affording relief from tax chargeable on the association.

(2) This section applies to a housing association at any time if, at that time—

(a) it is registered;

(b) it does not trade for profit; and

(c) it is not approved for the purposes of section 488 of the Income and Corporation Taxes Act 1988 (tax treatment of cooperative housing associations).

(3) References in this section to tax chargeable on an association are to income tax (other than income tax which the association is entitled to deduct on making any payment) and corporation tax.

(4) A grant under this section may be made—

(a) in a case falling within subsection (1)(a) above, for affording relief from any tax chargeable on the association for the period in respect of which the claim is made; and

(b) in a case falling within subsection (1)(b) above, for affording relief from such part of any tax so chargeable as the Secretary of State considers appropriate having regard to the other functions of the association;

and in any case shall be of such amount, shall be made at such times and shall be subject to such conditions as the Secretary of State thinks fit.

(5) The conditions may include conditions for securing the repayment in whole or in part of a grant made to an association—

(a) in the event of tax in respect of which it was made being found not to be chargeable; or

(b) in such other events (including the association beginning to trade for profit) as the Secretary of State may determine.

(6) A claim under this section shall be made in such manner and shall be supported by such evidence as the Secretary of State may direct.

(7) The Commissioners of Inland Revenue and their officers may disclose to the Secretary of State such particulars as he may reasonably require for determining whether a grant should be made on a claim or whether a grant should be repaid or the amount of such grant or repayment.

(8) In this section 'letting' includes—

(a) in England and Wales, the grant of a shared ownership lease or a licence to occupy;

(b) in Scotland, disposal under a shared ownership agreement or the grant of a right or permission to occupy.

Surplus rental income
55.—(1) An association to which this section applies, that is to say, a registered housing association which has at any time received a payment in respect of—

(a) a grant under section 50 above, or

(b) a grant under section 41 of the 1985 Act or any enactment replaced by that section, or

(c) a grant under section 2(2) of the Housing (Scotland) Act 1988,

(in this section referred to as a 'relevant grant') shall show separately in its accounts for any period ending after the coming into force of this section the surpluses arising from increased rental income during that period from such housing activities to which the grant relates as the Secretary of State may from time to time determine.

(2) The surpluses shall be shown by each association in a fund to be known as its rent surplus fund; and the method of constituting that fund and of showing it in the association's accounts shall be as required by order of the Secretary of State under section 24 of the 1985 Act (general requirements as to accounts) and, notwithstnding anything in subsection (5) of that section, such an order may make provision applying to any period to which this section applies.

(3) The surpluses in respect of a period shall be calculated in such manner as the Secretary of State may from time to time determine; and a determination

under this subsection may provide that, in calculating surpluses, an association shall act on such assumptions (whether or not borne out or likely to be borne out by events) as may be specified in the determination.

(4) A determination under subsection (1) or (3) above may—

(a) make the same provision for all cases; or

(b) make different provision for different cases or descriptions of cases, including different provision for different areas or for different descriptions of housing associations or housing activities;

and for the purposes of this subsection descriptions may be framed by reference to any matters whatever, including in particular, in the case of housing activities, the manner in which they are financed.

(5) Before making a determination under subsection (1) or (3) above, the Secretary of State shall consult such bodies appearing to him to be representative of housing associations as he considers appropriate; and after making such a determination, the Secretary of State shall publish it in such manner as he considers appropriate for bringing it to the notice of the associations concerned.

(6) The Secretary of State may from time to time give notice to an association to which this section applies requiring it to pay to him, with interest if demanded, or to apply or appropriate for purposes he specifies, any sums standing in its rent surplus fund at the end of a period of account.

(7) Any interest demanded by such a notice is payable—

(a) at the rate or rates (whether fixed or variable) previously determined by the Secretary of State, with the consent of the Treasury, for housing associations generally and published by him or, if no such determination has been made, at the rate or rates (whether fixed or variable) specified with the consent of the Treasury in the notice; and

(b) either from the date of the notice or from such other date, not earlier than the end of the period of account, as may be specified in the notice.

(8) A notice under subsection (6) above demanding interest may with the consent of the Treasury provide that, if the sums required by the notice to be paid to the Secretary of State are paid before a date specified in the notice—

(a) no interest shall be payable for any period after the date of the notice; and

(b) any interest payable shall be payable at a rate or rates lower than the rate or rates given by subsection (7) above.

(9) The Secretary of State may from time to time give notice—

(a) to all associations to which this section applies,

(b) to associations to which this section applies of a particular description, or

(c) to particular associations to which this section applies,

requiring them to furnish him with such information as he may reasonably require in connection with the exercise of his functions under this section; and a notice under paragraph (a) or (b) above may be given by publication in such manner as the Secretary of State considers appropriate for bringing it to the attention of the associations concerned.

(10) Where—

(a) an association has received a payment in respect of a relevant grant, and

(b) at any time property to which the grant relates becomes vested in, or is leased for a term of years to, or reverts to, some other registered housing association, or trustees for some other such association,

this section (including this subsection) shall have effect in relation to periods after that time as if the payment, or such proportion of it as may be determined by the Secretary of State to be appropriate, had been made to that other association.

Miscellaneous and supplemental

Duty of Housing Corporation and Housing for Wales in relation to racial discrimination

56. At the end of section 75 of the 1985 Act (general functions of the Corporation) there shall be added the following subsection—

'(5) Section 71 of the Race Relations Act 1976 (local authorities: general statutory duty) shall apply to the Corporation as it applies to a local authority.'

Delegation of certain functions

57. The Secretary of State may delegate to the Corporation, to such extent and subject to such conditions as he may specify, any of his functions under—

(a) section 54 or 55 above;

(b) sections 53 (recoupment of surplus rental income), 54 to 57 (deficit grants) and 62 (grants for affording tax relief) of the 1985 Act, so far as continuing in force after the passing of this Act; and

(c) Parts I and II of Schedule 5 to the 1985 Act (residual subsidies); and

where he does so, references to him in those provisions shall be construed accordingly.

Application of Housing Acts to certain transactions

58.—(1) This section applies to any tenant of a publicly funded house who, but for paragraph 1 of Schedule 5 to the Housing Act 1985 (no right to buy where landlord a charitable housing trust or housing association), would have the right to buy under Part V of the Housing Act 1985.

(2) A house is publicly funded for the purposes of subsection (1) above if a grant under section 50 above, or a grant under section 41 of the 1985 Act or any enactment replaced by that section, has been paid in respect of a project which included—

(a) the acquisition of the house;

(b) the acquisition of a building and the provision of the house by means of the conversion of the building; or

(c) the acquisition of land and the construction of the house on the land.

(3)   Where a registered housing association contracts for the acquisition of a house and, without taking the conveyance, grant or assignment, disposes of its interest at a discount to a tenant to whom this section applies, the provisions mentioned in subsection (4) below shall have effect as if the association first acquired the house and then disposed of it to the tenant.

(4)   The said provisions are—

section 4 of the 1985 Act (eligibility for registration);
section 8 of that Act (disposal of land by registered housing associations);
section 9 of that Act (consent of Corporation to disposals);
section 79(2) of that Act (power of Corporation to lend to person acquiring interest from registered housing association);
Schedule 2 to that Act (covenants for repayments of discount on early disposal and restricting disposal of houses in National Parks etc.); and
section 130 of the Housing Act 1985 (reduction of discount on exercise of right to buy where previous discount given).

Interpretation of Part II and amendments of Housing Associations Act 1985
59.—(1)   In this Part of this Act—

(a)   'the 1985 Act' means the Housing Associations Act 1985; and
(b)   except as provided in section 50(1) above, 'the Corporation' and other expressions used in this Part have the same meaning as in the 1985 Act.

(2)   The 1985 Act shall have effect subject to the amendments in Schedule 6 to this Act, being amendments—

(a)   extending the supervisory powers conferred by Part I of the 1985 Act;
(b)   making provision incidental to and consequential upon the establishment by this Part of this Act of Housing for Wales and the establishment by the Housing (Scotland) Act 1988 of Scottish Homes;
(c)   making provision incidental to and consequential upon other provisions of this Part of this Act and the provisions of Part IV of this Act; and
(d)   varying the grounds on which the Secretary of State may remove a member of the Housing Corporation from office.

(3)   In Schedule 6 to this Act,—

(a)   Part I contains amendments of Part I of the 1985 Act, including amendments which reproduce the effect of amendments made by Schedule 3 to the Housing (Scotland) Act 1988 with respect to Scottish Homes; and
(b)   Parts II and III contain amendments of Parts II and III respectively of the 1985 Act.

(4)   Without prejudice to the operation of Schedule 3 to the Housing (Scotland) Act 1988 in relation to anything done before the day appointed for the coming into force of this section, for the purpose of giving effect to the amendments in Part I of Schedule 6 to this Act, the said Schedule 3 shall be deemed never to have come into force.

Part III Housing action trust areas

Areas and trusts

Housing action trust areas

60.—(1) Subject to section 61 below, the Secretary of State may by order designate an area of land for which, in his opinion, it is expedient that a corporation, to be known as a housing action trust, having the functions specified in this Part of this Act, should be established.

(2) The area designated by an order under this section may comprise two or more parcels of land which—

    (a) need not be contiguous; and

    (b) need not be in the district of the same local housing authority.

(3) An order under this section shall be made by statutory instrument but no such order shall be made unless a draft of it has been laid before, and approved by a resolution of, each House of Parliament.

(4) In deciding whether to make an order under this section designating any area of land, the Secretary of State shall have regard to such matters as he thinks fit.

(5) Without prejudice to the generality of subsection (4) above, among the matters to which the Secretary of State may have regard in deciding whether to include a particular area of land in an order under this section, are—

    (a) the extent to which the housing accommodation in the area as a whole is occupied by tenants or owner-occupiers and the extent to which it is local authority housing;

    (b) the physical state and design of the housing accommodation in the area and any need to repair or improve it;

    (c) the way in which the local authority housing in the area is being managed; and

    (d) the living conditions of those who live in the area and the social conditions and general environment of the area.

(6) An area designated by an order under this section shall be known as a housing action trust area and in the following provisions of this Part of this Act—

    (a) such an area is referred to as a 'designated area'; and

    (b) an order under this section is referred to as a 'designation order'.

Consultation and publicity

61.—(1) Before making a designation order, the Secretary of State shall consult every local housing authority any part of whose district is to be included in the proposed designated area.

(2) Where the Secretary of State is considering a proposal to make a designation order, he shall use his best endeavours to secure that notice of the proposal is given to all tenants of houses in the area proposed to be designated who are either secure tenants or tenants of such description as may be prescribed by regulations.

(3) After having taken the action required by subsection (2) above, the Secretary of State shall either—

(a) make arrangements for such independent persons as appear to him to be appropriate to conduct, in such manner as seems best to them, a ballot or poll of the tenants who have been given notice of the proposal as mentioned in that subsection with a view to establishing their opinions about the proposal to make a designation order; or

(b) if it seems appropriate to him to do so, arrange for the conduct of a ballot or poll of those tenants in such manner as appears to him best suited to establish their opinions about the proposal.

(4) If it appears from a ballot or poll conducted as mentioned in subsection (3) above that a majority of the tenants who, on that ballot or poll, express an opinion about the proposal to make the designation order are opposed to it, the Secretary of State shall not make the order proposed.

(5) The power to make regulations under subsection (2) above shall be exercisable by the Secretary of State by statutory instrument which shall be subject to annulment in pursuance of a resolution of either House of Parliament.

(6) Consultation undertaken before the passing of this Act shall constitute as effective compliance with subsection (1) above as if undertaken after that passing.

Housing action trusts
62.—(1) Subject to subsection (2) below, where the Secretary of State makes a designation order, he shall, in that order or by a separate order, either—

(a) establish a housing action trust for the designated area; or

(b) specify as the housing action trust for the designated area a housing action trust already established for another designated area.

(2) Such a separate order as is referred to in subsection (1) above shall be made by statutory instrument but no such order shall be made unless a draft of it has been laid before, and approved by a resolution of, each House of Parliament.

(3) Subject to subsection (4) below, a housing action trust shall be a body corporate by such name as may be prescribed by the order establishing it.

(4) Where the Secretary of State makes the provision referred to in subsection (1)(b) above,—

(a) the housing action trust specified in the order shall, by virtue of the order, be treated as established for the new designated area (as well as for any designated area for which it is already established); and

(b) the order may alter the name of the trust to take account of the addition of the new designated area.

(5) Schedule 7 to this Act shall have effect with respect to the constitution of housing action trusts and Schedule 8 to this Act shall have effect with respect to their finances.

(6) It is hereby declared that a housing action trust is not to be regarded as the servant or agent of the Crown or as enjoying any status, immunity or privilege of the Crown and that the trust's property is not to be regarded as the property of, or property held on behalf of, the Crown.

(7) At the end of section 4 of the Housing Act 1985 (descriptions of authority) there shall be added—

'(f)   "housing action trust" means a housing action trust established under Part III of the Housing Act 1988';

and at the end of section 14 of the Rent Act 1977 (landlord's interest belonging to local authority etc.) there shall be added—

'(h)   a housing action trust established under Part III of the Housing Act 1988'.

Objects and general powers of housing action trusts
63.—(1)   The primary objects of a housing action trust in relation to the designated area for which it is established shall be—

(a)   to secure the repair or improvement of housing accommodation for the time being held by the trust;

(b)   to secure the proper and effective management and use of that housing accommodation;

(c)   to encourage diversity in the interests by virtue of which housing accommodation in the area is occupied and, in the case of accommodation which is occupied under tenancies, diversity in the identity of the landlords; and

(d)   generally to secure or facilitate the improvement of living conditions in the area and the social conditions and general environment of the area.

(2)   Without prejudice to subsection (1) above, a housing action trust may—

(a)   provide and maintain housing accommodation; and

(b)   facilitate the provision of shops, advice centres and other facilities for the benefit of the community or communities who live in the designated area.

(3)   For the purpose of achieving its objects and exercising the powers conferred on it by subsection (2) above, a housing action trust may—

(a)   acquire, hold, manage, reclaim and dispose of land and other property;

(b)   carry out building and other operations;

(c)   seek to ensure the provision of water, electricity, gas, sewerage and other services; and

(d)   carry on any business or undertaking;

and may generally do anything necessary or expedient for the purposes of those objects and powers or for purposes incidental thereto.

(4)   For the avoidance of doubt it is hereby declared that subsection (3) above relates only to the capacity of a housing action trust as a statutory corporation; and nothing in this section authorises such a trust to disregard any enactment or rule of law.

(5)   Section 71 of the Race Relations Act 1976 (local authorities: general statutory duty) shall apply to a housing action trust as it applies to a local authority.

(6)   A transaction between any person and a housing action trust shall not be invalidated by reason of any failure by the trust to observe the objects in subsection (1) above or the requirement that the trust shall exercise the powers conferred by subsections (2) and (3) above for the purpose referred to in that subsection.

The housing action trust's proposals for its area

64.—(1) As soon as practicable after a housing action trust has been established for a designated area, the trust shall prepare a statement of its proposals with regard to the exercise of its functions in the area.

(2) The trust shall consult every local housing authority or county council, any part of whose area lies within the designated area, with regard to the proposals contained in the statement prepared under subsection (1) above.

(3) A housing action trust shall take such steps as it considers appropriate to secure—

(a) that adequate publicity is given in the designated area to the proposals contained in the statement prepared under subsection (1) above;

(b) that those who live in the designated area are made aware that they have an opportunity to make, within such time as the trust may specify, representations to the trust with respect to those proposals; and

(c) that those who live in the designated area are given an adequate opportunity of making such representations;

and the trust shall consider any such representations as may be made within the time specified.

(4) As soon as may be after a housing action trust has complied with the requirements of subsections (1) to (3) above it shall send to the Secretary of State a copy of the statement prepared under subsection (1) above together with a report of—

(a) the steps the trust has taken to consult as mentioned in subsection (2) above and to secure the matters referred to in subsection (3) above; and

(b) the consideration it has given to points raised in the course of consultation and to representations received.

(5) At such times as a housing action trust considers appropriate or as it may be directed by the Secretary of State, the trust shall prepare a further statement of its proposals with regard to the exercise of its functions in its area; and subsections (2) and (4) above shall again apply as they applied in relation to the first statement.

Functions

Housing action trust as housing authority etc.

65.—(1) If the Secretary of State so provides by order, in a designated area or, as the case may be, in such part of the area as may be specified in the order, the housing action trust for the area shall have such of the functions described in subsection (2) below as may be so specified.

(2) The functions referred to in subsection (1) above are—

(a) the functions conferred on a local housing authority by Parts II, VI, VII and IX to XII and XVI of the Housing Act 1985 and section 3(1) of the Chronically Sick and Disabled Persons Act 1970;

(b) the functions conferred by Part II of the Housing Associations Act 1985 on a local authority, within the meaning of that Act; and

(c) the functions conferred by sections 39 to 41 of the Land Compensation

Act 1973 on the authority which is 'the relevant authority' for the purposes of section 39 of that Act.

(3)   As respects the designated area or part thereof to which an order under this section applies, on the coming into force of the order, any function conferred on a housing action trust by the order shall, according to the terms of the order, be exercisable either—

(a)   by the trust instead of by the authority by which, apart from the order, the function would be exercisable; or

(b)   by the trust concurrently with that authority.

(4)   Any enactment under which a housing action trust is to exercise a function by virtue of an order under this section shall have effect—

(a)   in relation to the trust, and

(b)   where the trust is to have the function concurrently with another authority, in relation to that authority,

subject to such modifications (if any) as may be specified in the order.

(5)   Where a housing action trust is to exercise functions conferred on a local housing authority by any of Parts VI, VII, IX and XI of the Housing Act 1985, section 36 of the Local Government Act 1974 (recovery by local authorities of establishment charges) shall apply to the housing action trust as if it were a local authority within the meaning of that section.

(6)   Such (if any) of the provisions of Parts XVII and XVIII of the Housing Act 1985 (compulsory purchase, land acquisition and general provisions) as may be specified in an order under this section shall have effect in relation to a housing action trust subject to such modifications as may be specified in the order.

(7)   An order under this section—

(a)   may contain such savings and transitional and supplementary provisions as appear to the Secretary of State to be appropriate; and

(b)   shall be made by statutory instrument which shall be subject to annulment in pursuance of a resolution of either House of Parliament.

Planning control

66.—(1)   A housing action trust may submit to the Secretary of State proposals for the development of land within its designated area and the Secretary of State, after consultation with the local planning authority within whose area the land is situated and with any other local authority which appears to him to be concerned, may approve any such proposals either with or without modification.

(2)   Without prejudice to the generality of the powers conferred by section 24 of the 1971 Act, a special development order made by the Secretary of State under that section with respect to a designated area may grant permission for any development of land in accordance with proposals approved under subsection (1) above, subject to such conditions, if any (including conditions requiring details of any proposed development to be submitted to the local planning authority), as may be specified in the order.

(3)   The Secretary of State shall give to a housing action trust such directions with regard to the disposal of land held by it and with respect to the development

by it of such land as appear to him to be necessary or expedient for securing, so far as practicable, the preservation of any features of special architectural or historical interest and, in particular, of any buildings included in any list compiled or approved or having effect as if compiled or approved under section 54(1) of the 1971 Act (which relates to the compilation or approval by the Secretary of State of lists of buildings of special architectural or historical interest).

(4)   Any reference in this section to the local planning authority,—

(a)   in relation to land in Greater London or a metropolitan county, is a reference to the authority which is the local planning authority as ascertained in accordance with section 1 of the 1971 Act; and

(b)   in relation to other land, is a reference to the district planning authority and also (in relation to proposals for any development which is a county matter, as defined in paragraph 32 of Schedule 16 to the Local Government Act 1972) to the county planning authority.

Housing action trust as planning authority
67.—(1)   If the Secretary of State so provides by order, for such purposes of Part III of the 1971 Act and in relation to such kinds of development as may be specified in the order, a housing action trust shall be the local planning authority for the whole or such part as may be so specified of its designated area in place of any authority which would otherwise be the local planning authority.

(2)   An order under subsection (1) above may provide—

(a)   that any enactment relating to local planning authorities shall not apply to the trust; and

(b)   that any such enactment which applies to the trust shall apply to it subject to such modifications as may be specified in the order.

(3)   An order made by the Secretary of State may provide—

(a)   that, subject to any modifications specified in the order, a housing action trust specified in the order shall have, in the whole or any part of its designated area and in place of any authority (except the Secretary of State) which would otherwise have them, such of the functions conferred by Parts IV, V and XV of the 1971 Act as may be so specified; and

(b)   that such of the provisions of Part IX and sections 212 and 214 of the 1971 Act as are mentioned in the order shall have effect, in relation to the housing action trust specified in the order and to land in the trust's area, subject to the modifications there specified.

(4)   An order under subsection (3) above may provide that, for the purposes of any of the provisions specified in the order, any enactment relating to local planning authorities shall apply to the housing action trust specified in the order subject to such modifications as may be so specified.

(5)   In relation to a housing action trust which, by virtue of an order under subsection (1) above, is the local planning authority for the whole or part of its area, section 270 of the 1971 Act (application to local planning authorities of provisions as to planning control and enforcement) shall have effect for the

purposes of Part III of the 1971 Act prescribed by that order, and in relation to the kinds of development so prescribed, as if—

(a) in subsection (1) the reference to the development by local authorities of land in respect of which they are the local planning authorities included a reference to the development by the trust of land in respect of which it is the local planning authority;

(b) in subsection (2),—

(i) in paragraph (a) for the words 'such an authority' there were substituted 'housing action trust' and for the words 'local planning authority' there were substituted 'housing action trust'; and

(ii) in paragraph (b) for the words 'local planning authority' there were substituted 'housing action trust'.

(6) If, by virtue of an order under subsection (1) above, a housing action trust is the local planning authority in relation to all kinds of development for the whole or part of its area, it shall be the hazardous substances authority for that area or, as the case may be, that part for the purposes of the 1971 Act.

(7) Any power to make an order under this section shall be exercisable by statutory instrument which shall be subject to annulment in pursuance of a resolution of either House of Parliament; and any such order shall have effect subject to such savings and transitional provisions as may be specified in the order.

Public health

68.—(1) The Secretary of State may by order provide that, in relation to premises comprising or consisting of housing accommodation, a housing action trust shall have in its designated area (or in such part of its designated area as may be specified in the order) the functions conferred on a local authority—

(a) by sections 83 and 84 of the Public Health Act 1936 (the '1936 Act') and section 36 of the Public Health Act 1961 (all of which relate to filthy or verminous premises or articles);

(b) by any enactment contained in Part III (nuisances and offensive trades) of the 1936 Act;

(c) by so much of Part XII of the 1936 Act as relates to any of the enactments mentioned in paragraphs (a) and (b) above; and

(d) by Part I of the Prevention of Damage by Pests Act 1949 (rats and mice).

(2) On the order coming into force, the trust shall have the functions conferred in relation to the designated area (or part) instead of or concurrently with any such authority, depending on the terms of the order.

(3) The order may provide that any enactment under which the trust is to exercise functions by virtue of the order shall have effect in relation to the trust and, where the trust is to have any function concurrently with another authority, in relation to that authority, as modified by the order.

(4) Where an order under this section provides that a housing action trust shall have the functions conferred upon a local authority by Part III of the 1936 Act, section 36 of the Local Government Act 1974 (recovery by local authorities

of establishment charges) shall apply to the housing action trust as if it were a local authority within the meaning of that section.

(5)   The order shall have effect subject to such savings and transitional and supplementary provisions as may be specified in the order.

(6)   The power to make an order under this section shall be exercisable by statutory instrument which shall be subject to annulment in pursuance of a resolution of either House of Parliament.

Highways

69.—(1)   When any street works have been executed in a private street (or part of a private street) in a designated area, the housing action trust may serve a notice on the street works authority requiring it to declare the street (or part) to be a highway which for the purposes of the Highways Act 1980 is a highway maintainable at the public expense.

(2)   Within the period of two months beginning on the date of the service of a notice under subsection (1) above, the street works authority may appeal against the notice to the Secretary of State on grounds relating to all or any of the following matters—

   (a)   the construction of the street (or part);
   (b)   its design;
   (c)   its layout; and
   (d)   the state of its maintenance.

(3)   After considering any representations made to him by the housing action trust and the street works authority, the Secretary of State shall determine an appeal under subsection (2) above by setting aside or confirming the notice under subsection (1) above (with or without modifications).

(4)   Where, under subsection (3) above, the Secretary of State confirms a notice,—

   (a)   he may at the same time impose conditions (including financial conditions) upon the housing action trust with which the trust must comply in order for the notice to take effect, and

   (b)   the highway (or part) shall become a highway maintainable at the public expense with effect from such date as the Secretary of State may specify.

(5)   Where a street works authority neither complies with the notice under subsection (1) above, nor appeals under subsection (2) above, the street (or part) concerned shall become a highway maintainable at the public expense upon the expiry of the period of two months referred to in subsection (2) above.

(6)   In this section 'private street' and 'street works authority' have the same meanings as in Part XI of the Highways Act 1980.

Cooperation on homelessness between local housing authorities and housing action trusts

70.   In paragraph (a) of section 72 of the Housing Act 1985 (which provides that, on a request by a local housing authority for assistance in the discharge of certain statutory functions relating to homelessness, or threatened homelessness, a body of a description specified in the paragraph shall cooperate in rendering such assistance as is reasonable in the circumstances) after the words 'a registered housing association' there shall be inserted 'a housing action trust'; and in the words following paragraph (c) of that section after the word 'authority' there shall be inserted 'or other body'.

Power to give financial assistance
71.—(1) For the purpose of achieving its objects a housing action trust may, with the consent of the Secretary of State, give financial assistance to any person.

(2) Financial assistance under subsection (1) above may be given in any form and, in particular, may be given by way of—

    (a) grants,
    (b) loans,
    (c) guarantees,
    (d) incurring expenditure for the benefit of the person assisted, or
    (e) purchasing loan or share capital in a company.

(3) Financial assistance under subsection (1) above may be given on such terms as the housing action trust, with the consent of the Secretary of State, considers appropriate.

(4) Any consent under this section—

    (a) may be given either unconditionally or subject to conditions; and
    (b) may be given in relation to a particular case or in relation to such description of cases as may be specified in the consent;

and the reference in subsection (3) above to the consent of the Secretary of State is a reference to his consent given with the approval of the Treasury.

(5) The terms referred to in subsection (3) above may, in particular, include provision as to—

    (a) the circumstances in which the assistance must be repaid or otherwise made good to the housing action trust and the manner in which that is to be done; or
    (b) the circumstances in which the housing action trust is entitled to recover the proceeds or part of the proceeds of any disposal of land or buildings in respect of which assistance was provided.

(6) Any person receiving assistance under subsection (1) above shall comply with the terms on which it is given and compliance may be enforced by the housing action trust.

Directions as to exercise of functions
72.—(1) In the exercise of its functions, a housing action trust shall comply with any directions given by the Secretary of State.

(2) Directions given by the Secretary of State may be of a general or particular character and may be varied or revoked by subsequent directions.

(3) The Secretary of State shall publish any direction given under this section.

(4) A transaction between any person and a housing action trust acting in purported exercise of its powers under this Part of this Act shall not be void by reason only that the transaction was carried out in contravention of a direction given under this section; and a person dealing with a housing action trust shall

not be concerned to see or enquire whether a direction under this section has been given or complied with.

Transfer of functions
73.—(1) If, in the case of any designated area, it appears to the Secretary of State that it is expedient that the functions of a housing action trust established for the area should be transferred—

    (a)   to the housing action trust established for another designated area, or
    (b)   to a new housing action trust to be established for the area,

he may by order provide for the dissolution of the first-mentioned trust and for the transfer of its functions, property, rights and liabilities to the trust referred to in paragraph (a) above, or, as the case may be, to a new housing action trust established for the area by the order.

(2)   Where an order under this section provides for the functions of a housing action trust established for a designated area to be transferred to the housing action trust established for another designated area—

    (a)   the latter trust shall, by virtue of the order, be treated as established for the first-mentioned designated area (as well as the area referred to in subsection (1)(a) above); and
    (b)   the order may alter the name of the latter trust in such manner as appears to the Secretary of State to be expedient.

(3)   Before making an order under this section the Secretary of State shall consult the housing action trust whose functions are to be transferred and also, in a case falling within subsection (1)(a) above, the housing action trust to whom the functions are to be transferred.

(4)   An order under this section shall be made by statutory instrument but no such order shall be made unless a draft of it has been laid before, and approved by a resolution of, each House of Parliament.

Transfer of housing accommodation etc.

Transfer of land and other property to housing action trusts
74.—(1) The Secretary of State may by order provide for the transfer from a local housing authority to a housing action trust of—

    (a)   all or any of the authority's local authority housing situated in the designated area; and
    (b)   any other land held or provided in connection with that local authority housing.

(2)   Without prejudice to the powers under subsection (1) above, if in the opinion of the Secretary of State a housing action trust requires for the purposes of its functions any land which, though not falling within that subsection, is situated in the designated area and held (for whatever purpose) by a local authority, the Secretary of State may by order provide for the transfer of that land to the trust.

(3)   The Secretary of State may by order transfer from a local housing authority or other local authority to a housing action trust so much as appears to

him to be appropriate of any property which is held or used by the authority in connection with any local authority housing or other land transferred to the trust under subsection (1) or subsection (2) above; and for this purpose 'property' includes chattels of any description and rights and liabilities, whether arising by contract or otherwise.

(4)   A transfer of any local authority housing or other land or property under the preceding provisions of this section shall be on such terms, including financial terms, as the Secretary of State thinks fit; and an order under this section may provide that, notwithstanding anything in section 141 of the Law of Property Act 1925 (rent and benefit of lessee's covenants to run with the reversion), any rent or other sum which—

(a)   arises under a tenancy of any local authority housing or other land transferred to the housing action trust under subsection (1) or subsection (2) above, and

(b)   falls due before the date of the transfer,

shall continue to be recoverable by the local housing authority or, as the case may be, the local authority to the exclusion of the trust and of any other person in whom the reversion on the tenancy may become vested.

(5)   Without prejudice to the generality of subsection (4) above, the financial terms referred to in that subsection may include provision for payments by a local authority (as well as or instead of payments to a local authority); and the transfer from a local housing authority or other local authority of any local authority housing or other land or property by virtue of this section shall not be taken to give rise to any right to compensation.

(6)   Where an order is made under this section—

(a)   payments made by a local authority as mentioned in subsection (5) above shall be prescribed expenditure for the purposes of Part VIII of the Local Government, Planning and Land Act 1980 (capital expenditure of local authorities); and

(b)   unless the order otherwise provides, payments made to a local authority as mentioned in subsection (5) above shall be regarded for the purposes of that Part as sums received by the authority in respect of a disposal falling within section 75(2) of that Act.

(7)   Any power to make an order under this section shall be exercisable by statutory instrument which shall be subject to annulment in pursuance of a resolution of either House of Parliament.

(8)   In this section 'local authority' means any of the following—

(a)   a local housing authority;

(b)   the council of a county;

(c)   the Inner London Education Authority;

(d)   an authority established by an order under section 10(1) of the Local Government Act 1985 (waste disposal);

(e)   a joint authority established by Part IV of that Act; and

(f)   a residuary body established by Part VII of that Act.

Supplementary provisions as to transfer orders
75.—(1) In this section a 'transfer order' means an order under any of subsections (1) to (3) of section 74 above and, in relation to a transfer order, 'the transferor authority' means the local housing authority or other local authority from whom local authority housing or other land or property is or is to be transferred by the order.

(2) Before making a transfer order, the Secretary of State shall consult the transferor authority with respect to—

(a) the local authority housing or other land or property which it is proposed should be transferred by the order; and

(b) the terms of the proposed transfer.

(3) Before making a transfer order with respect to any local authority housing or other land, the Secretary of State shall take such steps as appear to him to be appropriate to bring the proposed transfer to the attention of any secure tenant or other person (other than a local authority) having an interest in the property proposed to be transferred as lessor, lessee, mortgagor or mortgagee.

(4) In connection with any transfer made by it, a transfer order may contain such incidental, consequential, transitional or supplementary provisions as appear to the Secretary of State to be necessary or expedient and, in particular, may—

(a) apply, with or without modification, any provision made by or under any enactment; and

(b) modify the operation of any provision made by or under any enactment.

Vesting and acquistion of land

Vesting by order in housing action trust
76.—(1) Subject to subsections (2) and (3) below, the Secretary of State may by order provide that land specified in the order which is vested in statutory undertakers or any other public body or in a wholly-owned subsidiary of a public body shall vest in a housing action trust established or to be established for the designated area in which the land is situated.

(2) An order under this section may not specify land vested in statutory undertakers which is used for the purpose of carrying on their statutory undertakings or which is held for that purpose.

(3) In the case of land vested in statutory undertakers, the power to make an order under this section shall be exercisable by the Secretary of State and the appropriate Minister.

(4) Part I of Schedule 9 to this Act shall have effect for supplementing the preceding provisions of this section.

(5) An order under this section shall have the same effect as a declaration under the Compulsory Purchase (Vesting Declarations) Act 1981 except that, in relation to such an order, the enactments mentioned in Part II of Schedule 9 to this Act shall have effect subject to the modifications specified in that Part.

(6) Compensation under the Land Compensation Act 1961, as applied by subsection (5) above and Part II of Schedule 9 to this Act, shall be assessed by

reference to values current on the date the order under this section comes into force.

(7) An order under this section shall be made by statutory instrument but no such order shall be made unless a draft of it has been laid before, and approved by a resolution of, each House of Parliament.

Acquisition by housing action trust
77.—(1) For the purposes of achieving its objects (and performing any of its functions), a housing action trust may acquire land within its designated area by agreement or, on being authorised to do so by the Secretary of State, compulsorily.

(2) A housing action trust may acquire (by agreement or, on being authorised to do so by the Secretary of State, compulsorily)—

(a) land adjacent to the designated area which the trust requires for purposes connected with the discharge of its functions in the area; and
(b) land outside the designated area (whether or not adjacent to it) which the trust requires for the provision of services in connection with the discharge of its functions in the area.

(3) Where a housing action trust exercises its powers under subsection (1) or subsection (2) above in relation to land which forms part of a common or open space or fuel or field garden allotment, the trust may acquire (by agreement or, on being authorised to do so by the Secretary of State, compulsorily) land for giving in exchange for the land acquired.

(4) Subject to section 78 below, the Acquisition of Land Act 1981 shall apply in relation to the compulsory acquisition of land in pursuance of the preceding provisions of this section.

(5) A housing action trust may be authorised by the Secretary of State, by means of a compulsory purchase order, to purchase compulsorily such new rights as are specified in the order—

(a) being rights over land in the designated area and which the trust requires for the purposes of its functions;
(b) being rights over land adjacent to the designated area and which the trust requires for purposes connected with the discharge of its functions in the area; and
(c) being rights over land outside the designated area (whether or not adjacent to it) and which the trust requires for the provision of services in connection with the discharge of its functions in the area.

(6) In subsection (5) above—

(a) 'new rights' means rights which are not in existence when the order specifying them is made; and
(b) 'compulsory purchase order' has the same meaning as in the Acquisition of Land Act 1981;

and Schedule 3 to that Act shall apply to a compulsory purchase of a right by virtue of subsection (5) above.

(7) The provisions of Part I of the Compulsory Purchase Act 1965 (so far as

applicable), other than section 31, shall apply in relation to the acquisition of land by agreement under this section; and in that Part as so applied 'land' has the meaning given by the Interpretation Act 1978.

Supplementary provisions as to vesting, acquisition and compensation
78.—(1)   The Acquisition of Land Act 1981, as applied by section 77 above, shall have effect subject to the modifications in Part I of Schedule 10 to this Act.

(2)   The supplementary provisions in Parts II and III of that Schedule shall have effect, being,—

(a)   as to those in Part II, provisions about land vested in or acquired by a housing action trust under this Part of this Act; and

(b)   as to those in Part III, provisions about the acquisition by a housing action trust of rights over land under section 77(5) above.

(3)   In Schedule 1 to the Land Compensation Act 1961 (actual or prospective development which is not to be taken into account in assessing compensation in certain cases or the effect of which is to reduce compensation in certain cases of adjacent land in the same ownership), the following paragraph shall be added after the paragraph 4A inserted by section 145 of the Local Government, Planning and Land Act 1980:

'4B. Where any of the relevant land forms part of a housing action trust area established under Part III of the Housing Act 1988.	Development of any land other than the relevant land in the course of the development or redevelopment of the area as a housing action trust area.'

(4)   In section 6 of the Land Compensation Act 1961 (disregard of actual or prospective development in certain cases) in subsection (1)(b) for '4A' there shall be substituted '4B'.

Disposals of land

Disposal of land by housing action trusts
79.—(1)   Subject to subsection (2) below and any directions given by the Secretary of State, a housing action trust may, with the consent of the Secretary of State, dispose of any land for the time being held by it to such persons, in such manner and on such terms as it considers expedient for the purpose of achieving its objects.

(2)   A housing action trust may not dispose of a house which is for the time being subject to a secure tenancy except—

(a)   to a person who is for the time being approved by the Corporation either under this section or under section 94 below, or

(b)   to a local housing authority or other local authority in accordance with section 84 below;

but this subsection does not apply to a disposal under Part V of the Housing Act 1985 (the right to buy).

(3)   The reference in subsection (1) above to disposing of land includes a

reference to granting an interest in or right over land and, in particular, the granting of an option to purchase the freehold of, or any other interest in, land is a disposal for the purposes of that subsection; and a consent under that subsection given to such a disposal extends to a disposal made in pursuance of the option.

(4)   The consent of the Secretary of State referred to in subsection (1) above may be given—

(a)   either generally to all housing action trusts or to a particular trust or description of trust;

(b)   either in relation to particular land or in relation to land of a particular description; and

(c)   subject to conditions.

(5)   Without prejudice to the generality of subsection (4)(c) above, consent under subsection (1) above may, in particular, be given subject to conditions as to the price, premium or rent to be obtained by the housing action trust on the disposal, including conditions as to the amount by which, on the disposal of a house by way of sale or by the grant or assignment of a lease at a premium, the price or premium is to be, or may be, discounted by the housing action trust.

(6)   The Corporation shall not under this section approve—

(a)   a public sector landlord; or

(b)   the council of a county; or

(c)   any other body which the Corporation have reason to believe might not be independent of such a landlord or council;

and, for the purposes of paragraph (c) above, a body shall not be regarded as independent of a public sector landlord or the council of a county if the body is or appears likely to be under the control of, or subject to influence from, such a landlord or council or particular members or officers of such a landlord or council.

(7)   In subsection (6) above 'public sector landlord' means—

(a)   a local housing authority;

(b)   a new town corporation within the meaning of section 4(b) of the Housing Act 1985; and

(c)   the Development Board for Rural Wales.

(8)   The Corporation shall establish (and may from time to time vary) criteria to be satisfied by a person seeking approval under this section and, in deciding whether to give such approval, the Corporation shall have regard to whether the person satisfies the criteria.

(9)   Subject to any directions under section 76 of the Housing Associations Act 1985 (directions by the Secretary of State),—

(a)   an approval under this section shall not be given except to a person making an application accompanied by such fee as the Corporation, with the consent of the Secretary of State, may specify; and

(b)   an approval under this section may be made conditional upon the person or persons concerned entering into such undertakings as may be specified by the Corporation; and

(c) if it appears to the Corporation appropriate to do so (whether by reason of a failure to honour an undertaking or to meet any criteria or for any other reason) the Corporation may revoke an approval given under this section by notice in writing served on the approved person, but such a revocation shall not affect any transaction completed before the service of the notice;

and different fees may be specified under paragraph (a) above for different descriptions of cases.

(10) The Housing Corporation and Housing for Wales shall each maintain a register of persons for the time being approved by it under this section; and each register so maintained shall be open to inspection at the head office of the Corporation by which it is maintained at all reasonable times.

(11) In section 45(2)(b) of the Housing Act 1985 (which defines 'public sector authority' for the purposes of provisions of that Act restricting service charges payable after disposal of a house) after the entry 'an urban development corporation' there shall be inserted 'a housing action trust'.

(12) A housing action trust shall be treated as a local authority for the purposes of sections 18 to 30 of the Landlord and Tenant Act 1985 (service charges).

(13) The provisions of Schedule 11 to this Act shall have effect in the case of certain disposals of houses by a housing action trust.

Disposals made without consent
80.—(1) Any disposal of a house by a housing action trust which is made without the consent required by section 79(1) above is void unless—

    (a) the disposal is to an individual (or to two or more individuals); and
    (b) the disposal does not extend to any other house.

(2) Subject to subsection (1) above,—

    (a) a disposal of any land made by a housing action trust shall not be invalid by reason only that it is made without the consent required by section 79(1) above; and
    (b) a person dealing with a housing action trust or with a person claiming under such a trust shall not be concerned to see or enquire whether any consent required by section 79(1) above has been obtained.

Consent required for certain subsequent disposals
81.—(1) If, by a material disposal, a housing action trust disposes of a house which is for the time being subject to a secure tenancy to such a person as is mentioned in section 79(2)(a) above (in this section referred to as an 'approved person'), the conveyance shall contain a statement that the requirement of this section as to consent applies to a subsequent disposal of the house by the approved person.

(2) For the purposes of this section a 'material disposal' is—

    (a) the transfer of the fee simple;
    (b) the transfer of an existing lease; or
    (c) the grant of a new lease;

and 'the conveyance' means the instrument by which such a disposal is effected.

(3)   An approved person who acquires a house on a material disposal falling within subsection (1) above shall not dispose of it except with the consent of the Secretary of State which may be given either unconditionally or subject to conditions; but nothing in this subsection shall apply in relation to an exempt disposal as defined in subsection (8) below.

(4)   Where an estate or interest in a house acquired by an approved person as mentioned in subsection (3) above has been mortgaged or charged, the prohibition in that subsection applies also to a disposal by the mortgagee or chargee in exercise of a power of sale or leasing, whether or not the disposal is in the name of the approved person; and in any case where—

(a)   by operation of law or by virtue of an order of a court, property which has been acquired by an approved person passes or is transferred to another person, and

(b)   that passing or transfer does not constitute a disposal for which consent is required under subsection (3) above,

this section (including, where there is more than one such passing or transfer, this subsection) shall apply as if the other person to whom the property passes or is transferred were the approved person.

(5)   Before giving consent in respect of a disposal to which subsection (3) above applies, the Secretary of State—

(a)   shall satisfy himself that the person who is seeking the consent has taken appropriate steps to consult every tenant of any house proposed to be disposed of; and

(b)   shall have regard to the responses of any such tenants to that consultation.

(6)   If, apart from subsection (7) below, the consent of the Corporation would be required under section 9 of the Housing Associations Act 1985 (control of dispositions of land by housing associations) for a disposal to which subsection (3) above applies, the Secretary of State shall consult the Corporation before giving his consent in respect of the disposal for the purposes of this section.

(7)   No consent shall be required under the said section 9 for any disposal in respect of which consent is given in accordance with subsection (6) above.

(8)   In this section an 'exempt disposal' means—

(a)   the disposal of a dwelling-house to a person having the right to buy it under Part V of the Housing Act 1985 (whether the disposal is in fact made under that Part or otherwise);

(b)   a compulsory disposal, within the meaning of Part V of the Housing Act 1985;

(c)   the disposal of an easement or rentcharge;

(d)   the disposal of an interest by way of security for a loan;

(e)   the grant of a secure tenancy or what would be a secure tenancy but for any of paragraphs 2 to 12 of Schedule 1 to the Housing Act 1985;

(f)   the grant of an assured tenancy or an assured agricultural occupancy, within the meaning of Part I of this Act, or what would be such a tenancy or occupancy but for any of paragraphs 4 to 8 of Schedule 1 to this Act; and

(g) the transfer of an interest held on trust for any person where the disposal is made in connection with the appointment of a new trustee or in connection with the discharge of any trustee.

(9) Where the title of a housing action trust to a house which is disposed of by a material disposal falling within subsection (1) above is not registered—

(a) section 123 of the Land Registration Act 1925 (compulsory registration of title) applies in relation to the conveyance whether or not the house is in an area in which an Order in Council under section 120 of that Act (areas of compulsory registration) is in force;

(b) the housing action trust shall give the approved person a certificate stating that it is entitled to make the disposal subject only to such encumbrances, rights and interests as are stated in the conveyance or summarised in the certificate; and

(c) for the purpose of registration of title, the Chief Land Registrar shall accept such a certificate as evidence of the facts stated in it, but if as a result he has to meet a claim against him under the Land Registration Acts 1925 to 1986 the housing action trust is liable to indemnify him.

(10) On an application being made for registration of a disposition of registered land or, as the case may be, of the approved person's title under a disposition of unregistered land, if the conveyance contains the statement required by subsection (1) above, the Chief Land Registrar shall enter in the register a restriction stating the requirement of this section as to consent to a subsequent disposal.

(11) In this section references to disposing of a house include references to—

(a) granting or disposing of any interest in the house;

(b) entering into a contract to dispose of the house or to grant or dispose of any such interest; and

(c) granting an option to acquire the house or any such interest;

and any reference to a statement or certificate is a reference to a statement or, as the case may be, certificate in a form approved by the Chief Land Registrar.

Power of Corporation to provide legal assistance to tenants after disposal
82.—(1) This section applies where a house has been disposed of by a disposal falling within section 79(2) above and, in relation to a house which has been so disposed of, a 'transferred tenant' means a tenant of it who either—

(a) was the secure tenant of the house immediately before the disposal; or

(b) is the widow or widower of the person who was then the secure tenant of it.

(2) On an application by a transferred tenant of a house who is a party or a prospective party to proceedings or prospective proceedings to determine any dispute between himself and the person who acquired the house on the disposal referred to in subsection (1) above, the Corporation may give assistance to the transferred tenant if it thinks fit to do so—

(a) on the ground that the case raises a question of principle; or

(b) on the ground that it is unreasonable, having regard to the complexity

of the case, or to any other matter, to expect the transferred tenant to deal with it
without assistance; or

(c)   by reason of any other special consideration.

(3)   Assistance given by the Corporation under this section may include—

(a)   giving advice;

(b)   procuring or attempting to procure the settlement of the matter in
dispute;

(c)   arranging for the giving of advice or assistance by a solicitor or counsel;

(d)   arranging for representation by a solicitor or counsel, including such
assistance as is usually given by a solicitor or counsel in the steps preliminary or
incidental to any proceedings, or in arriving at or giving effect to a compromise to
avoid or bring to an end any proceedings; and

(e)   any other form of assistance which the Corporation may consider
appropriate;

but paragraph (d) above does not affect the law and practice regulating the
descriptions of persons who may appear in, conduct, defend and address the
court in any proceedings.

(4)   In so far as expenses are incurred by the Corporation in providing a
transferred tenant with assistance under this section, the recovery of those
expenses (as taxed or assessed in such manner as may be prescribed by rules of
court) shall constitute a first charge for the benefit of the Corporation—

(a)   on any costs which (whether by virtue of a judgment or order of a court
or an agreement or otherwise) are payable to the tenant by any other person in
respect of the matter in connection with which the assistance was given, and

(b)   so far as relates to any costs, on his rights under any compromise or
settlement arrived at in connection with that matter to avoid or bring to an end
any proceedings;

but subject to any charge under the Legal Aid Act 1988 and to any provision of
that Act for payment of any sum to the Legal Aid Board.

Secure tenancies and right to buy

Application of Parts IV and V of Housing Act 1985
83.—(1)   Parts IV and V of the Housing Act 1985 (secure tenancies and the right
to buy) shall be amended in accordance with this section.

(2)   In section 80(1) (which lists the landlords whose tenancies can qualify as
secure tenancies), after the entry specifying a new town corporation there shall be
inserted—

'a housing action trust'.

(3)   In section 108 (heating charges to secure tenants), in paragraph (a) of
subsection (5) (the definition of 'heating authority') after the words 'housing
authority' there shall be inserted 'or housing action trust'.

(4)   In section 114 (meaning of 'landlord authority' for the purposes of that
Part), in each of subsections (1) and (2), after the entry specifying a development
corporation, there shall be inserted—

'a housing action trust'.

(5)   In section 171 (power to extend right to buy where certain bodies hold an interest in a dwelling-house), in subsection (2), after the entry specifying a new town corporation there shall be inserted—

'a housing action trust'.

(6)   In each of the following provisions (all of which relate to cases where premises are or were let to a person in consequence of employment), namely—

(a)   paragraph 2(1) of Schedule 1 (tenancies which are not secure tenancies),

(b)   Grounds 7 and 12 of Schedule 2 (grounds for possession of dwelling-houses let under secure tenancies),

(c)   Ground 5 of Schedule 3 (grounds for withholding consent to assignment by way of exchange), and

(d)   paragraph 5 of Schedule 5 (exceptions to the right to buy),

after the entry specifying a new town corporation there shall be inserted—

'a housing action trust'.

(7)   In Schedule 4 (qualifying period for right to buy and discount), in paragraph 7 (the landlord condition) after the entry specifying a new town corporation there shall be inserted—

'a housing action trust'.

Provisions applicable to disposals of dwelling-houses subject to secure tenancies
84.—(1)   The provisions of this section apply in any case where a housing action trust proposes to make a disposal of one or more houses let on secure tenancies which would result in a person who, before the disposal, is a secure tenant of the trust becoming, after the disposal, the tenant of another person.

(2)   Before applying to the Secretary of State for consent to the proposed disposal or serving notice under subsection (4) below, the housing action trust shall serve notice in writing—

(a)   on any local housing authority in whose area any houses falling within subsection (1) above are situated, and

(b)   if any such houses were transferred to the trust from another local housing authority or other local authority under section 74 above, on that authority,

informing the authority of the proposed disposal, specifying the houses concerned, and requiring the authority within such period, being not less than 28 days, as may be specified in the notice, to serve on the trust a notice under subsection (3) below.

(3)   A notice by a local housing authority or other local authority under this subsection shall inform the housing action trust, with respect to each of the houses specified in the notice under subsection (2) above which is in the authority's area or, as the case may be, which was transferred from the authority as mentioned in paragraph (b) of that subsection,—

(a)   that the authority wishes to acquire the house or is considering its acquisition; or

(b)   that the authority does not wish to acquire the house;

and where the authority serves notice as mentioned in paragraph (a) above with respect to any house, the notice shall give information as to the likely consequences for the tenant if the house were to be acquired by the authority.

(4)   Before applying to the Secretary of State for consent to the proposed disposal, and after the expiry of the period specified in the notice under subsection (2) above, the housing action trust shall serve notice in writing on the secure tenant—

(a)   informing him of the proposed disposal and of the name of the person to whom the disposal is to be made;

(b)   containing such other details of the disposal as seem to the trust to be appropriate;

(c)   informing him of the likely consequences of the disposal on his position as a secure tenant and, if appropriate, of the effect of sections 171A to 171H of the Housing Act 1985 (preservation of right to buy on disposal to private sector landlord);

(d)   informing him, with respect to the house of which he is tenant, of the wishes of the local housing authority and of any other authority which has served a notice under subsection (3) above;

(e)   if an authority has served notice under paragraph (a) of subsection (3) above with respect to that house, informing him (in accordance with the information given in the notice) of the likely consequences for him if the house were to be acquired by that authority and also, if he wishes to become a tenant of that authority, of his right to make representations to that effect under paragraph (f) below; and

(f)   informing him of his right to make representations to the trust with respect to the proposed disposal within such period, being not less than 28 days, as may be specified in the notice.

(5)   The housing action trust shall consider any representations made to it in accordance with subsection (4)(f) above and, if it considers it appropriate having regard to—

(a)   any representations so made, and

(b)   any further information which may be provided by an authority which served a notice under subsection (3)(a) above that it was considering the acquisition of a house,

the trust may amend its proposals with respect to the disposal and, in such a case, shall serve a further notice under subsection (4) above (in relation to which this subsection will again apply).

(6)   When applying to the Secretary of State for consent to the proposed disposal (as amended, where appropriate, by virtue of subsection (5) above) the housing action trust shall furnish to him—

(a)   a copy of any notice served on it under subsection (3) above or served by it under subsection (4) above;

    (b)   a copy of any representations received by the trust; and

    (c)   a statement of the consideration given by the trust to those representations.

(7)   Without prejudice to the generality of section 72 above, where an application is made to the Secretary of State for consent to a disposal to which this section applies, the Secretary of State may, by a direction under that section, require the housing action trust—

    (a)   to carry out such further consultation with respect to the proposed disposal as may be specified in the direction; and

    (b)   to furnish to him such information as may be so specified with respect to the results of that consultation.

(8)   Notwithstanding the application to a housing action trust of Part IV of the Housing Act 1985 (secure tenancies) a disposal falling within subsection (1) above shall be treated as not being a matter of housing management to which section 105 of that Act applies.

Rents

Rents generally
85.—(1)   A housing action trust may make such reasonable charges as it may determine for the tenancy or occupation of housing accommodation for the time being held by it.

(2)   A housing action trust shall from time to time review rents and make such changes, either of rents generally or of particular rents, as circumstances may require.

Increase of rent where tenancy not secure
86.—(1)   This section applies where a dwelling-house is let by a housing action trust on a periodic tenancy which is not a secure tenancy.

(2)   The rent payable under the tenancy may, without the tenancy being terminated, be increased with effect from the beginning of a rental period by a written notice of increase given by the housing action trust to the tenant.

(3)   A notice under subsection (2) above is not effective unless—

    (a)   it is given at least four weeks before the first day of the rental period, or any earlier day on which the payment of rent in respect of that period falls to be made;

    (b)   it tells the tenant of his right to terminate the tenancy and of the steps to be taken by him if he wishes to do so; and

    (c)   it gives him the dates by which, if (by virtue of subsection (4) below) the increase is not to be effective, a notice to quit must be received by the trust and the tenancy be made to terminate.

(4)   Where a notice is given under subsection (2) above specifying an increase in rent with effect from the beginning of a rental period and the tenancy continues into that period, the notice shall not have effect if—

    (a)   the tenancy is terminated by notice to quit given by the tenant in accordance with the provisions (express or implied) of the tenancy;

(b)   the notice to quit is given before the expiry of the period of two weeks beginning on the day following the date on which the notice of increase is given, or before the expiry of such longer period as may be allowed by the notice of increase; and

(c)   the date on which the tenancy is made to terminate is not later than the earliest day on which the tenancy could be terminated by a notice to quit given by the tenant on the last day of that rental period.

(5)   In this section 'rental period' means a period in respect of which a payment of rent falls to be made.

Agency and dissolution

Agency agreements

87.—(1)   With the approval of the Secretary of State, a housing action trust may enter into an agreement with another person whereby, in relation to any housing accommodation or other land held by the trust which is specified in the agreement that other person shall exercise, as agent of the trust, such of the functions of the trust as are so specified.

(2)   An agreement under subsection (1) above shall set out the terms on which the functions of the housing action trust are exercisable by the person who, under the agreement, is the agent of the trust (in this Part of this Act referred to as 'the agent').

(3)   Where the agent is a body or association, an agreement under subsection (1) above may provide that the functions of the agent under the agreement may be performed by a committee or sub-committee, or by an officer, of the body or association.

(4)   The approval of the Secretary of State under subsection (1) above may be given unconditionally or subject to conditions.

(5)   References in this section to the functions of a housing action trust in relation to housing accommodation or other land include—

(a)   functions conferred by any statutory provision, and

(b)   the powers and duties of the trust as holder of an estate or interest in the housing accommodation or land in question.

Dissolution of housing action trust

88.—(1)   A housing action trust shall use its best endeavours to secure that its objects are achieved as soon as practicable.

(2)   Where it appears to a trust that its objects have been substantially achieved, it shall—

(a)   so far as practicable, dispose or arrange to dispose of any remaining property, rights or liabilities of the trust in accordance with the preceding provisions of this Part of this Act; and

(b)   submit proposals to the Secretary of State for—

(i)   the dissolution of the trust;

(ii)   the disposal to any person of any remaining property, rights or liabilities of the trust which it has not been able to dispose of or arrange to dispose of under paragraph (a) above; and

(iii) the transfer of any function exercisable by the trust to another person (including, where appropriate, a person with whom the trust has entered into an agreement under section 87 above).

(3) The Secretary of State may by order provide for the dissolution of a housing action trust and for any such disposal or transfer as is mentioned in subsection (2)(b) above, whether by way of giving effect (with or without modifications) to any proposals submitted to him under subsection (2) above or otherwise.

(4) Any order under this section—

(a) where it provides for any such disposal or transfer as is mentioned in subsection (2)(b) above, may be on such terms, including financial terms, as the Secretary of State thinks fit and may create or impose such new rights or liabilities in respect of what is transferred as appear to him to be necessary or expedient;

(b) may contain such supplementary and transitional provisions as the Secretary of State thinks necessary or expedient, including provisions amending any enactment or any instrument made under any enactment or establishing new bodies corporate to receive any functions, property, rights or liabilities transferred by the order; and

(c) shall be made by statutory instrument which shall be subject to annulment in pursuance of a resolution of either House of Parliament.

Miscellaneous and general

Supply of goods and services
89.—(1) A housing action trust and an urban development corporation established by an order under section 135 of the Local Government, Planning and Land Act 1980, may enter into any agreement with each other for all or any of the purposes set out in section 1(1) of the Local Authorities (Goods and Services) Act 1970, as if they were local authorities within the meaning of section 1 of that Act.

(2) Without prejudice to subsection (1) above, in section 1(4) of the Local Authorities (Goods and Services) Act 1970 (supply of goods and services by local authorities to public bodies), after the words '"public body" means any local authority' there shall be inserted 'housing action trust established under Part III of the Housing Act 1988'.

Information
90.—(1) If required to do so by notice in writing given by the Secretary of State for any of the purposes mentioned in subsection (3) below, a local authority,—

(a) at such time and place as may be specified in the notice, shall produce any document; or

(b) within such period as may be so specified, or such longer period as the Secretary of State may allow, shall furnish a copy of any document or supply any information;

being a document, copy or information of a description specified in the notice.

(2) Where notice is given to a local authority under subsection (1) above, any officer of the authority—

(a)   who has the custody or control of any document to which the notice relates, or

(b)   who is in a position to give information to which the notice relates,

shall take all reasonable steps to ensure that the notice is complied with.

(3)   The purposes referred to in subsection (1) above are—

(a)   determining whether the Secretary of State should make a designation order in respect of any area;

(b)   where a designation order is to be or has been made, determining whether, and to what extent, he should exercise any of his other powers under this Part of this Act; and

(c)   enabling him to provide information to a housing action trust the better to enable it to carry out its functions.

(4)   Without prejudice to the generality of subsection (1) above, among the information which may be required by a notice under that subsection is information with respect to the interests in, and the occupation of, land held by a local authority and, in particular, information with respect to any matter entered in a register kept under the Land Registration Act 1925 or the Land Charges Act 1972.

(5)   To any extent to which, apart from this subsection, he would not be able to do so, the Secretary of State may use, for any of the purposes mentioned in subsection (3) above, any information obtained by him under, or in connection with his functions under, the Housing Act 1985 or any other enactment.

(6)   If the Secretary of State considers it necessary or desirable to do so in order the better to enable a housing action trust to carry out its functions, he may disclose to the trust any information originally obtained by him for a purpose falling within paragraph (a) or paragraph (b) of subsection (3) above as well as information obtained for the purpose referred to in paragraph (c) of that subsection.

(7)   In this section 'local authority' has the same meaning as in section 74 above.

Service of notices
91.—(1)   This section has effect in relation to any notice required or authorised by this Part of this Act to be served on any person by a housing action trust.

(2)   Any such notice may be served on the person in question either by delivering it to him, or by leaving it at his proper address, or by sending it by post to him at that address.

(3)   Any such notice may—

(a)   in the case of a body corporate, be given to or served on the secretary or clerk of that body; and

(b)   in the case of a partnership, be given to or served on a partner or a person having the control or management of the partnership business.

(4)   For the purposes of this section and of section 7 of the Interpretation Act 1978 (service of documents by post) in its application to this section, the proper address of any person to or on whom a notice is to be given or served shall be his last known address, except that—

(a) in the case of a body corporate or its secretary or clerk, it shall be the address of the registered or principal office of that body; and

(b) in the case of a partnership or a person having the control or management of the partnership business, it shall be that of the principal office of the partnership;

and for the purposes of this subsection the principal office of a company registered outside the United Kingdom or of a partnership carrying on business outside the United Kingdom shall be its principal office within the United Kingdom.

(5) If the person to be given or served with any notice mentioned in subsection (1) above has specified an address within the United Kingdom other than his proper address within the meaning of subsection (4) above as the one at which he or someone on his behalf will accept documents of the same description as that notice, that address shall also be treated for the purposes of this section and section 7 of the Interpretation Act 1978 as his proper address.

(6) If the name or address of any owner, lessee or occupier of land to or on whom any notice mentioned in subsection (1) above is to be served cannot after reasonable inquiry be ascertained, the document may be served either by leaving it in the hands of a person who is or appears to be resident or employed on the land or by leaving it conspicuously affixed to some building or object on the land.

Interpretation of Part III

92.—(1) In this Part of this Act, except where the context otherwise requires,—

(a) 'designated area' and 'designation order' have the meaning assigned by section 60(6) above;

(b) any reference to a 'house' includes a reference to a flat and to any yard, garden, outhouses and appurtenances belonging to the house or flat or usually enjoyed with it;

(c) 'housing accommodation' includes flats, lodging-houses and hostels;

(d) 'local housing authority' has the same meaning as in the Housing Act 1985 and section 2 of that Act (the district of a local housing authority) has effect in relation to this Part of this Act as it has effect in relation to that Act;

(e) 'local authority housing' means housing accommodation provided by a local housing authority (whether in its own district or not);

(f) 'secure tenancy' has the meaning assigned by section 79 of the Housing Act 1985 and 'secure tenant' shall be construed accordingly; and

(g) 'the 1971 Act' means the Town and Country Planning Act 1971.

(2) In this Part of this Act 'the Corporation' means the Housing Corporation or Housing for Wales but—

(a) an approval given by the Housing Corporation shall not have effect in relation to buildings or other property in Wales; and

(b) an approval given by Housing for Wales shall not have effect in relation to buildings or other property in England.

Part IV Change of landlord: secure tenants

Preliminary

Right conferred by Part IV

93.—(1)   This Part has effect for the purpose of conferring on any person who has been approved under section 94 below the right to acquire from a public sector landlord, subject to and in accordance with the provisions of this Part—

(a)   the fee simple estate in any buildings each of which comprises or contains one or more dwelling-houses which on the relevant date are occupied by qualifying tenants of the public sector landlord; and

(b)   the fee simple estate in any other property which is reasonably required for occupation with buildings falling within paragraph (a) above.

(2)   The following are public sector landlords for the purposes of this Part, namely—

(a)   a local housing authority within the meaning of section 1 of the Housing Act 1985 (in this Part referred to as 'the 1985 Act');

(b)   a new town corporation within the meaning of section 4(b) of that Act;

(c)   a housing action trust within the meaning of Part III of this Act; and

(d)   the Development Board for Rural Wales.

(3)   Subject to subsection (4) below, a secure tenant of a public sector landlord is a qualifying tenant for the purposes of this Part if (and only if) his secure tenancy is held directly from the landlord as owner of the fee simple estate and, in relation to any acquisition or proposed acquisition under this Part, any reference in the following provisions of this Part to qualifying tenant is a reference only to a qualifying tenant of the public sector landlord from whom the acquisition is or is proposed to be made.

(4)   A secure tenant is not a qualifying tenant for the purposes of this Part if—

(a)   he is obliged to give up possession of the dwelling-house in pursuance of an order of the court or will be so obliged at a date specified in such an order; or

(b)   the circumstances are as set out in any of paragraphs 5 to 11 of Schedule 5 to the 1985 Act (exceptions to right to buy).

(5)   In this Part 'the relevant date', in relation to an acquisition or proposed acquisition under this Part, means the date on which is made the application under section 96 below claiming to exercise the right conferred by this Part.

Persons by whom right may be exercised

94.—(1)   The right conferred by this Part shall not be exercisable except by a person who is for the time being approved by the Corporation under this section; and neither a public sector landlord nor the council of a county nor any other body which the Corporation have reason to believe might not be independent of such a landlord or council may be approved under this section.

(2)   For the purposes of subsection (1) above, a body shall not be regarded as independent of a public sector landlord or the council of a county if the body is or appears likely to be under the control of, or subject to influence from, such a landlord or council or particular members or officers of such a landlord or council.

(3) The Corporation shall establish (and may from time to time vary) criteria to be satisfied by a person seeking approval under this section and, without prejudice to subsections (1) and (2) above, in deciding whether to give such approval, the Corporation shall have regard to whether the person satisfies those criteria.

(4) Subject to any directions under section 76 of the Housing Associations Act 1985 (directions by the Secretary of State), an approval under this section—

(a) shall not be given except to a person making an application accompanied by such fee as the Corporation, with the consent of the Secretary of State, may specify; and

(b) may be given to a particular person or to persons of a particular description; and

(c) may apply either in relation to acquisitions generally or in relation to a particular acquisition or acquisitions or in relation to acquisitions made in a particular area or within a particular period; and

(d) may be made conditional upon the person or persons concerned entering into such undertakings as may be specified by the Corporation;

and different fees may be specified under paragraph (a) above for different descriptions of cases.

(5) Subject to any directions under section 76 of the Housing Associations Act 1985, if it appears to the Corporation appropriate to do so (whether by reason of a failure to honour an undertaking or to meet any criteria or for any other reason), the Corporation may revoke an approval given under this section by notice in writing served on the approved person; and where such a notice of revocation is served—

(a) the revocation shall be provisional until the expiry of such period, being not less than 14 days, as may be specified in the notice;

(b) if the Corporation withdraws the notice at any time during the specified period, the approval shall be treated as never having been revoked; and

(c) subject to paragraph (b) above, after the date of service of the notice, the person concerned may not take any steps in connection with a claim to exercise the right conferred by this Part;

but the service of a notice under this subsection shall not affect any transaction completed before the service of the notice.

(6) In the case of a body which has been approved under this section which does not have a registered office (at which documents can be served) and which appears to the Corporation to have ceased to exist or not to operate, notice under subsection (5) above shall be deemed to be served on the body if it is served at the address last known to the Corporation to be the principal place of business of the body.

(7) The Housing Corporation and Housing for Wales shall each maintain a register of persons for the time being approved by it under this section, specifying the extent of the approval given in each case; and each register so maintained shall be open to inspection at the head office of the Corporation by which it is maintained at all reasonable times.

Property excluded from right
95.—(1) A building shall be excluded from an acquisition under this Part if on the relevant date—

(a) any part or parts of the building is or are occupied or intended to be occupied otherwise than for residential purposes; and

(b) the internal floor area of that part or those parts (taken together) exceeds 50 per cent of the internal floor area of the building (taken as a whole);

and for the purposes of this subsection the internal floor area of any common parts or common facilities shall be disregarded.

(2) In the application of subsection (1) above to property falling within section 93(1)(b) above, a building or part of a building which, apart from this subsection, would not be regarded as occupied for residential purposes shall be so regarded if—

(a) it is or is intended to be occupied together with dwelling-house and used for purposes connected with the occupation of the dwelling-house; or

(b) it is or is intended to be used for the provision of services to a dwelling-house which is comprised in a building falling within section 93(1)(a) above.

(3) A building shall be excluded from an acquisition under this Part if—

(a) it contains two or more dwelling-houses which on the relevant date are occupied by secure tenants who are not qualifying tenants; and

(b) the number of dwelling-houses which on that date are occupied by such tenants exceeds 50 per cent of the total number of dwelling-houses in the building.

(4) A dwelling-house shall be excluded from an acquisition under this Part if it is a house and it is occupied on the relevant date by—

(a) a secure tenant who is precluded from being a qualifying tenant by section 93(4)(b) above; or

(b) a tenant who is not a secure tenant.

(5) A building or other property shall be excluded from an acquisition under this Part if—

(a) it was specified in some other application made under section 96 below made before the relevant date; and

(b) that other application has not been disposed of.

(6) Except to the extent that it comprises or is let together with a dwelling-house, property shall be excluded from an acquisition under this Part if it is land held—

(a) for the purposes of section 164 of the Public Health Act 1875 (pleasure grounds); or

(b) in accordance with section 10 of the Open Spaces Act 1906 (duty of local authority to maintain open spaces and burial grounds).

(7) The Secretary of State may by order substitute for the percentage for the

time being specified in subsection (1)(b) above such other percentage as is specified in the order.

Initial procedures

Application to exercise right
96.—(1)   An application claiming to exercise the right conferred by this Part—

(a)   shall be made in the prescribed form to the public sector landlord concerned; and

(b)   shall specify and be accompanied by a plan which shows—

(i)   the buildings proposed to be acquired by virtue of paragraph (a) of subsection (1) of section 93 above; and

(ii)   the property proposed to be acquired by virtue of paragraph (b) of that subsection.

(2)   Where an application claiming to exercise the right conferred by this Part specifies, as a building proposed to be acquired by virtue of section 93(1)(a) above, a building containing a dwelling-house which is subject to an approved cooperative management agreement, the application—

(a)   shall specify all the buildings which contain dwelling-houses subject to the agreement and in which the public sector landlord has the fee simple estate; and

(b)   shall not specify (by virtue of paragraph (a) or paragraph (b) of subsection (1) of section 93 above) any building which contains dwelling-houses if none of them is subject to the agreement.

(3)   For the purposes of subsection (2) above, an approved cooperative management agreement is an agreement—

(a)   which is made with the approval of the Secretary of State under section 27 of the Housing Act 1985, either as originally enacted or as substituted by section 10 of the Housing and Planning Act 1986; and

(b)   under which the body exercising functions of the local housing authority is a society, company or body of trustees approved by the Secretary of State for the purposes of subsection (2) above.

Information etc. for applicant
97.—(1)   Within four weeks of the relevant date, the landlord shall serve on the applicant a notice specifying—

(a)   the name and address of every tenant or licensee of a dwelling-house which the buildings proposed to be acquired by virtue of section 93(1)(a) above comprise or contain; and

(b)   the general nature of his tenancy or licence.

(2)   As from four weeks after that date, the applicant shall have the following rights, namely—

(a)   a right of access, at any reasonable time and on giving reasonable notice, to any property proposed to be acquired which is not subject to a tenancy;

(b)   a right, on giving reasonable notice, to be provided with a list of any documents to which subsection (3) below applies;

(c)　a right to inspect, at any reasonable time and on giving reasonable notice, any documents to which that subsection applies; and

(d)　a right, on payment of a reasonable fee, to be provided with a copy of any documents inspected under paragraph (c) above.

(3)　This subsection applies to any document in the possession of the landlord—

(a)　sight of which is reasonably required for the purpose of pursuing the application; and

(b)　which, on a proposed sale by a willing vendor to a willing purchaser of the property proposed to be acquired, the landlord, as vendor, would be expected to make available to the purchaser (whether at or before contract or completion).

(4)　In this section 'document' has the same meaning as in Part I of the Civil Evidence Act 1968.

Determination of property to be included

98.—(1)　Within twelve weeks of the relevant date, the landlord shall serve on the applicant a notice stating—

(a)　which (if any) of the buildings proposed to be acquired by virtue of paragraph (a) of subsection (1) of section 93 above should be excluded from the acquisition on the ground that they do not comprise or contain one or more dwelling-houses which on the relevant date were occupied by qualifying tenants;

(b)　which (if any) property proposed to be acquired by virtue of paragraph (b) of that subsection should be excluded from the acquisition on the ground that it is not reasonably required for occupation with any of the buildings proposed to be acquired by virtue of paragraph (a) of that subsection or that it is reasonably required for occupation with such of those buildings as should be excluded from the acquisition on the ground mentioned in paragraph (a) above;

(c)　which (if any) property proposed to be acquired by virtue of either paragraph of that subsection should be excluded from the acquisition on the ground that its inclusion is precluded by section 95 above or that it is reasonably required for occupation with property the inclusion of which is so precluded or that it is a building which is excluded from the acquisition by virtue of section 96(2)(b) above;

(d)　which property (if any) the landlord desires to have included in the acquisition on the ground that it cannot otherwise be reasonably managed or maintained;

(e)　which rights (if any) the landlord desires to retain over property included in the acquisition on the ground that they are necessary for the proper management or maintenance of land to be retained by the landlord;

(f)　the other proposed terms of the conveyance; and

(g)　such other particulars as may be prescribed.

(2)　A building which is excluded from an acquisition by virtue of section 95 or section 96(2)(b) above may not be included by virtue of subsection (1)(d) above.

(3)　Where a notice under subsection (1) above specifies property falling within paragraph (d) of that subsection, the applicant shall have a right of access, at any reasonable time and on giving reasonable notice, to any of that property which is not subject to a tenancy.

(4)   Within four weeks of service of the notice under subsection (1) above, the applicant shall notify the landlord in writing of any matters stated in that notice which he does not accept.

(5)   Any dispute as to any matters stated in a notice under subsection (1) above shall be determined—

(a)   by a person agreed to by the parties or, in default of agreement, appointed by the Secretary of State; and

(b)   in accordance with such provisions (including provisions as to costs) as may be prescribed.

(6)   In relation to a proposed acquisition under this Part, any reference in the following provisions of this Part to the property to which the acquisition relates is a reference to the whole of the property which, in accordance with the provisions of this section, is to be acquired, disregarding the effect of any exclusion by virtue of regulations under section 100 below.

Determination of purchase price
99.—(1)   Within eight weeks of—

(a)   if there is no dispute as to any of the matters stated in the notice under section 98(1) above, the service of that notice, or

(b)   if there is such a dispute, the determination of the dispute,

the landlord shall serve on the applicant a notice specifying—

(i)   the price which, disregarding sections 100(3) and 103(1) below, it considers should be payable for the property to be acquired or, as the case may be, the disposal cost which, disregarding section 100(3) below, is attributable to the property to be acquired by virtue of subsection (3) below; and

(ii)   if the property to which the acquisition relates includes dwelling-houses which are houses as well as other property, an amount which the landlord considers to be the amount attributable to houses as defined in section 100(4)(b) below.

(2)   Subject to sections 100(3) and 103(1) below, the price payable for the property to be acquired shall be the price which on the relevant date the property to which the acquisition relates would realise if sold on the open market by a willing vendor on the following assumptions, namely—

(a)   that it was sold subject to any tenancies subsisting on that date but otherwise with vacant possession;

(b)   that it was to be conveyed with the same rights and subject to the same burdens as it would be in pursuance of the right of acquisition;

(c)   that the only bidders in the market were persons who on that date either were approved under section 94 above or fulfilled the criteria for approval established under subsection (3) of that section;

(d)   that the applicant would, within a reasonable period, carry out such works as are reasonably necessary to put the buildings included in the acquisition into the state of repair required by the landlord's repairing obligations; and

(e) that the applicant would not be required to grant any leases in pursuance of regulations made under section 100 below.

(3) Subject to section 100(3) below, there is a disposal cost attributable to the property to be acquired if, having regard to the expense likely to be incurred in carrying out the works referred to in paragraph (d) of subsection (2) above, the property to which the acquisition relates would not realise any price in the circumstances specified in that subsection; and that disposal cost is the amount by which the expense likely to be so incurred exceeds what would be determined under that subsection as the price if those works had already been carried out.

(4) The notice under subsection (1) above shall contain sufficient information to enable the applicant to see how the price or, as the case may be, disposal cost and any amount referred to in sub-paragraphs (i) and (ii) of subsection (1) above were arrived at and, if the property to which the acquisition relates consists of or includes any dwelling-houses which are houses, the notice shall also contain a list of the addresses of the houses together with the number of habitable rooms in each of them.

(5) Within four weeks of service of the notice under subsection (1) above, the applicant shall notify the landlord in writing of any matters stated in that notice which he does not accept.

(6) Any dispute as to any matters stated in a notice under subsection (1) above shall be determined by the district valuer, in accordance with such provisions (including provisions as to costs) as may be prescribed.

Special cases

Tenants continuing as tenants of landlord
100.—(1) The Secretary of State shall make regulations imposing the following requirements in relation to any acquisition under this Part, namely—

(a) that any dwelling-house which is a house and is occupied by a tenant to whom subsection (2) below applies shall be excluded from the acquisition; and

(b) that a lease of any dwelling-house which is a flat and is occupied by a tenant to whom subsection (2) below applies or by a tenant of a description prescribed for the purposes of this paragraph shall be granted by the applicant to the landlord immediately after the acquisition.

(2) This subsection applies—

(a) to any qualifying tenant whose tenancy commenced before the relevant date, and

(b) to any tenant of a description prescribed for the purposes of this subsection,

being, in either case, a tenant who, before the end of the period mentioned in section 102 below and in response to the consultation under that section, gives notice as mentioned in section 103(2) below of his wish to continue as a tenant of the landlord.

(3) If, by virtue of regulations under this section, any houses fall to be excluded from the acquisition—

(a)   there shall be determined the sum (in this subsection referred to as 'the sum referable to excluded houses') which represents that proportion of the amount attributable to houses which the number of habitable rooms in the houses which fall to be so excluded bears to the number of habitable rooms in all of the houses comprised in the property to which the acquisition relates; and

(b)   if the amount attributable to houses is a price, the sum referable to excluded houses shall be applied as a deduction from any price payable for the property to be acquired, as determined under section 99 above, and as an increase in any disposal cost attributable to that property; and

(c)   if the amount attributable to houses is a disposal cost, the sum referable to excluded houses shall be applied as an increase in any price payable for the property to be acquired, as determined under section 99 above, and as a deduction from any disposal cost attributable to that property.

(4)   In section 99(1)(ii) and subsection (3) above, 'the amount attributable to houses', in relation to an acquisition under this Part, means,—

(a)   if the property to which the acquisition relates consists of dwelling-houses which are houses and no other property, the price or, as the case may be, disposal cost specified in accordance with section 99(1)(i) above; and

(b)   in any other case, the price or disposal cost which, under subsection (2) or subsection (3) of section 99 above, would be payable for, or attributable to, the property to which the acquisition relates if there were excluded from that property all property other than dwelling-houses which are houses.

Tenancies granted after relevant date
101.—(1)   Subject to subsection (4)(a) below, this section applies to any tenancy of or licence to occupy any part of the property proposed to be acquired, being a tenancy or licence commencing,—

(a)   in the case of property falling within paragraph (d) of subsection (1) of section 98 above, after the date of the notice under that subsection;
(b)   in any other case, after the relevant date.

(2)   Notwithstanding anything in any enactment, a tenancy or licence to which this section applies—

(a)   shall not be a secure tenancy, and
(b)   shall not be capable of becoming an assured tenancy or an assured agricultural occupancy,

and neither Part II of the Landlord and Tenant Act 1954 (business tenancies) nor Parts III to VI of the Agricultural Holdings Act 1986 (tenancies of agricultural holdings, including market gardens and smallholdings) shall apply to a tenancy or licence to which this section applies.

(3)   Every tenancy or licence to which this section applies shall be determinable by the landlord or licensor by giving not less than four weeks' notice to quit expiring at any time during the tenancy; and this subsection has effect whether or not the tenancy or licence is periodic and, if it is periodic, regardless of the length of the period.

(4)   The Secretary of State may make regulations—

(a)   excluding from the tenancies and licences to which this section applies a tenancy or licence of a description specified in the regulations;

(b)   requiring the public sector landlord to give notice to the applicant of the grant of any tenancy or licence to which this section applies;

(c)   requiring the public sector landlord to give notice of the effect of this section to any tenant or licensee under a tenancy or licence to which this section applies;

(d)   for securing that, on the transfer of the property included in the acquisition to the applicant, the public sector landlord gives vacant possession of any property subject to a tenancy or licence to which this section applies;

(e)   that, in so far as vacant possession is not so given, any costs or expenses attributable to the recovery of vacant possession by the applicant and any losses consequent upon the failure of the public sector landlord to give vacant possession are recoverable by the applicant from that landlord as a simple contract debt; and

(f)   making provision for and in connection with the disapplication of this section in any case where the applicant does not proceed with the acquisition.

Final procedures

Consultations by applicant

102.—(1)   During such period as may be prescribed beginning with,—

(a)   if there is a determination by the district valuer under section 99 above, notification to the applicant of that determination,

(b)   if there is no such determination, service of the landlord's notice under that section,

the applicant shall consult, in accordance with such provisions as may be prescribed, tenants to whom this section applies.

(2)   This section applies—

(a)   to any qualifying tenant, or tenant under a long tenancy, who on the relevant date occupied a dwelling-house proposed to be included in the acquisition and continued to occupy the dwelling during the period referred to in subsection (1) above; and

(b)   to any tenant of a description prescribed for the purposes of section 100(2) above; and

(c)   to any tenant of a description prescribed for the purposes of this section.

Notice by applicant of intention to proceed

103.—(1)   Subject to subsection (2) below, the applicant may, within two weeks of the end of the period mentioned in section 102 above, serve on the landlord notice of his intention to proceed with the acquisition; and in that notice the applicant, in such circumstances as may be prescribed, may inform the landlord—

(a)   that he wishes to enter into a prescribed covenant to make payments to the landlord on the occasion of any prescribed disposal (occurring after the date of the acquisition) of a dwelling-house comprised in the property to be acquired; and

(b)   that he requires the value of that covenant to be taken into account in reducing the price which would otherwise be payable for the property to be acquired.

(2)   The applicant shall not be entitled to serve a notice under subsection (1) above if, in response to the consultation under section 102 above,—

(a)   less than 50 per cent of the tenants to whom that section applies have given notice of their wishes in such manner as may be prescribed; or

(b)   the number of tenants to whom that section applies who have given notice in that manner of their wish to continue as tenants of the landlord exceeds 50 per cent of the total number of tenants to whom that section applies.

(3)   In any case where a tenancy is held by two or more persons jointly, those persons shall be regarded as a single tenant for the purposes of subsection (2) above and, accordingly, any notice given in response to the consultation under section 102 above shall be of no effect for the purposes of subsection (2) above unless it is given by or on behalf of all the joint tenants.

(4)   A notice under subsection (1) above shall contain—

(a)   a list of the names and addresses of tenants to whom section 102 above applies (if any) who have given notice as mentioned in subsection (2)(b) above;

(b)   a list of the houses (if any) which are, by virtue of regulations under section 100 above, to be excluded from the acquisition;

(c)   a list of flats (if any) of which the applicant is required, by virtue of such regulations, to grant leases to the landlord and a statement of the proposed terms of those leases;

(d)   such information as may be necessary to show how the lists mentioned in paragraphs (a), (b) and (c) above were established; and

(e)   the price payable for the property to be acquired (disregarding any reduction by virtue of such a covenant as is referred to in subsection (1) above) or, as the case may be, the disposal cost attributable to that property.

(5)   Within two weeks of service of the notice under subsection (1) above, the landlord shall notify the applicant in writing of any matters stated in that notice which it does not accept.

(6)   Where a notice has been served under subsection (1) above, every tenant to whom section 102 above applies and who has not given notice as mentioned in subsection (2)(b) above shall be taken to have accepted, and to have given consideration for, any offer which—

(a)   relates to the terms on which, after the acquisition, he is to occupy the dwelling-house occupied by him on the relevant date;

(b)   was made to him by the applicant either in the course of the consultation required by subsection (1) of section 102 above or otherwise before the end of the period referred to in that subsection; and

(c)   was neither withdrawn by the applicant nor rejected by the tenant before the end of that period.

(7)   Regulations prescribing any of the matters referred to in subsection (1) above shall also make provision with respect to the determination of the amounts

which are to be payable on the occasion of prescribed disposals; and the amount of any reduction in the price payable for the property to be acquired which is attributable to such a covenant as is referred to in that subsection shall be determined by the district valuer.

Duty to complete and consequences of completion
104.—(1)   Where the applicant has served on the landlord a notice under section 103(1) above, then, as soon as any dispute as to any matters stated in that notice has been determined and, where appropriate, any determination has been made under section 103(7) above—

(a)   the landlord shall make to the applicant a grant of the property included in the acquisition for an estate in fee simple absolute, but subject to any rights to be retained by the landlord; and

(b)   the applicant shall grant to the landlord leases of any flats of which he is required to grant leases by regulations under section 100 above.

(2)   The terms of any grant or lease under subsection (1) above shall comply with such requirements as may be prescribed.

(3)   The duties imposed by the preceding provisions of this section are enforceable by injunction.

(4)   Notwithstanding anything in section 141 of the Law of Property Act 1925 (rent and benefit of lessee's covenants to run with the reversion) any rent or other sum which—

(a)   arises under a tenancy of any property included in the acquisition, and

(b)   falls due before the date of the grant under subsection (1) above,

shall continue to be recoverable by the landlord to the exclusion of the applicant and of any other person in whom the reversion on the tenancy may become vested.

(5)   Without prejudice to the application of Part VIII of the Local Government, Planning and Land Act 1980 (capital expenditure of local authorities) to the price received by the landlord on the disposal (as mentioned in subsection (1)(a) above) of the property included in the acquisition, where there is a disposal cost attributable to that property any payments made by the landlord in respect of that cost shall be prescribed expenditure for the purposes of that Part.

Subsequent disposals

Consent required for subsequent disposals
105.—(1)   A person who acquires any property under this Part (in this section referred to as 'the new landlord') shall not dispose of it except with the consent of the Secretary of State; but nothing in this subsection shall apply in relation to an exempt disposal, as defined in subsection (7) below.

(2)   Where an estate or interest in property acquired by the new landlord has been mortgaged or charged, the prohibition in subsection (1) above on disposal of the property without consent applies also to a disposal by the mortgagee or chargee in exercise of a power of sale or leasing, whether or not the disposal is in the name of the new landlord.

(3)   In any case where—

(a) by operation of law or by virtue of an order of a court property which has been acquired by the new landlord passes or is transferred to another person, and

(b) that passing or transfer does not constitute a disposal for which consent is required under subsection (1) above,

this section (including, where there is more than one such passing or transfer, this subsection) shall apply as if the other person to whom the property passes or is transferred were the new landlord.

(4) Any consent for the purposes of subsection (1) above may be given either unconditionally or subject to conditions; but, before giving any such consent, the Secretary of State—

(a) shall satisfy himself that the person who is seeking the consent has taken appropriate steps to consult every tenant of the whole or any part of the property proposed to be disposed of; and

(b) shall have regard to the responses of any such tenants to that consultation.

(5) If, apart from subsection (6) below, the consent of the Housing Corporation or Housing for Wales would be required under section 9 of the Housing Associations Act 1985 (control of dispositions of land by housing associations) for a disposal to which subsection (1) above applies, the Secretary of State shall consult that body before giving his consent in respect of that disposal for the purposes of that subsection.

(6) No consent shall be required under the said section 9 for any disposal in respect of which consent is given in accordance with subsection (5) above.

(7) In this section an 'exempt disposal' means—

(a) the grant of a lease pursuant to such a requirement as is referred to in section 100(1)(b) above;

(b) the disposal of a dwelling-house to a person having the right to buy it under Part V of the 1985 Act (whether the disposal is in fact made under that Part or otherwise);

(c) a compulsory disposal, within the meaning of Part V of the 1985 Act;

(d) the disposal of an easement or rentcharge;

(e) the disposal of an interest by way of security for a loan;

(f) the grant of a secure tenancy or what would be a secure tenancy but for any of paragraphs 2 to 12 of Schedule 1 to the 1985 Act;

(g) the grant of an assured tenancy, within the meaning of Part I of this Act, or what would be such a tenancy but for any of paragraphs 4 to 8 of Schedule 1 to this Act; and

(h) the transfer of an interest which is held on trust where the disposal is made in connection with the appointment of a new trustee or in connection with the discharge of any trustee.

(8) In this section references to disposing of property include references to—

(a) granting or disposing of any interest in property;

(b) entering into a contract to dispose of property or to grant or dispose of any such interest; and

(c) granting an option to acquire property or any such interest.

Supplemental

Service of information, advice and assistance

106.—(1) The Corporation may provide in connection with this Part a service of information, advice and assistance to, and for the benefit of,—

(a) persons who have been approved or are considering applying for approval under section 94 above; and

(b) persons who are tenants of public sector landlords.

(2) The Corporation may make charges for information, advice and assistance provided under this section otherwise than to persons falling within subsection (1)(b) above.

(3) The powers conferred on the Corporation by this section may be exercised by the Housing Corporation and Housing for Wales acting jointly.

Power of Corporation to provide legal assistance to tenants in relation to acquisitions

107.—(1) On an application by the tenant of a dwelling-house who is a party or a prospective party to proceedings or prospective proceedings falling within subsection (2) below, the Corporation may give assistance to the tenant if it thinks fit to do so—

(a) on the ground that the case raises a question of principle; or

(b) on the ground that it is unreasonable, having regard to the complexity of the case, or to any other matter, to expect the tenant to deal with it without assistance; or

(c) by reason of any other special consideration.

(2) The proceedings referred to in subsection (1) above are—

(a) proceedings to determine any question arising in relation to an acquisition or proposed acquisition under this Part; and

(b) proceedings to determine any dispute arising after an acquisition under this Part between a transferred tenant of a dwelling-house included in the acquisition and the body by which the acquisition was made;

and for the purposes of paragraph (b) above a tenant of a dwelling-house is a transferred tenant of it if he was the qualifying tenant of it at the time of the acquisition or is the widow or widower of the person who was then the qualifying tenant of it.

(3) Assistance given by the Corporation under this section may include—

(a) giving advice;

(b) procuring or attempting to procure the settlement of the matter in dispute;

(c) arranging for the giving of advice or assistance by a solicitor or counsel;

(d) arranging for representation by a solicitor or counsel, including such assistance as is usually given by a solicitor or counsel in the steps preliminary or incidental to any proceedings, or in arriving at or giving effect to a compromise to avoid or bring to an end any proceedings; and

(e)   any other form of assistance which the Corporation may consider appropriate;

but paragraph (d) above does not affect the law and practice regulating the descriptions of persons who may appear in, conduct, defend and address the court in any proceedings.

(4)   In so far as expenses are incurred by the Corporation in providing the tenant with assistance under this section, the recovery of those expenses (as taxed or assessed in such manner as may be prescribed by rules of court) shall constitute a first charge for the benefit of the Corporation—

(a)   on any costs which (whether by virtue of a judgment or order of a court or an agreement or otherwise) are payable to the tenant by any other person in respect of the matter in connection with which the assistance was given; and

(b)   so far as relates to any costs, on his rights under any compromise or settlement arrived at in connection with that matter to avoid or bring to an end any proceedings;

but subject to any charge under the Legal Aid Act 1988 and to any provision of that Act for payment of any sum to the Legal Aid Board.

Registration of title and related matters
108.   Schedule 12 to this Act shall have effect with respect to registration of title and related matters arising on acquisitions of property under this Part and disposals of property so acquired.

Public open space etc.
109.—(1)   To the extent that any land held—

(a)   for the purposes of section 164 of the Public Health Act 1875 (pleasure grounds), or
(b)   in accordance with section 10 of the Open Spaces Act 1906 (duty of local authority to maintain open spaces and burial grounds),

is included in an acquisition under this Part, it shall be deemed to be freed from any trust arising solely by virtue of its being land held in trust for enjoyment by the public in accordance with that section.

(2)   Nothing in section 5 of the Green Belt (London and Home Counties) Act 1938 (restrictions on alienation of land by local authorities) applies in relation to a disposal of land included in an acquisition under this Part.

Extension etc. of relevant periods
110.—(1)   In this section 'relevant period' means any period within which anything is required by this Part to be done by either of the parties, that is to say, the applicant and the landlord.

(2)   At any time before the end of any relevant period, or any such period as previously extended under this subsection, the other party may, by a written notice served on the party to whom the requirement relates, extend or further extend that period.

(3)   Where a notice of revocation of the applicant's approval is served under subsection (5) of section 94 above and subsequently withdrawn as mentioned in paragraph (b) of that subsection, any relevant period which, apart from this

subsection, would have expired before the withdrawal shall be taken to be extended by a period equal to that beginning with the date of the service of the notice of revocation and ending on the date of the withdrawal.

(4) Where—

(a) the applicant is the party to whom the requirement relates, and

(b) the relevant period, or that period as extended under subsection (2) above, expires without his doing what he is required by this Part to do within that period,

his application claiming to exercise the right conferred by this Part shall be deemed to be withdrawn, but without prejudice to his making a further such application.

Power to prescribe forms etc.
111. The Secretary of State may by regulations prescribe—

(a) anything which by this Part is to be prescribed; and

(b) the form of any notice, statement or other document which is required or authorised to be used under or for the purposes of this Part.

Orders and regulations
112.—(1) Any power of the Secretary of State to make orders or regulations under this Part shall be exercised by statutory instrument.

(2) A statutory instrument containing any order or regulations under this Part, other than regulations under section 111(b) above, shall be subject to annulment in pursuance of a resolution of either House of Parliament.

(3) Orders or regulations under this Part may make different provision for different cases or circumstances or different areas and may contain such incidental, supplemental or transitional provisions as the Secretary of State thinks fit.

Jurisdiction of county court
113.—(1) Subject to sections 98(5) and 99(6) above, a county court has jurisdiction—

(a) to entertain any proceedings brought under this Part; and

(b) to determine any question arising under this Part.

(2) The jurisdiction conferred by this section includes jurisdiction to entertain proceedings on any such question as is mentioned in subsection (1) above notwithstanding that no other relief is sought than a declaration.

(3) If a person takes in the High Court proceedings which, by virtue of this section, he could have taken in the county court, he shall not be entitled to recover any more costs of those proceedings than those to which he would have been entitled if the proceedings had been taken in a county court.

(4) In a case falling within subsection (3) above the taxing master shall have the same power of directing on what scale costs are to be allowed, and of allowing any item of costs, as the judge would have had if the proceedings had been taken in a county court.

Interpretation of Part IV
114.—(1) In this Part—

'the 1985 Act' means the Housing Act 1985;
'the Corporation' means the Housing Corporation or Housing for Wales
but—

(a) an approval given by the Housing Corporation shall not have effect
in relation to buildings or other property in Wales; and

(b) an approval given by Housing for Wales shall not have effect in
relation to buildings or other property in England;

'qualifying tenant' shall be construed in accordance with subsections (3) and
(4) of section 93 above;
'prescribed' means prescribed by regulations made by the Secretary of State;
'property' means land with or without buildings;
'public sector landlord' has the meaning given by section 93(2) above;
'the relevant date' has the meaning given by section 93(5) above; and
'habitable room', in relation to a house, means a room used, or intended for
use, as a bedroom, living room, dining room or kitchen.

(2) Subject to subsection (1) above, in this Part expressions which are also
used in Part V of the 1985 Act have the same meaning as in that Part.

Part V Miscellaneous and general

Leases

Premiums on long leases
115.—(1) With respect to—

(a) any premium received or required to be paid after the commencement
of this Act, or

(b) any loan required to be made after that commencement,

section 127 of the Rent Act 1977 (allowable premiums in relation to certain long
tenancies) shall have effect subject to the amendments in subsections (2) and (3)
below.

(2) For subsections (2) and (3) there shall be substituted the following
subsections—

'(2) The conditions mentioned in subsection (1)(a) above are—

(a) that the landlord has no power to determine the tenancy at any
time within 20 years beginning on the date when it was granted; and

(b) that the terms of the tenancy do not inhibit both the assignment
and the underletting of the whole of the premises comprised in the tenancy;

but for the purpose of paragraph (b) above there shall be disregarded any
term of the tenancy which inhibits assignment and underletting only during
a period which is or falls within the final seven years of the term for which
the tenancy was granted.

(3) The reference in subsection (2) above to a power of the landlord to
determine a tenancy does not include a reference to a power of re-entry or
forfeiture for breach of any term or condition of the tenancy.'

(3)   Subsections (3C) and (3D) shall be omitted and in subsection (5) for '(2)(c)' there shall be substituted '(2)(b)'.

(4)   Expressions used in subsection (1) above have the same meaning as in Part IX of the Rent Act 1977.

Repairing obligations in short leases

116.—(1)   In section 11 of the Landlord and Tenant Act 1985 (repairing obligations in short leases) after subsection (1) there shall be inserted the following subsections—

'(1A)   If a lease to which this section applies is a lease of a dwelling-house which forms part only of a building, then, subject to subsection (1B), the covenant implied by subsection (1) shall have effect as if—

(a)   the reference in paragraph (a) of that subsection to the dwelling-house included a reference to any part of the building in which the lessor has an estate or interest; and

(b)   any reference in paragraphs (b) and (c) of that subsection to an installation in the dwelling-house included a reference to an installation which, directly or indirectly, serves the dwelling-house and which either—

(i)   forms part of any part of a building in which the lessor has an estate or interest; or

(ii)   is owned by the lessor or under his control.

(1B)   Nothing in subsection (1A) shall be construed as requiring the lessor to carry out any works or repairs unless the disrepair (or failure to maintain in working order) is such as to affect the lessee's enjoyment of the dwelling-house or of any common parts, as defined in section 60(1) of the Landlord and Tenant Act 1987, which the lessee, as such, is entitled to use.'

(2)   After subsection (3) of that section there shall be inserted the following subsection—

'(3A)   In any case where—

(a)   the lessor's repairing covenant has effect as mentioned in subsection (1A), and

(b)   in order to comply with the covenant the lessor needs to carry out works or repairs otherwise than in, or to an installation in, the dwelling-house, and

(c)   the lessor does not have a sufficient right in the part of the building or the installation concerned to enable him to carry out the required works or repairs,

then, in any proceedings relating to a failure to comply with the lessor's repairing covenant, so far as it requires the lessor to carry out the works or repairs in question, it shall be a defence for the lessor to prove that he used all reasonable endeavours to obtain, but was unable to obtain, such rights as would be adequate to enable him to carry out the works or repairs.'

(3)   At the end of section 14(4) of the said Act of 1985 (which excludes from section 11 certain leases granted to various bodies) there shall be added—

'a housing action trust established under Part III of the Housing Act 1988'.

(4) The amendments made by this section do not have effect with respect to—

(a)   a lease entered into before the commencement of this Act; or

(b)   a lease entered into pursuant to a contract made before the commencement of this Act.

Certain tenancies excluded from bankrupt's estate
117.—(1) In section 283 of the Insolvency Act 1986 (definition of bankrupt's estate) at the end of subsection (3) (property excluded from the estate) there shall be inserted the following subsection—

'(3A) Subject to section 308A in Chapter IV, subsection (1) does not apply to—

(a)   a tenancy which is an assured tenancy or an assured agricultural occupancy, within the meaning of Part I of the Housing Act 1988, and the terms of which inhibit an assignment as mentioned in section 127(5) of the Rent Act 1977, or

(b)   a protected tenancy, within the meaning of the Rent Act 1977, in respect of which, by virtue of any provision of Part IX of that Act, no premium can lawfully be required as a condition of assignment, or

(c)   a tenancy of a dwelling-house by virtue of which the bankrupt is, within the meaning of the Rent (Agriculture) Act 1976, a protected occupier of the dwelling-house, and the terms of which inhibit an assignment as mentioned in section 127(5) of the Rent Act 1977, or

(d)   a secure tenancy, within the meaning of Part IV of the Housing Act 1985, which is not capable of being assigned, except in the cases mentioned in section 91(3) of that Act.'

(2) After section 308 of that Act there shall be inserted the following section—

'Vesting in trustee of certain tenancies
308A. Upon the service on the bankrupt by the trustee of a notice in writing under this section, any tenancy—

(a)   which is excluded by virtue of section 283(3A) from the bankrupt's estate, and

(b)   to which the notice relates,

vests in the trustee as part of the bankrupt's estate; and, except against a purchaser in good faith, for value and without notice of the bankruptcy, the trustee's title to that tenancy has relation back to the commencement of the bankruptcy.'

(3) In section 309 of that Act (time-limit for certain notices) in subsection (1)(b)—

(a)   after the words 'section 308' there shall be inserted 'or section 308A';
and

(b)   after the words 'the property' there shall be inserted 'or tenancy'.

(4)   In section 315 of that Act (disclaimer (general power)), in subsection (4) after the words 'reasonable replacement value)' there shall be inserted 'or 308A'.

Certain tenancies excluded from debtor's estate: Scotland
118.—(1)   In section 31 of the Bankruptcy (Scotland) Act 1985 (vesting of debtor's estate at date of sequestration) in subsection (8) after the word 'means' there shall be inserted the words ', subject to subsection (9) below,'.

(2)   After the said subsection (8) there shall be added the following subsections—

'(9)   Subject to subsection (10) below, the 'whole estate of the debtor' does not include any interest of the debtor as tenant under any of the following tenancies—

(a)   a tenancy which is an assured tenancy within the meaning of Part II of the Housing (Scotland) Act 1988, or

(b)   a protected tenancy within the meaning of the Rent (Scotland) Act 1984 in respect of which, by virtue of any provision of Part VIII of that Act, no premium can lawfully be required as a condition of the assignation, or

(c)   a secure tenancy within the meaning of Part III of the Housing (Scotland) Act 1987.

(10)   On the date on which the permanent trustee serves notice to that effect on the debtor, the interest of the debtor as tenant under any of the tenancies referred to in subsection (9) above shall form part of his estate and vest in the permanent trustee as if it had vested in him under section 32(6) of this Act.'

Amendment of Landlord and Tenant Act 1987
119.   The Landlord and Tenant Act 1987 shall have effect subject to the amendments in Schedule 13 to this Act.

Rent officers

Appointment etc. of rent officers
120.   Section 63 of the Rent Act 1977 (schemes for the appointment of rent officers) shall have effect subject to the amendments in Part I of Schedule 14 to this Act and after section 64 of that Act there shall be inserted the sections set out in Part II of that Schedule.

Rent officers: additional functions relating to housing benefit etc.
121.—(1)   The Secretary of State may by order require rent officers to carry out such functions as may be specified in the order in connection with housing benefit and rent allowance subsidy.

(2)   An order under this section—

(a)   shall be made by statutory instrument which, except in the case of the first order to be made, shall be subject to annulment in pursuance of a resolution of either House of Parliament;

(b)   may make different provision for different cases or classes of case and for different areas; and

(c) may contain such transitional, incidental and supplementary provisions as appear to the Secretary of State to be desirable;

and the first order under this section shall not be made unless a draft of it has been laid before, and approved by a resolution of, each House of Parliament.

(3) In subsection (7) of section 63 of the Rent Act 1977 (expenditure arising in connection with rent officers etc.), in paragraph (a) after the words 'this section' there shall be inserted 'or an order under section 121 of the Housing Act 1988'.

(4) At the end of section 21(6) of the Social Security Act 1986 (regulations prescribing maximum family credit and maximum housing benefit) there shall be added the words 'and regulations prescribing the appropriate maximum housing benefit may provide for benefit to be limited by reference to determinations made by rent officers in exercise of functions conferred under section 121 of the Housing Act 1988'.

(5) In section 30 of that Act (housing benefit finance) at the end of subsection (2) there shall be added the words 'and, in relation to rent allowance subsidy, the Secretary of State may exercise his discretion as to what is unreasonable for the purposes of paragraph (b) above by reference to determinations made by rent officers in exercise of functions conferred under section 121 of the Housing Act 1988'.

(6) In section 51(1)(h) of that Act (regulations may require information etc. needed for determination of a claim) the reference to information or evidence needed for the determination of a claim includes a reference to information or evidence required by a rent officer for the purpose of a function conferred on him under this section.

(7) In this section 'housing benefit' and 'rent allowance subsidy' have the same meaning as in Part II of the Social Security Act 1986.

Right to buy etc. and grants to obtain accommodation

Variation of cost floor for right-to-buy discount
122.—(1) Section 131 of the Housing Act 1985 (limits on amount of discount in relation to the right to buy) shall be amended in accordance with subsections (2) and (3) below.

(2) In subsection (1) (the cost floor provision) for paragraph (a) there shall be substituted the following paragraph—

'(a) is to be treated as incurred at or after the beginning of that period of account of the landlord in which falls the date which is eight years, or such other period of time as may be specified in an order made by the Secretary of State, earlier than the relevant time, and'.

(3) After subsection (1) there shall be inserted the following subsection—

'(1A) In subsection (1)(a) above "period of account", in relation to any costs, means the period for which the landlord made up those of its accounts in which account is taken of those costs.'

(4) This section has effect in relation to the determination of discount in any case where—

(a)   the relevant time falls on or after the date on which this section comes into force; or

(b)   paragraph (a) above does not apply but the landlord has not before that date served on the tenant a notice complying with section 125 of the Housing Act 1985; or

(c)   the tenant has before that date claimed to exercise the right to be granted a shared ownership lease but the landlord has not before that date served on the tenant a notice complying with section 147 of that Act; or

(d)   the tenant has before that date served a notice under paragraph 1 of Schedule 8 to that Act (claiming to exercise the right to acquire an additional share under a shared ownership lease) but the landlord has not before that date served a notice under subparagraph (3) of that paragraph;

and, for the purposes of this subsection, no account shall be taken of any steps taken under section 177 of that Act (amendment or withdrawal and re-service of notice to correct mistakes).

(5)   Expressions used in subsection (4) above have the same meaning as in Part V of the Housing Act 1985.

Amendment of Schedule 5 to Housing Act 1985
123.—(1)   Schedule 5 of the Housing Act 1985 (exceptions to the right to buy) shall be amended in accordance with this section.

(2)   Paragraphs 6 and 8 shall be omitted.

(3)   The repeal by this Act of paragraphs 6 and 8 of Schedule 5 shall not affect the operation of either of those paragraphs in any case where the tenant's notice claiming to exercise the right to buy was served before the repeal comes into force unless, at that time, no notice in response had been served under section 124 of the Housing Act 1985 (landlord's notice admitting or denying right to buy).

(4)   For the purposes of subsection (3) above, no account shall be taken of any steps taken under section 177 of the Housing Act 1985 (amendment or withdrawal and re-service of notice to correct mistakes).

Right to buy: tenant's sanction for landlord's delays
124.   After section 153 of the Housing Act 1985 there shall be inserted the following sections—

'Tenant's notices of delay
153A.—(1)   Where a secure tenant has claimed to exercise the right to buy, he may serve on his landlord a notice (in this section referred to as an "initial notice of delay") in any of the following cases, namely,—

(a)   where the landlord has failed to serve a notice under section 124 within the period appropriate under subsection (2) of that section;

(b)   where the tenant's right to buy has been established and the landlord has failed to serve a notice under section 125 within the period appropriate under subsection (1) of that section;

(c)   where the tenant has claimed to exercise the right to be granted a shared ownership lease and the landlord has failed to serve a notice under section 146 within the period of the four weeks required by that section;

(d)   where the tenant's right to a shared ownership lease has been established and the landlord has failed to serve a notice under section 147 within the period of the eight weeks required by that section; or

(e)   where the tenant considers that delays on the part of the landlord are preventing him from exercising expeditiously his right to buy or his right to be granted a shared ownership lease;

and where an initial notice of delay specifies any of the cases in paragraphs (a) to (d), any reference in this section or section 153B to the default date is a reference to the end of the period referred to in the paragraph in question or, if it is later, the day appointed for the coming into force of section 124 of the Housing Act 1988.

(2)   An initial notice of delay—

(a)   shall specify the most recent action of which the tenant is aware which has been taken by the landlord pursuant to this Part of this Act; and

(b)   shall specify a period (in this section referred to as "the response period"), not being less than one month, beginning on the date of service of the notice, within which the service by the landlord of a counter-notice under subsection (3) will have the effect of cancelling the initial notice of delay.

(3)   Within the response period specified in an initial notice of delay or at any time thereafter, the landlord may serve on the tenant a counter-notice in either of the following circumstances—

(a)   if the initial notice specifies any of the cases in paragraphs (a) to (d) of subsection (1) and the landlord has served, or is serving together with the counter-notice, the required notice under section 124, section 125, section 146 or section 147, as the case may be; or

(b)   if the initial notice specifies the case in subsection (1)(e) and there is no action under this Part which, at the beginning of the response period, it was for the landlord to take in order to allow the tenant expeditiously to exercise his right to buy or his right to be granted a shared ownership lease and which remains to be taken at the time of service of the counter-notice.

(4)   A counter-notice under subsection (3) shall specify the circumstances by virtue of which it is served.

(5)   At any time when—

(a)   the response period specified in an initial notice of delay has expired, and

(b)   the landlord has not served a counter-notice under subsection (3),

the tenant may serve on the landlord a notice (in this section and section 153B referred to as an "operative notice of delay") which shall state that section 153B will apply to payments of rent made by the tenant on or after the default date or, if the initial notice of delay specified the case in subsection (1)(e), the date of the service of the notice.

(6)   If, after a tenant has served an initial notice of delay, a counter-notice has been served under subsection (3), then, whether or not

the tenant has also served an operative notice of delay, if any of the cases in subsection (1) again arises, the tenant may serve a further initial notice of delay and the provisions of this section shall apply again accordingly.

Payments of rent attributable to purchase price etc.
153B.—(1)   Where a secure tenant has served on his landlord an operative notice of delay, this section applies to any payment of rent which is made on or after the default date or, as the case may be, the date of the service of the notice and before the occurrence of any of the following events (and, if more than one event occurs, before the earliest to occur)—

(a)   the service by the landlord of a counter-notice under section 153A(3);

(b)   the date on which the landlord makes to the tenant the grant required by section 138 or, as the case may be, section 150;

(c)   the date on which the tenant serves notice under section 142(2) (claiming to be entitled to defer completion);

(d)   the date on which the tenant withdraws or is deemed to have withdrawn the notice claiming to exercise the right to buy or, as the case may be, the notice claiming to exercise the right to be granted a shared ownership lease; and

(e)   the date on which the tenant ceases to be entitled to exercise the right to buy.

(2)   Except where this section ceases to apply on a date determined under any of paragraphs (c) to (e) of subsection (1), so much of any payment of rent to which this section applies as does not consist of—

(a)   a sum due on account of rates, or

(b)   a service charge (as defined in section 621A),

shall be treated not only as a payment of rent but also as a payment on account by the tenant which is to be taken into account in accordance with subsection (3).

(3)   In a case where subsection (2) applies, the amount which, apart from this section, would be the purchase price or, as the case may be, the tenant's initial contribution for the grant of a shared ownership lease shall be reduced by an amount equal to the aggregate of—

(a)   the total of any payments on account treated as having been paid by the tenant by virtue of subsection (2); and

(b)   if those payments on account are derived from payments of rent referable to a period of more than 12 months, a sum equal to the appropriate percentage of the total referred to in paragraph (a).

(4)   In subsection (3)(b) "the appropriate percentage" means 50 per cent or such other percentage as may be prescribed.'

Restriction on letting etc. of certain houses in National Parks etc.
125.—(1)   Section 37 of the Housing Act 1985 (restriction on disposals of dwelling-houses in National Parks etc.) shall be amended in accordance with this section.

(2)   In subsection (2) (the convenanted limitation) after the word 'his' there shall be inserted '(a)' and at the end there shall be added

'and

(b)   there will be no disposal by way of tenancy or licence without the written consent of the authority unless the disposal is to a person satisfying that condition or by a person whose only or principal home is and, throughout the duration of the tenancy or licence, remains the house'.

(3)   In subsection (3) (disposals limited to persons employed or living locally) after the words 'application for consent' there shall be inserted the words 'or, in the case of a disposal by way of tenancy or licence, preceding the disposal'.

(4)   At the end of subsection (4) (disposals in breach of covenant to be void) there shall be added

'and, so far as it relates to disposals by way of tenancy or licence, such a covenant may be enforced by the local authority as if—

(a)   the authority were possessed of land adjacent to the house concerned; and

(b)   the covenant were expressed to be made for the benefit of such adjacent land'.

(5)   After subsection (4) there shall be inserted the following subsection—

'(4A)   Any reference in the preceding provisions of this section to a disposal by way of tenancy or licence does not include a reference to a relevant disposal or an exempted disposal.'

(6)   This section has effect where the conveyance, grant or assignment referred to in subsection (1) of section 37 is executed on or after the commencement of this Act.

Restriction on disposal of dwelling-houses in National Parks etc. acquired under the right to buy
126.—(1)   In Part V of the Housing Act 1985 (the right to buy), section 157 (restriction on disposal of dwelling-houses in National Parks etc.) shall be amended in accordance with this section.

(2)   In subsection (2) (the covenanted limitation) after the word 'his' there shall be inserted '(a)' and at the end there shall be added

'and

(b)   there will be no disposal by way of tenancy or licence without the written consent of the landlord unless the disposal is to a person satisfying that condition or by a person whose only or principal home is and, throughout the duration of the tenancy or licence, remains the dwelling-house'.

(3)   In subsection (3) (disposals limited to persons employed or living locally) after the words 'application for consent' there shall be inserted the words 'or, in the case of a disposal by way of tenancy or licence, preceding the disposal'.

(4)   At the end of subsection (6) (disposals in breach of covenant to be void) there shall be added

'and, so far as it relates to disposals by way of tenancy or licence, such a covenant may be enforced by the landlord as if—

(a)   the landlord were possessed of land adjacent to the house concerned; and

(b)   the covenant were expressed to be made for the benefit of such adjacent land'.

(5)   After subsection (6) there shall be inserted the following subsection—

'(6A)   Any reference in the preceding provisions of this section to a disposal by way of tenancy or licence does not include a reference to a relevant disposal or an exempted disposal.'

(6)   This section has effect where the conveyance or grant referred to in subsection (1) of section 157 is executed on or after the commencement of this Act.

Preserved right to buy
127.—(1)   In subsection (4) of section 171B of the Housing Act 1985 for paragraph (a) there shall be substituted the following paragraphs—

'(a)   where the former secure tenancy was not a joint tenancy and, immediately before his death, the former secure tenant was tenant under an assured tenancy of a dwelling-house in relation to which he had the preserved right to buy, a member of the former secure tenant's family who acquired that assured tenancy under the will or intestacy of the former secure tenant;

(aa)   where the former secure tenancy was not a joint tenancy, a member of the former secure tenant's family to whom the former secure tenant assigned his assured tenancy of a dwelling-house in relation to which, immediately before the assignment, he had the preserved right to buy'.

(2)   In subsection (2)(a) of section 171C of that Act after the word 'paragraphs' there shall be inserted '1, 3 and'.

(3)   After subsection (4) of that section there shall be added the following subsection—

'(5)   The disapplication by the regulations of paragraph 1 of Schedule 5 shall not be taken to authorise any action on the part of a charity which would conflict with the trusts of the charity.'

Preservation of right to buy on disposal to private sector landlord: Scotland
128.   After section 81 of the Housing (Scotland) Act 1987 there shall be inserted the following section—

'*Preservation of right to buy on disposal to private sector landlord*

Preservation of right to buy on disposal to private sector landlord
81A.—(1)   The right-to-buy provisions shall continue to apply where a

person ceases to be a secure tenant of a house by reason of the disposal by the landlord of an interest in the house to a private sector landlord.

(2) The right-to-buy provisions shall not, however, continue to apply under subsection (1) in such circumstances as may be prescribed.

(3) The continued application under subsection (1) of the right-to-buy provisions shall be in accordance with and subject to such provision as is prescribed which may—

(a) include—

(i) such additions and exceptions to, and adaptations and modifications of, the right-to-buy provisions in their continued application by virtue of this section; and

(ii) such incidental, supplementary and transitional provisions;

as the Secretary of State considers appropriate;

(b) differ as between different cases or descriptions of case and as between different areas;

(c) relate to a particular disposal.

(4) Without prejudice to the generality of subsection (3), provision may be made by virtue of it—

(a) specifying the persons entitled to the benefit of the right-to-buy provisions in their continued application by virtue of this section;

(b) preventing, except with the consent of the Secretary of State, the disposal by the private sector landlord of less than his whole interest in a house in relation to which the right-to-buy provisions continue to apply by virtue of this section;

(c) ensuring that where, under Ground 9 of Schedule 5 to the Housing (Scotland) Act 1988 (availability of suitable alternative accommodation), the sheriff makes an order for possession of a house in relation to which the right-to-buy provisions continue to apply by virtue of this section and the tenant would not have the right under this Part (other than this section) to buy the house which is or will be available by way of alternative accommodation, these provisions as so continued will apply in relation to the house which is or will be so available.

(5) In this section—

(a) "secure tenant" means a tenant under a secure tenancy;

(b) "private sector landlord" means a landlord other than one of those set out in subparagraphs (i) to (iv) and (viii) and (ix) of paragraph (a) of subsection (2) of section 61;

(c) the "right-to-buy provisions" means the provisions of this Act relating to the right of a tenant of a house to purchase it under this Part and to his rights in respect of a loan.'

Schemes for payments to assist local housing authority tenants to obtain other accommodation

129.—(1) In accordance with a scheme made by a local housing authority and approved by the Secretary of State under this section, the authority may make grants to or for the benefit of qualifying tenants or licensees of the authority with a view to assisting each person to whom or for whose benefit a grant is made to obtain accommodation otherwise than as a tenant or licensee of the authority either—

    (a) by acquiring an interest in a dwelling-house; or

    (b) by carrying out works to a dwelling-house to provide additional accommodation; or

    (c) by both of those means.

(2) A scheme under this section shall contain such provisions as the local housing authority considers appropriate together with any which the Secretary of State may require as a condition of his approval and, without prejudice to the generality, a scheme may include provisions specifying, or providing for the determination of—

    (a) the persons who are qualifying tenants or licensees for the purposes of the scheme;

    (b) the interests which qualifying tenants or licensees may be assisted to acquire;

    (c) the works for the carrying out of which grants may be made;

    (d) the circumstances in which a grant may be made for the benefit of a qualifying tenant or licensee;

    (e) the amount of the grant which may be made in any particular case and the terms on which it may be made;

    (f) the limits on the total number and amount of grants which may be made; and

    (g) the period within which the scheme is to apply.

(3) The Secretary of State may approve a scheme made by a local housing authority under this section with or without conditions and, where a scheme has been approved, the authority shall take such steps as it considers appropriate to bring the scheme to the attention of persons likely to be able to benefit from it and shall take such other steps (if any) as the Secretary of State may direct in any particular case to secure publicity for the scheme.

(4) The Secretary of State may revoke an approval of a scheme under this section by a notice given to the local housing authority concerned; and, where such a notice is given, the revocation shall not affect the operation of the scheme in relation to any grants made or agreed before the date of the notice.

(5) Any grant made pursuant to a scheme under this section—

    (a) shall be regarded as a grant of a capital nature for the purposes of Part VIII of the Local Government, Planning and Land Act 1980 (capital expenditure of local authorities); and

    (b) shall be regarded as expenditure on management for the purposes of Part II of Schedule 14 to the Housing Act 1985 (debits to the Housing Revenue Account).

(6) Where a scheme made by a local housing authority under this section has been approved, a person dealing with the authority shall not be concerned to see or enquire whether the terms of the scheme have been or are being complied with;

and any failure to comply with the terms of a scheme shall not invalidate any grant purporting to be made in accordance with the scheme unless the person to whom the grant is made has actual notice of the failure.

(7)   In this section—

(a)   'local housing authority' has the meaning assigned by section 1 of the Housing Act 1985;

(b)   'dwelling-house' has the meaning assigned by section 112 of that Act; and

(c)   'tenant' does not include a tenant under a long tenancy, as defined in section 115 of that Act.

Repair notices and improvement grants

Repair notices

130.—(1)   Part VI of the Housing Act 1985 (repair notices) shall have effect subject to the amendments in Schedule 15 to this Act.

(2)   In section 604 of that Act (fitness for human habitation) after subsection (1) there shall be inserted the following subsection—

'(1A)   In the application, for the purposes of Part VI, of subsection (1) to premises consisting of a flat, within the meaning of that Part, regard shall be had not only to the condition of the flat itself but also to the condition of any other part of the building as it affects the flat and, accordingly, the flat may be deemed to be unfit by reference to the defective condition of a part of the building outside the flat (whether or not that part is itself used, or suitable for use, as a dwelling).'

(3)   The amendments in subsection (2) above and Schedule 15 to this Act do not have effect in relation to any repair notice, within the meaning of the said Part VI, served before this section comes into force.

Letting conditions applicable to improvement grants etc.

131.—(1)   With respect to applications for grants approved after the commencement of this Act, Part XV of the Housing Act 1985 (grants for works of improvement, repair and conversion) shall have effect subject to the following provisions of this section.

(2)   In each of the following provisions—

(a)   section 464 (preliminary condition: certificates as to future occupation), in subsection (5) (certificate of availability for letting), and

(b)   section 501 (condition as to availability for letting), in subsection (2) (the terms of the condition),

in paragraph (a) after the word 'holiday' there shall be inserted 'on a tenancy which is not a long tenancy and'.

(3)   After the words 'Rent (Agriculture) Act 1976', in each place where they occur in—

(a)   section 464(5),

(b)   section 501(2), and

(c)   subsection (2)(d) of section 503 (restriction on imposition of further conditions in relation to certain grants),

there shall be inserted 'or is occupied under an assured agricultural occupancy, within the meaning of Part I of the Housing Act 1988'.

(4) In section 504 (further conditions as to letting of dwelling), at the beginning of subsection (1) there shall be inserted the words 'Subject to subsection (1A)'; in paragraph (a) of that subsection after the word 'letting' there shall be inserted 'on an assured tenancy which is not a long tenancy or'; and at the end of that subsection there shall be inserted the following subsection—

'(1A) Paragraphs (d) to (f) of subsection (1) do not apply in the case of a dwelling which is or is to be let or available for letting on an assured tenancy.'

(5) In subsection (2) of section 504 (definitions) after the words 'subsection (1)' there shall be inserted 'and subsection (1A)' and before paragraph (a) there shall be inserted the following paragraph—

'(aa) "assured tenancy" means a tenancy which is an assured tenancy within the meaning of Part I of the Housing Act 1988 or would be such a tenancy if paragraphs 3, 6, 7 and 10 of Schedule 1 to that Act were omitted'.

(6) In section 526 (index of defined expressions in Part XV), after the entry relating to 'local housing authority' there shall be inserted—

'long tenancy ....section 115'.

(7) Without prejudice to subsection (1) above, where an application for a grant—

(a) was made but not approved before the commencement of this Act, and

(b) was accompanied by a certificate of availability for letting in a form which does not take account of the amendments of section 464(5) by subsections (2) and (3) above,

the certificate shall be treated as it it were in a form which takes account of the amendments made by those subsections.

(8) Without prejudice to subsection (1) above, where a grant has been approved before the commencement of this Act and—

(a) section 501(2) applies to impose a condition of the grant, or

(b) conditions have been imposed in terms of section 504(1),

the condition or conditions shall have effect as if it or they were in a form which takes account of the amendments made by subsection (3) or, as the case may be, subsections (4) and (5) above.

Disposals of housing stock

Consents to disposals of housing stock and application of receipts
132.—(1) At the end of subsection (4) of section 34 of the Housing Act 1985 (consent to disposals of land held for the purposes of Part II— provision of housing accommodation) and at the end of subsection (4) of section 43 of that Act (consent for certain disposals of other houses) there shall be inserted the subsections set out in subsection (2) below.

(2)   The subsections referred to in subsection (1) above and subsection (3) below are as follows—

'(4A)   The matters to which the Secretary of State may have regard in determining whether to give consent and, if so, to what conditions consent should be subject shall include—

(a)   the extent (if any) to which the person to whom the proposed disposal is to be made (in this subsection referred to as "the intending purchaser") is, or is likely to be, dependent upon, controlled by or subject to influence from the local authority making the disposal or any members or officers of that authority;

(b)   the extent (if any) to which the proposed disposal would result in the intending purchaser becoming the predominant or a substantial owner in any area of housing accommodation let on tenancies or subject to licences;

(c)   the terms of the proposed disposal; and

(d)   any other matters whatsoever which he considers relevant.

(4B)   Where the Secretary of State gives consent to a disposal by a local authority, he may give directions as to the purpose for which any capital money received by the authority in respect of the disposal is to be applied and, where any such directions are given, nothing in any enactment shall require his consent to be given for the application of the capital money concerned in accordance with the directions.'

(3)   Section 13 of the Housing (Scotland) Act 1987 (power of Secretary of State to impose conditions in sale of local authority houses) shall be renumbered as subsection (1) of that section and after that subsection there shall be inserted as subsections (2) and (3) the subsections which are set out in subsection (2) above and there numbered (4A) and (4B).

(4)   In section 153 of the Local Government Act 1972 (application of capital money on disposal of land), in subsection (1) after the words '127(4) above' there shall be inserted 'to any directions given in respect of the disposal under section 43(4B) of the Housing Act 1985'.

(5)   In section 430 of the Housing Act 1985 (application of capital money received on disposal of land), in subsection (1) after the word 'applied', in the first place where it occurs, there shall be inserted 'in accordance with any directions given in respect of the disposal under section 34(4B) or section 43(4B) and, subject thereto'.

(6)   In section 208 of the Housing (Scotland) Act 1987 (application of receipts from disposal of certain land), in subsection (2) there shall be inserted at the end the words 'or has made directions under section 13(3)'.

(7)   In section 26 of the Local Government Act 1988 (provisions as to consents under section 25 for provision of financial assistance etc.), in subsection (5) (which excludes consent under various enactments where consent is given to a disposal of land under section 25) after the words 'such a consent' there shall be inserted 'then, if the consent given for the purposes of section 25 above so provides'.

(8)   This section shall be deemed to have come into force on 9 June 1988.

Consent required for certain subsequent disposals
133.—(1)   Where consent is required for a disposal (in this section referred to as 'the original disposal') by virtue of section 32 or section 43 of the Housing Act 1985 and that consent does not provide otherwise, the person who acquires the land or house on the disposal shall not dispose of it except with the consent of the Secretary of State; but nothing in this section shall apply in relation to an exempt disposal as defined in section 81(8) above.

(2)   Where an estate or interest of the person who acquired the land or house on the original disposal has been mortgaged or charged, the prohibition in subsection (1) above applies also to a disposal by the mortgagee or chargee in exercise of a power of sale or leasing, whether or not the disposal is in the name of the person who so acquired the land or house; and in any case where—

(a)   by operation of law or by virtue of an order of a court, the land or house which has been acquired passes or is transferred from the person who so acquired it to another person, and

(b)   that passing or transfer does not constitute a disposal for which consent is required under this section,

this section (including, where there is more than one such passing or transfer, this subsection) shall apply as if the other person to whom the land or house passes or is transferred were the person who acquired it on the original disposal.

(3)   Where subsection (1) above applies—

(a)   if section 34 of the Housing Act 1985 applies to the consent given to the original disposal, subsections (2)(b) and (3) to (4A) of that section shall also apply to any consent required by virtue of this section;

(b)   if the consent to the original disposal was given under section 43 of that Act, subsections (2)(b) and (3) to (4A) of that section shall also apply to any consent required by virtue of this section;

(c)   in the application of subsection (4A) of section 34 or section 43 to any consent required by virtue of this section, any reference to the local authority making the disposal shall be construed as a reference to the local authority making the original disposal; and

(d)   the instrument by which the original disposal is effected shall contain a statement in a form approved by the Chief Land Registrar that the requirement of this section as to consent applies to a subsequent disposal of the land or house by the person to whom the original disposal was made.

(4)   Subsection (4) of section 32 of the Housing Act 1985 or, as the case may be, subsection (5) of section 43 of that Act (options to purchase as disposals) applies for the purposes of this section.

(5)   Before giving any consent required by virtue of this section, the Secretary of State—

(a)   shall satisfy himself that the person who is seeking the consent has taken appropriate steps to consult every tenant of any land or house proposed to be disposed of; and

(b)   shall have regard to the responses of any such tenants to that consultation.

(6) If, apart from subsection (7) below, the consent of the Housing Corporation or Housing for Wales would be required under section 9 of the Housing Associations Act 1985 (control of dispositions of land by housing associations) for a disposal in respect of which, by virtue of subsection (1) above, the consent of the Secretary of State is required, the Secretary of State shall consult that body before giving his consent for the purposes of this section.

(7) No consent shall be required under the said section 9 for any disposal in respect of which consent is given in accordance with subsection (6) above.

(8) Where the title of the authority to the land or house which is disposed of by the original disposal is not registered, and the original disposal is a conveyance, grant or assignment of a description mentioned in section 123 of the Land Registration Act 1925 (compulsory registration of title)—

(a) that section applies in relation to the instrument by which the original disposal is effected whether or not the land or house is in an area in which an Order in Council under section 120 of that Act (areas of compulsory registration) is in force;

(b) the authority shall give to the person to whom the original disposal is made a certificate in a form approved by the Chief Land Registrar stating that the authority is entitled to make the disposal subject only to such encumbrances, rights and interests as are stated in the instrument by which the original disposal is effected or summarised in the certificate; and

(c) for the purpose of registration of title, the Chief Land Registrar shall accept such a certificate as evidence of the facts stated in it, but if as a result he has to meet a claim against him under the Land Registration Acts 1925 to 1986 the authority by whom the original disposal was made is liable to indemnify him.

(9) On an application being made for registration of a disposition of registered land or, as the case may be, of the title under a disposition of unregistered land, if the instrument by which the original disposal is effected contains the statement required by subsection (3)(d) above, the Chief Land Registrar shall enter in the register a restriction stating the requirement of this section as to consent to a subsequent disposal.

(10) In every case where the consent of the Secretary of State is required for the original disposal by virtue of section 32 or section 43 of the Housing Act 1985 (whether or not consent is required under this section to a subsequent disposal), the authority by which the original disposal is made shall furnish to the person to whom it is made a copy of that consent.

Consent required for certain subsequent disposals: Scotland
134. In Part I of the Housing (Scotland) Act 1987 (provision of housing) after section 12 there shall be inserted the following section—

'*Consent of Secretary of State required for certain subsequent disposals*
12A.—(1) Where a person acquires any land or house from a local authority under section 12(1)(c) or (d) above and the consent of the Secretary of State is required under section 12(7) above to the local authority's disposal of the land or house to that person, that person shall not dispose of the land or house without the consent in writing of the Secretary of State.

(2)　Any consent for the purposes of subsection (1) above may be given either in respect of a particular disposal or in respect of disposals of any class or description (including disposals in particular areas) and either unconditionally or subject to conditions.

(3)　Before giving any consent for the purposes of subsection (1) above, the Secretary of State—

(a)　shall satisfy himself that the person who is seeking the consent has taken appropriate steps to consult every tenant of any land or house proposed to be disposed of; and

(b)　shall have regard to the responses of any such tenants to that consultation.

(4)　The consent of Scottish Homes under section 9 of the Housing Associations Act 1985 (control of dispositions) is not required for any disposal, or disposals of any class or description, in respect of which consent is given under subsection (1) above.

(5)　In this section references to disposing of property include references to—

(a)　granting or disposing of any interest in property;

(b)　entering into a contract to dispose of property or to grant or dispose of any such interest; and

(c)　granting an option to acquire property or any such interest.'

Consultation before disposal: Scotland
135.—(1)　In Part III of the Housing (Scotland) Act 1987 (rights of public sector tenants) after section 81 there shall be inserted the following section—

'Consultation before disposal to private sector landlord

Consultation before disposal to private sector landlord
81B.　The provisions of Schedule 6A have effect with respect to the duties of—

(a)　a local authority proposing to dispose of houses let on secure tenancies;

(b)　the Secretary of State in considering whether to give his consent under section 12(7) to such a disposal,

to have regard to the views of tenants liable as a result of the disposal to cease to be secure tenants (that is to say, tenants under secure tenancies).'

(2)　After Schedule 6 to the Housing (Scotland) Act 1987 there shall be inserted, as Schedule 6A, the Schedule set out in Schedule 16 to this Act.

(3)　The amendments made by this section apply to disposals after the coming into force of this section.

Application of capital money to meet costs of disposals of land
136.—(1)　At the end of section 430 of the Housing Act 1985 (application of capital money received on disposal of land) there shall be inserted the following subsection—

'(3)   In the case of capital money received by a local authority in respect of—

    (a)   disposals of land held for the purposes of Part II (provision of housing), and

    (b)   any other disposals of land made by virtue of Part V (the right to buy) which do not fall within paragraph (a),

the reference in subsection (1) to any other purpose for which capital money may properly be applied includes a reference to the purpose of meeting the administrative costs of and incidental to such disposals; and, accordingly, the reference in subsection (2) to subsection (1) includes a reference to that subsection as extended by virtue of this subsection.'

(2)   In section 72 of the Local Government, Planning and Land Act 1980 (expenditure which authorities may make), in subsection (7) (net capital receipts for any year defined as the receipts which are capital receipts for the purposes of Part VIII of that Act, reduced by certain payments) after the words 'reduced by' there shall be inserted—

'(a)   any amount of capital money which in that year is applied for the purpose specified in section 430(3) of the Housing Act 1985 (meeting administrative costs of and incidental to certain disposals of land); and
    (b)'.

Codes of practice

Codes of practice in field of rented housing
137.—(1)   Section 47 of the Race Relations Act 1976 (codes of practice) shall be amended in accordance with the following provisions of this section.

(2)   In subsection (1) for the words 'either or both' there shall be substituted the words 'all or any' and at the end there shall be added the following paragraphs—

'(c)   the elimination of discrimination in the field of housing let on tenancies or occupied under licences ("the field of rented housing");

    (d)   the promotion of equality of opportunity in the field of rented housing between persons of different racial groups'.

(3)   In subsection (3), after the words 'code of practice' there shall be inserted 'relating to the field of employment' and after that subsection there shall be inserted the following subsection—

'(3A)   In the course of preparing any draft code of practice relating to the field of rented housing for eventual publication under subsection (2) the Commission shall consult with such organisations or bodies as appear to the Commission to be appropriate having regard to the content of the draft code.'

(4)   In subsection (4) for the words 'the draft' there shall be substituted 'a draft code of practice'.

(5)   In subsection (10) after the words 'industrial tribunal' there shall be

inserted 'a county court or, in Scotland, a sheriff court' and after the words 'the tribunal' there shall be inserted 'or the court'.

Supplementary

Financial provisions

138.—(1)   There shall be paid out of money provided by Parliament—

(a)   any sums required for the payment by the Secretary of State of grants under this Act;

(b)   any sums required to enable the Secretary of State to make payments to housing action trusts established under Part III of this Act;

(c)   any other expenses of the Secretary of State under this Act; and

(d)   any increase attributable to this Act in the sums so payable under any other enactment.

(2)   Any sums received by the Secretary of State under this Act, other than those required to be paid into the National Loans Fund, shall be paid into the Consolidated Fund.

Application to Isles of Scilly

139.—(1)   This Act applies to the Isles of Scilly subject to such exceptions, adaptations and modifications as the Secretary of State may by order direct.

(2)   The power to make an order under this section shall be exercisable by statutory instrument which shall be subject to annulment in pursuance of a resolution of either House of Parliament.

Amendments and repeals

140.—(1)   Schedule 17 to this Act, which contains minor amendments and amendments consequential on the provisions of this Act and the Housing (Scotland) Act 1988, shall have effect and in that Schedule Part I contains general amendments and Part II contains amendments consequential on the establishment of Housing for Wales.

(2)   The enactments specified in Schedule 18 to this Act, which include some that are spent, are hereby repealed to the extent specified in the third column of that Schedule, but subject to any provision at the end of that Schedule and to any saving in Chapter V of Part I of or Schedule 17 to this Act.

Short title, commencement and extent

141.—(1)   This Act may be cited as the Housing Act 1988.

(2)   The provisions of Parts II and IV of this Act and sections 119, 122, 124, 128, 129, 135 and 140 above shall come into force on such day as the Secretary of State may by order made by statutory instrument appoint, and different days may be so appointed for different provisions or for different purposes.

(3)   Part I and this Part of this Act, other than sections 119, 122, 124, 128, 129, 132, 133, 134, 135 and 138 onwards, shall come into force at the expiry of the period of two months beginning on the day it is passed; and any reference in those provisions to the commencement of this Act shall be construed accordingly.

(4)   An order under subsection (2) above may make such transitional provisions as appear to the Secretary of State necessary or expedient in connection with the provisions brought into force by the order.

(5)   Parts I, III and IV of this Act and this Part, except sections 118, 128, 132, 134, 135 and 137 onwards, extend to England and Wales only.

(6)   This Act does not extend to Northern Ireland.

Schedule 1 Tenancies which cannot be assured tenancies

Part I The tenancies

Tenancies entered into before commencement

1.   A tenancy which is entered into before, or pursuant to a contract made before, the commencement of this Act.

Tenancies of dwelling-houses with high rateable values

2.   A tenancy under which the dwelling-house has for the time being a rateable value which,—

     (a)   if it is in Greater London, exceeds £1,500; and

     (b)   if it is elsewhere, exceeds £750.

Tenancies at a low rent

3.—(1)   A tenancy under which either no rent is payable or the rent payable is less than two thirds of the rateable value of the dwelling-house for the time being.

(2)   In determining whether the rent under a tenancy falls within subparagraph (1) above, there shall be disregarded such part (if any) of the sums payable by the tenant as is expressed (in whatever terms) to be payable in respect of rates, services, management, repairs, maintenance or insurance, unless it could not have been regarded by the parties to the tenancy as a part so payable.

Business tenancies

4.   A tenancy to which Part II of the Landlord and Tenant Act 1954 applies (business tenancies).

Licensed premises

5.   A tenancy under which the dwelling-house consists of or comprises premises licensed for the sale of intoxicating liquors for consumption on the premises.

Tenancies of agricultural land

6.—(1)   A tenancy under which agricultural land, exceeding two acres, is let together with the dwelling-house.

(2)   In this paragraph 'agricultural land' has the meaning set out in section 26(3)(a) of the General Rate Act 1967 (exclusion of agricultural land and premises from liability for rating).

Tenancies of agricultural holdings

7.   A tenancy under which the dwelling-house—

     (a)   is comprised in an agricultural holding (within the meaning of the Agricultural Holdings Act 1986); and

(b)   is occupied by the person responsible for the control (whether as tenant or as servant or agent of the tenant) of the farming of the holding.

Lettings to students

8.—(1)   A tenancy which is granted to a person who is pursuing, or intends to pursue, a course of study provided by a specified educational institution and is so granted either by that institution or by another specified institution or body of persons.

(2)   In subparagraph (1) above 'specified' means specified, or of a class specified, for the purposes of this paragraph by regulations made by the Secretary of State by statutory instrument.

(3)   A statutory instrument made in the exercise of the power conferred by subparagraph (2) above shall be subject to annulment in pursuance of a resolution of either House of Parliament.

Holiday lettings

9.   A tenancy the purpose of which is to confer on the tenant the right to occupy the dwelling-house for a holiday.

Resident landlords

10.—(1)   A tenancy in respect of which the following conditions are fulfilled—

(a)   that the dwelling-house forms part only of a building and, except in a case where the dwelling-house also forms part of a flat, the building is not a purpose-built block of flats; and

(b)   that, subject to Part III of this Schedule, the tenancy was granted by an individual who, at the time when the tenancy was granted, occupied as his only or principal home another dwelling-house which,—

(i)   in the case mentioned in paragraph (a) above, also forms part of the flat; or

(ii)   in any other case, also forms part of the building; and

(c)   that, subject to Part III of this Schedule, at all times since the tenancy was granted the interest of the landlord under the tenancy has belonged to an individual who, at the time he owned that interest, occupied as his only or principal home another dwelling-house which,—

(i)   in the case mentioned in paragraph (a) above, also formed part of the flat; or

(ii)   in any other case, also formed part of the building; and

(d)   that the tenancy is not one which is excluded from this subparagraph by subparagraph (3) below.

(2)   If a tenancy was granted by two or more persons jointly, the reference in subparagraph (1)(b) above to an individual is a reference to any one of those persons and if the interest of the landlord is for the time being held by two or more persons jointly, the reference in subparagraph (1)(c) above to an individual is a reference to any one of those persons.

(3)   A tenancy (in this subparagraph referred to as 'the new tenancy') is excluded from subparagraph (1) above if—

(a)   it is granted to a person (alone, or jointly with others) who, immediately before it was granted, was a tenant under an assured tenancy (in this subparagraph referred to as 'the former tenancy') of the same dwelling-house or of another dwelling-house which forms part of the building in question; and

(b)   the landlord under the new tenancy and under the former tenancy is the same person or, if either of those tenancies is or was granted by two or more persons jointly, the same person is the landlord or one of the landlords under each tenancy.

Crown tenancies

11.—(1)   A tenancy under which the interest of the landlord belongs to Her Majesty in right of the Crown or to a government department or is held in trust for Her Majesty for the purposes of a government department.

(2)   The reference in subparagraph (1) above to the case where the interest of the landlord belongs to Her Majesty in right of the Crown does not include the case where that interest is under the management of the Crown Estate Commissioners.

Local authority tenancies etc.

12.—(1)   A tenancy under which the interest of the landlord belongs to—

(a)   a local authority, as defined in subparagraph (2) below;
(b)   the Commission for the New Towns;
(c)   the Development Board for Rural Wales;
(d)   an urban development corporation established by an order under section 135 of the Local Government, Planning and Land Act 1980;
(e)   a development corporation, within the meaning of the New Towns Act 1981;
(f)   an authority established under section 10 of the Local Government Act 1985 (waste disposal authorities);
(g)   a residuary body, within the meaning of the Local Government Act 1985;
(h)   a fully mutual housing association; or
(i)   a housing action trust established under Part III of this Act.

(2)   The following are local authorities for the purposes of subparagraph (1)(a) above—

(a)   the council of a county, district or London borough;
(b)   the Common Council of the City of London;
(c)   the Council of the Isles of Scilly;
(d)   the Broads Authority;
(e)   the Inner London Education Authority; and
(f)   a joint authority, within the meaning of the Local Government Act 1985.

Transitional cases

13.—(1)   A protected tenancy, within the meaning of the Rent Act 1977.

(2)   A housing association tenancy, within the meaning of Part VI of that Act.

(3)   A secure tenancy.

(4)   Where a person is a protected occupier of a dwelling-house, within the meaning of the Rent (Agriculture) Act 1976, the relevant tenancy, within the meaning of that Act, by virtue of which he occupies the dwelling-house.

Part II Rateable values

14.—(1)   The rateable value of a dwelling-house at any time shall be ascertained for the purposes of Part I of this Schedule as follows—

(a)   if the dwelling-house is a hereditament for which a rateable value is then shown in the valuation list, it shall be that rateable value;

(b)   if the dwelling-house forms part only of such a hereditament or consists of or forms part of more than one such hereditament, its rateable value shall be taken to be such value as is found by a proper apportionment or aggregation of the rateable value or values so shown.

(2)   Any question arising under this Part of this Schedule as to the proper apportionment or aggregation of any value or values shall be determined by the county court and the decision of that court shall be final.

15.   Where, after the time at which the rateable value of a dwelling-house is material for the purposes of any provision of Part I of this Schedule, the valuation list is altered so as to vary the rateable value of the hereditament of which the dwelling-house consists (in whole or in part) or forms part and the alteration has effect from that time or from an earlier time, the rateable value of the dwelling-house at the material time shall be ascertained as if the value shown in the valuation list at the material time had been the value shown in the list as altered.

16.   Paragraphs 14 and 15 above apply in relation to any other land which, under section 2 of this Act, is treated as part of a dwelling-house as they apply in relation to the dwelling-house itself.

Part III Provisions for determining application of paragraph 10
(resident landlords)

17.—(1)   In determining whether the condition in paragraph 10(1)(c) above is at any time fulfilled with respect to a tenancy, there shall be disregarded—

(a)   any period of not more than twenty-eight days, beginning with the date on which the interest of the landlord under the tenancy becomes vested at law and in equity in an individual who, during that period, does not occupy as his only or principal home another dwelling-house which forms part of the building or, as the case may be, flat concerned;

(b)   if, within a period falling within paragraph (a) above, the individual concerned notifies the tenant in writing of his intention to occupy as his only or principal home another dwelling-house in the building or, as the case may be, flat concerned, the period beginning with the date on which the interest of the landlord under the tenancy becomes vested in that individual as mentioned in that paragraph and ending—

    (i)   at the expiry of the period of six months beginning on that date, or

    (ii) on the date on which that interest ceases to be so vested, or

    (iii)   on the date on which that interest becomes again vested in such an individual as is mentioned in paragraph 10(1)(c) or the condition in that paragraph becomes deemed to be fulfilled by virtue of paragraph 18(1) or paragraph 20 below,

whichever is the earlier; and

    (c)   any period of not more than two years beginning with the date on which the interest of the landlord under the tenancy becomes, and during which it remains, vested—

    (i)   in trustees as such; or

    (ii)   by virtue of section 9 of the Administration of Estates Act 1925, in the Probate Judge, within the meaning of that Act.

(2)   Where the interest of the landlord under a tenancy becomes vested at law and in equity in two or more persons jointly, of whom at least one was an individual, subparagraph (1) above shall have effect subject to the following modifications—

    (a)   in paragraph (a) for the words from 'an individual' to 'occupy' there shall be substituted 'the joint landlords if, during that period none of them occupies'; and

    (b)   in paragraph (b) for the words 'the individual concerned' there shall be substituted 'any of the joint landlords who is an individual' and for the words 'that individual' there shall be substituted 'the joint landlords'.

18.—(1)   During any period when—

    (a)   the interest of the landlord under the tenancy referred to in paragraph 10 above is vested in trustees as such, and

    (b)   that interest is or, if it is held on trust for sale, the proceeds of its sale are held on trust for any person who or for two or more persons of whom at least one occupies as his only or principal home a dwelling-house which forms part of the building or, as the case may be, flat referred to in paragraph 10(1)(a),

the condition in paragraph 10(1)(c) shall be deemed to be fulfilled and accordingly, no part of that period shall be disregarded by virtue of paragraph 17 above.

(2)   If a period during which the condition in paragraph 10(1)(c) is deemed to be fulfilled by virtue of subparagraph (1) above comes to an end on the death of a person who was in occupation of a dwelling-house as mentioned in paragraph (b) of that subparagraph, then, in determining whether that condition is at any time thereafter fulfilled, there shall be disregarded any period—

    (a)   which begins on the date of the death;

(b)   during which the interest of the landlord remains vested as mentioned in subparagraph (1)(a) above; and

(c)   which ends at the expiry of the period of two years beginning on the date of the death or on any earlier date on which the condition in paragraph 10(1)(c) becomes again deemed to be fulfilled by virtue of subparagraph (1) above.

19.   In any case where—

(a)   immediately before a tenancy comes to an end the condition in paragraph 10(1)(c) is deemed to be fulfilled by virtue of paragraph 18(1) above, and

(b)   on the coming to an end of that tenancy the trustees in whom the interest of the landlord is vested grant a new tenancy of the same or substantially the same dwelling-house to a person (alone or jointly with others) who was the tenant or one of the tenants under the previous tenancy,

the condition in paragraph 10(1)(b) above shall be deemed to be fulfilled with respect to the new tenancy.

20.—(1)   The tenancy referred to in paragraph 10 above falls within this paragraph if the interest of the landlord under the tenancy becomes vested in the personal representatives of a deceased person acting in that capacity.

(2)   If the tenancy falls within this paragraph, the condition in paragraph 10(1)(c) shall be deemed to be fulfilled for any period, beginning with the date on which the interest becomes vested in the personal representatives and not exceeding two years, during which the interest of the landlord remains so vested.

21.   Throughout any period which, by virtue of paragraph 17 or paragraph 18(2) above, falls to be disregarded for the purpose of determining whether the condition in paragraph 10(1)(c) is fulfilled with respect to a tenancy, no order shall be made for possession of the dwelling-house subject to that tenancy, other than an order which might be made if that tenancy were or, as the case may be, had been an assured tenancy.

22.   For the purposes of paragraph 10 above, a building is a purpose-built block of flats if as constructed it contained, and it contains, two or more flats; and for this purpose 'flat' means a dwelling-house which—

(a)   forms part only of a building; and

(b)   is separated horizontally from another dwelling-house which forms part of the same building.

Schedule 2 Grounds for possession of dwelling-houses let on assured tenancies

Part I Grounds on which court must order possession

Ground 1

Not later than the beginning of the tenancy the landlord gave notice in writing to the tenant that possession might be recovered on this ground or the court is of the opinion that it is just and equitable to dispense with the requirement of notice and (in either case)—

(a)　at some time before the beginning of the tenancy, the landlord who is seeking possession or, in the case of joint landlords seeking possession, at least one of them occupied the dwelling-house as his only or principal home; or

(b)　the landlord who is seeking possession or, in the case of joint landlords seeking possession, at least one of them requires the dwelling-house as his or his spouse's only or principal home and neither the landlord (or, in the case of joint landlords, any one of them) nor any other person who, as landlord, derived title under the landlord who gave the notice mentioned above acquired the reversion on the tenancy for money or money's worth.

Ground 2

The dwelling-house is subject to a mortgage granted before the beginning of the tenancy and—

(a)　the mortgagee is entitled to exercise a power of sale conferred on him by the mortgage or by section 101 of the Law of Property Act 1925; and

(b)　the mortgagee requires possession of the dwelling-house for the purpose of disposing of it with vacant possession in exercise of that power; and

(c)　either notice was given as mentioned in Ground 1 above or the court is satisfied that it is just and equitable to dispense with the requirement of notice;

and for the purposes of this ground 'mortgage' includes a charge and 'mortgagee' shall be construed accordingly.

Ground 3

The tenancy is a fixed-term tenancy for a term not exceeding eight months and—

(a)　not later than the beginning of the tenancy the landlord gave notice in writing to the tenant that possession might be recovered on this ground; and

(b)　at some time within the period of twelve months ending with the beginning of the tenancy, the dwelling-house was occupied under a right to occupy it for a holiday.

Ground 4

The tenancy is a fixed-term tenancy for a term not exceeding twelve months and—

(a)　not later than the beginning of the tenancy the landlord gave notice in writing to the tenant that possession might be recovered on this ground; and

(b)　at some time within the period of twelve months ending with the beginning of the tenancy, the dwelling-house was let on a tenancy falling within paragraph 8 of Schedule 1 to this Act.

Ground 5

The dwelling-house is held for the purpose of being available for occupation by a minister of religion as a residence from which to perform the duties of his office and—

(a)　not later than the beginning of the tenancy the landlord gave notice in writing to the tenant that possession might be recovered on this ground; and

(b)   the court is satisfied that the dwelling-house is required for occupation by a minister of religion as such a residence.

Ground 6

The landlord who is seeking possession or, if that landlord is a registered housing association or charitable housing trust, a superior landlord intends to demolish or reconstruct the whole or a substantial part of the dwelling-house or to carry out substantial works on the dwelling-house or any part thereof or any building of which it forms part and the following conditions are fulfilled—

(a)   the intended work cannot reasonably be carried out without the tenant giving up possession of the dwelling-house because—

(i)   the tenant is not willing to agree to such a variation of the terms of the tenancy as would give such access and other facilities as would permit the intended work to be carried out, or

(ii)   the nature of the intended work is such that no such variation is practicable, or

(iii)   the tenant is not willing to accept an assured tenancy of such part only of the dwelling-house (in this subparagraph referred to as 'the reduced part') as would leave in the possession of his landlord so much of the dwelling-house as would be reasonable to enable the intended work to be carried out and, where appropriate, as would give such access and other facilities over the reduced part as would permit the intended work to be carried out, or

(iv)   the nature of the intended work is such that such a tenancy is not practicable; and

(b)   either the landlord seeking possession acquired his interest in the dwelling-house before the grant of the tenancy or that interest was in existence at the time of that grant and neither that landlord (or, in the case of joint landlords, any of them) nor any other person who, alone or jointly with others, has acquired that interest since that time acquired it for money or money's worth; and

(c)   the assured tenancy on which the dwelling-house is let did not come into being by virtue of any provision of Schedule 1 to the Rent Act 1977, as amended by Part I of Schedule 4 to this Act or, as the case may be, section 4 of the Rent (Agriculture) Act 1976, as amended by Part II of that Schedule.

For the purposes of this ground, if, immediately before the grant of the tenancy, the tenant to whom it was granted or, if it was granted to joint tenants, any of them was the tenant or one of the joint tenants under an earlier assured tenancy of the dwelling-house concerned, any reference in paragraph (b) above to the grant of the tenancy is a reference to the grant of that earlier assured tenancy.

For the purposes of this ground 'registered housing association' has the same meaning as in the Housing Associations Act 1985 and 'charitable housing trust' means a housing trust, within the meaning of that Act, which is a charity, within the meaning of the Charities Act 1960.

Ground 7

The tenancy is a periodic tenancy (including a statutory periodic tenancy) which has devolved under the will or intestacy of the former tenant and the proceedings for the recovery of possession are begun not later than 12 months after the death of the former tenant or, if the court so directs, after the date on which, in the opinion of the court, the landlord or, in the case of joint landlords, any one of them became aware of the former tenant's death.

For the purposes of this ground, the acceptance by the landlord of rent from a new tenant after the death of the former tenant shall not be regarded as creating a new periodic tenancy, unless the landlord agrees in writing to a change (as compared with the tenancy before the death) in the amount of the rent, the period of the tenancy, the premises which are let or any other term of the tenancy.

Ground 8

Both at the date of the service of the notice under section 8 of this Act relating to the proceedings for possession and at the date of the hearing—

    (a) if rent is payable weekly or fortnightly, at least 13 weeks' rent is unpaid;

    (b) if rent is payable monthly, at least three months' rent is unpaid;

    (c) if rent is payable quarterly, at least one quarter's rent is more than three months in arrears; and

    (d) if rent is payable yearly, at least three months' rent is more than three months in arrears;

and for the purpose of this ground 'rent' means rent lawfully due from the tenant.

Part II Grounds on which court may order possession

Ground 9

Suitable alternative accommodation is available for the tenant or will be available for him when the order for possession takes effect.

Ground 10

Some rent lawfully due from the tenant—

    (a) is unpaid on the date on which the proceedings for possession are begun; and

    (b) except where subsection (1)(b) of section 8 of this Act applies, was in arrears at the date of the service of the notice under that section relating to those proceedings.

Ground 11

Whether or not any rent is in arrears on the date on which proceedings for possession are begun, the tenant has persistently delayed paying rent which has become lawfully due.

Ground 12

Any obligation of the tenancy (other than one related to the payment of rent) has been broken or not performed.

Ground 13

The condition of the dwelling-house or any of the common parts has deteriorated owning to acts of waste by, or the neglect or default of, the tenant or any other person residing in the dwelling-house and, in the case of an act of waste by, or the neglect or default of, a person lodging with the tenant or a subtenant of his, the tenant has not taken such steps as he ought reasonably to have taken for the removal of the lodger or subtenant.

For the purposes of this ground, 'common parts' means any part of a building comprising the dwelling-house and any other premises which the tenant is entitled under the terms of the tenancy to use in common with the occupiers of other dwelling-houses in which the landlord has an estate or interest.

Ground 14

The tenant or any other person residing in the dwelling-house has been guilty of conduct which is a nuisance or annoyance to adjoining occupiers, or has been convicted of using the dwelling-house or allowing the dwelling-house to be used for immoral or illegal purposes.

Ground 15

The condition of any furniture provided for use under the tenancy has, in the opinion of the court, deteriorated owing to ill-treatment by the tenant or any other person residing in the dwelling-house and, in the case of ill-treatment by a person lodging with the tenant or by a subtenant of his, the tenant has not taken such steps as he ought reasonably to have taken for the removal of the lodger or subtenant.

Ground 16

The dwelling-house was let to the tenant in consequence of his employment by the landlord seeking possession or a previous landlord under the tenancy and the tenant has ceased to be in that employment.

Part III Suitable alternative accommodation

1. For the purposes of Ground 9 above, a certificate of the local housing authority for the district in which the dwelling-house in question is situated, certifying that the authority will provide suitable alternative accommodation for the tenant by a date specified in the certificate, shall be conclusive evidence that suitable alternative accommodation will be available for him by that date.

2. Where no such certificate as is mentioned in paragraph 1 above is produced to the court, accommodation shall be deemed to be suitable for the purposes of Ground 9 above if it consists of either—

(a) premises which are to be let as a separate dwelling such that they will then be let on an assured tenancy, other than—

(i) a tenancy in respect of which notice is given not later than the beginning of the tenancy that possession might be recovered on any of Grounds 1 to 5 above, or

(ii) an assured shorthold tenancy, within the meaning of Chapter II of Part I of this Act, or

(b) premises to be let as a separate dwelling on terms which will, in the opinion of the court, afford to the tenant security of tenure reasonably equivalent to the security afforded by Chapter I of Part I of this Act in the case of an assured tenancy of a kind mentioned in subparagraph (a) above,

and, in the opinion of the court, the accommodation fulfils the relevant conditions as defined in paragraph 3 below.

3.—(1) For the purposes of paragraph 2 above, the relevant conditions are that the accommodation is reasonably suitable to the needs of the tenant and his family as regards proximity to place of work, and either—

(a) similar as regards rental and extent to the accommodation afforded by dwelling-houses provided in the neighbourhood by any local housing authority for persons whose needs as regards extent are, in the opinion of the court, similar to those of the tenant and of his family; or

(b) reasonably suitable to the means of the tenant and to the needs of the tenant and his family as regards extent and character; and

that if any furniture was provided for use under the assured tenancy in question, furniture is provided for use in the accommodation which is either similar to that so provided or is reasonably suitable to the needs of the tenant and his family.

(2) For the purposes of subparagraph (1)(a) above, a certificate of a local housing authority stating—

(a) the extent of the accommodation afforded by dwelling-houses provided by the authority to meet the needs of tenants with families of such number as may be specified in the certificate, and

(b) the amount of the rent charged by the authority for dwelling-houses affording accommodation of that extent,

shall be conclusive evidence of the facts so stated.

4. Accommodation shall not be deemed to be suitable to the needs of the tenant and his family if the result of their occupation of the accommodation would be that it would be an overcrowded dwelling-house for the purposes of Part X of the Housing Act 1985.

5. Any document purporting to be a certificate of a local housing authority named therein issued for the purposes of this Part of this Schedule and to be signed by the proper officer of that authority shall be received in evidence and, unless the contrary is shown, shall be deemed to be such a certificate without further proof.

6. In this Part of this Schedule 'local housing authority' and 'district', in relation to such an authority, have the same meaning as in the Housing Act 1985.

Part IV Notices relating to recovery of possession

7. Any reference in Grounds 1 to 5 in Part I of this Schedule or in the following provisions of this Part to the landlord giving a notice in writing to the tenant is, in the case of joint landlords, a reference to at least one of the joint landlords giving such a notice.

8.—(1) If, not later than the beginning of a tenancy (in this paragraph referred to as 'the earlier tenancy'), the landlord gives such a notice in writing to the tenant as is mentioned in any of Grounds 1 to 5 in Part I of this Schedule, then, for the purposes of the ground in question and any further application of this paragraph, that notice shall also have effect as if it had been given immediately before the beginning of any later tenancy falling within subparagraph (2) below.

(2) Subject to subparagraph (3) below, subparagraph (1) above applies to a later tenancy—

(a) which takes effect immediately on the coming to an end of the earlier tenancy; and

(b) which is granted (or deemed to be granted) to the person who was the tenant under the earlier tenancy immediately before it came to an end; and

(c) which is of substantially the same dwelling-house as the earlier tenancy.

(3) Subparagraph (1) above does not apply in relation to a later tenancy if, not later than the beginning of the tenancy, the landlord gave notice in writing to the tenant that the tenancy is not one in respect of which possession can be recovered on the ground in question.

9. Where paragraph 8(1) above has effect in relation to a notice given as mentioned in Ground 1 in Part I of this Schedule, the reference in paragraph (b) of that ground to the reversion on the tenancy is a reference to the reversion on the earlier tenancy and on any later tenancy falling within paragraph 8(2) above.

10. Where paragraph 8(1) above has effect in relation to a notice given as mentioned in Ground 3 or Ground 4 in Part I of this Schedule, any second or subsequent tenancy in relation to which the notice has effect shall be treated for the purpose of that ground as beginning at the beginning of the tenancy in respect of which the notice was actually given.

11. Any reference in Grounds 1 to 5 in Part I of this Schedule to a notice being given not later than the beginning of the tenancy is a reference to its being given not later than the day on which the tenancy is entered into and, accordingly, section 45(2) of this Act shall not apply to any such reference.

Schedule 3 Agricultural worker conditions

Interpretation

1.—(1) In this Schedule—

'the 1976 Act' means the Rent (Agriculture) Act 1976;
'agriculture' has the same meaning as in the 1976 Act; and
'relevant tenancy or licence' means a tenancy or licence of a description specified in section 24(2) of this Act.

(2) In relation to a relevant tenancy or licence—

(a) 'the occupier' means the tenant or licensee; and
(b) 'the dwelling-house' means the dwelling-house which is let under the tenancy or, as the case may be, is occupied under the licence.

(3)   Schedule 3 to the 1976 Act applies for the purposes of this Schedule as it applies for the purposes of that Act and, accordingly, shall have effect to determine—

(a)   whether a person is a qualifying worker;

(b)   whether a person in incapable of whole-time work in agriculture, or work in agriculture as a permit worker, in consequence of a qualifying injury or disease; and

(c)   whether a dwelling-house is in qualifying ownership.

The conditions

2.   The agricultural worker condition is fulfilled with respect to a dwelling-house subject to a relevant tenancy or licence if—

(a)   the dwelling-house is or has been in qualifying ownership at any time during the subsistence of the tenancy or licence (whether or not it was at that time a relevant tenancy or licence); and

(b)   the occupier or, where there are joint occupiers, at least one of them—

(i)   is a qualifying worker or has been a qualifying worker at any time during the subsistence of the tenancy or licence (whether or not it was at that time a relevant tenancy or licence); or

(ii)   is incapable of whole-time work in agriculture or work in agriculture as a permit worker in consequence of a qualifying injury or disease.

3.—(1)   The agricultural worker condition is also fulfilled with respect to a dwelling-house subject to a relevant tenancy or licence if—

(a)   that condition was previously fulfilled with respect to the dwelling-house but the person who was then the occupier or, as the case may be, a person who was one of the joint occupiers (whether or not under the same relevant tenancy or licence) has died; and

(b)   that condition ceased to be fulfilled on the death of the occupier referred to in paragraph (a) above (hereinafter referred to as 'the previous qualifying occupier'); and

(c)   the occupier is either—

(i)   the qualifying widow or widower of the previous qualifying occupier; or

(ii)   the qualifying member of the previous qualifying occupier's family.

(2)   For the purposes of subparagraph (1)(c)(i) above and subparagraph (3) below a widow or widower of the previous qualifying occupier of the dwelling-house is a qualifying widow or widower if she or he was residing in the dwelling-house immediately before the previous qualifying occupier's death.

(3)   Subject to subparagraph (4) below, for the purposes of subparagraph (1)(c)(ii) above, a member of the family of the previous qualifying occupier of the dwelling-house is the qualifying member of the family if—

(a)   on the death of the previous qualifying occupier there was no qualifying widow or widower; and

(b)   the member of the family was residing in the dwelling-house with the previous qualifying occupier at the time of, and for the period of two years before, his death.

(4)   Not more than one member of the previous qualifying occupier's family may be taken into account in determining whether the agricultural worker condition is fulfilled by virtue of this paragraph and, accordingly, if there is more than one member of the family—

(a)   who is the occupier in relation to the relevant tenancy or licence, and
(b)   who, apart from this subparagraph, would be the qualifying member of the family by virtue of subparagraph (3) above,

only that one of those members of the family who may be decided by agreement or, in default of agreement by the county court, shall be the qualifying member.

(5)   For the purposes of the preceding provisions of this paragraph a person who, immediately before the previous qualifying occupier's death, was living with the previous occupier as his or her wife or husband shall be treated as the widow or widower of the previous occupier.

(6)   If, immediately before the death of the previous qualifying occupier, there is, by virtue of subparagraph (5) above, more than one person who falls within subparagraph (1)(c)(i) above, such one of them as may be decided by agreement or, in default of agreement, by the county court shall be treated as the qualifying widow or widower for the purposes of this paragraph.

4.   The agricultural worker condition is also fulfilled with respect to a dwelling-house subject to a relevant tenancy or licence if—

(a)   the tenancy or licence was granted to the occupier or, where there are joint occupiers, at least one of them in consideration of his giving up possession of another dwelling-house of which he was then occupier (or one of joint occupiers) under another relevant tenancy or licence; and

(b)   immediately before he gave up possession of that dwelling-house, as a result of his occupation the agricultural worker condition was fulfilled with respect to it (whether by virtue of paragraph 2 or paragraph 3 above or this paragraph);

and the reference in paragraph (a) above to a tenancy or licence granted to the occupier or at least one of joint occupiers includes a reference to the case where the grant is to him together with one or more other persons.

5.—(1)   This paragraph applies where—

(a)   by virtue of any of paragraphs 2 to 4 above, the agricultural worker condition is fulfilled with respect to a dwelling-house subject to a relevant tenancy or licence (in this paragraph referred to as 'the earlier tenancy or licence'); and

(b)   another relevant tenancy or licence of the same dwelling-house (in this paragraph referred to as 'the later tenancy or licence') is granted to the person who, immediately before the grant, was the occupier or one of the joint occupiers under the earlier tenancy or licence and as a result of whose occupation the agricultural worker condition was fulfilled as mentioned in paragraph (a) above;

and the reference in paragraph (b) above to the grant of the later tenancy or licence to the person mentioned in that paragraph includes a reference to the case where the grant is to that person together with one or more other persons.

(2) So long as a person as a result of whose occupation of the dwelling-house the agricultural worker condition was fulfilled with respect to the earlier tenancy or licence continues to be the occupier, or one of the joint occupiers, under the later tenancy or licence, the agricultural worker condition shall be fulfilled with respect to the dwelling-house.

(3) For the purposes of paragraphs 3 and 4 above and any further application of this paragraph, where subparagraph (2) above has effect, the agricultural worker condition shall be treated as fulfilled so far as concerns the later tenancy or licence by virtue of the same paragraph of this Schedule as was applicable (or, as the case may be, last applicable) in the case of the earlier tenancy or licence.

Schedule 4 Statutory tenants: succession

Part I Amendments of Schedule 1 to Rent Act 1977

1. In paragraph 1 the words 'or, as the case may be, paragraph 3' shall be omitted.

2. At the end of paragraph 2 there shall be inserted the following subparagraphs—

> '(2) For the purposes of this paragraph, a person who was living with the original tenant as his or her wife or husband shall be treated as the spouse of the original tenant.
>
> (3) If, immediately after the death of the original tenant, there is, by virtue of subparagraph (2) above, more than one person who fulfils the conditions in subparagraph (1) above, such one of them as may be decided by agreement or, in default of agreement, by the county court shall be treated as the surviving spouse for the purposes of this paragraph.'

3. In paragraph 3—

(a) after the words 'residing with him' there shall be inserted 'in the dwelling-house';

(b) for the words 'period of six months' there shall be substituted 'period of two years';

(c) for the words from 'the statutory tenant' onwards there shall be substituted 'entitled to an assured tenancy of the dwelling-house by succession'; and

(d) at the end there shall be added the following subparagraph—

> '(2) If the original tenant died within the period of 18 months beginning on the operative date, then, for the purposes of this paragraph, a person who was residing in the dwelling-house with the original tenant at the time of his death and for the period which began six months before the operative date and ended at the time of his death shall be taken to have been residing

with the original tenant for the period of two years immediately before his death.'

4.　In paragraph 4 the words 'or 3' shall be omitted.

5.　In paragraph 5—

　　(a)　for the words from 'or, as the case may be' to 'of this Act' there shall be substituted 'below shall have effect'; and

　　(b)　for the words 'the statutory tenant' there shall be substituted 'entitled to an assured tenancy of the dwelling-house by succession'.

6.　For paragraph 6 there shall be substituted the following paragraph—

　　'6.—(1)　Where a person who—

　　　　(a)　was a member of the original tenant's family immediately before that tenant's death, and

　　　　(b)　was a member of the first successor's family immediately before the first successor's death,

　　was residing in the dwelling-house with the first successor at the time of, and for the period of two years immediately before, the first successor's death, that person or, if there is more than one such person, such one of them as may be decided by agreement or, in default of agreement, by the county court shall be entitled to an assured tenancy of the dwelling-house by succession.

　　(2)　If the first successor died within the period of 18 months beginning on the operative date, then, for the purposes of this paragraph, a person who was residing in the dwelling-house with the first successor at the time of his death and for the period which began six months before the operative date and ended at the time of his death shall be taken to have been residing with the first successor for the period of two years immediately before his death.'

7.　Paragraph 7 shall be omitted.

8.　In paragraph 10(1)(a) for the words 'paragraphs 6 or 7' there shall be substituted 'paragraph 6'.

9.　At the end of paragraph 11 there shall be inserted the following paragraph—

　　'11A.　In this Part of this Schedule "the operative date" means the date on which Part I of the Housing Act 1988 came into force.'

Part II Amendments of section 4 of Rent (Agriculture) Act 1976

10.　In subsection (2) the words 'or, as the case may be, subsection (4)' shall be omitted.

11.　In subsection (4)—

　　(a)　in paragraph (b) after the words 'residing with him' there shall be inserted 'in the dwelling-house' and for the words 'period of six months' there shall be substituted 'period of two years'; and

(b) for the words from 'the statutory tenant' onwards there shall be substituted 'entitled to an assured tenancy of the dwelling-house by succession'.

12.   In subsection (5) for the words 'subsections (1), (3) and (4)' there shall be substituted 'subsections (1) and (3)' and after that subsection there shall be inserted the following subsections—

'(5A)   For the purposes of subsection (3) above, a person who was living with the original occupier as his or her wife or husband shall be treated as the spouse of the original occupier and, subject to subsection (5B) below, the references in subsection (3) above to a widow and in subsection (4) above to a surviving spouse shall be construed accordingly.

(5B)   If, immediately after the death of the original occupier, there is, by virtue of subsection (5A) above, more than one person who fulfils the conditions in subsection (3) above, such one of them as may be decided by agreement or, in default of agreement by the county court, shall be the statutory tenant by virtue of that subsection.

(5C)   If the original occupier died within the period of 18 months beginning on the operative date, then, for the purposes of subsection (3) above, a person who was residing in the dwelling-house with the original occupier at the time of his death and for the period which began six months before the operative date and ended at the time of his death shall be taken to have been residing with the original occupier for the period of two years immediately before his death; and in this subsection "the operative date" means the date on which Part I of the Housing Act 1988 came into force.'

Part III Modifications of section 7 and Schedule 2

13.—(1)   Subject to subparagraph (2) below, in relation to the assured tenancy to which the successor becomes entitled by succession, section 7 of this Act shall have effect as if in subsection (3) after the word 'established' there were inserted the words 'or that the circumstances are as specified in any of Cases 11, 12, 16, 17, 18 and 20 in Schedule 15 to the Rent Act 1977'.

(2)   Subparagraph (1) above does not apply if, by virtue of section 39(8) of this Act, the assured tenancy to which the successor becomes entitled is an assured agricultural occupancy.

14.   If by virtue of section 39(8) of this Act, the assured tenancy to which the successor becomes entitled is an assured agricultural occupancy, section 7 of this Act shall have effect in relation to that tenancy as if in subsection (3) after the word 'established' there were inserted the words 'or that the circumstances are as specified in Case XI or Case XII of the Rent (Agriculture) Act 1976'.

15.—(1)   In relation to the assured tenancy to which the successor becomes entitled by succession, any notice given to the predecessor for the purposes of Case 13, Case 14 or Case 15 in Schedule 15 to the Rent Act 1977 shall be treated as having been given for the purposes of whichever of Grounds 3 to 5 in Schedule 2 to this Act corresponds to the Case in question.

(2)   Where subparagraph (1) above applies, the regulated tenancy of the

predecessor shall be treated, in relation to the assured tenancy of the successor, as 'the earlier tenancy' for the purposes of Part IV of Schedule 2 to this Act.

Schedule 5 Housing for Wales

Status

1.—(1) Housing for Wales is a body corporate and is in this Schedule referred to as 'the Corporation'.

(2) The Corporation is a public body for the purposes of the Prevention of Corruption Acts 1889 to 1916.

(3) The Corporation shall not be regarded—

(a) as the servant or agent of the Crown; or

(b) as enjoying any status, immunity or privilege of the Crown; or

(c) as exempt from any tax, duty, rate, levy or other charge whatsoever, whether general or local;

and its property shall not be regarded as property of, or held on behalf of, the Crown.

Membership

2.—(1) The members of the Corporation shall be—

(a) not less than six nor more than eight persons appointed by the Secretary of State; and

(b) the chief executive of the Corporation appointed under paragraph 7 below;

and the members appointed under paragraph (a) above are in this Schedule referred to as the 'appointed members'.

(2) Before appointing a person to be a member of the Corporation the Secretary of State shall satisfy himself that he will have no financial or other interest likely to affect prejudicially the exercise of his functions as a member; and the Secretary of State may require a person whom he proposes to appoint to give him such information as he considers necessary for that purpose.

3.—(1) The appointed members shall hold and vacate office in accordance with the terms of their appointment, subject to the following provisions.

(2) A member may resign his membership by notice in writing addressed to the Secretary of State.

(3) The Secretary of State may remove a member from office if he is satisfied that—

(a) he has been adjudged bankrupt or made an arrangement with his creditors;

(b) he has been absent from meetings of the Corporation for a period longer than three consecutive months without the permission of the Corporation; or

(c) he is otherwise unable or unfit to discharge the functions of a member, or is unsuitable to continue as a member.

(4)   The Secretary of State shall satisfy himself from time to time with respect to every appointed member that he has no financial or other interest likely to affect prejudicially the exercise of his functions as a member; and he may require an appointed member to give him such information as he considers necessary for that purpose.

Chairman and Deputy Chairman

4.—(1)   The Secretary of State shall appoint one of the appointed members to be Chairman and may appoint one to be Deputy Chairman; and the members so appointed shall hold and vacate those offices in accordance with the terms of their appointment, subject to the following provisions.

(2)   The Chairman or Deputy Chairman may resign by notice in writing addressed to the Secretary of State.

(3)   If the Chairman or Deputy Chairman ceases to be a member of the Corporation, he also ceases to be Chairman or Deputy Chairman.

Remuneration and allowances

5.—(1)   The Secretary of State may pay the Chairman, Deputy Chairman and appointed members such remuneration as he may, with the consent of the Treasury, determine.

(2)   The Corporation may pay them such reasonable allowances as may be so determined in respect of expenses properly incurred by them in the performance of their duties.

Pensions

6.—(1)   The Secretary of State may, with the consent of the Treasury, determine to pay in respect of a person's office as Chairman, Deputy Chairman or appointed member—

(a)   such pension, allowance or gratuity to or in respect of that person on his retirement or death as may be so determined; or

(b)   such contributions or other payments towards provision for such pension, allowance or gratuity as may be so determined.

(2)   As soon as may be after the making of such a determination the Secretary of State shall lay before each House of Parliament a statement of the amount payable in pursuance of the determination.

(3)   Subparagraph (1) above does not apply in the case of a member who has been admitted in pursuance of regulations under section 7 of the Superannuation Act 1972 to participate in the benefits of a superannuation fund maintained by a local authority.

(4)   In such a case the Secretary of State shall make any payments required to be made to the fund in respect of the member by the employing authority and may make such deductions from his remuneration as the employing authority might make in respect of his contributions to the fund.

Staff

7.—(1)   There shall be a chief executive of the Corporation.

(2)   After consultation with the Chairman or person designated to be

chairman of the Corporation, the Secretary of State shall make the first appointment of the chief executive on such terms and conditions as he may, with the consent of the Treasury, determine.

(3) The Corporation, with the approval of the Secretary of State, may make subsequent appointments to the office of chief executive on such terms and conditions as the Corporation may, with the approval of the Secretary of State given with the consent of the Treasury, determine.

8.—(1) The Corporation may appoint, on such terms and conditions as it may, with the approval of the Secretary of State, determine, such other employees as it thinks fit.

(2) In respect of such of its employees as it may, with the approval of the Secretary of State, determine, the Corporation shall make such arrangements for providing pensions, allowances or gratuities as it may determine; and such arrangements may include the establishment and administration, by the Corporation or otherwise, of one or more pension schemes.

(3) The reference in subparagraph (2) above to pensions, allowances or gratuities to or in respect of employees of the Corporation includes a reference to pensions, allowances or gratuities by way of compensation to or in respect of any of the Corporation's employees who suffer loss of office or employment or loss or diminution of emoluments.

(4) The Secretary of State with the consent of the Treasury may, by statutory instrument subject to annulment in pursuance of a resolution of either House of Parliament, make regulations providing for—

(a) the transfer to, and administration by, Housing for Wales of any superannuation fund maintained by the Housing Corporation in terms of the provisions of any scheme made under section 7 of the Superannuation Act 1972; and

(b) the modification, for the purposes of the regulations, of that section or any scheme thereunder.

(5) If an employee of the Corporation becomes a member of the Corporation and was by reference to his employment by the Corporation a participant in a pension scheme administered by it for the benefit of its employees—

(a) the Corporation may determine that his service as a member shall be treated for the purposes of the scheme as service as an employee of the Corporation whether or not any benefits are to be payable to or in respect of him by virtue of paragraph 6 above; but

(b) if the Corporation does so determine, any discretion as to the benefits payable to or in respect of him which the scheme confers on the Corporation shall be exercised only with the approval of the Secretary of State.

(6) Any reference in the preceding provisions of this paragraph to the approval of the Secretary of State is a reference to that approval given with the consent of the Treasury.

9.—(1) Not later than such date as the Secretary of State may determine, the Corporation shall make an offer of employment by it to each person employed immediately before that date by the Housing Corporation in connection with functions in Wales; and any question as to the persons to whom an offer of employment is to be made under this paragraph shall be determined by the Secretary of State.

(2)   The terms of the offer shall be such that they are, taken as a whole, not less favourable to the person to whom the offer is made than the terms on which he is employed on the date on which the offer is made.

(3)   An offer made in pursuance of this paragraph shall not be revocable during the period of 3 months commencing with the date on which it is made.

10.—(1)   Where a person becomes an employee of the Corporation in consequence of an offer made under paragraph 9 above, then, for the purposes of the Employment Protection (Consolidation) Act 1978, his period of employment with the Housing Corporation shall count as a period of employment by the Corporation, and the change of employment shall not break the continuity of the period of employment.

(2)   Where an offer is made in pursuance of paragraph 9 above to any person employed as mentioned in that paragraph, none of the agreed redundancy procedures applicable to such a person shall apply to him; and where that person ceases to be so employed—

(a)   on becoming a member of the staff of the Corporation in consequence of that paragraph, or
(b)   having unreasonably refused the offer,

Part VI of the Employment Protection (Consolidation) Act 1978 shall not apply to him and he shall not be treated for the purposes of any scheme under section 24 of the Superannuation Act 1972 or any other scheme as having been retired on redundancy.

(3)   Without prejudice to subparagraph (2) above, where a person has unreasonably refused an offer made to him in pursuance of paragraph 9 above, the Housing Corporation shall not terminate that person's employment unless it has first had regard to the feasibility of employing him in a suitable alternative position with it.

(4)   Where a person continues in employment in the Housing Corporation either—

(a)   not having unreasonably refused an offer made to him in pursuance of this paragraph, or
(b)   not having been placed in a suitable alternative position as mentioned in subparagraph (3) above,

he shall be treated for all purposes as if the offer mentioned in paragraph 9 above had not been made.

11.—(1)   Any dispute as to whether an offer of employment complies with subparagraph (2) of paragraph 9 above shall be referred to and be determined by an industrial tribunal.

(2)   An industrial tribunal shall not consider a complaint referred to it under subparagraph (1) above unless the complaint is presented to the tribunal before the end of the period of three months beginning with the date of the offer of employment or, in a case where the tribunal is satisfied that it was not reasonably

practicable for the complaint to be presented before the end of the period of three months, within such further period as the tribunal considers reasonable.

(3) Subject to subparagraph (4) below, there shall be no appeal from the decision of an industrial tribunal under this paragraph.

(4) An appeal to the Employment Appeal Tribunal may be made only on a question of law arising from the decision of, or in proceedings before, an industrial tribunal under this paragraph.

Proceedings

12.—(1) The quorum of the Corporation and the arrangements relating to its meetings shall, subject to any directions given by the Secretary of State, be such as the Corporation may determine.

(2) The validity of proceedings of the Corporation is not affected by any defect in the appointment of any of its members.

13.—(1) Where a member of the Corporation is in any way directly or indirectly interested in a contract made or proposed to be made by the Corporation—

(a) he shall disclose the nature of his interest at a meeting of the Corporation, and the disclosure shall be recorded in the minutes of the Corporation; and

(b) he shall not take any part in any decision of the Corporation with respect to the contract.

(2) A general notice given by a member at a meeting of the Corporation to the effect that he is a member of a specified company or firm and is to be regarded as interested in any contract which may be made with the company or firm is a sufficient disclosure of his interest for the purposes of this paragraph in relation to a contract made after the date of the notice.

(3) A member need not attend in person at a meeting of the Corporation in order to make any disclosure which he is required to make under this paragraph provided he takes reasonable steps to secure that the disclosure is brought up and read at the meeting.

14.—(1) The fixing of the Corporation's seal may be authenticated by the signature of the Chairman or of any other person authorised for the purpose.

(2) A document purporting to be duly executed under the seal of the Corporation shall be received in evidence and be deemed to be so executed unless the contrary is proved.

Schedule 6 Amendments of Housing Associations Act 1985

Part I Amendments of Part I with respect to the Housing Corporation, Housing for Wales and Scottish Homes

1. After section 2 there shall be inserted the following section—

The Corporation

2A.—(1) In relation to a housing association which has its registered office for the purposes of the 1965 Act in Scotland, "the Corporation" means Scottish Homes.

(2)   In relation to a housing association—

(a)   which is a society registered under the 1965 Act and has its registered office for the purposes of that Act in Wales, or

(b)   which is a registered charity and has its address for the purposes of registration by the Charity Commissioners in Wales,

"the Corporation" means Housing for Wales.

(3)   In relation to any other housing association which is a society registered under the 1965 Act or a registered charity, "the Corporation" means the Housing Corporation.

(4)   Subject to subsections (1) to (3), in this Act, except where the context otherwise requires, "the Corporation" means the Housing Corporation, Scottish Homes or Housing for Wales and "the Corporations" means those three bodies.'

2.   Except as provided below, for the words 'Housing Corporation', in each place where they occur in Part I, there shall be substituted 'Corporation'.

3.—(1)   In section 3 (the register), in subsection (1)—

(a)   for the words 'the Housing Corporation' there shall be substituted 'each of the Corporations'; and

(b)   after the word 'Corporation', in the second place where it occurs, there shall be inserted 'by which it is maintained'.

(2)   After subsection (1) of that section there shall be inserted the following subsection—

'(1A)   In this Act "register", in relation to the Corporation, means the register maintained by the Corporation under this section.'

(3)   In subsection (2) of that section the words 'of housing associations maintained under this section' shall be omitted.

4.—(1)   In section 5 (registration) for subsection (2) there shall be substituted the following subsection—

'(2)   Nothing in subsection (1) shall require the Corporations to establish the same criteria; and each of them may vary any criteria established by it under that subsection.'

(2)   For subsection (4) of that section there shall be substituted the following subsection—

'(4)   Where at any time a body is, or was, on a register maintained under section 3, then, for all purposes other than rectification of that register, the body shall be conclusively presumed to be, or to have been, at that time a housing association eligible for registration in that register.'

5.   In section 6(4) (removal from register) for paragraphs (a) to (c) there shall be substituted the following paragraphs—

'(a)   a grant under section 41 (housing association grants),

(b)   a grant under section 54 (revenue deficit grants),

(c)   any such payment or loan as is mentioned in paragraph 2 or paragraph 3 of Schedule 1 (grant-aided land),

(d)   a grant or a loan under section 2(2) of the Housing (Scotland) Act 1988,

(e)   a grant under section 50 of the Housing Act 1988 (housing association grants), or

(f)   a grant under section 51 of that Act (revenue deficit grants)'.

6.   In section 7 (appeals against removal from the register), in subsection (1) for the words from 'to the High Court' onwards there shall be substituted,—

'(a)   where it is a decision of Scottish Homes, to the Court of Session; and

(b)   in any other case, to the High Court'.

7.—(1)   In section 9 (control by Corporation of disposition of land by housing associations) for subsection (1) there shall be substituted the following subsections—

'(1)   Subject to section 10 and sections 81(7), 105(6) and 133(7) of the Housing Act 1988, the consent of the Corporation is required for any disposition of land by a registered housing association.

(1A)   Subject to section 10, the consent of the relevant Corporation is required for any disposition of grant-aided land (as defined in Schedule 1) by an unregistered housing association; and for this purpose "the relevant Corporation" means,—

(a)   if the land is in England, the Housing Corporation;

(b)   if the land is in Scotland, Scottish Homes, and

(c)   if the land is in Wales, Housing for Wales.'

(2)   In subsection (3) of that section—

(a)   for the words 'the consent of the Corporation', in the first place where they occur, there shall be substituted 'consent'; and

(b)   for the words 'the consent of the Corporation', in the second place where they occur, there shall be substituted 'that consent'.

(3)   After subsection (5) of that section there shall be added—

'(6)   References in this section to consent are references,—

(a)   in the case of the Housing Corporation or Housing for Wales, to consent given by order under the seal of the Corporation; and

(b)   in the case of Scottish Homes, to consent in writing.'

8.—(1)   In section 10 (dispositions excepted from section 9), in subsection (1) for the words from 'the Charity Commissioners', in the second place where they occur, onwards there shall be substituted

'before making an order in such a case the Charity Commissioners shall consult,—

(a) in the case of dispositions of land in England, the Housing Corporation;

(b) in the case of dispositions of land in Scotland, Scottish Homes; and

(c) in the case of dispositions of land in Wales, Housing for Wales.'

(2) In subsection (2) of that section at the end of paragraph (b) there shall be inserted

'or

(c) a letting of land under an assured tenancy or an assured agricultural occupancy, or

(d) a letting of land in England or Wales under what would be an assured tenancy or an assured agricultural occupancy but for any of paragraphs 4 to 8 of Schedule 1 to the Housing Act 1988, or

(e) a letting of land in Scotland under what would be an assured tenancy but for any of paragraphs 3 to 8 and 12 of Schedule 4 to the Housing (Scotland) Act 1988.'

9.—(1) In section 15 (payments and benefits to committee members, etc.) at the end of subsection (2) there shall be inserted the following paragraphs—

'(f) except in the case of housing associations registered in the register maintained by Scottish Homes, payments made or benefits granted by an association in such class or classes of case as may be specified in a determination made by the Corporation with the approval of the Secretary of State;

(g) in the case of housing associations registered in the register maintained by Scottish Homes, payments made or benefits granted by such an association with the approval of Scottish Homes (which approval may be given only in relation to a class or classes of case).'

(2) After subsection (2) there shall be inserted the following subsection—

'(3) The Housing Corporation and Housing for Wales may make different determinations for the purposes of subsection (2)(f) above and, before making such a determination, the Corporation shall consult such bodies appearing to it to be representative of housing associations as it considers appropriate; and after making such a determination the Corporation shall publish the determination in such manner as it considers appropriate for bringing it to the notice of the associations concerned.'

10. For section 15A (which was inserted by section 14 of the Housing (Scotland) Act 1986) there shall be substituted the following section—

Payments etc. in community-based housing associations in Scotland
15A.—(1) In relation to a community-based housing association in Scotland the following are also permitted, notwithstanding section 15(1)—

(a) payments made by the association in respect of the purchase of a dwelling, or part of a dwelling, owned and occupied by a person described in subsection (2) who is not an employee of the association; but only if—

(i)   such payments constitute expenditure in connection with housing projects undertaken for the purpose of improving or repairing dwellings; and

(ii)   the purchase price does not exceed such value as may be placed on the dwelling, or as the case may be part, by the district valuer;

(b)   the granting of the tenancy of a dwelling, or part of a dwelling, to such a person; but only if the person—

(i)   lives in the dwelling or in another dwelling owned by the association; or

(ii)   has at any time within the period of twelve months immediately preceding the granting of the tenancy lived in the dwelling (or such other dwelling) whether or not it belonged to the housing association when he lived there.

(2)   The persons mentioned in subsection (1) are—

(a)   a committee member or voluntary officer of the association; or

(b)   a person who at any time in the 12 months preceding the payment (or as the case may be the granting of the tenancy) has been such a member or officer; or

(c)   a close relative of a person described in paragraph (a) or (b).

(3)   For the purposes of subsection (1), a housing association is "community-based" if—

(a)   prior to the specified date, it was designated as such by the Housing Corporation; or

(b)   on or after that date, it is designated as such by Scottish Homes;

and, in this subsection, "specified date" has the same meaning as in section 3 of the Housing (Scotland) Act 1988.

(4)   Scottish Homes—

(a)   shall make a designation under subsection (3) only if it considers that the activities of the housing association relate wholly or mainly to the improvement of dwellings, or the management of improved dwellings, within a particular community (whether or not identified by reference to a geographical area entirely within any one administrative area); and

(b)   may revoke such a designation (including a designation made by the Housing Corporation under subsection (3) above as originally enacted) if it considers, after giving the association an opportunity to make representations to it as regards such revocation, that the association's activities have ceased so to relate.'

11.   In section 16 (general power to remove committee member), in subsection (4) for the words from 'order to the High Court' onwards there shall be substituted

'order,—

(a)   if it is an order of the Housing Corporation or Housing for Wales, to the High Court, and

(b)   if it is an order of Scottish Homes, to the Court of Session.'

12.   In section 17 (power to appoint new committee members) at the end of subsection (1) there shall be added the words 'and the power conferred by paragraph (c) may be exercised notwithstanding that it will cause the maximum number of committee members permissible under the association's constitution to be exceeded'.

13.—(1)   In section 18 (exercise of powers in relation to registered charities), in subsection (1) immediately before the entry relating to section 41 of the 1985 Act there shall be inserted the following entries—

'section 50 of the Housing Act 1988 (housing association grants),
section 51 of that Act (revenue deficit grants)'.

(2)   In subsection (3) of that section (appointment by Corporation of trustees of associations which are registered charities: appointments not to exceed maximum number of trustees) the words from 'and the Corporation' onwards shall be omitted.

14.   In section 19 (change of rules under the 1965 Act), in subsection (3) for the words 'given by order under the seal of the Corporation' there shall be substituted

'given,—

(a)   in the case of the Housing Corporation or Housing for Wales, by order under the seal of the Corporation; and
(b)   in the case of Scottish Homes, by notice in writing.'

15.   In section 21 (amalgamation and dissolution under the 1965 Act), in subsection (6) for the words from 'are to an order' onwards there shall be substituted

'are,—

(a)   in the case of the Housing Corporation or Housing for Wales, to consent given by order under the seal of the Corporation; and
(b)   in the case of Scottish Homes, to consent given in writing.'

16.   In section 22 (Corporation's power to petition for winding up), in subsection (1) after the word 'applies' there shall be inserted '(a)' and at the end there shall be added

'or

(b)   on the ground that the association is unable to pay its debts within the meaning of section 518 of the Companies Act 1985.'.

17.—(1)   In section 24 (general requirements as to accounts and audit), in subsection (2) after the word 'association' there shall be inserted 'which is a registered charity'.

(2)   In subsection (5) of that section after the words 'different areas' there shall be inserted 'or for different descriptions of housing associations or housing activities'.

(3)   After subsection (5) of that section there shall be inserted the following subsection—

> '(6)   For the purposes of subsection (5)(a), descriptions may be framed by reference to any matters whatever, including in particular, in the case of housing activities, the manner in which they are financed.'

18.   In section 27 (responsibility for securing compliance with accounting requirements), in subsection (2) at the end of paragraph (c) there shall be added

> 'or

> (d)   section 55(9) of the Housing Act 1988 is not complied with'.

19.—(1)   In section 28 (Corporation may appoint a person to inquire into the affairs of a registered housing association), in subsection (1) for the words 'the Corporation's staff' there shall be substituted 'staff of any of the Corporations' and at the end of that subsection there shall be added 'and, if the appointed person considers it necessary for the purposes of the inquiry, he may also inquire into the business of any other body which, at a time which the appointed person considers material, is or was a subsidiary or associate of the association concerned'.

(2)   In subsection (2) of that section at the end of paragraph (b) there shall be added

> 'or

> (c)   any person who is, or has been, an officer, agent or member of a subsidiary or associate of the association; or

> (d)   any other person whom the appointed person has reason to believe is or may be in possession of information of relevance to the inquiry';

and in the words following paragraph (b) for the words 'the association's business' there shall be substituted 'the business of the association or any other such body as is referred to in subsection (1)'.

(3)   After subsection (3) of that section there shall be inserted the following subsections—

> '(3A)   Where, by virtue of subsection (2), any books, accounts or other documents are produced to the appointed person, he may take copies of or make extracts from them.

> (3B)   The appointed person may, if he thinks fit during the course of the inquiry, make one or more interim reports to the Corporation on such matters as appear to him to be appropriate.'

(4)   After subsection (5) of that section there shall be added the following subsections—

> '(6)   In this section, in relation to a housing association, "subsidiary" means a company with respect to which one of the following conditions is fulfilled,—

> (a)   the association is a member of the company and controls the composition of the board of directors; or

(b) the association holds more than half in nominal value of the company's equity share capital; or

(c) the company is a subsidiary, within the meaning of the Companies Act 1985 or the Friendly and Industrial and Provident Societies Act 1968, of another company which, by virtue of paragraph (a) or paragraph (b), is itself a subsidiary of the housing association;

and, in the case of a housing association which is a body of trustees, the reference in paragraph (a) or paragraph (b) to the association is a reference to the trustees acting as such and any reference in subsection (7) to the association shall be construed accordingly.

(7) For the purposes of subsection (6)(a), the composition of a company's board of directors shall be deemed to be controlled by a housing association if, but only if, the association, by the exercise of some power exercisable by the association without the consent or concurrence of any other person, can appoint or remove the holders of all or a majority of the directorships.

(8) In this section, in relation to a housing association, "associate" means—

(a) any body of which the association is a subsidiary, and

(b) any other subsidiary of such a body,

and in this subsection "subsidiary" has the same meaning as in the Companies Act 1985 or the Friendly and Industrial and Provident Societies Act 1968 or, in the case of a body which is itself a housing association, has the meaning assigned by subsection (6).

(9) In relation to a company which is an industrial and provident society,—

(a) any reference in subsection (6)(a) or subsection (7) to the board of directors is a reference to the committee of management of the society; and

(b) the reference in subsection (7) to the holders of all or a majority of the directorships is a reference to all or a majority of the members of the committee or, if the housing association is itself a member of the committee, such number as together with the association would constitute a majority.'

20.   In section 29(1) (extraordinary audit) after the words 'section 28' there shall be inserted 'into the affairs of a registered housing association'.

21.—(1)   In section 30 (general powers of Corporation as a result of an inquiry or audit) after subsection (1) there shall be inserted the following subsection—

'(1A) If at any time the appointed person makes an interim report under section 28(3B) and, as a result of that interim report, the Corporation is satisfied that there has been misconduct or mismanagement as mentioned in subsection (1),—

(a) the Corporation may at that time exercise any of the powers conferred by paragraphs (b) to (d) of that subsection; and

(b)   in relation to the exercise at that time of the power conferred by subsection (1)(b), the reference therein to a period of six months shall be construed as a reference to a period beginning at that time and ending six months after the date of the report under section 28(4).'

(2)   In subsection (4) of that section (appeal against certain orders) for the words from 'order to the High Court' onwards there shall be substituted

'order,—

(a)   if it is an order of the Housing Corporation or Housing for Wales, to the High Court; and

(b)   if it is an order of Scottish Homes, to the Court of Session.'

22.—(1)   In section 31 (exercise of powers in relation to registered charities), in subsection (1) immediately before the entry relating to section 41 of the 1985 Act there shall be inserted the following entries—

'section 50 of the Housing Act 1988 (housing association grants), section 51 of that Act (revenue deficit grants)'.

(2)   At the end of subsection (2)(b) of that section there shall be added the words 'and such other activities (if any) of the association as are incidental to or connected with its housing activities'.

23.   In section 33 (recognition of central association), in subsection (1) after 'housing associations' there shall be inserted 'in Great Britain or in any part of Great Britain'.

24.   After section 33 there shall be inserted the following section—

Provision of services between the Corporations
33A.   Any of the Corporations may enter into an agreement with the others or either of them for the provision of services of any description by the one to the other or others on such terms, as to payment or otherwise, as the parties to the agreement consider appropriate.'

25.   In section 39 (minor definitions) before the definition of 'mental disorder' there shall be inserted—

'"assured tenancy" has, in England and Wales, the same meaning as in Part I of the Housing Act 1988 and, in Scotland, the same meaning as in Part II of the Housing (Scotland) Act 1988;
"assured agricultural occupancy" has the same meaning as in Part I of the Housing Act 1988.'

26.   In section 40 (index of defined expressions in Part I)—

(a)   after the entry relating to 'appropriate registrar' there shall be inserted—

'"assured agricultural occupancy" ... section 39
"assured tenancy" ... ... section 39';

(b)   after the entry relating to 'the Companies Act' there shall be inserted—

'"the Corporation" ... ... section 2A';

and

(c) in the entry beginning 'register', in the second column for '3(2)' there shall be substituted '3'.

Part II Amendments of Part II
with respect to the Housing Corporation and Housing for Wales

27.—(1) In section 63 (building society advances) for the words 'the Housing Corporation', in each place where they occur in subsections (1) and (2), there shall be substituted 'one of the Corporations' and in subsection (1)(b) for the words 'the Corporation' there shall be substituted 'that one of the Corporations which is concerned'.

(2) After subsection (2) of that section there shall be inserted the following subsection—

'(2A) In this section "the Corporations" means the Housing Corporation and Housing for Wales'.

28.—(1) In section 69 (power to vary or terminate certain agreements) at the end of subsection (1)(a) there shall be added '(including such an agreement under which rights and obligations have been transferred to Housing for Wales)'.

(2) After subsection (2) of that section there shall be inserted the following subsection—

'(2A) In the case of an agreement under which rights and obligations have been transferred to Housing for Wales, the reference to a party to the agreement includes a reference to Housing for Wales.'

29. In section 69A (land subject to housing management agreement) for the words 'housing association grant, revenue deficit grant or hostel deficit grant' there shall be substituted 'grant under section 50 (housing association grant) or section 51 (revenue deficit grant) of the Housing Act 1988'.

30.—(1) In Part I of Schedule 5 (residual subsidies)—

(a) in paragraph 5(3) the words 'at such times and in such places as the Treasury may direct' and 'with the approval of the Treasury' shall be omitted; and

(b) at the end of paragraph 6(2)(b) there shall be added 'or Housing for Wales'.

(2) In Part II of that Schedule, in paragraph 5(3) the words 'at such times and in such places as the Treasury may direct' and 'with the approval of the Treasury' shall be omitted.

Part III Amendments of Part III
with respect to the Housing Corporation and Housing for Wales

31.—(1) In section 74 (constitution of Housing Corporation etc.), in subsection (1) after the words 'Housing Corporation' there shall be inserted 'and Housing for Wales, each of'.

(2) In subsection (2) of that section for the words 'the Corporation' there shall be substituted 'the Housing Corporation'.

(3) At the end of that section there shall be inserted the following subsections—

> '(3) In this Part "registered housing association" in relation to the Corporation, means a housing association registered in the register maintained by the Corporation.
>
> (4) In this Part,—
>
> > (a) in relation to land in Wales held by an unregistered housing association, "the Corporation" means Housing for Wales; and
> > (b) in relation to land outside Wales held by such an association, "the Corporation" means the Housing Corporation.'

32. In section 75 (general functions), in subsection (1)(c) for the words 'a register of housing associations' there shall be substituted 'the register of housing associations referred to in section 3'.

33. At the end of section 77 (advisory service) there shall be added the following subsection—

> '(3) The powers conferred on the Corporation by subsections (1) and (2) may be exercised by the Housing Corporation and Housing for Wales acting jointly'.

34.—(1) In section 83 (power to guarantee loans), in subsection (3) (maximum amount outstanding in respect of loans etc.) for the words 'the Corporation', in each place where they occur, there shall be substituted 'the Housing Corporation'.

(2) After subsection (3) of that section there shall be inserted the following subsection—

> '(3A) The aggregate amount outstanding in respect of—
>
> > (a) loans for which Housing for Wales has given a guarantee under this section, and
> > (b) payments made by Housing for Wales in meeting an obligation arising by virtue of such a guarantee and not repaid to Housing for Wales,
>
> shall not exceed £30 million or such greater sum not exceeding £50 million as the Secretary of State may specify by order made with the approval of the Treasury'.

(3) In subsection (4) of that section (procedure for orders of Secretary of State) after the words 'subsection (3)' there shall be inserted 'or subsection (3A)'.

35.—(1) In section 93 (limit on borrowing), in subsection (2) for the words from 'shall not exceed' onwards there shall be substituted 'shall not exceed the limit appropriate to the Corporation under subsection (2A)'.

(2) At the end of subsection (2) of that section there shall be inserted the following subsection—

> '(2A) The limit referred to in subsection (2) is,—
>
> > (a) in the case of the Housing Corporation, £2,000 million or such

greater sum not exceeding £3,000 million as the Secretary of State may specify by order made with the consent of the Treasury; and

(b) in the case of Housing for Wales, £250 million or such greater sum not exceeding £300 million as the Secretary of State may specify by order made with the consent of the Treasury.'

(3) In subsections (3) to (5) of that section for '(2)', in each place where it occurs, there shall be substituted '(2A)'.

36. In section 106(1) (minor definitions: general) for the definition of 'housing activities' there shall be substituted the following—

'"housing activities", in relation to a registered housing association, means all its activities in pursuance of such of its purposes, objects or powers as are of a description mentioned in section 1(1)(a) or subsections (2) to (4) of section 4.'

37. In Schedule 6, paragraph 3(3)(b) shall be omitted.

Schedule 7 Housing action trusts: constitution

Members

1. A housing action trust (in this Schedule referred to as a 'trust') shall consist of a chairman and such number of other members (not less than five but not exceeding eleven) as the Secretary of State may from time to time appoint.

2.—(1) In appointing members of a trust the Secretary of State shall have regard to the desirability of securing the services of persons who live in or have special knowledge of the locality in which the designated area is situated and before appointing any such person as a member he shall consult every local housing authority any part of whose district is included in the designated area.

(2) Before appointing a person to be a member of a trust the Secretary of State shall satisfy himself that that person will have no financial or other interest likely to affect prejudicially the exercise of his functions as a member; and the Secretary of State may require a person whom he proposes to appoint to give him such information as he considers necessary for that purpose.

(3) For the purposes of subparagraph (2) above, the fact that a person is or may become a tenant of a trust shall not be regarded as giving to that person an interest likely to affect prejudicially the exercise of his functions as a member.

(4) The Secretary of State shall appoint one of the members to be chairman and, if he thinks fit, another to be deputy chairman of the trust.

3. Subject to the following provisions of this Schedule, each member of the trust as such and the chairman and deputy chairman as such shall hold and vacate office in accordance with his appointment.

4. If the chairman or deputy chairman ceases to be a member of the trust, he shall also cease to be chairman or deputy chairman, as the case may be.

5. Any member of the trust may, by notice in writing addressed to the Secretary of State, resign his membership; and the chairman or deputy chairman may, by like notice, resign his office as such.

6.   If the Secretary of State is satisfied that a member of the trust (including the chairman or deputy chairman)—

    (a)   has become bankrupt or made an arrangement with his creditors, or
    (b)   has been absent from meetings of the trust for a period longer than three consecutive months without the permission of the trust, or
    (c)   is otherwise unable or unfit to discharge the functions of a member, or is unsuitable to continue as a member,

the Secretary of State may remove him from his office.

7.   A member of the trust who ceases to be a member or ceases to be chairman or deputy chairman shall be eligible for reappointment.

Remuneration

8.   The trust may pay to each member such remuneration and allowances as the Secretary of State may with the approval of the Treasury determine.

9.   The trust may pay or make provision for paying, to or in respect of any member, such sums by way of pensions, allowances and gratuities as the Secretary of State may with the approval of the Treasury determine and, with that approval, the Secretary of State may undertake to meet any liabilities arising in respect of such pensions, allowances or gratuities after the dissolution of the trust.

10.   Where a person ceases to be a member of a trust and it appears to the Secretary of State that there are special circumstances which make it right for him to receive compensation, the trust may make to him payment of such amount as the Secretary of State may with the approval of the Treasury determine.

Staff

11.—(1)   There shall be a chief officer of the trust who shall be appointed by the trust with the approval of the Secretary of State.
    (2)   The chief officer shall be responsible to the trust for the general exercise of the trust's functions.
    (3)   The trust may appoint such number of other employees as may be approved by the Secretary of State.
    (4)   References in paragraph 12 below to employees of the trust include references to the chief officer as well as other employees.

12.—(1)   Employees of the trust shall be appointed at such remuneration and on such other terms and conditions as the trust may determine.
    (2)   The trust may pay such pensions, allowances or gratuities as it may determine to or in respect of any of its employees, make such payments as it may determine towards the provision of pensions, allowances or gratuities to or in respect of any of its employees or provide and maintain such schemes as it may determine (whether contributory or not) for the payment of pensions, allowances or gratuities to or in respect of any of its employees; and with the approval of the Treasury the Secretary of State may undertake to meet any liabilities arising in respect of such pensions, allowances or gratuities after the dissolution of the trust.

(3)   The reference in subparagraph (2) above to pensions, allowances or gratuities to or in respect of any of the trust's employees includes a reference to pensions, allowances or gratuities by way of compensation to or in respect of any of the trust's employees who suffer loss of office or employment or loss or diminution of emoluments.

(4)   If an employee of the trust becomes a member and was by reference to his employment by the trust a participant in a pension scheme maintained by the trust for the benefit of any of its employees, the trust may determine that his service as a member shall be treated for the purposes of the scheme as service as an employee of the trust whether or not any benefits are to be payable to or in respect of him by virtue of paragraph 9 above.

(5)   A determination of the trust for the purposes of this paragraph is ineffective unless made with the approval of the Secretary of State given with the consent of the Treasury.

Meetings and proceedings

13.   The quorum of the trust and the arrangements relating to its meetings shall, subject to any directions given by the Secretary of State, be such as the trust may determine.

14.   The validity of any proceedings of the trust shall not be affected by any vacancy among its members or by any defect in the appointment of any of its members.

Instruments, etc.

15.   The fixing of the seal of the trust shall be authenticated by the signature of the chairman or of some other member authorised either generally or specially by the trust to act for that purpose.

16.   Any document purporting to be a document duly executed under the seal of the trust shall be received in evidence and shall, unless the contrary is proved, be deemed to be so executed.

17.   A document purporting to be signed on behalf of a trust shall be received in evidence and shall, unless the contrary is proved, be deemed to be so signed.

House of Commons disqualification

18.   In Part III of Schedule 1 to the House of Commons Disqualification Act 1975 (disqualifying offices), there shall be inserted at the appropriate place the following entry—

> 'Any member, in receipt of remuneration, of a housing action trust (within the meaning of Part III of the Housing Act 1988).'

Schedule 8 Housing action trusts: finance etc.

Part I Preliminary

1.—(1)   References in this Schedule to a trust are to a housing action trust.

(2)   The financial year of a trust shall begin with 1 April and references to a financial year in relation to a trust shall be construed accordingly.

Part II Finance

Financial duties

2.—(1)   After consultation with a trust, the Secretary of State may, with the Treasury's approval, determine the financial duties of the trust, and different determinations may be made in relation to different trusts or for different functions and activities of the same trust.

(2)   The Secretary of State shall give the trust notice of every determination, and a determination may—

    (a)   relate to a period beginning before the date on which it is made;
    (b)   contain incidental or supplementary provisions; and
    (c)   be varied by a subsequent determination.

Government grants

3.—(1)   The Secretary of State may (out of moneys provided by Parliament and with the consent of the Treasury) pay to a trust, in respect of the exercise of its functions and in respect of its administrative expenses, such sums as he may (with the approval of the Treasury) determine.

(2)   The payment may be made on such terms as the Secretary of State (with the approval of the Treasury) provides.

Borrowing

4.—(1)   A trust may borrow temporarily, by way of overdraft or otherwise, such sums as it may require for meeting its obligations and discharging its functions—

    (a)   in sterling from the Secretary of State; or
    (b)   with the consent of the Secretary of State, or in accordance with any general authority given by the Secretary of State, either in sterling or in currency other than sterling from a person other than the Secretary of State.

(2)   A trust may borrow otherwise than by way of temporary loan such sums as the trust may require—

    (a)   in sterling from the Secretary of State; or
    (b)   with the consent of the Secretary of State, in a currency other than sterling from a person other than the Secretary of State.

(3)   The Secretary of State may lend to a trust any sums it has power to borrow from him under subparagraph (1) or subparagraph (2) above.

(4)   The Treasury may issue to the Secretary of State out of the National Loans Fund any sums necessary to enable him to make loans under subparagraph (3) above.

(5)   Loans made under subparagraph (3) above shall be repaid to the Secretary of State at such times and by such methods, and interest on the loans shall be paid to him at such times and at such rates, as he may determine.

(6)   All sums received by the Secretary of State under subparagraph (5) above shall be paid into the National Loans Fund.

(7) References in this paragraph to the Secretary of State are references to him acting with the approval of the Treasury.

Guarantees

5.—(1) The Treasury may guarantee, in such manner and on such conditions as they think fit, the repayment of the principal of and the payment of interest on any sums which a trust borrows from a person or body other than the Secretary of State.

(2) Immediately after a guarantee is given under this paragraph, the Treasury shall lay a statement of the guarantee before each House of Parliament; and where any sum is issued for fulfilling a guarantee so given, the Treasury shall lay before each House of Parliament a statement relating to that sum, as soon as possible after the end of each financial year, beginning with that in which the sum is issued and ending with that in which all liability in respect of the principal of the sum and in respect of interest on it is finally discharged.

(3) Any sums required by the Treasury for fulfilling a guarantee under this paragraph shall be charged on and issued out of the Consolidated Fund.

(4) If any sums are issued in fulfilment of a guarantee given under this paragraph, the trust shall make to the Treasury, at such times and in such manner as the Treasury may from time to time direct, payments of such amounts as the Treasury so direct in or towards repayment of the sums so issued and payments of interest, at such rates as the Treasury so direct, on what is outstanding for the time being in respect of sums so issued.

(5) Any sums received by the Treasury in pursuance of subparagraph (4) above shall be paid into the Consolidated Fund.

Assumed debt

6.—(1) On any acquisition to which this paragraph applies, a trust shall assume a debt to the Secretary of State of such amount as may be notified to the trust in writing by him, with the approval of the Treasury.

(2) This paragraph applies to any acquisition by the trust of property held—

    (a) by or on behalf of the Crown; or
    (b) by a company all of whose shares are held by or on behalf of the Crown or by a wholly owned subsidiary of such a company.

(3) Subject to subparagraph (4) below, the amount to be notified is the aggregate of the following—

    (a) the consideration given when the property was first brought into public ownership; and
    (b) the costs and expenses of and incidental to its being brought into public ownership.

(4) If it appears to the Secretary of State that there has been such a change in circumstances since the property was first brought into public ownership that its true value would not be reflected by reference to the consideration mentioned in subparagraph (3) above, the Secretary of State, with the approval of the Treasury, shall determine the amount to be notified.

(5) The rate of interest payable on the debt assumed by a trust under this

paragraph, and the date from which interest is to begin to accrue, the arrangements for paying off the principal, and the other terms of the debt shall be such as the Secretary of State, with the approval of the Treasury, may from time to time determine.

(6) Different rates and dates may be determined under subparagraph (5) above with respect to different portions of the debt.

(7) Any sums received by the Secretary of State under subparagraph (5) above shall be paid into the National Loans Fund.

Surplus funds

7.—(1) Where it appears to the Secretary of State, after consultation with the Treasury and the trust, that a trust has a surplus, whether on capital or on revenue account, after making allowance by way of transfer to reserve or otherwise for its future requirements, the trust shall, if the Secretary of State with the approval of the Treasury and after consultation with the trust so directs, pay to the Secretary of State such sum not exceeding the amount of that surplus as may be specified in the direction.

(2) Any sum received by the Secretary of State under this paragraph shall, subject to subparagraph (4) below, be paid into the Consolidated Fund.

(3) The whole or part of any payment made to the Secretary of State by a trust under subparagraph (1) above shall, if the Secretary of State with the approval of the Treasury so determines, be treated as made by way of repayment of such part of the principal of loans under paragraph 4(3) above, and as made in respect of the repayments due at such times, as may be so determined.

(4) Any sum treated under subparagraph (3) above as a repayment of a loan shall be paid by the Secretary of State into the National Loans Fund.

Financial limits

8.—(1) The aggregate amount of the sums mentioned in subparagraph (2) below shall not exceed such sum as the Secretary of State, with the consent of the Treasury, may by order made by statutory instrument specify.

(2) The sums are—

(a) sums borrowed by all trusts under paragraph 4 above minus repayments made in respect of the sums; and

(b) sums issued by the Treasury in fulfilment of guarantees under paragraph 5 above of debts of all trusts.

(3) No order shall be made under subparagraph (1) above unless a draft of it has been laid before, and approved by a resolution of, the House of Commons.

Grants and loans: accounts

9.—(1) The Secretary of State shall prepare in respect of each financial year an account—

(a) of the sums paid to trusts under paragraph 3 above;

(b) of the sums issued to him under paragraph 4(4) above and the sums received by him under paragraph 4(5) above and of the disposal by him of those sums; and

(c)   of the sums paid into the Consolidated Fund or National Loans Fund under paragraph 7 above.

(2)   The Secretary of State shall send the account to the Comptroller and Auditor General before the end of the month of November next following the end of that year.

(3)   The Comptroller and Auditor General shall examine, certify and report on the account and lay copies of it and of his report before each House of Parliament.

(4)   The form of the account and the manner of preparing it shall be such as the Treasury may direct.

Part III General accounts etc.

Accounts

10.—(1)   A trust shall keep proper accounts and other records in relation to them.

(2)   The accounts and records shall show, in respect of the financial year to which they relate, a true and fair view of the trust's activities.

(3)   A trust shall prepare in respect of each financial year a statement of accounts complying with any requirement which the Secretary of State has (with the consent of the Treasury) notified in writing to the trust relating to—

(a)   the information to be contained in the statement;

(b)   the manner in which the information is to be presented; and

(c)   the methods and principles according to which the statement is to be prepared.

(4)   Subject to any requirement notified to the trust under subparagraph (3) above, in preparing any statement of accounts in accordance with that subparagraph the trust shall follow, with respect to each of the matters specified in paragraphs (a) to (c) of that subparagraph, such course as may for the time being be approved by the Secretary of State with the consent of the Treasury.

(5)   Section 6 of the National Audit Act 1983 (which enables the Comptroller and Auditor General to conduct examinations into the economy, efficiency and effectiveness with which certain departments, authorities and bodies have used their resources) shall apply to a trust.

Audit

11.—(1)   The trust's accounts and statements of accounts shall be audited by an auditor to be appointed annually by the Secretary of State in relation to the trust.

(2)   A person shall not be qualified for appointment under subparagraph (1) above unless he is qualified for appointment as auditor of a company under section 389 of the Companies Act 1985.

(3)   A person shall not be qualified for appointment under subparagraph (1) above if the person is—

(a)   a member, officer or servant of the trust,

(b)   a partner of, or employed by, a member, officer or servant of the trust, or

(c)   a body corporate.

Transmission to Secretary of State

12.   As soon as the accounts and statement of accounts of the trust for any financial year have been audited, the trust shall send to the Secretary of State a copy of the statement, together with a copy of any report made by the auditor on the statement or on the accounts.

Reports

13.—(1)   As soon as possible after the end of each financial year, a trust shall make to the Secretary of State a report dealing generally with the trust's operations during the year, and shall include in the report a copy of its audited statement of accounts for that year.

(2)   Without prejudice to the generality of subparagraph (1) above, a report shall give particulars of the name and address of every person who, in the financial year to which the report relates, has received financial assistance from the trust under section 71(1) of this Act, together with particulars of the form of the assistance, the amount involved and the purpose for which the assistance was given.

(3)   The Secretary of State shall lay a copy of the report before each House of Parliament.

Information

14.   Without prejudice to paragraph 13 above, a trust shall provide the Secretary of State with such information relating to its activities as he may require, and for that purpose shall permit any person authorised by the Secretary of State to inspect and make copies of the accounts, books, documents or papers of the trust and shall afford such explanation of them as that person or the Secretary of State may reasonably require.

Schedule 9 Orders vesting land in housing action trusts

Part I Provisions supplementing section 76(1) to (3)

1.   In this Part of this Schedule 'the principal section' means section 76 of this Act.

2.—(1)   In the principal section and paragraph 3 below, 'statutory undertakers' and 'statutory undertaking' shall be construed in accordance with paragraph 4 below.

(2)   In the principal section and the following provisions of this Part of this Schedule, 'wholly owned subsidiary' has the meaning given by section 736 of the Companies Act 1985.

3.—(1)   In subsection (3) of the principal section the reference to the Secretary of State and the appropriate Minister—

(a)   in relation to statutory undertakers who are also statutory undertakers for the purposes of any provision of Part XI of the Town and Country Planning Act 1971, shall be construed as if contained in that Part; and

(b) in relation to any other statutory undertakers shall be construed in accordance with an order made by the Secretary of State.

(2) If, for the purposes of subsection (3) of the principal section, any question arises as to which Minister is the appropriate Minister in relation to any statutory undertakers, that question shall be determined by the Treasury.

4. In the principal section and, except where the context otherwise requires, in paragraph 3 above 'statutory undertakers' means—

(a) persons authorised by any enactment to carry on any railway, light railway, tramway, road transport, water transport, canal, inland navigation, dock, harbour, pier or lighthouse undertaking, or any undertaking for the supply of electricity, hydraulic power or water;

(b) British Shipbuilders, the British Steel Corporation, the Civil Aviation Authority, the British Coal Corporation, the National Enterprise Board, the Post Office and any other authority, body or undertakers which, by virtue of any enactment, are to be treated as statutory undertakers for any of the purposes of the Town and Country Planning Act 1971;

(c) any other authority, body or undertakers specified in an order made by the Secretary of State; and

(d) any wholly owned subsidiary of any person, authority, body or undertakers mentioned in subparagraphs (a) and (b) above or specified in an order made under subparagraph (c) above;

and 'statutory undertaking' shall be construed accordingly.

5. An order under any provision of this Part of this Schedule shall be made by statutory instrument which shall be subject to annulment in pursuance of a resolution of either House of Parliament.

Part II Modifications of enactments

Land Compensation Act 1961

6. The Land Compensation Act 1961 shall have effect in relation to orders under section 76 of this Act subject to the modifications in paragraphs 7 to 11 below.

7. References to the date of service of a notice to treat shall be treated as references to the date on which an order under section 76 of this Act comes into force.

8. Section 17(2) shall be treated as if for the words 'the authority proposing to acquire it have served a notice to treat in respect thereof, or an agreement has been made for the sale thereof to that authority' there were substituted the words 'an order under section 76 of the Housing Act 1988 vesting the land in which the interest subsists in a housing action trust has come into force, or an agreement has been made for the sale of the interest to such a trust'.

9. In section 22—

(a) subsection (2) shall be treated as if at the end of paragraph (c) there were added the words 'or

    (cc)   where an order has been made under section 76 of the Housing Act 1988 vesting the land in which the interest subsists in a housing action trust';

and

    (b)   subsection (3) shall be treated as if, in paragraph (a), after the words 'paragraph (b)' there were inserted 'or paragraph (cc)'.

10.   Any reference to a notice to treat in section 39(2) shall be treated as a reference to an order under section 76 of this Act.

11.   In Schedule 2, paragraph 1(2) shall be treated as if at the end there were added the following paragraph—

    '(k)   an acquisition by means of an order under section 76 of the Housing Act 1988 vesting land in a housing action trust.'

Compulsory Purchase (Vesting Declarations) Act 1981

12.—(1)   In Schedule 2 to the Compulsory Purchase (Vesting Declarations) Act 1981 (vesting of land in urban development corporation), in paragraph 1 after the world 'declaration)' there shall be inserted 'or under section 76 of the Housing Act 1988 (subsection (5) of which contains similar provision)'.

    (2)   At the end of subparagraph (a) of paragraph 3 of that Schedule there shall be added 'or, as the case may be, the housing action trust'.

Schedule 10 Housing action trusts: land

Part I Modifications of Acquisition of Land Act 1981

1.   The Acquisition of Land Act 1981 (in this Part referred to as 'the 1981 Act') shall apply in relation to the compulsory acquisition of land under section 77 of this Act with the modifications made by this Part of this Schedule.

2.—(1)   Where a compulsory purchase order authorising the acquisition of any land is submitted to the Secretary of State in accordance with section 2(2) of the 1981 Act then, if the Secretary of State—

    (a)   is satisfied that the order ought to be confirmed so far as it relates to part of the land comprised in it, but

    (b)   has not for the time being determined whether it ought to be confirmed so far as it relates to any other such land,

he may confirm the order so far as it relates to the land mentioned in paragraph (a) above, and give directions postponing the consideration of the order, so far as it relates to any other land specified in the directions, until such time as may be so specified.

    (2)   Where the Secretary of State gives directions under subparagraph (1) above, the notices required by section 15 of the 1981 Act to be published and served shall include a statement of the effect of the directions.

3.   The reference in section 17(3) of the 1981 Act to statutory undertakers includes a reference to a housing action trust.

Part II Land: supplementary

Extinguishment of rights over land

4.—(1)   Subject to this paragraph, on an order under section 76 of this Act coming into force or the completion by a housing action trust of a compulsory acquisition of land under Part III of this Act, all private rights of way and rights of laying down, erecting, continuing or maintaining any apparatus on, under or over the land shall be extinguished, and any such apparatus shall vest in the trust.

(2)   Subparagraph (1) above does not apply—

(a)   to any right vested in, or apparatus belonging to, statutory undertakers for the purpose of carrying on their undertaking; or

(b)   to any right conferred by or in accordance with the telecommunications code on the operator of a telecommunications code system or to any telecommunications apparatus kept installed for the purposes of any such system.

(3)   In respect of any right or apparatus not falling within subparagraph (2) above, subparagraph (1) above shall have effect subject—

(a)   to any direction given by the Secretary of State before the coming into force of the order (or, as the case may be, by the trust before the completion of the acquisition) that subparagraph (1) above shall not apply to any right or apparatus specified in the direction, and

(b)   to any agreement which may be made (whether before or after the coming into force of the order or completion of the acquisition) between the Secretary of State (or trust) and the person in or to whom the right or apparatus in question is vested or belongs.

(4)   Any person who suffers loss by the extinguishment of a right or the vesting of any apparatus under this paragraph shall be entitled to compensation from the trust.

(5)   Any compensation payable under this paragraph shall be determined in accordance with the Land Compensation Act 1961.

Power to override easements

5.—(1)   The erection, construction or carrying out, or maintenance of any building or work on land which has been vested in or acquired by a housing action trust for the purposes of Part III of this Act, whether done by the trust or by any other person, is authorised by virtue of this paragraph if it is done in accordance with planning permission, notwithstanding that it involves interference with an interest or right to which this paragraph applies, or involves a breach of a restriction as to the user of land arising by virtue of a contract.

(2)   Nothing in subparagraph (1) above shall authorise interference with any right of way or right of laying down, erecting, continuing or maintaining apparatus on, under or over land, being a right vested in or belonging to statutory undertakers for the purpose of the carrying on of their undertaking or a right conferred by or in accordance with the telecommunications code on the operator of a telecommunications code system.

(3)   This paragraph applies to the following interests and rights, that is to say, any easement, liberty, privilege, right or advantage annexed to land and adversely affecting other land, including any natural right to support.

(4)   In respect of any interference or breach in pursuance of subparagraph (1) above, compensation shall be payable under section 7 or section 10 of the Compulsory Purchase Act 1965, to be assessed in the same manner and subject to the same rules as in the case of other compensation under those sections in respect of injurious affection where the compensation is to be estimated in connection with a purchase by a housing action trust or the injury arises from the execution of works on land acquired by such a trust.

(5)   Where a person other than the housing action trust by or in whom the land in question was acquired or vested is liable to pay compensation by virtue of subparagraph (4) above and fails to discharge that liability, the liability shall (subject to subparagraph (6) below) be enforceable against the trust.

(6)   Nothing in subparagraph (5) above shall be construed as affecting any agreement between the trust and any other person for indemnifying the trust against any liability under that subparagraph.

(7)   Nothing in this paragraph shall be construed as authorising any act or omission on the part of any person which is actionable at the suit of any person on any grounds other than such an interference or breach as is mentioned in subparagraph (1) above.

(8)   Nothing in this paragraph shall be construed as authorising any act or omission on the part of a housing action trust, or of any body corporate, in contravention of any limitation imposed by law on its capacity by virtue of the constitution of the trust or body.

Consecrated land and burial grounds

6.—(1)   Any consecrated land, whether including a building or not, which has been vested in or acquired by a housing action trust for the purposes of Part III of this Act may (subject to the following provisions of this paragraph) be used by the trust, or by any other person, in any manner in accordance with planning permission, notwithstanding any obligation or restriction imposed under ecclesiastical law or otherwise in respect of consecrated land.

(2)   Subparagraph (1) above does not apply to land which consists or forms part of a burial ground.

(3)   Any use of consecrated land authorised by subparagraph (1) above, and the use of any land, not being consecrated land, vested or acquired as mentioned in that subparagraph which at the time of acquisition included a church or other building used or formerly used for religious worship or the site thereof, shall be subject to compliance with the prescribed requirements with respect to the removal and reinterment of any human remains, and the disposal of monuments and fixtures and furnishings; and, in the case of consecrated land, shall be subject to such provisions as may be prescribed for prohibiting or restricting the use of the land, either absolutely or until the prescribed consent has been obtained, so long as any church or other building used or formerly used for religious worship, or any part thereof, remains on the land.

(4)   Any regulations made for the purposes of subparagraph (3) above—

(a)   shall contain such provisions as appear to the Secretary of State to be requisite for securing that any use of land which is subject to compliance with the regulations shall, as nearly as may be, be subject to the like control as is imposed by law in the case of a similar use authorised by an enactment not contained in this Act or by a Measure, or as it would be proper to impose on a disposal of the land in question otherwise than in pursuance of an enactment or Measure;

(b)   shall contain requirements relating to the disposal of any such land as is mentioned in subparagraph (3) above such as appear to the Secretary of State requisite for securing that the provisions of that subparagraph shall be complied with in relation to the use of the land; and

(c)   may contain such incidental and consequential provisions (including provision as to the closing of registers) as appear to the Secretary of State to be expedient for the purposes of the regulations.

(5)   Any land consisting of a burial ground or part of a burial ground which has been vested in or acquired by a housing action trust for the purposes of Part III of this Act may be used by the trust in any manner in accordance with planning permission, notwithstanding anything in any enactment relating to burial grounds or any obligation or restriction imposed under ecclesiastical law or otherwise in respect of burial grounds.

(6)   Subparagraph (5) above shall not have effect in respect of any land which has been used for the burial of the dead until the prescribed requirements with respect to the removal and reinterment of human remains and the disposal of monuments in or upon the land have been complied with.

(7)   Provision shall be made by any regulations made for the purposes of subparagraphs (3) and (6) above—

(a)   for requiring the persons in whom the land is vested to publish notice of their intention to carry out the removal and reinterment of any human remains or the disposal of any monuments; and

(b)   for enabling the personal representatives or relatives of any deceased person themselves to undertake the removal and reinterment of the remains of the deceased and the disposal of any monument commemorating the deceased, and for requiring the persons in whom the land is vested to defray the expenses of such removal, reinterment and disposal, not exceeding such amount as may be prescribed; and

(c)   for requiring compliance with such reasonable conditions (if any) as may be imposed, in the case of consecrated land, by the bishop of the diocese, with respect to the manner of removal and the place and manner of reinterment of any human remains and the disposal of any monuments; and

(d)   for requiring compliance with any directions given in any case by the Secretary of State with respect to the removal and reinterment of any human remains.

(8)   Subject to the provisions of any such regulations as are referred to in subparagraph (7) above, no faculty shall be required for the removal and reinterment in accordance with the regulations of any human remains or for the removal or disposal of any monuments, and the provisions of section 25 of the Burial Act 1857 (which prohibits the removal of human remains without the licence of the Secretary of State except in certain cases) shall not apply to a removal carried out in accordance with the regulations.

(9)   Any power conferred by this paragraph to use land in a manner therein mentioned shall be construed as a power so to use the land, whether it involves the erection, construction or carrying out of any building or work, or the maintenance of any building or work, or not.

(10)   Nothing in this paragraph shall be construed as authorising any act or omission on the part of any person which is actionable at the suit of any person on any grounds other than contravention of any such obligation, restriction or enactment as is mentioned in subparagraph 1 or subparagraph (5) above.

(11)   Subparagraph (8) of paragraph 5 above shall apply in relation to this paragraph as it applies in relation to that.

(12)   In this paragraph 'burial ground' includes any churchyard, cemetery or other ground, whether consecrated or not, which has at any time been set apart for the purposes of interment, and 'monument' includes a tombstone or other memorial.

(13)   In this paragraph 'prescribed' means prescribed by regulations made by the Secretary of State.

(14)   The power to make regulations under this paragraph shall be exercisable by statutory instrument which shall be subject to annulment in pursuance of a resolution of either House of Parliament.

Open spaces

7.—(1)   Any land being, or forming part of, a common, open space or fuel or field garden allotment, which has been vested in or acquired by a housing action trust for the purposes of Part III of this Act may be used by the trust, or by any other person, in any manner in accordance with planning permission, notwithstanding anything in any enactment relating to land of that kind, or in any enactment by which the land is specially regulated.

(2)   Nothing in this paragraph shall be construed as authorising any act or omission on the part of any person which is actionable at the suit of any person on any grounds other than contravention of any such enactment as is mentioned in subparagraph (1) above.

(3)   Subparagraph (8) of paragraph 5 above shall apply in relation to this paragraph as it applies in relation to that.

Displacement of persons

8.   If the Secretary of State certifies that possession of a house which has been vested in or acquired by a housing action trust for the purposes of Part III of this Act and is for the time being held by that trust for the purposes for which it was acquired, is immediately required for those purposes, nothing in the Rent (Agriculture) Act 1976 or the Rent Act 1977 or this Act shall prevent that trust from obtaining possession of the house.

Extinguishment of public rights of way

9.—(1)   Where any land has been vested in or acquired by a housing action trust for the purposes of Part III of this Act and is for the time being held by that trust for those purposes, the Secretary of State may by order extinguish any public right of way over the land.

(2)   Where the Secretary of State proposes to make an order under this

paragraph, he shall publish in such manner as appears to him to be requisite a notice—

    (a)   stating the effect of the order, and

    (b)   specifying the time (not being less than 28 days from the publication of the notice) within which, and the manner in which, objections to the proposal may be made,

and shall serve a like notice—

    (i)   on the local planning authority in whose area the land is situated; and

    (ii)   on the relevant highway authority.

(3)   In subparagraph (2) above 'the relevant highway authority' means any authority which is a highway authority in relation to the right of way proposed to be extinguished by the order under this paragraph.

(4)   Where an objection to a proposal to make an order under this paragraph is duly made and is not withdrawn, the provisions of paragraph 10 below shall have effect in relation to the proposal.

(5)   For the purposes of this paragraph an objection to such a proposal shall not be treated as duly made unless—

    (a)   it is made within the time and in the manner specified in the notice required by this paragraph; and

    (b)   a statement in writing of the grounds of the objection is comprised in or submitted with the objection.

(6)   Where it is proposed to make an order under this paragraph extinguishing a public right of way over a road on land acquired for the purposes of this Act by a housing action trust and compensation in respect of restrictions imposed under section 1 or section 2 of the Restriction of Ribbon Development Act 1935 in respect of that road has been paid by the highway authority (or, in the case of a trunk road, by the authority which, when the compensation was paid, was the authority for the purposes of section 4 of the Trunk Roads Act 1936), the order may provide for the payment by the housing action trust to that authority, in respect of the compensation so paid, of such sums as the Secretary of State, with the consent of the Treasury, may determine.

(7)   Where the Secretary of State makes an order under this paragraph on the application of a housing action trust, he shall send a copy of it to the Post Office.

10.—(1)   In this paragraph any reference to making a final decision, in relation to an order, is a reference to deciding whether to make the order or what modification, if any, ought to be made.

(2)   Unless the Secretary of State decides apart from the objection not to make the order, or decides to make a modification which is agreed to by the objector as meeting the objection, the Secretary of State shall, before making a final decision, consider the grounds of the objection as set out in the statement comprised in or submitted with the objection, and may, if he thinks fit, require the objector to submit within a specified period a further statement in writing as to any of the matters to which the objection relates.

(3)   In so far as the Secretary of State, after considering the grounds of the objection as set out in the original statement and in any such further statement, is

satisfied that the objection relates to a matter which can be dealt with in the assessment of compensation, the Secretary of State may treat the objection as irrelevant for the purpose of making a final decision.

(4)   If, after considering the grounds of the objection as set out in the original statement and in any such further statement, the Secretary of State is satisfied that, for the purpose of making a final decision, he is sufficiently informed as to the matters to which the objection relates, or if, where a further statement has been required, it is not submitted within the specified period, the Secretary of State may make a final decision without further investigation as to those matters.

(5)   Subject to subparagraphs (3) and (4) above, the Secretary of State, before making a final decision, shall afford to the objector an opportunity of appearing before, and being heard by, a person appointed for the purpose by the Secretary of State; and if the objector avails himself of that opportunity, the Secretary of State shall afford an opportunity of appearing and being heard on the same occasion to the housing action trust on whose representation the order is proposed to be made, and to any other persons to whom it appears to the Secretary of State to be expedient to afford such an opportunity.

(6)   Notwithstanding anything in the preceding provisions of this paragraph, if it appears to the Secretary of State that the matters to which the objection relates are such as to require investigation by public local inquiry before he makes a final decision, he shall cause such an inquiry to be held; and where he determines to cause such an inquiry to be held, any of the requirements of those provisions to which effect has not been given at the time of that determination shall be dispensed with.

Telegraphic lines

11.—(1)   Where an order under paragraph 9 above extinguishing a public right of way is made on the application of a housing action trust and at the time of the publication of the notice required by subparagraph (2) of that paragraph any telecommunication apparatus was kept installed for the purposes of a telecommunications code system under, in, on, over, along or across the land over which the right of way subsisted—

(a)   the power of the operator of the system to remove the apparatus shall, notwithstanding the making of the order, be exercisable at any time not later than the end of the period of three months from the date on which the right of way is extinguished and shall be exercisable in respect of the whole or any part of the apparatus after the end of that period if before the end of that period the operator of the system has given notice to the trust of his intention to remove the apparatus or that part of it, as the case may be;

(b)   the operator of the system may by notice given in that behalf to the trust not later than the end of the said period of three months abandon the telecommunication apparatus or any part of it;

(c)   subject to paragraph (b) above, the operator of the system shall be deemed at the end of that period to have abandoned any part of the apparatus which he has then neither removed nor given notice of his intention to remove;

(d)   the operator of the system shall be entitled to recover from the trust the expense of providing, in substitution for the apparatus and any other telecommunication apparatus connected with it which is rendered useless in consequence of the removal or abandonment of the first-mentioned apparatus, any telecommunication apparatus in such other place as the operator may require; and

(e) where under the preceding provisions of this subparagraph the operator of the system has abandoned the whole or any part of any telecommunication apparatus, that apparatus or that part of it shall vest in the trust and shall be deemed, with its abandonment, to cease to be kept installed for the purposes of a telecommunications code system.

(2) As soon as practicable after the making of an order under paragraph 9 above extinguishing a public right of way in circumstances in which subparagraph (1) above applies in relation to the operator of any telecommunications code system, the Secretary of State shall give notice to the operator of the making of the order.

Statutory undertakers

12.—(1) Where any land has been acquired by a housing action trust under section 77 of this Act and—

(a) there subsists over that land a right vested in or belonging to statutory undertakers for the purpose of the carrying on of their undertaking, being a right of way or a right of laying down, erecting, continuing or maintaining apparatus on, under or over that land, or

(b) there is on, under or over the land apparatus vested in or belonging to statutory undertakers for the purpose of the carrying on of their undertaking,

the trust, if satisfied that the extinguishment of the right or, as the case may be, the removal of the apparatus, is necessary for the purpose of carrying out any development, may serve on the statutory undertakers a notice stating that, at the end of the period of 28 days from the date of service of the notice or such longer period as may be specified therein, the right will be extinguished or requiring that, before the end of that period, the apparatus shall be removed.

(2) The statutory undertakers on whom a notice is served under subparagraph (1) above may, before the end of the period of 28 days from the service of the notice, serve a counter-notice on the trust stating that they object to all or any provisions of the notice and specifying the grounds of their objection.

(3) If no counter-notice is served under subparagraph (2) above—

(a) any right to which the notice relates shall be extinguished at the end of the period specified in that behalf in the notice; and

(b) if, at the end of the period so specified in relation to any apparatus, any requirement of the notice as to the removal of the apparatus has not been complied with, the trust may remove the apparatus and dispose of it in any way it may think fit.

(4) If a counter-notice is served under subparagraph (2) above on a trust, the trust may either withdraw the notice (without prejudice to the service of a further notice) or may apply to the Secretary of State and the appropriate Minister for an order under this paragraph embodying the provisions of the notice with or without modification.

(5) Where by virtue of this paragraph any right vested in or belonging to statutory undertakers is extinguished, or any requirement is imposed on

statutory undertakers, those undertakers shall be entitled to compensation from the trust.

(6) Sections 238 and 240 of the Town and Country Planning Act 1971 (measure of compensation to statutory undertakers) shall apply to compensation under subparagraph (5) above as they apply to compensation under section 237(2) of that Act.

(7) Except in a case in which paragraph 11 above has effect—

(a) the reference in paragraph (a) of subparagraph (1) above to a right vested in or belonging to statutory undertakers for the purpose of the carrying on of their undertaking shall include a reference to a right conferred by or in accordance with the telecommunications code on the operator of a telecommunications code system; and

(b) the reference in paragraph (b) of that subparagraph to apparatus vested in or belonging to statutory undertakers for the purpose of the carrying on of their undertaking shall include a reference to telecommunication apparatus kept installed for the purposes of any such system.

(8) Where paragraph (a) or paragraph (b) of subparagraph (1) above has effect as mentioned in subparagraph (7) above, in the rest of this paragraph and in paragraph 13 below,—

(a) any reference to statutory undertakers shall have effect as a reference to the operator of any such system as is referred to in subparagraph (7) above; and

(b) any reference to the appropriate Minister shall have effect as a reference to the Secretary of State for Trade and Industry.

13.—(1) Before making an order under paragraph 12(4) above the Ministers proposing to make the order—

(a) shall afford to the statutory undertakers on whom notice was served under paragraph 12(1) above an opportunity of objecting to the application for the order; and

(b) if any objection is made, shall consider the objection and afford to those statutory undertakers and to the trust on whom the counter-notice was served, an opportunity of appearing before and being heard by a person appointed by the Secretary of State and the appropriate Minister for the purpose;

and the Ministers may then, if they think fit, make the order in accordance with the application either with or without modification.

(2) Where an order is made under paragraph 12(4) above—

(a) any right to which the order relates shall be extinguished at the end of the period specified in that behalf in the order; and

(b) if, at the end of the period so specified in relation to any apparatus, any requirement of the order as to the removal of the apparatus has not been complied with, the trust may remove the apparatus and dispose of it in any way it may think fit.

14.—(1) Subject to this paragraph, where any land has been acquired by a housing action trust under section 77 of this Act and—

(a)   there is on, under or over the land apparatus vested in or belonging to statutory undertakers, and

(b)   the undertakers claim that development to be carried out on the land is such as to require, on technical or other grounds connected with the carrying on of their undertaking, the removal or resiting of the apparatus affected by the development,

the undertakers may serve on the trust a notice claiming the right to enter on the land and carry out such works for the removal or resiting of the apparatus or any part of it as may be specified in the notice.

(2)   Where, after the land has been acquired as mentioned in subparagraph (1) above, development of the land is begun to be carried out, no notice under this paragraph shall be served later than 21 days after the beginning of the development.

(3)   Where a notice is served under this paragraph the trust on which it is served may, before the end of the period of 28 days from the date of service, serve on the statutory undertakers a counter-notice stating that it objects to all or any of the provisions of the notice and specifying the grounds of its objection.

(4)   If no counter-notice is served under subparagraph (3) above, the statutory undertakers shall, after the end of the said period of 28 days, have the rights claimed in their notice.

(5)   If a counter-notice is served under subparagraph (3) above, the statutory undertakers who served the notice under this paragraph may either withdraw it or may apply to the Secretary of State and the appropriate Minister for an order under this paragraph conferring on the undertakers the rights claimed in the notice or such modified rights as the Secretary of State and the appropriate Minister think it expedient to confer on them.

(6)   Where by virtue of this paragraph or an order of Ministers made under it, statutory undertakers have the right to execute works for the removal or resiting of apparatus, they may arrange with the trust for the works to be carried out by the trust, under the superintendence of the undertakers, instead of by the undertakers themselves.

(7)   Where works are carried out for the removal or resiting of statutory undertakers' apparatus, being works which the undertakers have the right to carry out by virtue of this paragraph or an order of Ministers made under it, the undertakers shall be entitled to compensation from the trust.

(8)   Sections 238 and 240 of the Town and Country Planning Act 1971 (measure of compensation to statutory undertakers) shall apply to compensation under subparagraph (7) above as they apply to compensation under section 237(3) of that Act.

(9)   In subparagraph (1)(a) above, the reference to apparatus vested in or belonging to statutory undertakers shall include a reference to telecommunication apparatus kept installed for the purposes of a telecommunications code system.

(10)   Where subparagraph (1)(a) above has effect as mentioned in subparagraph (9) above, in the rest of this paragraph—

(a)   any reference to statutory undertakers shall have effect as a reference to the operator of any such system as is referred to in subparagraph (9) above; and

(b) any reference to the appropriate Minister shall have effect as a reference to the Secretary of State for Trade and Industry.

15.—(1) The powers conferred by this paragraph shall be exercisable where, on a representation made by statutory undertakers, it appears to the Secretary of State and the appropriate Minister to be expedient that the powers and duties of those undertakers should be extended or modified, in order—

(a) to secure the provision for a designated area of services which would not otherwise be provided, or which would not otherwise be satisfactorily provided; or

(b) to facilitate an adjustment of the carrying on of the undertaking necessitated by any of the acts and events mentioned in subparagraph (2) below.

(2) The said acts and events are—

(a) the acquisition under Part III of this Act of any land in which an interest was held, or which was used, for the purpose of the carrying on of the undertaking of the statutory undertakers in question; and

(b) the extinguishment of a right or the imposition of any requirements by virtue of paragraph 12 above.

(3) The powers conferred by this paragraph shall also be exercisable where, on a representation made by a housing action trust, it appears to the Secretary of State and the appropriate Minister to be expedient that the powers and duties of statutory undertakers should be extended or modified, in order to secure the provision of new services, or the extension of existing services, for the purposes of a designated area under Part III of this Act.

(4) Where the powers conferred by this paragraph are exercisable, the Secretary of State and the appropriate Minister may, if they think fit, by order provide for such extension or modification of the powers and duties of the statutory undertakers as appears to them to be requisite in order to secure the provision of the services in question, as mentioned in subparagraph (1)(a) or subparagraph (3) above, or to secure the adjustment in question, as mentioned in subparagraph (1)(b) above, as the case may be.

(5) Without prejudice to the generality of subparagraph (4) above, an order under this paragraph may make provision—

(a) for empowering the statutory undertakers to acquire (whether compulsorily or by agreement) any land specified in the order, and to erect or construct any buildings or works so specified;

(b) for applying, in relation to the acquisition of any such land or the construction of any such works, enactments relating to the acquisition of land and the construction of works;

(c) where it has been represented that the making of the order is expedient for the purposes mentioned in subparagraph (1)(a) or subparagraph (3) above, for giving effect to such financial arrangements between the housing action trust and the statutory undertakers as they may agree, or as, in default of agreement, may be determined to be equitable in such manner and by such tribunal as may be specified in the order; and

(d) for such incidental and supplemental matters as appear to the

Secretary of State and the appropriate Minister to be expedient for the purposes
of the order.

16.—(1)   As soon as may be after making such a representation as is mentioned
in subparagraph (1) or subparagraph (3) of paragraph 15 above—

   (a)   the statutory undertakers, in a case falling within subparagraph (1), or
   (b)   the housing action trust, in a case falling within subparagraph (3),

shall publish, in such form and manner as may be directed by the Secretary of
State and the appropriate Minister, a notice giving such particulars as may be so
directed of the matters to which representation relates, and specifying the time
within which, and the manner in which, objections to the making of an order on
the representation may be made, and shall also, if it is so directed by the Secretary
of State and the appropriate Minister, serve a like notice on such persons, or
persons of such classes, as may be so directed.

   (2)   Orders under paragraph 15 above shall be subject to special parliamentary procedure.

17.—(1)   Where, on a representation made by statutory undertakers, the
appropriate Minister is satisfied that the fulfilment of any obligations incurred by
those undertakers in connection with the carrying on of their undertaking has
been rendered impracticable by an act or event to which this subparagraph
applies, the appropriate Minister may, if he thinks fit, by order direct that the
statutory undertakers shall be relieved of the fulfilment of that obligation, either
absolutely or to such extent as may be specified in the order.

   (2)   Subparagraph (1) above applies to the following acts and events—

   (a)   the compulsory acquisition under this Part of this Act of any land in
which an interest was held, or which was used, for the purpose of the carrying on
of the undertaking of the statutory undertakers; and

   (b)   the extinguishment of a right or the imposition of any requirement by
virtue of paragraph 12 above.

   (3)   As soon as may be after making a representation to the appropriate
Minister under subparagraph (1) above, the appropriate statutory undertakers
shall, as may be directed by the appropriate Minister, either publish (in such form
and manner as may be so directed) a notice giving such particulars as may be so
directed of the matters to which the representation relates, and specifying the
time within which, and the manner in which, objections to the making of an order
on the representation may be made, or service such a notice on such persons, or
persons of such classes, as may be so directed, or both publish and serve such
notices.

   (4)   If any objection to the making of an order under this paragraph is duly
made and is not withdrawn before the order is made, the order shall be subject to
special parliamentary procedure.

   (5)   Immediately after an order is made under this paragraph by the
appropriate Minister, he shall publish a notice stating that the order has been
made and naming a place where a copy of it may be seen at all reasonable hours,
and shall serve a like notice—

(a)   on any person who duly made an objection to the order and has sent to the appropriate Minister a request in writing to serve him with the notice required by this subparagraph, specifying an address for service; and

(b)   on such other persons (if any) as the appropriate Minister thinks fit.

(6)   Subject to the following provisions of this paragraph, an order under this paragraph shall become operative on the date on which the notice required by subparagraph (5) above is first published.

(7)   Where in accordance with subparagraph (4) above the order is subject to special parliamentary procedure, subparagraph (6) above shall not apply.

(8)   If any person aggrieved by an order under this paragraph wishes to question the validity of the order on the ground that it is not within the powers conferred by this paragraph, or that any requirement of this paragraph has not been complied with in relation to the order, he may, within six weeks from the date on which the notice required by subparagraph (5) above is first published, make an application to the High Court under this paragraph.

(9)   On any application under subparagraph (8) above the High Court—

(a)   may by interim order wholly or in part suspend the operation of the order, either generally or in so far as it affects any property of the applicant, until the final determination of the proceedings; and

(b)   if satisfied that the order is wholly or to any extent outside the powers conferred by this paragraph, or that the interests of the applicant have been substantially prejudiced by the failure to comply with any requirement of this paragraph, may wholly or in part quash the order, either generally or in so far as it affects any property of the applicant.

(10)   Subject to subparagraph (8) above, the validity of an order under this paragraph shall not be questioned in any legal proceedings whatsoever, either before or after the order has been made.

18.—(1)   For the purposes of paragraphs 15 and 17 above, an objection to the making of an order thereunder shall not be treated as duly made unless—

(a)   the objection is made within the time and in the manner specified in the notice required by paragraph 16 or (as the case may be) paragraph 17 above; and

(b)   a statement in writing of the grounds of the objection is comprised in or submitted with the objection.

(2)   Where an objection to the making of such an order is duly made in accordance with subparagraph (1) above and is not withdrawn, the following provisions of this paragraph shall have effect in relation thereto; but, in the application of those provisions to an order under paragraph 15 above, any reference to the appropriate Minister shall be construed as a reference to the Secretary of State and the appropriate Minister.

(3)   Unless the appropriate Minister decides apart from the objection not to make the order, or decides to make a modification which is agreed to by the objector as meeting the objection, the appropriate Minister, before making a final decision, shall consider the grounds of the objection as set out in the statement, and may, if he thinks fit, require the objector to submit within a

specified period a further statement in writing as to any of the matters to which the objection relates.

(4) In so far as the appropriate Minister after considering the grounds of the objection as set out in the original statement and in any such further statement, is satisfied that the objection relates to a matter which can be dealt with in the assessment of compensation, the appropriate Minister may treat the objection as irrelevant for the purpose of making a final decision.

(5) If, after considering the grounds of the objection as set out in the original statement and in any such further statement, the appropriate Minister is satisfied that, for the purpose of making a final decision, he is sufficiently informed as to the matters to which the objection relates, or if, where a further statement has been required it is not submitted within the specified period, the appropriate Minister may make a final decision without further investigation as to those matters.

(6) Subject to subparagraphs (4) and (5) above, the appropriate Minister, before making a final decision, shall afford to the objector an opportunity of appearing before, and being heard by, a person appointed for the purpose by the appropriate Minister; and if the objector avails himself of that opportunity, the appropriate Minister shall afford an opportunity of appearing and being heard on the same occasion to the statutory undertakers, local authority or Minister on whose representation the order is proposed to be made, and to any other persons to whom it appears to the appropriate Minister to be expedient to afford such an opportunity.

(7) Notwithstanding anything in the preceding provisions of this paragraph, if it appears to the appropriate Minister that the matters to which the objection relates are such as to require investigation by public local inquiry before he makes a final decision, he shall cause such an inquiry to be held; and where he determines to cause such an inquiry to be held, any of the requirements of those provisions to which effect has not been given at the time of that determination shall be dispensed with.

(8) In this paragraph any reference to making a final decision, in relation to an order, is a reference to deciding whether to make the order or what modification (if any) ought to be made.

Interpretation

19. Any expression used in this Part of the Schedule to which a meaning is assigned by paragraph 1 of Schedule 4 to the Telecommunications Act 1984 has that meaning in this Part.

Part III Acquisition of rights

20.—(1) The Compulsory Purchase Act 1965 (in this Part of the Schedule referred to as 'the 1965 Act') shall have effect with the modifications necessary to make it apply to the compulsory purchase of rights by virtue of section 77(5) of this Act as it applies to the compulsory purchase of land so that, in appropriate contexts, references in the 1965 Act to land are read as referring, or as including references, to the rights or to land over which the rights are or are to be exercisable, according to the requirements of the particular context.

(2)   Without prejudice to the generality of subparagraph (1) above, in relation to the purchase of rights in pursuance of section 77(5) of this Act—

(a)   Part I of the 1965 Act (which relates to compulsory purchases under the Acquisition of Land Act 1981) shall have effect with the modifications specified in paragraphs 21 to 23 below; and

(b)   the enactments relating to compensation for the compulsory purchase of land shall apply with the necessary modifications as they apply to such compensation.

21.—(1)   For section 7 of the 1965 Act (which relates to compensation) there shall be substituted the following—

'**7.**—(1)   In assessing the compensation to be paid by the acquiring authority under this Act regard shall be had not only to the extent, if any, to which the value of the land over which the right is purchased is depreciated by the purchase but also to the damage, if any, to be sustained by the owner of the land by reason of injurious affection of other land of the owner by the exercise of the right.

(2)   The modifications subject to which subsection (1) of section 44 of the Land Compensation Act 1973 is to have effect, as applied by subsection (2) of that section to compensation for injurious affection under this section, are that for the words "land is acquired or taken" there shall be substituted the words "a right over land is purchased" and for the words "acquired or taken from him" there shall be substituted the words "over which the right is exercisable".'

22.   For section 8 of the 1965 Act (which relates to cases in which a vendor cannot be required to sell part only of a building or garden) there shall be substituted the following—

'**8.**—(1)   Where in consequence of the service on a person in pursuance of section 5 of this Act of a notice to treat in respect of a right over land consisting of a house, building or manufactory or of a park or garden belonging to a house (hereafter in this subsection referred to as "the relevant land")—

(a)   a question of disputed compensation in respect of the purchase of the right would apart from this section fall to be determined by the Lands Tribunal (hereafter in this section referred to as "the Tribunal"); and

(b)   before the Tribunal has determined that question the person satisfies the Tribunal that he has an interest which he is able and willing to sell in the whole of the relevant land and—

(i)   where that land consists of a house, building or manufactory, that the right cannot be purchased without material detriment to that land, or

(ii)   where that land consists of such a park or garden, that the right cannot be purchased without seriously affecting the amenity or convenience of the house to which that land belongs,

the compulsory purchase order to which the notice to treat relates shall, in relation to that person, cease to authorise the purchase of the right and be deemed to authorise the purchase of that person's interest in the whole of the relevant land including, where the land consists of such a park or garden, the house to which it belongs, and the notice shall be deemed to have been served in respect of that interest on such date as the Tribunal directs.

(2)   Any question as to the extent of the land in which a compulsory purchase order is deemed to authorise the purchase of an interest by virtue of the preceding subsection shall be determined by the Tribunal.

(3)   Where in consequence of a determination of the Tribunal that it is satisfied as mentioned in subsection (1) of this section a compulsory purchase order is deemed by virtue of that subsection to authorise the purchase of an interest in land, the acquiring authority may, at any time within the period of six weeks beginning with the date of the determination, withdraw the notice to treat in consequence of which the determination was made; but nothing in this subsection prejudices any other power of the authority to withdraw the notice.

(4)   The modifications subject to which subsection (1) of section 58 of the Land Compensation Act 1973 is to have effect, as applied by subsection (2) of that section to the duty of the Tribunal in determining whether it is satisfied as mentioned in subsection (1) of this section, are that at the beginning of paragraphs (a) and (b) there shall be inserted the words "a right over", for the word "severance" there shall be substituted the words "right on the whole of the house, building or manufactory or of the house and the park or garden" and for the words "part proposed" and "part is" there shall be substituted respectively the words "right proposed" and "right is".'

23.—(1)   The following provisions of the 1965 Act (which state the effect of a deed poll executed in various circumstances where there is no conveyance by persons with interests in the land), namely—

section 9(4) (failure of owners to convey),
paragraph 10(3) of Schedule 1 (owners under incapacity),
paragraph 2(3) of Schedule 2 (absent and untraced owners), and
paragraphs 2(3) and 7(2) of Schedule 4 (common land),

shall be so modified as to secure that, as against persons with interests in the land which are expressed to be overridden by the deed, the right which is to be purchased compulsorily is vested absolutely in the acquiring authority.

(2)   Section 11 of the 1965 Act (powers of entry) shall be so modified as to secure that, as from the date on which the acquiring authority has served notice to treat in respect of any right, it has power, exercisable in the like circumstances and subject to the like conditions, to enter for the purpose of exercising that right (which shall be deemed for this purpose to have been created on the date of service of the notice); and sections 12 (penalty for unauthorised entry) and 13 (entry on sheriff's warrant in the event of obstruction) of the Act shall be modified correspondingly.

(3)   Section 20 of the 1965 Act (compensation for short-term tenants) shall

apply with the modifications necessary to secure that persons with such interests as are mentioned in that section are compensated in a manner corresponding to that in which they would be compensated on a compulsory acquisition of the interests but taking into account only the extent (if any) of such interference with such interests as is actually caused, or likely to be caused, by the exercise of the right in question.

(4)   Section 22 of the 1965 Act (protection of acquiring authority's possession of land where by inadvertence an interest in the land has not been purchased) shall be so modified as to enable the acquiring authority, in circumstances corresponding to those referred to in that section, to continue to be entitled to exercise the right in question, subject to compliance with that section as respects compensation.

Schedule 11 Provisions applicable to certain disposals of houses

Repayment of discount on early disposal

1.—(1)   This paragraph applies where, on the disposal of a house under section 79 of this Act, a discount is given to the purchaser by the housing action trust in accordance with a consent given by the Secretary of State under subsection (1) of that section and that consent does not exclude the application of this paragraph.

(2)   On the disposal, the conveyance, grant or assignment shall contain a covenant binding on the purchaser and his successors in title to pay to the housing action trust on demand, if within a period of three years there is a relevant disposal which is not an exempted disposal (but if there is more than one such disposal then only on the first of them), an amount equal to the discount, reduced by one third for each complete year which has elapsed after the conveyance, grant or assignment and before the further disposal.

Obligation to repay a charge on the house

2.—(1)   The liability that may arise under the covenant required by paragraph 1 above is a charge on the house, taking effect as if it had been created by deed expressed to be by way of legal mortgage.

(2)   The charge has priority immediately after any legal charge securing an amount—

(a)   left outstanding by the purchaser; or

(b)   advanced to him by an approved lending institution for the purpose of enabling him to acquire the interest disposed of on the first disposal; or

(c)   further advanced to him by that institution;

but the housing action trust may at any time by written notice served on an approved lending institution postpone the charge taking effect by virtue of this paragraph to a legal charge securing an amount advanced or further advanced to the purchaser by that institution.

(3)   A charge taking effect by virtue of this paragraph is a land charge for the purposes of section 59 of the Land Registration Act 1925 notwithstanding subsection (5) of that section (exclusion of mortgages), and subsection (2) of that section applies accordingly with respect to its protection and realisation.

(4) The covenant required by paragraph 1 above does not, by virtue of its binding successors in title of the purchaser, bind a person exercising rights under a charge having priority over the charge taking effect by virtue of this paragraph, or a person deriving title under him; and a provision of the conveyance, grant or assignment, or of a collateral agreement, is void in so far as it purports to authorise a forfeiture, or to impose a penalty or disability, in the event of any such person failing to comply with the covenant.

(5) The approved lending institutions for the purposes of this paragraph are—

    (a)   a building society;
    (b)   a bank;
    (c)   an insurance company;
    (d)   a friendly society; and
    (e)   any body specified, or of a class or description specified, in an order

made under section 156 of the Housing Act 1985 (which makes provision in relation to disposals in pursuance of the right to buy corresponding to that made by this paragraph).

Relevant disposals

3.—(1) A disposal, whether of the whole or part of the house, is a relevant disposal for the purpose of this Schedule if it is—

    (a)   a conveyance of the freehold or an assignment of the lease; or
    (b)   the grant of a lease or sublease (other than a mortgage term) for a term

of more than 21 years otherwise than at a rack rent.

(2) For the purposes of subparagraph (1)(b) above it shall be assumed—

    (a)   that any option to renew or extend a lease or sublease, whether or not

forming part of a series of options, is exercised; and

    (b)   that any option to terminate a lease or sublease is not exercised.

Exempted disposals

4.—(1) A disposal is an exempted disposal for the purposes of this Schedule if—

    (a)   it is a disposal of the whole of the house and a conveyance of the freehold or an assignment of the lease and the person or each of the persons to whom it is made is a qualifying person (as defined in subparagraph (2) below);

    (b)   it is a vesting of the whole of the house in a person taking under a will or on an intestacy;

    (c)   it is a disposal of the whole of the house in pursuance of an order made under section 24 of the Matrimonial Causes Act 1973 (property adjustment orders in connection with matrimonial proceedings) or section 2 of the Inheritance (Provision for Family and Dependants) Act 1975 (orders as to financial provision to be made from estate);

    (d)   it is a compulsory disposal; or

    (e)   the property disposed of is property included with the house as being such a yard, garden, outhouse or appurtenance as is referred to in section 92(1)(b) of this Act.

(2)   For the purposes of subparagraph (1)(a) above, a person is a qualifying person in relation to a disposal if—

(a)   he is the person or one of the persons by whom the disposal is made;

(b)   he is the spouse or a former spouse of that person or one of those persons; or

(c)   he is a member of the family of that person or one of those persons and has resided with him throughout the period of 12 months ending with the disposal.

(3)   Section 186 of the Housing Act 1985 applies to determine whether a person is a member of another person's family for the purposes of subparagraph (2)(c) above.

Compulsory disposal

5.   In this Schedule a 'compulsory disposal' means a disposal of property which is acquired compulsorily, or is acquired by a person who has made or would have made, or for whom another person has made or would have made, a compulsory purchase order authorising its compulsory purchase for the purposes for which it is acquired.

Exempted disposals ending obligation under covenants

6.   Where there is a relevant disposal which is an exempted disposal by virtue of paragraph 4(1)(d) or paragraph 4(1)(e) above—

(a)   the covenant required by paragraph 1 above is not binding on the person to whom the disposal is made or any successor in title of his; and

(b)   that covenant and the charge taking effect by virtue of paragraph 2 above cease to apply in relation to the property disposed of.

Treatment of options

7.   For the purpose of this Schedule, the grant of an option enabling a person to call for a relevant disposal which is not an exempted disposal shall be treated as such a disposal made to him.

Schedule 12 Registration of title and related matters

Interpretation

1.   In this Schedule—

'transferred property' means property which is the subject of a grant under section 104(1)(a) of this Act;

'transferee', in relation to any transferred property, means the person to whom the grant is made;

'conveyance' means the instrument by which the grant is effected; and

other expressions have the same meaning as in section 104 of this Act.

Acquisitions under section 104(1)(a)

2.—(1)   Where a landlord makes a grant of transferred property, it shall ensure—

(a) that the conveyance contains a statement that the grant is made under section 104(1)(a) of this Act; and

(b) that all deeds and other documents relating to land (including, in the case of registered land, the land certificate) which are in its possession or under its control and which the transferee reasonably requires on or in connection with the grant of the transferred property are made available to him for this purpose.

(2) Where the landlord's title to the whole or any part of the transferred property is not registered—

(a) section 123 of the Land Registration Act 1925 (compulsory registration of title) applies in relation to the conveyance whether or not the transferred property is in an area in which an Order in Council under section 120 of that Act (areas of compulsory registration) is in force; and

(b) the landlord shall give the transferee a certificate stating that it is entitled to convey the freehold subject only to such incumbrances, rights and interests as are stated in the conveyance or summarised in the certificate.

(3) The Chief Land Registrar shall, for the purpose of the registration of title, accept such a certificate as is referred to in subparagraph (2)(b) above as sufficient evidence of the facts stated in it; but if as a result he has to meet a claim under the Land Registration Acts 1925 to 1986 the landlord is liable to indemnify him.

(4) On an application being made for registration of a disposition of registered land or, as the case may be, of the transferee's title under a disposition of unregistered land, the Chief Land Registrar shall, if the conveyance contains the statement required by subparagraph (1)(a) above, enter in the register a restriction stating the requirement under section 105 of this Act of consent to subsequent disposals.

(5) Any reference in the preceding provisions of this paragraph to a statement or a certificate is a reference to a statement or, as the case may be, certificate in a form approved by the Chief Land Registrar.

Procedures on termination of leases granted under section 104(1)(b)

3.—(1) If a lease granted under section 104(1)(b) of this Act comes to an end in such circumstances as may be prescribed, the public sector landlord which was the lessee under the lease shall, at such time as may be prescribed, furnish to the Chief Land Registrar such statement as may be prescribed.

(2) In any case where—

(a) under section 104(1)(b) of this Act the applicant has granted a lease of a flat (in this subparagraph referred to as 'the landlord's lease'), and

(b) under Part V of the Housing Act 1985 (the right to buy) a lease of the flat (in this subparagraph referred to as 'the right-to-buy lease') has been granted to a qualifying tenant, and

(c) by virtue of requirements prescribed under section 104(2) of this Act and related to the grant of the right-to-buy lease, the landlord's lease comes to an end,

then, notwithstanding anything in section 64 of the Land Registration Act 1925 (production of land certificate), notice of the grant of the right-to-buy lease may be entered in the register without production of the applicant's land certificate, but without prejudice to the power of the Chief Land Registrar to compel production of the certificate.

Schedule 13 Amendments of Landlord and Tenant Act 1987

1. In Part I of the Landlord and Tenant Act 1987 (tenants' rights of first refusal), in section 2 (landlords for the purposes of Part I), in subsection (1) after '(2)' there shall be inserted 'and section 4(1A)'.

2.—(1) In section 3 of that Act (qualifying tenants), in subsection (1) (paragraphs (a) to (c) of which exclude certain tenants) the word 'or' immediately preceding paragraph (c) shall be omitted and at the end of that paragraph there shall be added

'or
      (d) an assured tenancy or assured agricultural occupancy within the meaning of Part I of the Housing Act 1988'.

(2) In subsection (2) of that section (which excludes persons having interests going beyond a particular flat), for paragraphs (a) and (b) there shall be substituted the words 'by virtue of one or more tenancies none of which falls within paragraphs (a) to (d) of subsection (1), he is the tenant not only of the flat in question but also of at least two other flats contained in those premises'; and in subsection (3) of that section for '(2)(b)' there shall be substituted '(2)'.

3.—(1) In section 4 of that Act (relevant disposals) after subsection (1) there shall be inserted the following subsection—

'(1A) Where an estate or interest of the landlord has been mortgaged, the reference in subsection (1) above to the disposal of an estate or interest by the landlord includes a reference to its disposal by the mortgagee in exercise of a power of sale or leasing, whether or not the disposal is made in the name of the landlord; and, in relation to such a proposed disposal by the mortgagee, any reference in the following provisions of this Part to the landlord shall be construed as a reference to the mortgagee.'

(2) In subsection (2) of that section, in paragraph (a), at the end of subparagraph (i) there shall be inserted 'or', subparagraph (ii) shall be omitted and at the end of that paragraph there shall be inserted—

'(aa) a disposal consisting of the creation of an estate or interest by way of security for a loan'.

4.—(1) In Part III of that Act (compulsory acquisition by tenants of their landlord's interest), in section 26 (qualifying tenants), in subsection (2) (which excludes persons having interests going beyond a particular flat) for the words following 'if' there shall be substituted 'by virtue of one or more long leases none of which constitutes a tenancy to which Part II of the Landlord and Tenant Act 1954 applies, he is the tenant not only of the flat in question but also of at least two other flats contained in those premises'.

(2)   At the end of the said section 26 there shall be added the following subsection—

'(4)   For the purposes of subsection (2) any tenant of a flat contained in the premises in question who is a body corporate shall be treated as the tenant of any other flat so contained and let to an associated company, as defined in section 20(1).'

5.   In Part IV of that Act (variation of leases), for subsections (6) and (7) of section 35 (which make provision about long leases) there shall be substituted the following subsection—

'(6)   For the purposes of this Part a long lease shall not be regarded as a long lease of a flat if—

(a)   the demised premises consist of or include three or more flats contained in the same building; or

(b)   the lease constitutes a tenancy to which Part II of the Landlord and Tenant Act 1954 applies.'

6.   In section 40 (application for variation of insurance provisions of lease of dwelling other than a flat) for subsection (4) (which makes provision about long leases) there shall be substituted the following subsections—

'(4)   For the purpose of this section, a long lease shall not be regarded as a long lease of a dwelling if—

(a)   the demised premises consist of three or more dwellings; or

(b)   the lease constitutes a tenancy to which Part II of the Landlord and Tenant Act 1954 applies.

(4A)   Without prejudice to subsection (4), an application under subsection (1) may not be made by a person who is a tenant under a long lease of a dwelling if, by virtue of that lease and one or more other long leases of dwellings, he is also a tenant from the same landlord of at least two other dwellings.

(4B)   For the purposes of subsection (4A), any tenant of a dwelling who is a body corporate shall be treated as a tenant of any other dwelling held from the same landlord which is let under a long lease to an associated company, as defined in section 20(1).'

7.   In Part VII of that Act (general), in section 58 (exempt landlords), in subsection (1) after paragraph (c) there shall be inserted the following paragraph—

'(ca)   a housing action trust established under Part III of the Housing Act 1988.'

Schedule 14 Appointment etc. of rent officers

Part I Amendments of section 63 of Rent Act 1977

1.   In subsection (1), paragraph (b) and the word 'and' immediately preceding it shall be omitted.

2.   In subsection (2)—

    (a)   in paragraph (a) the words 'and deputy rent officers' shall be omitted;

    (b)   in paragraph (b) the words 'or deputy rent officer' shall be omitted;

    (c)   in paragraph (d) the words 'and deputy rent officers' and the word 'and' at the end of the paragraph shall be omitted; and

    (d)   paragraph (e) shall be omitted.

3.   After subsection (2) there shall be inserted the following subsection—

    '(2A)   A scheme under this section may make all or any of the following provisions—

    (a)   provision requiring the consent of the Secretary of State to the appointment of rent officers;

    (b)   provision with respect to the appointment of rent officers for fixed periods;

    (c)   provision for the proper officer of the local authority, in such circumstances and subject to such conditions (as to consent or otherwise) as may be specified in the scheme,—

        (i)   to designate a person appointed or to be appointed a rent officer as chief rent officer and to designate one or more such persons as senior rent officers;

        (ii)   to delegate to a person so designated as chief rent officer such functions as may be specified in the scheme; and

        (iii)   to revoke a designation under subparagraph (i) above and to revoke or vary a delegation under subparagraph (ii) above;

    (d)   provision with respect to the delegation of functions by a chief rent officer to other rent officers (whether designated as senior rent officers or not);

    (e)   provision as to the circumstances in which and the terms on which a rent officer appointed by the scheme may undertake functions outside the area to which the scheme relates in accordance with paragraph (f) below;

    (f)   provision under which a rent officer appointed for an area other than that to which the scheme relates may undertake functions in the area to which the scheme relates and for such a rent officer to be treated for such purposes as may be specified in the scheme (which may include the purposes of paragraphs (c) and (d) above and paragraphs (c) and (d) of subsection (2) above) as if he were a rent officer appointed under the scheme; and

    (g)   provision conferring functions on the proper officer of a local authority with respect to the matters referred to in paragraphs (d) to (f) above.'

4.   In subsection (3) the words 'and deputy rent officers' shall be omitted.

5.   In subsection (7)—

    (a)   in paragraph (b) the words 'and deputy rent officers' shall be omitted, after the words 'section 7' there shall be inserted 'or section 24' and for the words following '1972' there shall be substituted 'or'; and

(b)   at the end of paragraph (b) there shall be inserted the following paragraph—

'(c)   incurred in respect of increases of pensions payable to or in respect of rent officers (so appointed) by virtue of the Pensions (Increase) Act 1971'.

Part II Sections to be inserted in Rent Act 1977 after section 64

'Amalgamation schemes

64A.—(1)   If the Secretary of State is of the opinion—

(a)   that there is at any time insufficient work in two or more registration areas to justify the existence of a separate service of rent officers for each area, or

(b)   that it would at any time be beneficial for the efficient administration of the service provided by rent officers in two or more registration areas,

he may, after consultation with the local authorities concerned, make a scheme under section 63 above designating as an amalgamated registration area the areas of those authorities and making provision accordingly for that amalgamated area.

(2)   Any reference in the following provisions of this Chapter to a registration area includes a reference to an amalgamated registration area and, in relation to such an area, "the constituent authorities" means the local authorities whose areas make up the amalgamated area.

(3)   A scheme under section 63 above made for an amalgamated registration area—

(a)   shall confer on the proper officer of one of the constituent authorities all or any of the functions which, in accordance with section 63 above, fall to be exercisable by the proper officer of the local authority for the registration area;

(b)   may provide that any rent officer previously appointed for the area of any one of the constituent authorities shall be treated for such purposes as may be specified in the scheme as a rent officer appointed for the amalgamated registration area; and

(c)   shall make such provision as appears to the Secretary of State to be appropriate for the payment by one or more of the constituent authorities of the remunerations, allowances and other expenditure which under section 63 above is to be paid by the local authority for the area.

(4)   A scheme under section 63 above made for an amalgamated registration area may contain such incidental, transitional and supplementary provisions as appear to the Secretary of State to be necessary or expedient.

New basis for administration of rent officer service

64B.—(1)   If, with respect to registration areas generally or any particular registration area or areas, it appears to the Secretary of State that it is no longer appropriate for the appointment, remuneration and administration of rent officers to be a function of local authorities, he may by order—

(a)   provide that no scheme under section 63 above shall be made for the area or areas specified in the order; and

(b)   make, with respect to the area or areas so specified, such provision as appears to him to be appropriate with respect to the appointment, remuneration and administration of rent officers and the payment of pensions, allowances or gratuities to or in respect of them.

(2)   An order under this section shall make provision for any expenditure attributable to the provisions of the order to be met by the Secretary of State in such manner as may be specified in the order (whether by way of grant, reimbursement or otherwise); and any expenditure incurred by the Secretary of State by virtue of this subsection shall be paid out of money provided by Parliament.

(3)   An order under this section—

(a)   may contain such incidental, transitional and supplementary provisions as appear to the Secretary of State to be appropriate, including provisions amending this Part of this Act; and

(b)   shall be made by statutory instrument which shall be subject to annulment in pursuance of a resolution of either House of Parliament.'

Schedule 15 Repair notices: amendments of Housing Act 1985, Part VI

1.—(1)   In section 189 (repair notice in respect of unfit house), in subsection (1)—

(a)   at the beginning there shall be inserted the words 'Subject to subsection (1A)'; and

(b)   for the word 'house', in each place where it occurs, there shall be substituted 'dwelling-house'.

(2)   At the end of subsection (1) of that section there shall be inserted the following subsection—

'(1A)   Where the local housing authority are satisfied that a dwelling-house which is a flat is unfit for human habitation by reason of the defective condition of a part of the building outside the flat, they shall serve a repair notice on the person having control of that part of the building, unless they are satisfied that the works which would be required to that part are such that the flat is not capable of being rendered so fit at reasonable expense.'

(3)   In subsection (2) of that section—

(a)   in paragraph (a) for the words from 'within such reasonable time' onwards there shall be substituted the words 'and to begin those works not later than such reasonable date, being not earlier than the seventh day after the notice becomes operative, as is specified in the notice and to complete those works within such reasonable time as is so specified, and'; and

(b) in paragraph (b) for the word 'house' there shall be substituted 'dwelling-house'.

(4) In subsection (3) of that section for the words 'the house', in each place where they occur, there shall be substituted 'the dwelling-house or part of the building concerned', for the word 'may' there shall be substituted 'shall' and for the words 'lessee or otherwise' there shall be substituted 'or lessee'.

(5) At the end of that section there shall be added the following subsection—

'(5) A repair notice under this section which has become operative is a local land charge.'

2.—(1) In section 190 (repair notice in respect of house in state of disrepair, but not unfit), in subsection (1),—

(a) for the word 'house', in each place where it occurs, there shall be substituted 'dwelling-house';

(b) in paragraph (b), after the word 'satisfied' there shall be inserted 'whether' and after the word 'tenant', in the first place where it occurs, there shall be inserted 'or otherwise'.

(2) At the end of subsection (1) of that section there shall be inserted the following subsection—

'(1A) Where the local housing authority—

(a) are satisfied that a building containing a flat is in such a state of disrepair that, although the flat is not unfit for human habitation, substantial repairs are necessary to a part of the building outside the flat to bring the flat up to a reasonable standard, having regard to its age, character and locality, or

(b) are satisfied, whether on a representation made by an occupying tenant or otherwise, that a building containing a flat is in such a state of disrepair that, although the flat is not unfit for human habitation, the condition of a part of the building outside the flat is such as to interfere materially with the personal comfort of the occupying tenant,

they may serve a repair notice on the person having control of the part of the building concerned.'

(3) In subsection (2) of that section for the words from 'within such reasonable time' onwards there shall be substituted

'to execute the works specified in the notice, not being works of internal decorative repair, and—

(a) to begin those works not later than such reasonable date, being not earlier than the seventh day after the notice becomes operative, as is specified in the notice; and

(b) to complete those works within such reasonable time as is so specified.'

(4) In subsection (3) of that section for the words 'the house', in each place where they occur, there shall be substituted 'the dwelling-house or part of the

building concerned', for the word 'may' there shall be substituted 'shall' and for the words 'lessee or otherwise' there shall be substituted 'or lessee'.

(5)   At the end of that section there shall be added the following subsection—

'(5)   A repair notice under this section which has become operative is a local land charge.'

3.—(1)   In section 191 (appeals against repair notices), after subsection (1) there shall be inserted the following subsection—

'(1A)   Without prejudice to the generality of subsection (1), it shall be a ground of appeal that some person other than the appellant, being a person who is an owner in relation to the dwelling-house or part of the building concerned, ought to execute the works or pay the whole or part of the cost of executing them.'

(2)   In subsection (3) of that section for the words 'the house' there shall be substituted 'the dwelling-house'.

(3)   After subsection (3) of that section there shall be inserted the following subsections—

'(3A)   Where the grounds on which an appeal is brought are or include that specified in subsection (1A), the appellant shall serve a copy of his notice of appeal on each other person referred to; and on the hearing of the appeal the court may—

(a)   vary the repair notice so as to require the works to be executed by any such other person; or

(b)   make such order as it thinks fit with respect to the payment to be made by any such other person to the appellant or, where the works are executed by the local housing authority, to the authority.

(3B)   In the exercise of its powers under subsection (3A), the court shall take into account, as between the appellant and any such other person as is referred to in that subsection,—

(a)   their relative interests in the dwelling-house or part of the building concerned (considering both the nature of the interests and the rights and obligations arising under or by virtue of them);

(b)   their relative responsibility for the state of the dwelling-house or building which gives rise to the need for the execution of the works; and

(c)   the relative degree of benefit to be derived from the execution of the works.

(3C)   If, by virtue of the exercise of the court's powers under subsection (3A), a person other than the appellant is required to execute the works specified in a repair notice, then, so long as that other person continues to be an owner in relation to the premises to which the notice relates, he shall be regarded as the person having control of those premises for the purposes of the following provisions of this Part.'

4.—(1)   In section 192 (power to purchase houses found on appeal to be unfit etc.), in subsections (1) and (2) for the words 'the house', in each place where they occur, there shall be substituted 'the dwelling-house'.

(2)   In subsection (3) of that section for the words 'the house' there shall be substituted 'the dwelling-house or part of the building in question'.

(3)   In subsection (4) of that section for the words 'the house' there shall be substituted 'the dwelling-house'.

5.—(1)   In section 193 (power of local housing authority to execute works) for subsection (2) there shall be substituted the following subsections—

'(2)   For the purpose of this Part compliance with the notice means beginning and completing the works specified in the notice,—

(a)   if no appeal is brought against the notice, not later than such date and within such period as is specified in the notice;

(b)   if an appeal is brought against the notice and is not withdrawn, not later than such date and within such period as may be fixed by the court determining the appeal; and

(c)   if an appeal brought against the notice is withdrawn, not later than the twenty-first day after the date on which the notice becomes operative and within such period (beginning on that twenty-first day) as is specified in the notice.

(2A)   If, before the expiry of the period which under subsection (2) is appropriate for completion of the works specified in the notice, it appears to the local housing authority that reasonable progress is not being made towards compliance with the notice, the authority may themselves do the work required to be done by the notice.'

(2)   At the end of that section there shall be added the following subsection—

'(4)   If, after the local housing authority have given notice under section 194 of their intention to enter and do any works, the works are in fact carried out by the person having control of the dwelling-house or part of the building in question, any administrative and other expenses incurred by the authority with a view to doing the works themselves shall be treated for the purposes of Schedule 10 as expenses incurred by them under this section in carrying out works in default of the person on whom the repair notice was served.'

6.—(1)   In section 194 (notice of authority's intention to execute works), in subsection (1)—

(a)   for the words 'a house' there shall be substituted 'any premises';

(b)   for the word 'may' there shall be substituted 'shall'; and

(c)   for the words 'the house', in each place where they occur, there shall be substituted 'the premises'.

(2)   In subsection (2) of that section for the words 'the house', in each place where they occur, there shall be substituted 'the premises'.

7.   In section 198 (penalty for obstruction), in subsection (2) for the words 'level 2' there shall be substituted 'level 3'.

8. After section 198 there shall be inserted the following section—

'Penalty for failure to execute works

198A.—(1) A person having control of premises to which a repair notice relates who intentionally fails to comply with the notice commits a summary offence and is liable on conviction to a fine not exceeding level 4 on the standard scale.

(2) The obligation to execute the works specified in the notice continues nothwithstanding that the period for completion of the works has expired.

(3) Section 193(2) shall have effect to determine whether a person has failed to comply with a notice and what is the period for completion of any works.

(4) The provisions of this section are without prejudice to the exercise by the local housing authority of the powers conferred by the preceding provisions of this Part.'

9. Sections 199 to 201 (recovery by lessee of proportion of works and provisions as to charging orders) shall cease to have effect.

10. In section 203 (saving for rights arising from breach of covenant, etc.), in subsection (3) for the words 'a house' there shall be substituted 'any premises'.

11. In section 205 (application of provisions to parts of buildings and temporary or movable structures) paragraph (a) shall be omitted and for the word 'house' there shall be substituted 'dwelling-house'.

12.—(1) In section 207 (definitions)—

(a) for the definition beginning 'house' there shall be substituted—

'"dwelling-house" and "flat" shall be construed in accordance with subsection (2) and "the building", in relation to a flat, means the building containing the flat';

(b) in the definition of 'person having control' for the words 'in relation to premises' there shall be substituted

'subject to section 191(3A),—

(a) in relation to a dwelling-house';

(c) at the end of that definition there shall be added

'and

(b) in relation to a part of a building to which relates a repair notice served under subsection (1A) of section 189 or section 190, means a person who is an owner in relation to that part of the building (or the building as a whole) and who, in the opinion of the authority by whom the notice is served, ought to execute the works specified in the notice';

and

(d) after the definition of 'person having control' there shall be inserted—

'"premises" includes a dwelling-house or part of a building and, in relation to any premises, any reference to a person having control shall be construed accordingly'.

(2) At the end of that section there shall be inserted the following subsection—

'(2) For the purposes of this Part a "dwelling-house" includes any yard, garden, outhouses and appurtenances belonging to it or usually enjoyed with it and section 183 shall have effect to determine whether a dwelling-house is a flat.'

13.—(1) In Schedule 10 (recovery of expenses incurred by local housing authority), in paragraph 2, in subparagraph (1) for the words following 'authority' there shall be substituted—

'(a) where the works were required by a notice under section 189 or section 190 (repair notices), from the person having control of the dwelling-house or part of the building to which the notice relates; and

(b) in any other case, from the person on whom the notice was served;

and in the following provisions of this paragraph the person from whom expenses are recoverable by virtue of this subparagraph is referred to as "the person primarily liable".'

(2) In subparagraphs (2) and (3) of paragraph 2 of that Schedule for the words 'on whom the notice was served', in each place where they occur, there shall be substituted 'primarily liable'.

(3) In paragraph 6 of that Schedule (appeals) after subparagraph (1) there shall be inserted the following subparagraph—

'(1A) Where the demand for recovery of expenses relates to works carried out by virtue of section 193(2A), it shall be a ground of appeal that, at the time the local housing authority gave notice under section 194 of their intention to enter and do the works, reasonable progress was being made towards compliance with the repair notice.'

Schedule 16 Schedule to be inserted in the Housing (Scotland) Act 1987

'Schedule 6A Consultation before disposal to private sector landlord

Disposals to which this Schedule applies

1.—(1) This Schedule applies to the disposal by a local authority of an interest in land as a result of which a secure tenant of the local authority will become the tenant of a private sector landlord.

(2) For the purposes of this Schedule the grant of an option which if exercised would result in a secure tenant of a local authority becoming the tenant of a private sector landlord shall be treated as a disposal of the interest which is the subject of the option.

(3) Where a disposal of land by a local authority is in part a disposal to

which this Schedule applies, the provisions of this Schedule apply to that part as to a separate disposal.

(4)   In this paragraph 'private sector landlord' means a person other than one of those set out in subparagraphs (i) to (iv) and (viii) and (ix) of paragraph (a) of subsection (2) of section 61.

Application for Secretary of State's consent

2.—(1)   The Secretary of State shall not entertain an application for his consent under section 12(7) to a disposal to which this Schedule applies unless the local authority certify either—

(a)   that the requirements of paragraph 3 as to consultation have been complied with, or

(b)   that the requirements of that paragraph as to consultation have been complied with except in relation to tenants expected to have vacated the house in question before the disposal;

and the certificate shall be accompanied by a copy of the notices given by the local authority in accordance with that paragraph.

(2)   Where the certificate is in the latter form, the Secretary of State shall not determine the application until the local authority certify as regards the tenants not originally consulted—

(a)   that they have vacated the house in question, or

(b)   that the requirements of paragraph 3 as to consultation have been complied with;

and a certificate under subparagraph (b) shall be accompanied by a copy of the notices given by the local authority in accordance with paragraph 3.

Requirements as to consultation

3.—(1)   The requirements as to consultation referred to above are as follows.

(2)   The local authority shall serve notice in writing on the tenant informing him of—

(a)   such details of their proposal as the local authority consider appropriate, but including the identity of the person to whom the disposal is to be made,

(b)   the likely consequences of the disposal for the tenant, and

(c)   the effect of section 81A and the provision made under it (preservation of right to buy on disposal to private sector landlord) and of this Schedule,

and informing him that he may, within such reasonable period as may be specified in the notice, which must be at least 28 days after the service of the notice, make representations to the local authority.

(3)   The local authority shall consider any representations made to them within that period and shall serve a further written notice on the tenant informing him—

(a)   of any significant changes in their proposal, and

(b) that he may within such period as is specified (which must be at least 28 days after the service of the notice) communicate to the Secretary of State his objection to the proposal,

and informing him of the effect of paragraph 5 (consent to be withheld if majority of tenants are opposed).

Power to require further consultation

4.   The Secretary of State may require the local authority to carry out such further consultation with their tenants, and to give him such information as to the results of that consultation, as he may direct.

Consent to be withheld if majority of tenants are opposed

5.—(1) The Secretary of State shall not give his consent if it appears to him that a majority of the tenants of the houses to which the application relates do not wish the disposal to proceed; but this does not affect his general discretion to refuse consent on grounds relating to whether a disposal has the support of the tenants or on any other ground.

(2) In making his decision the Secretary of State may have regard to any information available to him; and the local authority shall give him such information as to the representations made to them by tenants and others, and other relevant matters, as he may require.

Protection of purchasers

6.   The Secretary of State's consent to a disposal is not invalidated by a failure on his part or that of the local authority to comply with the requirements of this Schedule.'

Schedule 17 Minor and consequential amendments

Part I General amendments

The Reserve and Auxiliary Forces (Protection of Civil Interests) Act 1951

1.   In section 4 of the Reserve and Auxiliary Forces (Protection of Civil Interests) Act 1951 (recovery of possession of dwelling-houses in default of payment of rent precluded in certain cases) after subsection (2) there shall be inserted the following subsection—

'(2A) For the purposes of the foregoing provisions of this Act, a judgment or order for the recovery of possession of a dwelling-house let on an assured tenancy within the meaning of Part I of the Housing Act 1988 shall be regarded as a judgment or order for the recovery of possession in default of payment of rent if the judgment or order was made on any of Ground 8, 10 and 11 in Schedule 2 to that Act and not on any other ground.'

2.   For section 16 of that Act (protection of tenure of rented premises by extension of Rent Acts), as it applies otherwise than to Scotland, there shall be substituted the following section—

'Protection of tenure of certain rented premises by extension of Housing Act 1988

16.—(1)   Subject to subsection (2) of section 14 of this Act and subsection (3) below, if at any time during a service man's period of residence protection—

(a)   a tenancy qualifying for protection which is a fixed-term tenancy ends without being continued or renewed by agreement (whether on the same or different terms and conditions), and

(b)   by reason only of such circumstances as are mentioned in subsection (4) below, on the ending of that tenancy no statutory periodic tenancy of the rented family residence would arise, apart from the provisions of this section,

Chapter I of Part I of the Housing Act 1988 shall, during the remainder of the period of protection, apply in relation to the rented family residence as if those circumstances did not exist and had not existed immediately before the ending of that tenancy and, accordingly, as if on the ending of that tenancy there arose a statutory periodic tenancy which is an assured tenancy during the remainder of that period.

(2)   Subject to subsection (2) of section 14 of this Act and subsection (3) below, if at any time during a service man's period of residence protection—

(a)   a tenancy qualifying for protection which is a periodic tenancy would come to an end, apart from the provisions of this section, and

(b)   by reason only of such circumstances as are mentioned in subsection (4) below that tenancy is not an assured tenancy, and

(c)   if that tenancy had been an assured tenancy, it would not have come to an end at that time,

Chapter I of Part I of the Housing Act 1988 shall, during the remainder of the period of protection, apply in relation to the rented family residence as if those circumstances did not exist and, accordingly, as if the tenancy had become an assured tenancy immediately before it would otherwise have come to an end.

(3)   Neither subsection (1) nor subsection (2) above applies if, on the ending of the tenancy qualifying for protection, a statutory tenancy arises.

(4)   The circumstances referred to in subsections (1) and (2) above are any one or more of the following, that is to say,—

(a)   that the tenancy was entered into before, or pursuant to a contract made before, Part I of the Housing Act 1988 came into force;

(b)   that the rateable value (as defined for the purposes of that Act) of the premises which are the rented family residence, or of property of which those premises form part, exceeded the relevant limit specified in paragraph 2 of Schedule 1 to that Act;

(c)   that the circumstances mentioned in paragraph 3 or paragraph 6 of that Schedule applied with respect to the tenancy qualifying for protection; and

(d)   that the reversion immediately expectant on the tenancy qualifying for protection belongs to any of the bodies specified in paragraph 12 of that Schedule.'

3.   For the said section 16, as it applies to Scotland, there shall be substituted the following section—

Protection of tenure of certain rented premises by extension of Housing (Scotland) Act 1988
16.—(1)   Subject to subsection (2) of section 14 of this Act and subsection (3) below, if at any time during a service man's period of residence protection—

(a)   a tenancy qualifying for protection ends without being continued or renewed by agreement (whether on the same or different terms and conditions), and

(b)   by reason only of such circumstances as are mentioned in subsection (4) below, on the ending of that tenancy no statutory tenancy of the rented family residence would arise, apart from the provisions of this section,

sections 12 to 31 of the Housing (Scotland) Act 1988 shall, during the remainder of the period of protection, apply in relation to the rented family residence as if those circumstances did not exist and had not existed immediately before the ending of that tenancy and, accordingly, as if on the ending of that tenancy there arose a statutory assured tenancy during the remainder of that period.

(2)   Subject to subsection (2) of section 14 of this Act and subsection (3) below, if at any time during a service man's period of residence protection—

(a)   a tenancy qualifying for protection would come to an end, apart from the provisions of this section,

(b)   by reason only of such circumstances as are mentioned in subsection (4) below that tenancy is not an assured tenancy, and

(c)   if that tenancy had been an assured tenancy, it would not have come to an end at that time,

sections 12 to 31 of the Housing (Scotland) Act 1988 shall, during the remainder of the period of protection, apply in relation to the rented family residence as if those circumstances did not exist and, accordingly, as if the tenancy had become an assured tenancy immediately before it would otherwise have come to an end.

(3)   Neither subsection (1) nor subsection (2) above applies if, on the ending of the tenancy qualifying for protection, a statutory tenancy arises.

(4)   The circumstances referred to in subsections (1) and (2) above are one or more of the following, that is to say—

(a)   that the circumstances mentioned in paragraph 2 of Schedule 4 to the Housing (Scotland) Act 1988 applied with respect to the tenancy qualifying for protection;

(b)   that the circumstances mentioned in paragraph 5 of that Schedule applied with respect to the tenancy qualifying for protection; and

(c)   that the reversion immediately expectant on the tenancy qualifying for protection belongs to any of the bodies specified in paragraph 11 of that Schedule.'

4.—(1)   Section 17 of that Act (provisions in case of rented premises which include accommodation shared otherwise than with landlord), as it applies otherwise than to Scotland, shall be amended in accordance with this paragraph.

(2)   In subsection (1)—

(a)   after the words 'qualifying for protection' there shall be inserted 'which is a fixed-term tenancy';

(b)   in paragraph (b) for the words from 'subsection (2)' to '1977' there shall be substituted 'section 16(4) above, subsection (1) of section 3 of the Housing Act 1988';

(c)   for the words 'said section 22' there shall be substituted 'said section 3'; and

(d)   at the end there shall be added 'and, accordingly, as if on the ending of the tenancy there arose a statutory periodic tenancy which is an assured tenancy during the remainder of that period'.

(3)   For subsection (2) there shall be substituted the following subsections—

'(2)   Where, at any time during a service man's period of residence protection—

(a)   a tenancy qualifying for protection which is a periodic tenancy would come to an end, apart from the provisions of this section and section 16 above, and

(b)   paragraphs (a) and (b) of subsection (1) above apply,

section 3 of the Housing Act 1988 shall, during the remainder of the period of protection, apply in relation to the separate accommodation as if the circumstances referred to in subsection (1)(b) above did not exist and, accordingly, as if the tenancy had become an assured tenancy immediately before it would otherwise have come to an end.

(3)   Neither subsection (1) nor subsection (2) above applies if, on the ending of the tenancy qualifying for protection, a statutory tenancy arises.'

5.—(1)   The said section 17, as it applies to Scotland, shall be amended in accordance with this paragraph.

(2)   In subsection (1)—

(a)   in paragraph (b) for the words from 'subsection (2)' to '1977' there shall be substituted the words 'section 16(4) above, subsection (1) of section 14 of the Housing (Scotland) Act 1988';

(b)   for the words 'said section 97' there shall be substituted the words 'said section 14'; and

(c)   at the end there shall be added the words 'and, accordingly, as if on the ending of the tenancy there arose a statutory assured tenancy during the remainder of that period'.

'(2)   Where, at any time during a service man's period of residence protection—

(a)   a tenancy qualifying for protection would come to an end, apart from the provisions of this section and section 16 above, and
(b)   paragraphs (a) and (b) of subsection (1) above apply,

section 14 of the Housing (Scotland) Act 1988 shall, during the remainder of the period of protection, apply in relation to the separate accommodation as if the circumstances in subsection (1)(b) above did not exist and, accordingly, as if the tenancy had become an assured tenancy immediately before it would otherwise come to an end.

(3)   Neither subsection (1) nor subsection (2) above applies if, on the ending of the tenancy qualifying for protection, a statutory tenancy arises.'

6.—(1)   In section 18 of that Act (protection of tenure, in connection with employment, under a licence or rent-free letting), in subsection (1), as it applies otherwise than to Scotland,—

(a)   for the words 'Part VII of the Rent Act 1977' there shall be substituted 'Chapter I of Part I of the Housing Act 1988'; and
(b)   for the words 'subject to a statutory tenancy within the meaning of the Rent Act 1977' there shall be substituted 'let on a statutory periodic tenancy which is an assured tenancy'.

(2)   In that subsection, as it applies to Scotland,—

(a)   for the words 'the Rent (Scotland) Act 1971' there shall be substituted the words 'sections 12 to 31 of the Housing (Scotland) Act 1988', and
(b)   for the words 'subject to a statutory tenancy within the meaning of the Rent (Scotland) Act 1971' there shall be substituted the words 'let on a statutory assured tenancy'.

(3)   Subsection (2) of that section shall be omitted.
(4)   In subsection (3) of that section, as it applies otherwise than to Scotland, at the end of paragraph (c) there shall be added

'or
(d)   is a dwelling-house which is let on or subject to an assured agricultural occupancy within the meaning of Part I of the Housing Act 1988 which is not an assured tenancy.'

7.   For section 19 of that Act (limitation on application of Rent Acts by virtue of sections 16 to 18), as it applies otherwise than to Scotland, there shall be substituted the following section—

'Limitation on application of Housing Act 1988 by virtue of sections 16 to 18
19.   Where by virtue of sections 16 to 18 above, the operation of Chapter I of Part I of the Housing Act 1988 in relation to any premises is extended or modified, the extension or modification shall not affect—

(a)   any tenancy of those premises other than the statutory periodic tenancy which is deemed to arise or, as the case may be, the tenancy which is for any period deemed to be an assured tenancy by virtue of any of those provisions; or

(b) any rent payable in respect of a period beginning before the time when that statutory periodic tenancy was deemed to arise or, as the case may be, before that tenancy became deemed to be an assured tenancy; or

(c) anything done or omitted to be done before the time referred to in paragraph (b) above.'

8. For the said section 19, as it applies to Scotland, there shall be substituted the following section—

'Limitation on application of Housing (Scotland) Act 1988 by virtue of sections 16 to 18

19. Where by virtue of sections 16 to 18 above, the operation of sections 12 to 31 of the Housing (Scotland) Act 1988 in relation to any premises is extended or modified, the extension or modification shall not affect—

(a) any tenancy of those premises other than the statutory assured tenancy which is deemed to arise or, as the case may be, the tenancy which is for any period deemed to be an assured tenancy by virtue of any of those provisions; or

(b) any rent payable in respect of a period beginning before the time when that statutory assured tenancy was deemed to arise or, as the case may be, before that tenancy became deemed to be an assured tenancy; or

(c) anything done or omitted to be done before the time referred to in paragraph (b) above.'

9.—(1) Section 20 of that Act (modification of Rent Acts as respects occupation by employees), as it applies otherwise than to Scotland, shall be amended in accordance with this paragraph.

(2) In subsection (1) after the words 'Case I in Schedule 15 to the Rent Act 1977' there shall be inserted 'or Ground 12 in Schedule 2 to the Housing Act 1988'.

(3) In subsection (2) after the words 'Case 8 in the said Schedule 15' there shall be inserted 'or, as the case may be, Ground 16 in the said Schedule 2' and for paragraph (b) there shall be substituted the following paragraph—

'(b) Chapter I of Part I of the Housing Act 1988 applies in relation to the premises as mentioned in section 18(1) of this Act and a dependant or dependants of the service man is or are living in the premises or in part thereof in right of the statutory periodic tenancy or assured tenancy referred to in section 19(a) of this Act'.

(4) In subsection (3)—

(a) after the words 'the Cases in Part I of the said Schedule 15' there shall be inserted 'or, as the case may be, Grounds 10 to 16 in Part II of the said Schedule 2'; and

(b) after the words 'section 98(1) of the Rent Act 1977' there shall be inserted 'or, as the case may be, section 7(4) of the Housing Act 1988'.

10.—(1) The said section 20, as it applies to Scotland, shall be amended in accordance with this paragraph.

(2)　In subsection (1) after the words 'Case 1 in Schedule 2 to the Rent (Scotland) Act 1984' there shall be inserted the words 'or Ground 13 in Schedule 5 to the Housing (Scotland) Act 1988'.

(3)　In subsection (2) after the words 'Case 7 in the said Schedule 2' there shall be inserted the words 'or, as the case may be, Ground 17 in the said Schedule 5' and for paragraph (b) there shall be substituted the following paragraph—

> '(b)　sections 12 to 31 of the Housing (Scotland) Act 1988 apply in relation to the premises as mentioned in section 18(1) of this Act and a dependant or dependants of the service man is or are living in the premises or in part thereof in right of the statutory assured tenancy or assured tenancy referred to in paragraph (a) of section 19 of this Act'.

(4)　In subsection (3)—

(a)　after the words 'the Cases in Part I of the said Schedule 2' there shall be inserted the words 'or, as the case may be, Grounds 10 to 17 in Part II of the said Schedule 5'; and

(b)　after the words 'section 11 of the Rent (Scotland) Act 1984' there shall be inserted the words 'or, as the case may be, section 18(4) of the Housing (Scotland) Act 1988'.

11.　In section 22 of that Act (facilities for action on behalf of men serving abroad in proceedings as to tenancies), as it applies otherwise than to Scotland, in subsection (1)—

(a)　after the words 'Rent Act 1977' there shall be inserted 'or under Part I of the Housing Act 1988';

(b)　for the words 'Part V of that Act' there shall be substituted 'Part V of the Rent Act 1977 or Part I of the Housing Act 1988'; and

(c)　in paragraph (a) after the word 'tenancy' there shall be inserted 'or licence'.

12.　In the said section 22, as it applies to Scotland, in subsection (1),—

(a)　for the words 'Part III of the Rent Act 1965 or under the Rent (Scotland) Act 1971' there shall be substituted the words 'the Rent (Scotland) Act 1984 or under Part II of the Housing (Scotland) Act 1988';

(b)　for the words 'rent tribunal' there shall be substituted the words 'rent assessment committee' and for the words 'or tribunal' there shall be substituted the words 'or committee';

(c)　for the words 'Part VII of that Act' there shall be substituted the words 'Part VII of the said Act of 1984 or under Part II of the Housing (Scotland) Act 1988'; and

(d)　in paragraph (a) after the word 'tenancy' there shall be inserted the words 'or licence'.

13.—(1)　Section 23 of that Act (interpretation of Part II), as it applies otherwise than to Scotland, shall be amended in accordance with this paragraph.

(2)　In subsection (1)—

(a)　after the definition of 'agricultural land' there shall be inserted—

'"assured tenancy" has the same meaning as in Part I of the Housing Act 1988';

(b) after the definition of 'dependant' there shall be inserted—

'"fixed-term tenancy" means any tenancy other than a periodic tenancy';

(c) for the definition of 'landlord' and 'tenant' there shall be substituted—

'in relation to a statutory tenancy or to a provision of the Rent Act 1977 "landlord" and "tenant" have the same meaning as in that Act but, subject to that, those expressions have the same meaning as in Part I of the Housing Act 1988';

and

(d) after the definition of 'relevant police authority' there shall be inserted—

'"statutory periodic tenancy" has the same meaning as in Part I of the Housing Act 1988'.

(3) At the end of subsection (1) there shall be inserted the following subsection—

'(1A) Any reference in this Part of this Act to Chapter I of Part I of the Housing Act 1988 includes a reference to the General Provisions of Chapter VI of that Part, so far as applicable to Chapter I.'

(4) In subsection (3) after the words 'Rent Act 1977' there shall be inserted 'or Chapter I of Part I of the Housing Act 1988'.

14.—(1) The said section 23, as it applies to Scotland, shall be amended in accordance with this paragraph.

(2) In subsection (1)—

(a) after the definition of "agricultural land" there shall be inserted—

'"assured tenancy" and "statutory assured tenancy" have the same meaning as in Part II of the Housing (Scotland) Act 1988';

(b) for the definition of 'landlord' and 'tenant' there shall be substituted—

'in relation to a statutory tenancy or to a provision of the Rent (Scotland) Act 1984 "landlord" and "tenant" have the same meaning as in that Act but, subject to that, those expressions have the same meaning as in Part II of the Housing (Scotland) Act 1988'.

(3) At the end of subsection (1) there shall be inserted the following subsection—

'(1A) Any reference in this Part of this Act to sections 12 to 31 of the Housing (Scotland) Act 1988 includes a reference to sections 47 to 55 of that Act so far as applicable to those sections.'

(4) In subsection (3) after the words 'Rent (Scotland) Act 1984' there shall be inserted the words 'or sections 12 to 31 of the Housing (Scotland) Act 1988'.

The Leasehold Reform Act 1967

15.   In section 28 of the Leasehold Reform Act 1967 (retention or resumption of land required for public purposes) at the end of subsection (5) (bodies to whom that section applies) there shall be added

'and

(g)   a housing action trust established under Part III of the Housing Act 1988.'

16.   In section 29 of that Act (reservation of future right to develop) after subsection (6B) there shall be inserted the following subsection—

'(6C)   Subsections (1) to (4) above shall have effect in relation to a housing action trust as if any reference in those subsections or in Part I of Schedule 4 to this Act to a local authority were a reference to the trust.'

17.—(1)   In Schedule 4A to that Act (which is set out in Schedule 4 to the Housing and Planning Act 1986 and excludes certain shared ownership leases from Part I of the 1967 Act) at the end of paragraph 2(1) there shall be added 'or to a person who acquired that interest in exercise of the right conferred by Part IV of the Housing Act 1988'.

(2)   In paragraph 2(2) of that Schedule, at the end of paragraph (e) there shall be added the following paragraph—

'(f)   a housing action trust established under Part III of the Housing Act 1988'.

The Town and Country Planning Act 1971

18.   In section 215 of the Town and Country Planning Act 1971 (procedure for making certain orders), in subsection (8) (definitions of 'relevant area' and 'local authority') after the words 'Part IV of the Local Government Act 1985' there shall be inserted 'a housing action trust established under Part III of the Housing Act 1988'.

The Local Government Act 1974

19.   In section 25 of the Local Government Act 1974 (local government administration: authorities subject to investigation), in subsection (1) after paragraph (bd) there shall be inserted the following paragraph—

'(be)   any housing action trust established under Part III of the Housing Act 1988'.

The Consumer Credit Act 1974

20.   In section 16 of the Consumer Credit Act 1974 (exempt agreements), in subsection (6B), in paragraph (a) after the words 'England and Wales,' there shall be inserted 'the Housing Corporation, Housing for Wales and'.

The Rent (Agriculture) Act 1976

21.   In section 28 of the Rent (Agriculture) Act 1976 (rehousing: duty of housing authority concerned), the following subsection shall be inserted after subsection (14) of that section—

'(14A)   Notwithstanding anything in section 127(1) of the Magistrates' Courts Act 1980, any information relating to an offence under this section may be tried if it is laid at any time within two years after the commission of the offence and within six months after the date on which evidence sufficient in the opinion of the housing authority concerned to justify the proceedings comes to its knowledge.'

The Rent Act 1977

22.   In the Rent Act 1977, sections 68 and 69, Part II of Schedule 11 and Schedule 12 (which provide for applications by a local authority for the determination of a fair rent and make provision about certificates of fair rent) shall cease to have effect except as respects applications made before the commencement of this Act.

23.   In section 77 of that Act (which provides for the reference of restricted contracts to rent tribunals by the lessor, the lessee or the local authority) the words 'or the local authority' shall be omitted.

24.   Section 89 of the Rent Act 1977 (which provides for the phasing of progression to a registered rent in the case of housing association tenancies) and Schedule 8 to that Act (phasing of rent increases: general provisions) shall cease to have effect except with respect to an increase in rent up to, or towards, a registered rent in relation to which the relevant date for the purposes of the said Schedule 8 falls before this Act comes into force.

25.   In section 137 of the Rent Act 1977 (effect on subtenancy of determination of superior tenancy), in subsection (1) the words 'this Part of' shall be omitted.

The Protection from Eviction Act 1977

26.   In section 7 of the Protection from Eviction Act 1977 (service of notices), in subsection (3)(c) (certain licensors treated as landlords for the purposes of the section) the words 'under a restricted contract (within the meaning of the Rent Act 1977)' shall be omitted.

The Justices of the Peace Act 1979

27.   In section 64 of the Justices of the Peace Act 1979 (disqualification in certain cases of justices who are members of local authorities) at the end of subsection (6) there shall be added the words 'and a housing action trust established under Part III of the Housing Act 1988'.

The Local Government, Planning and Land Act 1980

28.   In Schedule 16 to the Local Government, Planning and Land Act 1980 (bodies to whom Part X applies) after paragraph 8 there shall be inserted the following paragraph—

'8A.   A housing action trust established under Part III of the Housing Act 1988.'

29.   In Schedule 28 to the Local Government, Planning and Land Act 1980, in paragraph 10 after the words 'Rent Act 1977' there shall be inserted 'or the Housing Act 1988.'

The Highways Act 1980

30.   In Schedule 6 to the Highways Act 1980, in Part I, in paragraph 1(3)(b)(i) after the words 'Rent Act 1977' there shall be inserted 'and licensees under an assured agricultural occupancy within the meaning of Part I of the Housing Act 1988'.

The New Towns Act 1981

31.   In section 22 of the New Towns Act 1981 (possession of houses) after the words 'Rent Act 1977' there shall be inserted 'or Part I of the Housing Act 1988'.

The Acquisition of Land Act 1981

32.—(1)   In section 12(2) of the Acquisition of Land Act 1981 after the words 'Rent (Agriculture) Act 1976' there shall be inserted 'or a licensee under an assured agricultural occupancy within the meaning of Part I of the Housing Act 1988'.

(2)   In Schedule 1 to that Act, in paragraph 3(2) after the words 'Rent (Agriculture) Act 1976' there shall be inserted 'or a licensee under an assured agricultural occupancy within the meaning of Part I of the Housing Act 1988'.

The Matrimonial Homes Act 1983

33.   In section 1(6) of the Matrimonial Homes Act 1983 (occupation of one spouse by virtue of that section treated as occupation by the other for the purposes of certain enactments) after the words 'Housing Act 1985' there shall be inserted 'and Part I of the Housing Act 1988'.

34.—(1)   In Schedule 1 to that Act (transfer of certain tenancies on divorce, etc.), in paragraph 1—

(a)   at the end of paragraph (c) of subparagraph (1) there shall be inserted 'or

(d)   an assured tenancy or assured agricultural occupancy, within the meaning of Part I of the Housing Act 1988';

and

(b)   in subparagraph (2) after the words 'secure tenancy' there shall be inserted 'or an assured tenancy or assured agricultural occupancy'.

(2)   In paragraph 2 of that Schedule (orders transferring tenancies etc. from one spouse to another)—

(a)   in subparagraph (1) after the words 'Housing Act 1985' there shall be inserted 'or an assured tenancy or assured agricultural occupancy within the meaning of Part I of the Housing Act 1988'; and

(b)   at the end of subparagraph (3) there shall be inserted—

'(4)   Where the spouse so entitled is for the purposes of section 17 of the Housing Act 1988 a successor in relation to the tenancy or occupancy, his or her former spouse (or, in the case of judicial separation, his or her spouse) shall be deemed to be a successor in relation to the tenancy or occupancy for the purposes of that section.

(5) If the transfer under subparagraph (1) above is of an assured agricultural occupancy, then, for the purposes of Chapter III of Part I of the Housing Act 1988,—

(a) the agricultural worker condition shall be fulfilled with respect to the dwelling-house while the spouse to whom the assured agricultural occupancy is transferred continues to be the occupier under that occupancy; and

(b) that condition shall be treated as so fulfilled by virtue of the same paragraph of Schedule 3 to the Housing Act 1988 as was applicable before the transfer.'

The County Courts Act 1984

35.—(1) In section 66 of the County Courts Act 1984 (trial by jury: exceptions), in subsection (1) at the end of paragraph (b)(iii) there shall be inserted

'or

(iv) under Part I of the Housing Act 1988'.

(2) In section 77(6) of that Act (appeals: possession proceedings) after paragraph (e) there shall be inserted the following paragraph—

'(ee) section 7 of the Housing Act 1988, as it applies to the grounds in Part II of Schedule 2 to that Act; or'.

The Matrimonial and Family Proceedings Act 1984

36. In section 22 of the Matrimonial and Family Proceedings Act 1984 (powers of the court in relation to certain tenancies of dwelling-houses), in paragraph (a) after the word 'tenancy' there shall be inserted 'or assured agricultural occupancy'.

The Local Government Act 1985

37. In section 101 of the Local Government Act 1985 (power by order to make incidental, consequential, etc. provisions) in subsection (1)(b) after second 'Act' insert 'or the Housing Act 1988'.

The Housing Act 1985

38. In section 32(1) of the Housing Act 1985 (power to dispose of land) after '(the right to buy)' there shall be inserted 'and Part IV of the Housing Act 1988 (change of landlord: secure tenants)'.

39. In section 43(1) of that Act (consent required for certain disposals) after '(the right to buy)' there shall be inserted 'or Part IV of the Housing Act 1988 (change of landlord: secure tenants)'.

40. In section 115 of that Act (meaning of 'long tenancy') in subsection (2)(c) after '1980' there shall be inserted 'or paragraph 4(2)(b) of Schedule 4A to the Leasehold Reform Act 1967'.

41. In section 155 of that Act (repayment of discount on early disposal) after subsection (3) there shall be inserted the following subsection—

'(3A) Where a secure tenant has served on his landlord an operative notice of delay, as defined in section 153A,—

(a) the three years referred to in subsection (2) shall begin from a date which precedes the date of the conveyance of the freehold or grant of the lease by a period equal to the time (or, if there is more than one such notice, the aggregate of the times) during which, by virtue of section 153B, any payment of rent falls to be taken into account in accordance with subsection (3) of that section; and

(b) any reference in subsection (3) (other than paragraph (a) thereof) to the acquisition of the tenant's initial share shall be construed as a reference to a date which precedes that acquisition by the period referred to in paragraph (a) of this subsection.'

42. In section 171F of that Act (subsequent dealings after disposal of dwelling-house to private sector landlord: possession on grounds of suitable alternative accommodation) after 'Rent Act 1977' there shall be inserted 'or on Ground 9 in Schedule 2 to the Housing Act 1988'.

43. In section 236 of that Act at the end of subsection (2) (meaning of 'occupying tenant') there shall be added the words

'or

(e) is a licensee under an assured agricultural occupancy.'

44. In section 238 of that Act (index of defined expressions in Part VII) before the entry relating to 'clearance area' there shall be inserted—

'assured agricultural occupancy ...   . section 622'.

45. In section 247 of that Act (notification of certain disposals of land to the local housing authority), in subsection (5) (provision not to apply to certain disposals) after paragraph (c) there shall be inserted the following paragraph—

'(ca) the grant of an assured tenancy or assured agricultural occupancy, or of a tenancy which is not such a tenancy or occupancy by reason only of paragraph 10 of Schedule 1 to the Housing Act 1988 (resident landlords) or of that paragraph and the fact that the accommodation which is let is not let as a separate dwelling'.

46. In section 263 of that Act (index of defined expressions in Part VIII) before the entry relating to 'clearance area' there shall be inserted—

'assured agricultural occupancy ...   . section 622
assured tenancy   ...   . section 622'.

47. In Part IX of that Act (slum clearance) in the following provisions relating to the recovery of possession, namely, sections 264(5), 270(3), 276 and 286(3), after the words 'Rent Acts' there shall be inserted 'or Part I of the Housing Act 1988'.

48. In section 309 of that Act (recovery of possession of premises for purposes of approved redevelopment), in paragraph (a) of subsection (1) after the words 'the Rent Act 1977)' the following words shall be inserted 'or let on or subject to

an assured tenancy or assured agricultural occupancy'; and in the words following paragraph (b) of that subsection after the words 'section 98(1)(a) of the Rent Act 1977' there shall be inserted 'or section 7 of the Housing Act 1988'.

49.   In section 323 of that Act (index of defined expressions in Part IX) before the entry relating to 'clearance area' there shall be inserted—

'assured agricultural occupancy ...   . section 622
assured tenancy   ...   . section 622'.

50.   In section 368 of that Act (means of escape from fire: power to secure that part of house not used for human habitation), in subsection (6) after the words 'Rent Acts' there shall be inserted 'or Part I of the Housing Act 1988'.

51.   In section 381 of that Act (general effect of control order), in subsection (3) after the words 'Rent Acts' there shall be inserted 'and Part I of the Housing Act 1988'.

52.—(1)   In section 382 of that Act (effect of control order on persons occupying house) after subsection (3) there shall be inserted the following subsection—

'(3A)   Section 1(2) of and paragraph 12 of Part I of Schedule 1 to the Housing Act 1988 (which exclude local authority lettings from Part I of that Act) do not apply to a lease or agreement under which a person to whom this section applies is occupying part of the house.'

(2)   In subsection (4) of that section after paragraph (b) there shall be inserted

'or

(c)   an assured tenancy or assured agricultural occupancy within the meaning of Part I of the Housing Act 1988';

and for the words 'either of those Acts' there shall be substituted 'any of those Acts'.

53.   In section 400 of that Act (index of defined expressions for Part XI) after the entry relating to 'appropriate multiplier' there shall be inserted—

'assured tenancy   ...   . section 622
assured agricultural occupancy ...   . section 622'.

54.   In section 429A of that Act (housing management: financial assistance etc.) in subsection (2), in paragraph (a) after the words 'secure tenancies)' there shall be inserted 'or subsection (2A)' and at the end of that subsection there shall be inserted the following subsection—

'(2A)   Subsection (2)(a) applies to the following bodies—

(a)   the Housing Corporation;
(b)   Housing for Wales;
(c)   a housing trust which is a charity;
(d)   a registered housing association other than a cooperative housing association; and
(e)   an unregistered housing association which is a cooperative housing association.'

55.   In section 434 of that Act (index of defined expressions for Part XIII) there shall be inserted, in the appropriate places in alphabetical order, the following entries—

'charity   ...   . section 622'
'cooperative housing association   ...   . section 5(2)'
'housing association   ...   . section 5(1)'
'housing trust" ...   .   section 6'.

56.   In section 450A of that Act (right to a loan in certain cases after exercise of right to buy) in subsection (6), in the definition of 'housing authority' for the words from 'housing association' onwards there shall be substituted 'registered housing association other than a cooperative housing association and any unregistered housing association which is a cooperative housing association; and'.

57.   In section 450B of that Act (power to make loans in other cases) in subsection (4), in the definition of 'housing authority' for the words from 'housing association' onwards there shall be substituted 'registered housing association other than a cooperative housing association and any unregistered housing association which is a cooperative housing association; and'.

58.   In section 459 of that Act (index of defined expressions for Part XIV) after the entry relating to 'building society' there shall be inserted—

'cooperative housing association   ...   . section 5(2)'.

59.   In section 533 of that Act (assistance for owners of defective housing: exceptions to eligibility) after the words 'Rent (Agriculture) Act 1976' there shall be inserted 'or who occupies the dwelling under an assured agricultural occupancy which is not an assured tenancy'.

60.   In section 553 of that Act (effect of repurchase of defective dwellings on certain existing tenancies) in subsection (2)—

(a)   in paragraph (a) after the words 'protected tenancy' there shall be inserted 'or an assured tenancy';
(b)   at the end of paragraph (b) there shall be added the words 'or in accordance with any of Grounds 1, 3, 4 and 5 in Schedule 2 to the Housing Act 1988 (notice that possession might be recovered under that ground) or under section 20(1)(c) of that Act (notice served in respect of assured shorthold tenancies); and'; and
(c)   after paragraph (b) there shall be added—

'(c)   the tenancy is not an assured periodic tenancy which, by virtue of section 39(7) of the Housing Act 1988 (successors under the Rent Act 1977), is an assured shorthold tenancy'.

61.—(1)   In section 554 of that Act (grant of tenancy of defective dwelling to former owner-occupier) at the end of subsection (2) there shall be inserted the following subsection—

'(2A)   If the authority is a registered housing association, other than a housing cooperative, within the meaning of section 27B, their obligation is to grant a secure tenancy if the individual to whom a tenancy is to be granted—

(a) is a person who, immediately before he acquired his interest in the dwelling-house, was a secure tenant of it; or

(b) is the spouse or former spouse or widow or widower of a person falling within paragraph (a); or

(c) is a member of the family, within the meaning of section 186, of a person falling within paragraph (a) who has died, and was residing with that person in the dwelling-house at the time of and for the period of twelve months before his death.'

(2) In subsection (3) of that section, at the end of paragraph (b) there shall be inserted

'or

(c) an assured tenancy which is neither an assured shorthold tenancy, within the meaning of Part I of the Housing Act 1988, nor a tenancy under which the landlord might recover possession on any of Grounds 1 to 5 in Schedule 2 to that Act.'

62. In section 577 of that Act (index of defined expressions for Part XVI) after the entry relating to 'associated arrangement' there shall be inserted—

'assured agricultural occupancy   ...   . section 622
assured tenancy ...   . section 622'.

63. In section 612 of that Act (exclusion of Rent Act protection) after the words 'the Rent Acts' there shall be inserted 'or Part I of the Housing Act 1988'.

64. In section 622 of that Act (definitions: general) before the definition of 'bank' there shall be inserted—

'"assured tenancy" has the same meaning as in Part I of the Housing Act 1988;

"assured agricultural occupancy" has the same meaning as in Part I of the Housing Act 1988'.

65. In Schedule 2 to that Act, in Part IV (grounds for possession: suitability of alternative accommodation) in paragraph 1, at the end of subparagraph (b) there shall be added

'or

(c) which are to be let as a separate dwelling under an assured tenancy which is neither an assured shorthold tenancy, within the meaning of Part I of the Housing Act 1988, nor a tenancy under which the landlord might recover possession under any of Grounds 1 to 5 in Schedule 2 to that Act'.

66. In Schedule 5 to that Act, in paragraph 3, after the entry for section 58(2) of the Housing Associations Act 1985 there shall be inserted the following entries—

'section 50 of the Housing Act 1988 (housing association grants), or section 51 of that Act (revenue deficit grants).'

The Landlord and Tenant Act 1985

67.—(1)   In section 5 of the Landlord and Tenant Act 1985 (information to be contained in rent books), in subsection (1)(b) after the word 'tenancy' there shall be inserted 'or let on an assured tenancy within the meaning of Part I of the Housing Act 1988'.

(2)   In subsection (2) of that section after the word 'tenancy' there shall be added 'or let on an assured tenancy within the meaning of Part I of the Housing Act 1988'.

68.   In section 26 of that Act (tenants of certain public authorities excepted from provisions about service charges etc.) in subsection (3)(c) after the words 'Housing Act 1980' there shall be inserted 'or paragraph 4(2)(b) of Schedule 4A to the Leasehold Reform Act 1967'.

The Agricultural Holdings Act 1986

69.—(1)   In Schedule 3 to the Agricultural Holdings Act 1986 (cases where consent of Tribunal to operation of notice to quit is not required), in Part II (provisions applicable to Case A: suitable alternative accommodation), in paragraph 3 after paragraph (b) there shall be inserted

'or
    (c)   premises which are to be let as a separate dwelling such that they will then be let on an assured tenancy which is not an assured shorthold tenancy (construing those terms in accordance with Part I of the Housing Act 1988), or
    (d)   premises to be let as a separate dwelling on terms which will afford to the tenant security of tenure reasonably equivalent to the security afforded by Chapter I of Part I of that Act in the case of an assured tenancy which is not an assured shorthold tenancy.'

(2)   At the end of the said paragraph 3 there shall be added the following subparagraph—

'(2)   Any reference in subparagraph (1) above to an assured tenancy does not include a reference to a tenancy in respect of which possession might be recovered on any of Grounds 1 to 5 in Schedule 2 to the Housing Act 1988.'

70.   In Schedule 5 to that Act (notice to quit where tenant is a service man), in paragraph 2(2)(a) after the words 'Rent Act 1977' there shall be inserted 'or paragraph 7 of Schedule 1 to the Housing Act 1988'.

The Drug Trafficking Offences Act 1986

71.   In section 15 of the Drug Trafficking Offences Act 1986 (bankruptcy of defendant etc.), in subsection (2)(b) for the words 'or 308' there shall be substituted '308 or 308A' and after the word 'replacement' there shall be inserted 'and certain tenancies'.

72.   In section 16 of that Act (sequestration in Scotland of defendant), in subsection (2)(b) for the words 'under subsection (6) of that section' there shall be

substituted the words 'under subsection (10) of section 31 of that Act or subsection (6) of the said section 32 of that Act'.

The Insolvency Act 1986

73.   In section 308 of the Insolvency Act 1986 (vesting in trustee of certain items of excess value), in subsection (1), for the words 'the next section' there shall be substituted 'section 309'.

74.   In section 335 of that Act (adjustment between earlier and later bankruptcy estates), in subsection (4) after the words 'replacement value)' there shall be inserted the words 'or section 308A (vesting in trustee of certain tenancies)'.

75.   In section 351 of that Act (definitions), in paragraph (a), for the words 'or 308' there shall be substituted ', section 308' and after the words 'replacement value)' there shall be inserted 'or section 308A (vesting in trustee of certain tenancies)'.

The Social Security Act 1986

76.   In section 31 of the Social Security Act 1986 (information relating to housing benefit), in subsection (5) (information as to registered rents), after the words 'housing benefit scheme' there shall be inserted '(a)', and at the end there shall be added

'and
    (b)   where a rent is determined under section 14 or section 22 of the Housing Act 1988 or section 25 or section 34 of the Housing (Scotland) Act 1988 (determination of rents by rent assessment committee), the committee shall note in their determination the amount (if any) of the rent which, in the opinion of the committee, is fairly attributable to the provision of services, except where that amount is in their opinion negligible; and the amounts so noted may be included in the information specified in an order under section 42 of the Housing Act 1988 or, as the case may be, section 49 of the Housing (Scotland) Act 1988 (information to be publicly available)'.

The Housing (Scotland) Act 1987

77.   In section 12 of the Housing (Scotland) Act 1987 (which relates, amongst other things, to the disposal by local authorities of land acquired or appropriated for housing purposes and of houses)—

    (a)   in subsection (1)(c), for the words 'subsection (5)' there shall be substituted the words 'subsections (5) and (7)';
    (b)   in subsection (7)—

        (i)   for '(1)(d)' there shall be substituted '(1)(c) or (d)';
        (ii)   for the words 'house or any part share thereof' there shall be substituted the words 'land, house or part share therof';
        (iii)   for the words 'it is a house' there shall be substituted the words ', in the case of a house, it is one';

    (c)   in subsection (8) after the word 'apply' there shall be inserted the words ', in the case of a house,'.

78. In section 13 of that Act (power of Secretary of State in certain cases to impose conditions on sale of local authority's houses etc.) for the words 'land or dwelling' there shall be substituted the words 'or land'.

79. In section 61(4)(b) of the Housing (Scotland) Act 1987 after subparagraph (vi) there shall be inserted the following subparagraphs—

> '(vii) section 50 of the Housing Act 1988 (housing association grants); or
>
> (viii) section 51 of that Act (revenue deficit grants); or'.

The Access to Personal Files Act 1987

80. In Schedule 1 to the Access to Personal Files Act 1987 (accessible personal information: England and Wales), in paragraph 2 at the end of subparagraph (2) there shall be added 'and any housing action trust established under Part III of the Housing Act 1988.'

The Criminal Justice (Scotland) Act 1987

81. In section 33 of the Criminal Justice (Scotland) Act 1987 (sequestration of person holding realisable property), in subsection (2)(b) for the words 'under subsection (6) of that section' there shall be substituted the words 'under subsection (10) of section 31 of that Act or subsection (6) of the said section 32 of that Act'.

82. In section 34 of that Act (bankruptcy in England and Wales of person holding realisable property), in subsection (2)(b) for the words 'or 308' there shall be substituted '308 or 308A' and after the word 'replacement' there shall be inserted 'and certain tenancies'.

The Criminal Justice Act 1988

83. In section 84 of the Criminal Justice Act 1988 (bankruptcy of defendant etc.), in subsection (2)(b) for the words 'or 308' there shall be substituted '308 or 308A' and after the word 'replacement' there shall be inserted 'and certain tenancies'.

84. In section 85 of that Act (sequestration in Scotland of defendant), in subsection 2(b) for the words 'under subsection (6) of that section' there shall be substituted the words 'under subsection (10) of section 31 of that Act or subsection (6) of the said section 32 of that Act'.

The Housing (Scotland) Act 1988

85. In section 19 of the Housing (Scotland) Act 1988 (notice of proceedings for possession)—

> (a) in subsection (2) for the word 'is' there shall be substituted the words 'and particulars of it are';
>
> (b) in subsection (3) after the word 'one' where it first occurs there shall be inserted the words 'in the prescribed form'.

86. In section 36 of that Act (damages for unlawful eviction)—

(a)   in subsection (2) for the word 'calculated' there shall be substituted the word 'likely';

(b)   in subsection (7)(b)—

(i)   after the word 'of' where it first occurs there shall be inserted the words 'the doing of acts or';

(ii)   after the word 'for' there shall be inserted the words 'doing the acts or'.

87.   In section 38 of that Act (further offence of harassment)—

(a)   for the words from 'In section 22' to 'after subsection (2)' there shall be substituted the words—

'(1)   Subsection (2) of section 22 of the Rent (Scotland) Act 1984 (unlawful eviction and harassment of occupier) shall, as respects acts done after the commencement of this section, have effect with the substitution of the word "likely" for the word "calculated".

(2)   After that subsection';

(b)   after '(2A)' there shall be inserted the words 'Subject to subsection (2B) below';

(c)   for the word 'calculated' there shall be substituted the word 'likely';

(d)   the words 'subject to subsection (2B) below' and 'by reason only of conduct falling within paragraph (b) of that subsection' shall cease to have effect;

(e)   after the word 'for' where it second occurs there shall be inserted the words 'doing the acts or'.

88.   In section 36 of that Act (damages for unlawful eviction)—

(a)   in subsection (6), for the words 'proceedings are begun to enforce the liability' there shall be substituted the words 'the date on which the proceedings to enforce the liability are finally decided'; and

(b)   after subsection (6) there shall be inserted the following subsections—

'(6A)   For the purposes of subsection (6)(a) above, proceedings to enforce a liability are finally decided—

(a)   if no appeal may be made against the decision in these proceedings;

(b)   if an appeal may be made against the decision with leave and the time-limit for applications for leave expires and either no application has been made or leave has been refused;

(c)   if leave to appeal against the decision is granted or is not required and no appeal is made within the time-limit for appeals; or

(d)   if an appeal is made but is abandoned before it is determined.

(6B)   If, in proceedings to enforce a liability arising by virtue of subsection (3) above, it appears to the court—

(a)   that, prior to the event which gave rise to the liability, the conduct of the former residential occupier or any person living with him in the premises concerned was such that it is reasonable to mitigate the damages for which the landlord would otherwise be liable, or

(b)   that, before the proceedings were begun, the landlord offered to reinstate the former residential occupier in the premises in question and either it was unreasonable of the former residential occupier to refuse that offer or, if he had obtained alternative accommodation before the offer was made, it would have been unreasonable of him to refuse that offer if he had not obtained that accommodation,

the court may reduce the amount of damages which would otherwise be payable to such amount as it thinks appropriate.'.

89.   In section 63 of that Act (consent for subsequent disposals) after subsection (2) there shall be inserted the following subsection—

'(2A)   Before giving any consent for the purposes of subsection (1) above, Scottish Homes—

(a)   shall satisfy itself that the person who is seeking the consent has taken appropriate steps to consult the tenant of the house (or, as the case may be, each house) of which the property proposed to be disposed of consists; and

(b)   shall have regard to the response of such tenant to that consultation.'

90.   In Schedule 4 to that Act (tenancies which cannot be assured tenancies) after paragraph 11 there shall be inserted the following paragraph—

'Accommodation for homeless persons

11A.   A tenancy granted expressly on a temporary basis in the fulfilment of a duty imposed on a local authority by Part II of the Housing (Scotland) Act 1987.'

Part II Amendments consequential on the establishment of Housing for Wales

The Land Commission Act 1967

91.   In section 56(4) of the Land Commission Act 1967 (bodies exempted from betterment levy) after paragraph (e) there shall be inserted the following paragraph—

'(ea)   Housing for Wales'.

The Parliamentary Commissioner Act 1967

92.   In Schedule 2 to the Parliamentary Commissioner Act 1967 (departments etc. subject to investigation) after the entry 'Housing Corporation' there shall be inserted—

'Housing for Wales'.

The Income and Corporation Taxes Act 1970

93.   In section 342 of the Income and Corporation Taxes Act 1970 (disposals of land between Housing Corporation and housing societies) and in section 342A of that Act (disposals by certain housing associations) after the words 'Housing

Corporation' in each place where they occur there shall be inserted 'or Housing for Wales'.

The Land Compensation Act 1973

94. In section 32(7B)(b) of the Land Compensation Act 1973 (supplementary provisions about home loss payments) after the words 'Housing Corporation' there shall be inserted 'or Housing for Wales'.

The House of Commons Disqualification Act 1975

95. In Schedule 1 to the House of Commons Disqualification Act 1975, in Part II (bodies of which all members are disqualified) there shall be inserted at the appropriate place the following entry—

'Housing for Wales'.

The Statutory Corporations (Financial Provisions) Act 1975

96. In Schedule 2 to the Statutory Corporations (Financial Provisions) Act 1975 (bodies corporate affected by section 5 of that Act as to their power to borrow in currencies other than sterling) after the entry 'The Housing Corporation' there shall be inserted—

'Housing for Wales'.

The Development of Rural Wales Act 1976

97. In section 8(2) of the Development of Rural Wales Act 1976 (assistance to the Development Board for Rural Wales from public authorities and others) for the words 'the Housing Corporation' there shall be substituted 'Housing for Wales'.

The Rent (Agriculture) Act 1976

98. In section 5(3) of the Rent (Agriculture) Act 1976 (no statutory tenancy where landlord's interest belongs to Crown or to local authority etc.) after paragraph (d) there shall be inserted the following paragraph—

'(da) Housing for Wales'.

The Rent Act 1977

99. In section 15(2)(a) of the Rent Act 1977 (landlord's interest belonging to housing association etc.) after the words 'Housing Corporation' there shall be inserted—

'(aa) Housing for Wales'.

100. In each of the following provisions of that Act, that is to say, sections 86(2)(a) (tenancies to which Part VI applies), 93(1) (increase of rent without notice to quit) and Schedule 12 (certificates of fair rent), in paragraph 12 (meaning of 'secure tenancy'), after the words 'Housing Corporation' there shall be inserted 'or Housing for Wales'.

The Criminal Law Act 1977

101. In section 7(5) of the Criminal Law Act 1977 (authorities who may authorise occupation by protected intending occupier for purposes of offence of

adverse occupation of residential premises) after the words 'Housing Corporation' there shall be inserted—

'(ba)   Housing for Wales'.

The National Health Service Act 1977

102.   In section 28A(2)(e) of the National Health Service Act 1977 (power to make payments towards expenditure on community services) at the end there shall be added the following subparagraph

'and

(vii)   Housing for Wales.'

103.   In section 28B(1)(b)(v) of that Act (power of Secretary of State to make payments towards expenditure on community services in Wales) for the words 'the Housing Corporation' there shall be substituted 'Housing for Wales'.

The Local Government, Planning and Land Act 1980

104.   In Schedule 16 to the Local Government, Planning and Land Act 1980 (bodies to whom Part X of that Act applies) after paragraph 9 there shall be inserted the following paragraph—

'9a.   Housing for Wales.'

The Finance Act 1981

105.   In section 107(3) of the Finance Act 1981 (exemption from stamp duty in case of sale of houses at discount by local authorities etc.) after paragraph (c) there shall be inserted the following paragraph—

'(ca)   Housing for Wales.'

The Housing Act 1985

106.   In the Housing Act 1985 for the words 'Housing Corporation' in each place where they occur there shall be substituted 'Corporation'.

107.   In Part I of that Act (introductory provisions—authorities and bodies other than local housing authorities) after section 6 there shall be inserted the following section—

'**6A.**   In this Act "the Corporation" has the meaning assigned by section 2A of the Housing Associations Act 1985.'

108.   In section 57 of that Act (index of defined expressions: Part II) after the entry relating to 'compulsory disposal' there shall be inserted—

'the Corporation   section 6A'.

109.   In section 117 of that Act (index of defined expressions: Part IV) after the entry relating to 'cooperative housing association' there shall be inserted—

'the Corporation   section 6A'.

110.   In section 188 of that Act (index of defined expressions: Part V) after the entry relating to 'cooperative housing association' there shall be inserted—

'the Corporation   section 6A'.

111.   In section 238 of that Act (index of defined expressions: Part VII) after the entry relating to 'clearance area' there shall be inserted—

'the Corporation   section 6A'.

112.   In section 459 of that Act (index of defined expressions: Part XIV) after the entry relating to 'building society' there shall be inserted—

'the Corporation   section 6A'.

113.   In section 577 of that Act (index of defined expressions: Part XVI) after the entry relating to 'cooperative housing association' there shall be inserted—

'the Corporation   section 6A'.

The Landlord and Tenant Act 1987

114.   In section 58(1) of the Landlord and Tenant Act 1987 (exempt landlords) after paragraph (e) there shall be inserted the following paragraph—

'(ea)   Housing for Wales'.

The Income and Corporation Taxes Act 1988

115.   In section 376(4) of the Income and Corporation Taxes Act 1988 (qualifying borrowers and lenders) after paragraph (k) there shall be inserted the following paragraph—

'(ka)   Housing for Wales.'

116.   In section 560(2)(e) of that Act (persons who are subcontractors or contractors for the purposes of Chapter IV of Part XIII of that Act) after the words 'Housing Corporation' there shall be inserted 'Housing for Wales'.

Schedule 18 Enactments repealed

Chapter	Short title	Extent of repeal
14 & 15 Geo. VI c. 65.	The Reserve and Auxiliary Forces (Protection of Civil Interests) Act 1951.	Section 18(2).
1976 c.80.	The Rent (Agriculture) Act 1976.	In section 4(2) the words 'or, as the case may be, subsection (4)'. In section 13(3) the words '68, 69' and 'or Part II of Schedule 11 or Schedule 12 to that Act'. In Schedule 4, in Part I, paragraph 2(2).

Chapter	Short title	Extent of repeal
1977 c.42.	The Rent Act 1977.	Section 16A. Sections 19 to 21. In section 63, in subsection (1), paragraph (b) and the word 'and' immediately preceding it; in subsection (2) in paragraph (a), the words 'and deputy rent officers', in paragraph (b), the words 'or deputy rent officer', in paragraph (d) the words 'and deputy rent officers' and the word 'and' at the end of the paragraph, and paragraph (e); in subsection (3), the words 'and deputy rent officers'; and in subsection (7)(b), the words 'and deputy rent officers'. In section 67, in subsection (5), the words 'and sections 68 and 69 of this Act' and in subsection (7), the words 'Subject to section 69(4) of this Act.' Sections 68 and 69. In section 74, in subsection (2), in paragraph (a) '69', in paragraph (b) the words 'or II' and paragraph (c). In section 77(1) the words 'or the local authority'. In section 80(1) the words 'or the local authority'. Section 81A(1)(a). In section 87, in subsection (2), in paragraph (a) '69' and in paragraph (c) the words 'and 12'. In section 88(2) the words 'then, subject to section 89 of this Act'. Section 89. In section 103(1) the words 'or the local authority'. In section 137 the words 'this Part of'. In Schedule 1, in paragraph 1 the words 'or, as the case may be, paragraph 3', in paragraph 4, the words 'or 3', and paragraph 7. In Schedule 2, paragraph 6(3). Schedule 8.

Chapter	Short title	Extent of repeal
		In Schedule 11, Part II. Schedule 12. In Schedule 14, paragraph 4. In Schedule 15, in Part IV, paragraph 4(2). In Schedule 20, paragraph 2(2). In Schedule 24, paragraph 8(3).
1977 c. 43.	The Protection from Eviction Act 1977.	In section 7(3)(c) the words from 'under' to '1977)'.
1980 c.51.	The Housing Act 1980.	Section 52. Sections 56 to 58. Section 59(1). Section 60. Section 73(2). Section 76(2). In Schedule 9, paragraph 2. In Schedule 10, paragraph 2. In Schedule 25, paragraph 36, in paragraph 40 '68 (4)' and paragraphs 46 and 63.
1985 c. 51.	The Local Government Act 1985.	In Schedule 13, in paragraph 21, the words from 'and section 19(5)(aa)' onwards.
1985 c.68.	The Housing Act 1985.	In section 80, in subsection (1) the words from 'the Housing Corporation' to 'charity or', the words 'housing association or', and subsection (2). Sections 199 to 201. In Schedule 5, in paragraph 3 the word 'or' immediately following the entry for section 55 of the Housing Associations Act 1985; paragraphs 6 and 8.
1985 c.69.	The Housing Associations Act 1985.	In section 3(2) the words 'of housing associations maintained under this section'. In section 18(3) the words from 'and the Corporation' onwards. In section 40, the entries relating to housing association grant and revenue deficit grant.

Chapter	Short title	Extent of repeal
		Sections 41 to 57.
		Section 62.
		In section 73, the entries relating to approved development programme, hostel deficit grant, housing association grant, housing project, revenue deficit grant, shared ownership agreement and shared ownership lease.
		Section 75(1)(d).
		In section 87(1) the words 'registered housing associations and other'.
		In section 107, in subsection (3) the entries relating to sections 4, 44 and 45 and 52, and in subsection (4) the words 'section 4(3)(h)'.
		In Schedule 5, in paragraph 5(3) of Part I and in paragraph 5(3)) of Part II, the words 'at such times and in such places as the Treasury may direct, and' and the words 'with the approval of the Treasury'.
		In Schedule 6, paragraph 3(3)(b).
1986 c.63.	The Housing and Planning Act 1986.	Section 7.
		Section 12.
		In section 13, subsections (1) to (3) and (5).
		Section 19.
		In Schedule 4, paragraphs 1(3) and 10.
		In Schedule 5, paragraph 8.
1986 c.65.	The Housing (Scotland) Act 1986.	Section 13(1).
		Sections 14 to 16.
		In Schedule 2, in paragraph 4(8), subparagraph (a) and, in subparagraph (b), the words 'section 4(3)(h)'.
1987 c.26.	The Housing (Scotland) Act 1987.	In section 61(4)(b) the word 'or' at the end of subparagraph (v) and at the end of subparagraph (vi).
1987 c.31.	The Landlord and Tenant Act 1987.	In section 3(1)(b) the word 'or'.
		Section 4(2)(a)(ii).
		Section 45.

Chapter	Short title	Extent of repeal
		Section 60(2).
		In Schedule 4, paragraph 7.
1988 c.9.	The Local Government Act 1988.	Section 24(5)(b).
1988 c.43.	The Housing (Scotland) Act 1988.	Section 4(4).
		In section 38, the words 'subject to subsection (2B) below' and 'by reason only of conduct falling within paragraph (b) of that subsection'.
		Schedule 3.
		In Schedule 9, paragraphs 6(b) and 7.
		In Schedule 10, the entry relating to the Housing Associations Act 1985.

1.   The repeal of sections 19 to 21 of the Rent Act 1977 does not apply with respect to any tenancy or contract entered into before the coming into force of Part I of this Act nor to any other tenancy or contract which, having regard to section 36 of this Act, can be a restricted contract.

2.   The repeal of section 52 of the Housing Act 1980 (protected shorthold tenancies) does not apply with respect to any tenancy entered into before the coming into force of Part I of this Act nor to any other tenancy which, having regard to section 34 of this Act, can be a protected shorthold tenancy.

3.   The repeal of sections 56 to 58 of the Housing Act 1980 does not have effect in relation to any tenancy to which, by virtue of section 37(2) of this Act, section 1(3) of this Act does not apply.

4.   The repeals in section 80 of the Housing Act 1985—

(a)   have effect (subject to section 35(5) of this Act) in relation to any tenancy or licence entered into before the coming into force of Part I of this Act unless, immediately before that time, the landlord or, as the case may be, the licensor is a body which, in accordance with the repeals, would cease to be within the said section 80; and

(b)   do not have effect in relation to a tenancy or licence entered into on or after the coming into force of Part I of this Act if the tenancy or licence falls within any of paragraphs (c) to (f) of subsection (4) of section 35 of this Act.

Protection from Eviction Act 1977

The text of the Act printed here incorporates amendments made by statutes up to and including the Housing Act 1988.

Part I Unlawful eviction and harassment

Part II Notice to quit

Part III Supplemental provisions

c.43. An Act to consolidate section 16 of the Rent Act 1957 and Part III of the Rent Act 1965, and related enactments.   [Royal assent 29 July 1977]

Part I Unlawful eviction and harassment

Unlawful eviction and harassment of occupier

1.—(1) In this section 'residential occupier', in relation to any premises, means a person occupying the premises as a residence, whether under a contract or by virtue of any enactment or rule of law giving him the right to remain in occupation or restricting the right of any other person to recover possession of the premises.

(2) If any person unlawfully deprives the residential occupier of any premises of his occupation of the premises or any part thereof, or attempts to do so, he shall be guilty of an offence unless he proves that he believed, and had reasonable cause to believe, that the residential occupier had ceased to reside in the premises.

(3) If any person with intent to cause the residential occupier of any premises—

    (a) to give up the occupation of the premises or any part thereof, or

    (b) to refrain from exercising any right or pursuing any remedy in respect of the premises or part thereof;

does acts likely to interfere with the peace or comfort of the residential occupier or members of his household, or persistently withdraws or withholds services reasonably required for the occupation of the premises as a residence he shall be guilty of an offence.

(3A) Subject to subsection (3B) below, the landlord of a residential occupier or an agent of the landlord shall be guilty of an offence if—

    (a) he does acts likely to interfere with the peace or comfort of the residential occupier or members of his household, or

    (b) he persistently withdraws or withholds services reasonably required for the occupation of the premises in question as a residence,

and (in either case) he knows, or has reasonable cause to believe, that the conduct is likely to cause the residential occupier to give up the occupation of the whole or part of the premises or to refrain from exercising any right or pursuing any remedy in respect of the whole or part of the premises.

(3B) A person shall not be guilty of an offence under subsection (3A) above if he proves that he had reasonable grounds for doing the acts or withdrawing or withholding the services in question.

(3C) In subsection (3A) above 'landlord', in relation to a residential occupier of any premises, means the person who, but for—

    (a) the residential occupier's right to remain in occupation of the premises, or

    (b) a restriction on the person's right to recover possession of the premises,

would be entitled to occupation of the premises and any superior landlord under whom that person derives title.

(4) A person guilty of an offence under this section shall be liable—

    (a) on summary conviction, to a fine not exceeding the prescribed sum or to imprisonment for a term not exceeding six months or to both;

(b)   on conviction on indictment, to a fine or to imprisonment for a term not exceeding two years or to both.

(5)   Nothing in this section shall be taken to prejudice any liability or remedy to which a person guilty of an offence thereunder may be subject in civil proceedings.

(6)   Where an offence under this section committed by a body corporate is proved to have been committed with the consent or connivance of, or to be attributable to any neglect on the part of, any director, manager or secretary or other similar officer of the body corporate or any person who was purporting to act in any such capacity, he as well as the body corporate shall be guilty of that offence and shall be liable to be proceeded against and punished accordingly.

Restriction on re-entry without due process of law
2.   Where any premises are let as a dwelling on a lease which is subject to a right of re-entry or forfeiture it shall not be lawful to enforce that right otherwise than by proceedings in the court while any person is lawfully residing in the premises or part of them.

Prohibition of eviction without due process of law
3.—(1)   Where any premises have been let as a dwelling under a tenancy which is neither a statutorily protected tenancy nor an excluded tenancy and—

(a)   the tenancy (in this section referred to as the former tenancy) has come to an end, but
(b)   the occupier continues to reside in the premises or part of them,

it shall not be lawful for the owner to enforce against the occupier, otherwise than by proceedings in the court, his right to recover possession of the premises.

(2)   In this section 'the occupier', in relation to any premises, means any person lawfully residing in the premises or part of them at the termination of the former tenancy.

(2A)   Subsections (1) and (2) above apply in relation to any restricted contract (within the meaning of the Rent Act 1977) which—

(a)   creates a licence; and
(b)   is entered into after the commencement of section 69 of the Housing Act 1980;

as they apply in relation to a restricted contract which creates a tenancy.

(2B)   Subsections (1) and (2) above apply in relation to any premises occupied as a dwelling under a licence, other than an excluded licence, as they apply in relation to premises let as a dwelling under a tenancy, and in those subsections the expressions 'let' and 'tenancy' shall be construed accordingly.

(2C)   References in the preceding provisions of this section and section 4(2A) below to an excluded tenancy do not apply to—

(a)   a tenancy entered into before the date on which the Housing Act 1988 came into force, or
(b)   a tenancy entered into on or after that date but pursuant to a contract made before that date,

but, subject to that, 'excluded tenancy' and 'excluded licence' shall be construed in accordance with section 3A below.

(3) This section shall, with the necessary modifications, apply where the owner's right to recover possession arises on the death of the tenant under a statutory tenancy within the meaning of the Rent Act 1977 or the Rent (Agriculture) Act 1976.

Excluded tenancies and licences

3A.—(1) Any reference in this Act to an excluded tenancy or an excluded licence is a reference to a tenancy or licence which is excluded by virtue of any of the following provisions of this section.

(2) A tenancy or licence is excluded if—

(a) under its terms the occupier shares any accommodation with the landlord or licensor; and

(b) immediately before the tenancy or licence was granted and also at the time it comes to an end, the landlord or licensor occupied as his only or principal home premises of which the whole or part of the shared accommodation formed part.

(3) A tenancy or licence is also excluded if—

(a) under its terms the occupier shares any accommodation with a member of the family of the landlord or licensor;

(b) immediately before the tenancy or licence was granted and also at the time it comes to an end, the member of the family of the landlord or licensor occupied as his only or principal home premises of which the whole or part of the shared accommodation formed part; and

(c) immediately before the tenancy or licence was granted and also at the time it comes to an end, the landlord or licensor occupied as his only or principal home premises in the same building as the shared accommodation and that building is not a purpose-built block of flats.

(4) For the purposes of subsections (2) and (3) above, an occupier shares accommodation with another person if he has the use of it in common with that person (whether or not also in common with others) and any reference in those subsections to shared accommodation shall be construed accordingly, and if, in relation to any tenancy or licence, there is at any time more than one person who is the landlord or licensor, any reference in those subsections to the landlord or licensor shall be construed as a reference to any one of those persons.

(5) In subsections (2) to (4) above—

(a) 'accommodation' includes neither an area used for storage nor a staircase, passage, corridor or other means of access;

(b) 'occupier' means, in relation to a tenancy, the tenant and, in relation to a licence, the licensee; and

(c) 'purpose-built block of flats' has the same meaning as in Part III of Schedule 1 to the Housing Act 1988;

and section 113 of the Housing Act 1985 shall apply to determine whether a person is for the purposes of subsection (3) above a member of another's family as it applies for the purposes of Part IV of that Act.

(6)   A tenancy or licence is excluded if it was granted as a temporary expedient to a person who entered the premises in question or any other premises as a trespasser (whether or not, before the beginning of that tenancy or licence, another tenancy or licence to occupy the premises or any other premises had been granted to him).

(7)   A tenancy or licence is excluded if—

     (a)   it confers on the tenant or licensee the right to occupy the premises for a holiday only; or

     (b)   it is granted otherwise than for money or money's worth.

(8)   A licence is excluded if it confers rights of occupation in a hostel, within the meaning of the Housing Act 1985, which is provided by—

     (a)   the council of a county, district or London Borough, the Common Council of the City of London, the Council of the Isles of Scilly, the Inner London Education Authority, a joint authority within the meaning of the Local Government Act 1985 or a residuary body within the meaning of that Act;

     (b)   a development corporation within the meaning of the New Towns Act 1981;

     (c)   the Commission for the New Towns;

     (d)   an urban development corporation established by an order under section 135 of the Local Government, Planning and Land Act 1980;

     (e)   a housing action trust established under Part III of the Housing Act 1988;

     (f)   the Development Board for Rural Wales;

     (g)   the Housing Corporation or Housing for Wales;

     (h)   a housing trust which is a charity or a registered housing association, within the meaning of the Housing Associations Act 1985; or

     (i)   any other person who is, or who belongs to a class of person which is, specified in an order made by the Secretary of State.

(9)   The power to make an order under subsection (8)(i) above shall be exercisable by statutory instrument which shall be subject to annulment in pursuance of a resolution of either House of Parliament.

Special provisions for agricultural employees
4.—(1)   This section shall apply where the tenant under the former tenancy (within the meaning of section 3 of this Act) occupied the premises under the terms of his employment as a person employed in agriculture, as defined in section 1 of the Rent (Agriculture) Act 1976, but is not a statutory tenant as defined in that Act.

(2)   In this section 'the occupier', in relation to any premises means—

     (a)   the tenant under the former tenancy; or

     (b)   the widow or widower of the tenant under the former tenancy residing with him at his death or, if the former tenant leaves no such widow or widower, any member of his family residing with him at his death.

(2A)   In accordance with section 3(2B) above, any reference in subsections (1) and (2) above to the tenant under the former tenancy includes a reference to the licensee under a licence (other than an excluded licence) which has come to an end (being a licence to occupy premises as a dwelling); and in the following provisions of this section the expressions 'tenancy' and 'rent' and any other expressions referable to a tenancy shall be construed accordingly.

(3) Without prejudice to any power of the court apart from this section to postpone the operation or suspend the execution of an order for possession, if in proceedings by the owner against the occupier the court makes an order for the possession of the premises the court may suspend the execution of the order on such terms and conditions, including conditions as to the payment by the occupier of arrears of rent, mesne profits and otherwise as the court thinks reasonable.

(4)) Where the order for possession is made within the period of six months beginning with the date when the former tenancy came to an end, then, without prejudice to any powers of the court under the preceding provisions of this section or apart from this section to postpone the operation or suspend the execution of the order for a longer period, the court shall suspend the execution of the order for the remainder of the said period of six months unless the court—

(a)   is satisfied either—

(i)   that other suitable accommodation is, or will within that period be made, available to the occupier; or

(ii)   that the efficient management of any agricultural land or the efficient carrying on of any agricultural operations would be seriously prejudiced unless the premises are available for occupation by a person employed or to be employed by the owner; or

(iii)   that greater hardship (being hardship in respect of matters other than the carrying on of such a business as aforesaid) would be caused by the suspension of the order until the end of that period than by its execution within that period; or

(iv)   that the occupier, or any person residing or lodging with the occupier, has been causing damage to the premises or has been guilty of conduct which is a nuisance or annoyance to persons occupying other premises; and

(b)   considers that it would be reasonable not to suspend the execution of the order for the remainder of that period.

(5)   Where the court suspends the execution of an order for possession under subsection (4) above it shall do so on such terms and conditions, including conditions as to the payment by the occupier of arrears of rent, mesne profits and otherwise as the court thinks reasonable.

(6)   A decision of the court not to suspend the execution of the order under subsection (4) above shall not prejudice any other power of the court to postpone the operation or suspend the execution of the order for the whole or part of the period of six months mentioned in that subsection.

(7)   Where the court has, under the preceding provisions of this section, suspended the execution of an order for possession, it may from time to time vary the period of suspension or terminate it and may vary any terms and conditions imposed by virtue of this section.

(8) In considering whether or how to exercise its powers under subsection (3) above, the court shall have regard to all the circumstances and, in particular, to—

(a) whether other suitable accommodation is or can be made available to the occupier;

(b) whether the efficient management of any agricultural land or the efficient carrying on of any agricultural operations would be seriously prejudiced unless the premises were available for occupation by a person employed or to be employed by the owner; and

(c) whether greater hardship would be caused by the suspension of the execution of the order than by its execution without suspension or further suspension.

(9) Where in proceedings for the recovery of possession of the premises the court makes an order for possession but suspends the execution of the order under this section, it shall make no order for costs, unless it appears to the court, having regard to the conduct of the owner or of the occupier, that there are special reasons for making such an order.

(10) Where, in the case of an order for possession of the premises to which subsection (4) above applies, the execution of the order is not suspended under that subsection or, the execution of the order having been so suspended, the suspension is terminated, then, if it is subsequently made to appear to the court that the failure to suspend the execution of the order or, as the case may be, the termination of the suspension was—

(a) attributable to the provisions of paragraph (a)(ii) of subsection (4), and

(b) due to misrepresentation or concealment of material facts by the owner of the premises,

the court may order the owner to pay to the occupier such sum as appears sufficient as compensation for damage or loss sustained by the occupier as a result of that failure or termination.

Part II Notice to quit

Validity of notices to quit
5.—(1) Subject to subsection (1B) below no notice by a landlord or a tenant to quit any premises let (whether before or after the commencement of this Act) as a dwelling shall be valid unless—

(a) it is in writing and contains such information as may be prescribed, and

(b) it is given not less than four weeks before the date on which it is to take effect.

(1A) Subject to subsection (1B) below, no notice by a licensor or a licensee to determine a periodic licence to occupy premises as a dwelling (whether the licence was granted before or after the passing of this Act) shall be valid unless—

(a) it is in writing and contains such information as may be prescribed, and

(b) it is given not less than four weeks before the date on which it is to take effect.

(1B)   Nothing in subsection (1) or subsection (1A) above applies to—

(a)   premises let on an excluded tenancy which is entered into on or after the date on which the Housing Act 1988 came into force unless it is entered into pursuant to a contract made before that date; or
(b)   premises occupied under an excluded licence.

(2)   In this section 'prescribed' means prescribed by regulations made by the Secretary of State by statutory instrument, and a statutory instrument containing any such regulations shall be subject to annulment in pursuance of a resolution of either House of Parliament.

(3)   Regulations under this section may make different provision in relation to different descriptions of lettings and different circumstances.

Part III Supplemental provisions

Prosecution of offences
6.   Proceedings for an offence under this Act may be instituted by any of the following authorities:—

(a)   councils of districts and London boroughs;
(b)   the Common Council of the City of London;
(c)   the Council of the Isles of Scilly.

Service of notices
7.—(1)   If for the purpose of any proceedings (whether civil or criminal) brought or intended to be brought under this Act, any person serves upon—

(a)   any agent of the landlord named as such in the rent book or other similar document, or
(b)   the person who receives the rent of the dwelling,

a notice in writing requiring the agent or other person to disclose to him the full name and place of abode or place of business of the landlord, that agent or other person shall forthwith comply with the notice.

(2)   If any such agent or other person as is referred to in subsection (1) above fails or refuses forthwith to comply with a notice served on him under that subsection, he shall be liable on summary conviction to a fine not exceeding level 4 on the standard scale unless he shows to the satisfaction of the court that he did not know, and could not with reasonable diligence have ascertained, such of the facts required by the notice to be disclosed as were not disclosed by him.

(3)   In this section 'landlord' includes—

(a)   any person from time to time deriving title under the original landlord,
(b)   in relation to any dwelling-house, any person other than the tenant who is or, but for Part VII of the Rent Act 1977 would be, entitled to possession of the dwelling-house, and
(c)   any person who grants to another the right to occupy the dwelling in question as a residence and any person directly or indirectly deriving title from the grantor.

Interpretation

8.—(1) In this Act 'statutorily protected tenancy' means—

(a) a protected tenancy within the meaning of the Rent Act 1977 or a tenancy to which Part I of the Landlord and Tenant Act 1954 applies;

(b) a protected occupancy or statutory tenancy as defined in the Rent (Agriculture) Act 1976;

(c) a tenancy to which Part II of the Landlord and Tenant Act 1954 applies;

(d) a tenancy of an agricultural holding within the meaning of the Agricultural Holdings Act 1986;

(e) an assured tenancy or assured agricultural occupancy under Part I of the Housing Act 1988.

(2) For the purposes of Part I of this Act a person who, under the terms of his employment, had exclusive possession of any premises other than as a tenant shall be deemed to have been a tenant and the expressions 'let' and 'tenancy' shall be construed accordingly.

(3) In Part I of this Act 'the owner', in relation to any premises, means the person who, as against the occupier, is entitled to possession thereof.

(4) In this Act 'excluded tenancy' and 'excluded licence' have the meaning assigned by section 3A of this Act.

(5) If, on or after the date on which the Housing Act 1988 came into force, the terms of an excluded tenancy or excluded licence entered into before that date are varied, then—

(a) if the variation affects the amount of the rent which is payable under the tenancy or licence, the tenancy or licence shall be treated for the purposes of sections 3(2C) and 5(1B) above as a new tenancy or licence entered into at the time of the variation; and

(b) if the variation does not affect the amount of the rent which is so payable, nothing in this Act shall affect the determination of the question whether the variation is such as to give rise to a new tenancy or licence.

(6) Any reference in subsection (5) above to a variation affecting the amount of the rent which is payable under a tenancy or licence does not include a reference to—

(a) a reduction or increase effected under Part III or Part VI of the Rent Act 1977 (rents under regulated tenancies and housing association tenancies), section 78 of that Act (power of rent tribunal in relation to restricted contracts) or sections 11 to 14 of the Rent (Agriculture) Act 1976; or

(b) a variation which is made by the parties and has the effect of making the rent expressed to be payable under the tenancy or licence the same as a rent for the dwelling which is entered in the register under Part IV or section 79 of the Rent Act 1977.

The court for purposes of Part I

9.—(1) The court for the purposes of Part I of this Act shall, subject to this section, be—

(a) the county court, in relation to premises with respect to which the county court has for the time being jurisdiction in actions for the recovery of land; and

(b)   the High Court, in relation to other premises.

(2)   Any powers of a county court in proceedings for the recovery of possession of any premises in the circumstances mentioned in section 3(1) of this Act may be exercised with the leave of the judge by any registrar of the court, except in so far as rules of court otherwise provide.

(3)   Nothing in this Act shall affect the jurisdiction of the High Court in procedings to enforce a lessor's right of re-entry or forfeiture or to enforce a mortgagee's right of possession in a case where the former tenancy was not binding on the mortgagee.

(4)   Nothing in this Act shall affect the operation of—

(a)   section 59 of the Pluralities Act 1838;
(b)   section 19 of the Defence Act 1842;
(c)   section 6 of the Lecturers and Parish Clerks Act 1844;
(d)   paragraph 3 of Schedule 1 to the Sexual Offences Act 1956; or
(e)   section 13 of the Compulsory Purchase Act 1965.

Application to Crown
10.   In so far as this Act requires the taking of proceedings in the court for the recovery of possession or confers any powers on the court is shall (except in the case of section 4(10)) be binding on the Crown.

Application to Isles of Scilly
11.—(1)   In its application to the Isles of Scilly, this Act (except in the case of section 5) shall have effect subject to such exceptions, adaptations and modifications as the Secretary of State may by order direct.

(2)   The power to make an order under this section shall be exercisable by statutory instrument which shall be subject to annulment, in pursuance of a resolution of either House of Parliament.

(3)   An order under this section may be varied or revoked by a subsequent order.

Consequental amendments, etc.
12.—(1)   Schedule 1 to this Act contains amendments consequential on the provisions of this Act.

(2)   Schedule 2 to this Act contains transitional provisions and savings.

(3)   The enactments mentioned in Schedule 3 to this Act are hereby repealed to the extent specified in the third column of that Schedule.

(4)   The inclusion in this Act of any express savings, transitional provisions or amendment shall not be taken to affect the operation in relation to this Act of section 38 of the Interpretation Act 1889 (which relates to the effect of repeals).

Short title, etc.
13.—(1)   This Act may be cited as the Protection from Eviction Act 1977.

(2)   This Act shall come into force on the expiry of the period of one month beginning with the date on which it is passed.

(3)   This Act does not extend to Scotland or Northern Ireland.

(4)   References in this Act to any enactment are references to that enactment

as amended, and include references thereto as applied by any other enactment including, except where the context otherwise requires, this Act.

Schedule 2 Transitional provisions and savings

1.—(1) Insofar as anything done under an enactment repealed by this Act could have been done under a corresponding provision of this Act, it shall not be invalidated by the repeal but shall have effect as if done under that provision.

(2) Subparagraph (1) above applies, in particular, to any regulation, rule, notice or order.

2. The enactments mentioned in Schedule 6 to the Rent Act 1965 shall, notwithstanding the repeal of that Act by this Act, continue to have effect as they had effect immediately before the commencement of this Act.

Index